A COMMENTARY ON P

A Commentary on Propertius, Book 3

S. J. HEYWORTH
&
J. H. W. MORWOOD

OXFORD
UNIVERSITY PRESS

OXFORD
UNIVERSITY PRESS

Great Clarendon Street, Oxford OX2 6DP

Oxford University Press is a department of the University of Oxford.
It furthers the University's objective of excellence in research, scholarship,
and education by publishing worldwide in

Oxford New York

Auckland Cape Town Dar es Salaam Hong Kong Karachi
Kuala Lumpur Madrid Melbourne Mexico City Nairobi
New Delhi Shanghai Taipei Toronto

With offices in

Argentina Austria Brazil Chile Czech Republic France Greece
Guatemala Hungary Italy Japan Poland Portugal Singapore
South Korea Switzerland Thailand Turkey Ukraine Vietnam

Oxford is a registered trade mark of Oxford University Press
in the UK and in certain other countries

Published in the United States
by Oxford University Press Inc., New York

British Library Cataloguing in Publication Data

Data available

Library of Congress Cataloging in Publication Data

Data available

Typeset by SPI Publisher Services, Pondicherry, India
Printed in Great Britain
on acid-free paper by
MPG Books Group, Bodmin and King's Lynn

ISBN 978-0-19-957148-2 (Hbk.)
978-0-19-957149-9 (Pbk.)

1 3 5 7 9 10 8 6 4 2

To Wadham College
and
the Wadham Classicists

Contents

Preface

At a party in December 2007 to mark the publication of a new Oxford Classical Text of Propertius and a companion volume entitled *Cynthia*, Alex Smith, a Wadham alumnus from 1992–6, who had just moved from a career as a solicitor to teaching, revealed that some poems from Propertius 3 were shortly to appear on the syllabus for the A2 (i.e. school-leaving) examination in England. This seemed surprising: Propertius' Latin can be difficult; Book 3 requires a fair bit of knowledge of the literary tradition; and there was no accessible commentary more recent than Camps (1966), or, on the whole text, Richardson (1976). But the notion of filling the gap quickly became tempting. As editor of the Oxford text SJH had already done much of the work necessary to produce an edition for students; *Cynthia* provided a translation and discussions of difficult passages that could be mined for appropriate material; a year's leave was imminent; and in JHWM he had a prospective colleague who had spent decades thinking about how to explain linguistic difficulties in clear ways, and who had interests in Augustan poetry, including Propertius.

So, with the generous support of Hilary O'Shea and her colleagues, together with OUP's readers, we set out on our enjoyably collaborative journey. It should be said at the outset that despite the original stimulus this is not meant primarily as an edition for schools. Though we hope schoolteachers and some A2 students will find the book useful, the main audience we have had in mind is undergraduates, particularly those who have not been learning Latin for long, and for whom aspects of the ancient world, including its literature, may well be mysterious. We do not think that Propertius 3 is an easy text, but we have come to see it as rich in educational potential; while remaining grounded in the erotic tradition of Latin elegy, it touches on a very wide range of material: contemporary and earlier Roman history; art; ethical and natural philosophy; luxury; travel; the empire (and beyond). Within the literary sphere, it engages with epic (*Iliad* and *Odyssey*, Apollonius' *Argonautica*, Ennius' *Annales* and the still unpublished *Aeneid*); the recently published *Odes* of Horace; epigram; pastoral; the elegiac tradition, conjured up with the names of Callimachus and Philitas in the opening line; and above all the earlier works of Propertius himself. We have tried in the space available to us at appropriate places in the commentary to give a sense of fascinating topics such as *seruitium* and *militia amoris* [the slavery of love (3.6 intro) and the warfare of love (3.8)], patronage (3.9), diatribe (3.13), the ancient hymn (3.17), and the tradition of epigrams for those who have died at sea (3.7). And we have dedicated a major section of the introduction to an outline history of Roman politics between the assassination of Julius Caesar and the publication of Book 3.

Some aspects of how we see this working as an educational text can helpfully be explained here. We have freely used those technical terms we ourselves find useful, but we have tried to do so in ways that clarify the meaning, either in the commentary or in the glossary included in the Introduction: words to be found in the glossary are marked with an asterisk throughout. An appendix includes eighteen passages (each allocated a letter in bold) that we have found to be important as background to Propertius 3: these are passages from Hesiod through Callimachus to Lucretius, Gallus, Vergil, Horace, and Propertius himself, mainly of programmatic significance, each accompanied by a translation, as is the case with almost all Greek and Latin cited in the commentary: we believe students are more likely to inspect a piece of Latin if they are given some sense of what it means. Though we hope that the commentary will also be useful to more advanced scholars, we have not tried to serve their needs by giving exhaustive references; it is rare for us to mention bibliography in languages other than English.

We have been very fortunate in the enthusiastic assistance of many friends and colleagues. A continuing debt is owed to all whose help is acknowledged in the prefaces to *Cynthia* and the Oxford text of Propertius. Bryan Morwood drew the maps. Sections of the commentary and introduction were carefully read by Laurel Fulkerson, Adrian Hollis, Jennifer Ingleheart, Ted Kenney, John Murrell, Chris Parrott, Meghan Reedy, Alex Smith, and Katherine van Schaik.[1]

---

[1] Ted Kenney's involvement is a particular delight: he supervised us both long ago, in another place, in SJH's case as a doctoral student; an early title for the thesis that came to be primarily concerned with the manuscript tradition was 'A commentary on Propertius 3'.

We are very grateful to them all; they saved us from many errors and omissions, and the commentary has benefited from their sharp insights; if we had had more room, we would gladly have included more. Our thoughts on 3.4 and 3.5 were sharpened by the responses of audiences at the Universities of Amsterdam, Virginia, Colorado, Bologna, and Pisa. The commentary on 3.19 was presented to a day of discussion of poetic commentary organized by Bruce Gibson and Stephen Harrison, and held at Corpus Christi College, Oxford, on 14 March 2009; drafts on 3.2 and 3.16 were discussed on 13 December 2008 by a group of Wadham classicists, most of them schoolteachers; we are grateful to all who attended either event; and to Wadham students over the years for the ways they have stimulated us to think about ancient poetry.

Finally let us say that little of what is said in the commentary is proven fact: sometimes we mark particular uncertainties with 'perhaps', 'probably', 'it seems', or by offering an alternative reading. But the absence of such markers should not be taken as indicative of certainty on our part: far more statements could be hedged with such qualifications; and in any case, even when we feel confident in our view, we may well be wrong, and readers, especially students, should feel encouraged to doubt and to question anything they read in what follows.

Stephen Heyworth   Wadham College
James Morwood   Oxford
                                                   October 2009

Thanks are due also to Jane Burkowski and Andrew Hawkey (for OUP) for their sharp-eyed reading of the proofs.

S.J.H., J.H.W.M.
July 2010

INTRODUCTION

1. PROPERTIUS AND CYNTHIA

> CYNTHIA prima suis miserum me cepit ocellis,
>   contactum nullis ante Cupidinibus.
> tum mihi constantis deiecit lumina fastus
>   et caput impositis pressit Amor pedibus
> donec me docuit castas odisse Puellas   5
>   improbus et nullo uiuere consilio.
> ei mihi, iam toto furor hic non deficit anno,
>   cum tamen aduersos cogor habere deos.

Cynthia was the first; she caught me with her eyes and made me miserable—
I had never been infected with desire before. Love forced me to drop my look
of resolute pride, put his feet on my head and pressed it down, until he had
taught me to dislike the chaste girls [i.e. the Muses], the rogue, and to live
without set purpose. Alas, already a whole year has gone by and still the
madness has not left me; but all that time I have had to follow gods who are
against me.

So begins Propertius' first book, immediately conveying interests that
will be of key importance in what follows. In first place the name of
his beloved Cynthia, its primacy stressed by addition of *prima*. The
poet is unhappy (*miserum*, 1), disorganized (6), mad (7), and ill-
fated (8): this will turn out to be normal—love for him is never easy.
Verse 2 prepares for the notion of madness with a brief metaphor of
disease (*contactum*). The equally fleeting image of capture (*cepit*, 1) is
developed in verse 4, where Cupid, the God of Love, is presented as a
conquering general before whom the poet has to submit like a slave.
Such details get built up into what scholars call *militia amoris* (the
soldiery of love); though they are taken far further by Propertius and
his fellow elegists,[1] here they can clearly be seen to emanate from

---

[1] i.e. Tibullus and Ovid, the latter especially in his wonderfully extended comparison of lover and soldier in *Am.* 1.9, *Militat omnis amans*, 'Every lover is a soldier',
and *Am.* 2.12.

P.'s model, a six-line epigram by the Greek writer Meleager, *Anthologia Palatina* 12.101:[2]

I was unwounded by desires before, but Myiscus shot me deep in my heart **with his eyes,** and shouted out these words: 'I have **caught** the bold one; and that **arrogance** of sceptre-bearing wisdom [i.e. poetry], look, **I tread on it with my feet.**' And to him, I replied, scarcely breathing, 'Lovely boy, why are you surprised? Eros **captured** Zeus himself down from Olympus.'

In what follows in Book 1 we see the classic statement of the relationship between the elegist and mistress: passionate commitment constantly threatened by rivals and friends, by separations potential and actual. But there are also surprising aspects to the way the book develops. After the opening statement of hopeless longing, in 1.2 we find Cynthia addressed and advised on what she should wear: in the interstice* between the two poems, they have become a couple. The focus is not on the poet's happiness; instead P. fears that Cynthia's desire to dress up in imported finery shows that she seeks other lovers. His mistrust in 1.2 is matched by hers in 1.3: he tells the story of how he came home late and drunk, and far from assaulting her as she slept he gazed in worship on her beauty—until she woke up and criticized him for abandoning her.

The first three poems all use mythological *exempla** as part of their argumentation and poetic texture; the complexity involved in this device (especially in the use of multiple *exempla*) is a very marked part of P.'s style in Book 1. Elegy 1.3, for example, begins with three similes: the sleeping Cynthia was like Ariadne, Andromeda, and a Maenad.

> Qualis Thesea iacuit cedente carina
>   languida desertis Cnosia litoribus;
> qualis et accubuit primo Cepheïa somno
>   libera iam duris cotibus Andromede;
> nec minus assiduis Edonis fessa choreis   5
>   qualis in herboso concidit Apidano:
> talis uisa mihi mollem spirare quietem
>   Cynthia . . .

---

[2] Expressions in bold are reprised in P.'s version.
* Words marked with an asterisk are explained in the glossary.

Like the Cretan girl, lying languid on empty shores as Theseus' vessel departed; like Cepheus' daughter Andromeda too as she lay in her first sleep, now free from the harsh cliff; and also like the Maenad who tired by constant dancing collapses on grassy Apidanus: so Cynthia seemed to me, breathing soft sleep, . . .

The first of these evokes a passage of Catullus, his predecessor (who apparently died young *c.*53 BC) as a writer of passionate love poetry. Catullus writes about his emotional commitment to and estrangement from a woman he calls Lesbia (as well as a youth called Juventius), but poem 64 is a 400-line mythological poem, which includes a long account of a tapestry depicting Theseus' abandonment of Ariadne while she is sleeping on the seashore and her reaction on waking (64.52–250). Propertius not only mentions the myth, he alludes to specific phrasing: cf. 64.53, 132–3, 171–2, and 249:

> **These**a **cedent**em celeri cum classe tuetur . . .
> 'sicine me patriis avectam, perfide, ab aris,
> perfide, **desert**o liquisti in **litor**e, **Theseu**? . . .
> utinam ne tempore primo
> **Cnosi**a Cecropiae tetigissent **litor**a puppes. . . .'
> quae tum prospectans **cedent**em maesta **carinam** . . .

when she was watching Theseus departing with his swift fleet . . . 'Having carried me off, traitor, from the altars of my homeland, traitor, is this the way you have left me on the deserted shore, Theseus? . . . Would that the Athenian ships had not originally touched the shores of Crete. . . .' She then was looking out sadly on the departing boat . . .

Catullus' Ariadne is displayed on a coverlet with a loving Bacchus coming to rescue her (64.251–64): P. urged on by love and wine (1.3.13–14) clearly casts himself in the role of Bacchus (named in verse 9). But he approaches her only tentatively, fearing the row that will result if he disturbs her rest (17–18); and when Cynthia wakes up she attacks him as a treacherous Theseus figure, and curses him in terms like those Ariadne uses.[3] This early poem thus gives us a clear

[3] 1.3.39–40 *o utinam tales producas, improbe, noctes | me miseram quales semper habere iubes* [would that you might pass such nights, rogue, as you are always forcing unhappy me to have] picks up the structure of Ariadne's closing words, *quali solam Theseus me mente reliquit, | tali mente, deae, funestet seque suosque* [may Theseus bereave himself and his family, goddesses, with the same attitude with which he abandoned me: Cat. 64.200–1].

exhibition of the malleability of myth: an *exemplum* has to be interpreted, and one reader's interpretation may well differ from another's.

Other *exempla* introduce different complexities. One notable feature is the use of negation; this can be seen already in 1.1, where Milanion is introduced to show that *benefacta* (services rendered) and *preces* (prayers) can overcome the resistance of the wildest, most stubborn girl, but after five couplets (one now lost), P. announces that the familiar pattern simply does not work in his case (1.1.17–18):

> in me tardus Amor non ullas cogitat artes
> nec meminit notas, ut prius, ire uias.

In my case Love is slow and does not think up any tricks, nor does he remember to travel the old familiar courses.

Again, at 1.13.21–4 (*non sic... nec sic*) the passion of Gallus and his girlfriend exceeds that of Neptune with Tyro and of Hercules with Hebe: the *exempla* illustrate the heat of their love, but P.'s world goes beyond what is familiar from myth. When such negatives are addressed to Cynthia, they can have a rhetorical purpose. Thus in 1.2 Cynthia's[4] use of make-up and imported clothing is contrasted with the behaviour of some heroines from myth: unlike her (*non sic*, 15) Phoebe, Helaira, Marpessa, and Hippodamia attracted the attentions of lovers (and caused famous conflicts) without such tricks. And in 1.15 her willingness to spend time doing her hair and putting on jewellery sets her in opposition (*non sic*, 9; *nec sic*, 17) to Calypso and Hypsipyle, each perturbed by the departure of an epic hero (Odysseus or Jason). Just as similes complicate by introducing things that are like, but often very different (the Carthaginians building their city at *Aeneid* 1.423–36 are not really like bees), so dissimiles lay claim to a basic similarity at the same time as asserting difference. As he enhances the range of reference in his poetry P. seems to claim that the world of myth is not the equal of his world[5]—sometimes in ways that do not entirely please him.

[4] In fact the name does not appear in this poem, but the single-minded concentration on the one woman so named allows us to take any reference to his *uita* ('darling', lit. 'life': 1.2.1) or *domina* (1.7.6) or even *illa* (1.14.9) as implying Cynthia, unless there is good reason not to do so (see 3.20 intro.).

[5] Not so Lyne 1980: esp. 81–102.

In poems 1.4–7 the reader's understanding of the relationship is furthered less directly in a sequence addressed to the patronizing figure Tullus (1.6 [N]) and three rival poets, Bassus (1.4), Gallus[6] (1.5) and Ponticus (1.7). He sets each of these up as a contrast to himself: Tullus is able to travel to the East as part of his uncle's cohort, concerned not with *amor*, but for *arma* and his *patria* ('arms, i.e. military life' and 'the fatherland': 1.6.19–30). Bassus, we know from Ovid (*Tristia* 4.10.47), was an iambic poet, Ponticus a writer of epic; the *Thebaid* of the latter provides a striking antithesis to Propertian elegy: grandiose and grim, aspiring to compete with Homer (1.7.1–4), but having less appeal to readers (1.7.9–14, 21–6), and useless when the poet falls in love (1.7.15–20; 1.9).

Whereas the male addressees contrast with Propertius, Cynthia is repeatedly assimilated to him, and he to her. This is a literary effect, but we should not miss the real insight when he presents each lover as imitating the behaviour of the other. In 1.3, as we have seen, Cynthia treats the late arrival home of P. as a sign of betrayal—he's only come now because another woman has shut him out. In 1.15 it is the poet's voice that complains: he has summoned her for some urgent reason (*periclum*, 3), and when she is slow to respond (4–6), he too sees this as a sign of betrayal, whatever she says in denial. He is so perturbed that he forgets about the *periclum*; however, at the end he yields to her persuasive charm (*blanditiae*, 42). After describing in 1.6 his inability to leave Rome because that is where his love is, and the emotional reaction of Cynthia herself to such a departure (1.6.5–18), in 1.8A he responds emotionally to news that she may head East with another, and then in 1.8B reacts with delight to her decision to stay (31: *illi carus ego, et per me carissima Roma | dicitur*: 'I am dear to her, and thanks to me Rome is said to be most dear'). In the second half

---

[6] We take it that the name Gallus is expected to be read as the elegist Cornelius Gallus [F], though the issue is highly controversial: for a recent exposition and bibliography, see Cairns 2006: 70–82, revisiting arguments previously presented at *PLLS* 4 (1983), 83–96. Note especially the emphasis on their pairing, so evocative of the elegiac couplet, as well as elegiac love, in 1.5.29–30: *sed pariter miseri socio cogemur amore | alter in alterius mutua flere sinu* [but together unhappy in our shared love we will be forced to weep for one another each in the other's embrace]. Though like P. in his erotic engagement, the older poet is presented in 1.5, 10, 13, 20 as having much to learn from his younger colleague; but with so little surviving of his work there is much that we cannot comprehend.

of the book, however, Cynthia does leave Rome: 1.11 takes her to the resort of Baiae, famous for encouraging infidelity, described as an 'offence against love' (30: *crimen Amoris*); and in the following poem she is described as 'separated from my bed by as many miles as the Hypanis [*a river in the Ukraine*] is distant from the Venetian Po' (1.12.3–4: see intro. to 3.13). The reader may not be entirely surprised to find that despite his earlier protestations, Propertius too is seen outside the city: in 1.17 he has taken ship for foreign parts and is now marooned by a storm; and in 1.18 he is somewhere isolated in the woods, hoping (with obvious irony, in a published poem) that his inanimate audience of trees, breeze, and rocks can keep secret his complaints about Cynthia's disdainful behaviour. The two of them are equally committed, and equally liable to distrust the other—and to betray the other's trust.

The depiction of P.'s behaviour in 1.18 is based on a passage of the *Aetia* of the Hellenistic* Greek elegist Callimachus, where Acontius, lover of Cydippe, was described wandering in the wilderness, addressing the trees; this now survives only in fragments* (72–3) and through a paraphrase by the fifth-century prose author Aristaenetus.[7] However, imitation of Callimachus begins in the first word of the first poem, the very name of Cynthia recalling his epithet for Apollo, derived from the hill, Cynthos, in the centre of Delos, where Apollo and his sister (Artemis/Diana) were born. One occurrence comes at the start of the Acontius episode, fr. 67.1–6:

Αὐτὸς Ἔρως ἐδίδαξεν Ἀκόντιον, ὁππότε καλῆι
ἤιθετο Κυδίππηι παῖς ἐπὶ παρθενικῆι,
τέχνην (οὐ γὰρ ὅγ᾽ ἔσκε πολύκροτος) ὄφρα λέγοιτο
τοῦτο διὰ ζωῆς οὔνομα κουρίδιον.
ἦ γάρ, ἄναξ, ὁ μὲν ἦλθεν Ἰουλίδος, ἡ δ᾽ ἀπὸ Νάξου,
Κύνθιε, τὴν Δήλῳ σὴν ἐπὶ βουφονίην.

Love himself taught Acontius, when the boy was growing passionate over maidenly Cydippe, he taught him **artfulness**—for he was not very cunning—so that he might through his life be called this name of bridegroom. For, lord, he came from Iulis [i.e. the Aegean island of Ceos], she from Naxos, **Cynthius**, to your sacrifice on Delos.

[7] See F. Cairns, *CR* 19 (1969), 131–4.

It is typical of Latin poetic style that allusion* to this passage (the phrasing in bold is picked up in 1.1.1, 5, 18 *artes*) is combined with P.'s version of Meleager's epigram: both poets are important models in the writing of elegy, Meleager for his explorations of love of an individual over a series of poems, Callimachus for his learning and artistry and because he champions the small-scale over the grandiose. The interest in the Acontius episode of the *Aetia* is obviously due to its erotic content; and some have thought that this may have been the only passage of the poem read with any attention by Propertius. However, there is already in Book 1 a creative engagement with the aesthetic that is so prominent a part of Callimachus' appeal, most notably in the rejection of the military life and the military poetry of Tullus and Ponticus respectively (1.6; 1.7, 9); this will become more obvious in the later books, but 1.7 and 1.9 already establish a strong contrast between elegy and epic that is basic to the way that elegy develops in the hands of P. himself and Ovid. Modern readers have been particularly fascinated by the way in which Cynthia can immediately be read as a symbol for the elegies themselves: in dedicating himself to Cynthia, P. is also dedicating himself to elegy, another exacting mistress.[8] In publishing his *Cynthia*[9] he is also putting his Cynthia on public display, artfully dressed up in 'Coan' cloth (1.2.2), i.e. elegiac verse that imitates the tradition of Philitas of Cos, Callimachus' predecessor in the composition of artful elegy in the Hellenistic* age, who was regarded in Rome as the second of the great Greek elegists[10] (but of whose work virtually nothing now survives). Some have been so struck by the force of this allegory, and the obvious fictionality of Cynthia, whose identity is so vague, whose status and domestic arrangements shift from poem to poem,[11] that they prefer to set aside the notion of a love affair and concentrate on the poetics.[12] We think that is misguided: if the poetry is to be

---

[8] E.g. Ross 1975: 58–9, 70, 117; Wyke 2002: 46–77.

[9] Ancient books were regularly known by their first words: see e.g. E. J. Kenney, *CR* 20 (1970), 290.

[10] Quintilian 10.1.58; Ov. *Ars* 3.329; *Rem.* 760. For the fragments see e.g. Spanoudakis 2002.

[11] We are also given quite precise but inconsistent chronology: 3.15.7 n., 24.23 (= 25.3).

[12] E.g. Wyke 2002: 11–45; and Keith 2008, though she also thinks it might be possible to decode Cynthia as a Hostia (88–92).

read as poetry that explores what it is to be a committed lover in
Rome, the reader needs to go along with the fictional narrative, to
allow that it might be true. And some part of it in some way may be.

2. THE HISTORICAL CONTEXT[13]

Love and poetry are two of the major themes of Propertian elegy. The
third is politics. In Book 1 the political world is not obtrusive; for
example, the name of Caesar, i.e. Octavian, the future Augustus, already
master of the Roman world at the time of publication, does not appear
until the penultimate poem. He is mentioned there (1.21.7) by a dead
soldier, who has been killed by hands unknown after escaping through
Caesar's battle lines at the siege of Perusia in 41,[14] and now requests
burial from a comrade in arms. The poem is a sepulchral epigram, like
many transmitted in Meleager's *Garland* (the collection from which
significant parts of the extant Palatine and Planudean Anthologies
come), and it may partly owe its place in the book to the poet's desire
to mark again at the end his debt to elegiac epigram. But the following
poem provides a sharper reason for its presence here. The book ends
with a *sphragis** in which the poet answers questions about his family
and home by defining his origin in terms of the vicinity of the Perusine
War, in which a relative was killed and never buried (1.22.3–8): the
sequence forces the reader to identify this relative with the soldier of
1.21. A book that has been political only in its rejection of the service of
the state in 1.6 suddenly gets a keen edge: the poet's family has been
opposed to Octavian in the Perusine War—and this is something that
Propertius regards as important over a decade later.[15]

---

[13] We have found Osgood 2006 particularly helpful in the writing of this section.
Pelling provides a clear and masterly account of the period in the *CAH*, Vol. 10, 2nd
edn (1996), 1–69. Syme 1939 remains a classic treatment of these years. For an
account of the iconography, see Zanker 1988. Also recommended are K. A. Raaflaub
and M. Toher (eds.), *Between Republic and Empire, Interpretations of Augustus and his
Principate* (California, 1990); Gurval 1995; K. Galinsky (ed.), *The Cambridge Companion to the Age of Augustus* (Cambridge, 2005).

[14] Unless specified as AD, all dates in this section are BC.

[15] For a reading that takes the revelation of 1.21–2 as fundamental to reading
Propertius as a writer on politics, see Heyworth, *BICS* 50 (2007), 93–128.

Knowledge of the events of the twenty-five years after the assassination of Julius Caesar in 44 is vital for the understanding of Propertius. Any brief account is going to be tendentious, and serious study will consider more detailed, better annotated histories, as well as looking at the sources: literary, numismatic, epigraphic, and architectural. But we believe the following survey may be of some use to readers of this volume.

The dominance of Julius Caesar after his victories in the civil wars of 49–45 had given Rome a brief period of peace after fifty years of repeated warfare in Italy.[16] But on the Ides (15th) of March 44 he was assassinated by Brutus and Cassius and the rest of the conspirators. At the time, his mistress Cleopatra, the queen of Egypt, was living in Rome;[17] his fellow consul and close friend Mark Antony was also in the city; and his great-nephew, the eighteen-year-old Gaius Octavius, was with his future general Marcus Vipsanius Agrippa in Apollonia (in modern Albania) preparing to campaign with Caesar against the Parthians in requital for the massacre of Crassus' army and the capture of his standards at Carrhae nine years before. Cleopatra returned to Egypt the following month. Mark Antony played brilliantly on the emotions of the crowd to inflame it against the conspirators, who fled from Rome within a month of the Ides.[18] Octavius sailed back to Italy and discovered on landing near Brundisium that Caesar had adopted him and nominated him as his principal heir. Modern historians call him Octavian—after adoption he became Gaius Julius Caesar Octavianus—but in fact he made use of the magical name Caesar.[19]

In July Octavian celebrated funeral games in honour of his adoptive father. During this period a comet appeared; this was generally interpreted as a sign of Caesar's apotheosis, and became known as the

---

[16] The Social War (91–89), Sulla v Marius (88–81), revolt of Lepidus (78–77), Spartacus' revolt (73–71), the revolt of Catiline and Manlius (63–62), gang wars in Rome (much of the 50s), Caesar v Pompey, Cato, and others (49–45).

[17] Cic. *Att.* 14.8.1, Dio 43.27.

[18] For Caesar's funeral, Plut. *Ant.* 14.3–4, *Brut.* 20.2–6, App. *B.Civ.* 2.143–7. Suetonius (*Iul.* 84) does not believe that Antony played on the feelings of the crowd but cf. Cic. *Att.* 14.10.1, *Phil.* 2.91.

[19] Cic. *Att.* 14.12.2. The name Octavian is used today to avoid the confusion of referring to two different men as Caesar.

Julian star.[20] Soon afterwards Octavian put a star above the head of
the statue of Caesar which was placed in the temple of Venus (Plin.
Nat. 2.93–4, Suet. *Iul.* 88); the comet regularly features on coins; and
Augustan literature is full of allusions to it.[21] Tensions were not slow
to develop between the eighteen-year-old, referred to as 'the boy' by
some who underestimated him, and Mark Antony, who was now
approaching forty.

Viewing Antony as the enemy of the republic, the senate turned to
Octavian as their champion, and in the spring of 43 two battles were
fought in Cisalpine Gaul (northern Italy) at Forum Gallorum
(a particularly brutal encounter) and Mutina, in which the senat-
orial forces, commanded at the final stage by Octavian, defeated
Antony's.[22] Asinius Pollio wrote from Spain that 'the flower and
youth of our soldiers have perished' (Cic. *Fam.* 10.33.1).

With Antony thus humiliated, the senate now tried to brush the
young Octavian aside and to put its authority behind Caesar's assassins. Octavian, however, would have none of it. He controlled eight
legions and, in a pattern of events familiar in the history of the
century, he marched on Rome demanding the consulship. Despite
the fact that he was only nineteen, more than twenty years below the
legal age, he was declared consul in August.[23]

Then on 27 November 43, Octavian met with Antony and Marcus
Aemilius Lepidus, another leading politician and Caesar's former
Master of the Cavalry, at Bononia in Cisalpine Gaul. They appointed
themselves 'triumvirs for establishing a constitution' for a period of
five years and divided the empire between them. They wished to
dispose of their many political enemies and, even more importantly,
to raise money, and in order to do so, they reintroduced the grim
practice of proscription. This involved publishing a list of Roman
citizens who were declared outlaws. Whoever killed someone named
on the list would receive a reward and the state would confiscate the
dead man's property. Some 300 senators and 2,000 *equites* were

[20] See J. T. Ramsey and A. L. Licht, *The Comet of 44 BC and Caesar's Funeral Games*
(Atlanta, 1997).

[21] E.g. Verg. *Ecl.* 9.46–50; *Aen.* 8.681; Hor. *Odes* 1.12.46–8; Prop. 3.18.34, 4.6.59;
Ov. *Met.* 15.746–50, 840–51.

[22] Cic. *Fam.* 10.30.3 (an eyewitness account of the battle); App. *B.Civ.* 3.67–8, 71.

[23] Suet. *Aug.* 26.1, App. *B.Civ.* 3.88, Dio 46.43.

proscribed, and the most famous victim of the reign of terror that ensued was the great orator, philosopher and champion of the republic, Marcus Tullius Cicero, whose severed head and hands were displayed on the Speakers' Platform in Rome, a grisly demonstration of the extinction of freedom of speech.[24]

Brutus and Cassius, the assassins of Julius Caesar, were now gathering forces in the East for the inevitable showdown with Antony and Octavian. When Brutus was in Athens, he recruited among others the future poet Horace, then a student, who, if his poetry is to be believed, won the rank of tribune and commanded a legion at the battle of Philippi.[25] This battle, in which a survivor estimated that 24,000 were killed,[26] was fought in two stages during October 42 in northern Greece, about 200 miles from the site of the battle of Pharsalus in which Caesar had defeated the republican Pompey in 48: the coincidence allowed Vergil to confuse the two in the horrendous evocation of civil war and a world spinning out of control that ends Book 1 of his *Georgics* (489–514). Antony won; Brutus and Cassius committed suicide; Octavian was ill, according to hostile accounts, and, warned by his doctor's dream, he was carried out of his camp only a short time before the enemy overran it.[27] Horace fled the battlefield (*Odes* 2.7.9–10) and at some stage returned to Italy 'with his wings clipped' (*Epist.* 2.2.50). He was confronted with a grim situation.

For while Antony had the glory of a great victory and went off to the East to re-establish order and to raise money, Octavian took on the highly unpopular task of going back to Italy to confiscate land on which to settle the 50,000 veterans of the Philippi campaign.[28] He caused bitter anger. Large areas were confiscated from inhabitants of around forty cities, leading to violent protests and riots. The dispossessed landowners flocked to Rome to plead their cause and gained

[24] Sen. *Suas.* 6.17. For further horrific details of the proscriptions, see App. *B.Civ.* 4.8–35.

[25] Hor. *Epist.* 2.2.43–8, *Sat.* 1.6.47–8.

[26] Plut. *Brut.* 45.1, App. *B.Civ.* 4.112: the survivor was Messalla.

[27] Vell. Pat. 2.70.1. He may have taken refuge in a marsh (Plin. *Nat.* 7.148).

[28] P. Brunt, *Italian Manpower, 225 BC–AD 14* (Oxford, 1971), 488–98; L. Keppie, *Colonisation and Veteran Settlement in Italy: 47–14 BC* (London, 1983), 60.

the support of the people.[29] While the proscriptions had affected the upper classes, the confiscations uprooted vast numbers of ordinary people. Their huge scale is reflected in the remarkable fact that the three greatest poets of the period all hailed from areas that were affected.[30] Horace came from Venusia and it seems that his family lost its farm in the region: he says that the resulting poverty drove him to write poetry.[31] Vergil's family owned property near Mantua and he vividly conveys the chaos and misery caused by the confiscations in two of his Eclogues (1, 9). The unpredictability of fortune is shown in the first of these, in which a fictitious pastoral character named Tityrus is allowed to continue his old life by a young god in Rome (1.6, 42), presumably referring to Octavian, who was twenty-one at the time of the confiscations.[32] Thirdly, Propertius' family holdings were in Umbria, an area which suffered not only from the confiscations (4.1.121–30), but, as we shall soon see, from their appalling consequences.

The difficult relationship between Octavian and Antony was now put under new pressure. In 41 Antony's brother Lucius and his own wife Fulvia gathered a force of six legions from the disaffected, and occupied Rome in protest at what Octavian was doing. The latter soon drove them out of the city and later in the year Lucius' forces took refuge in Perusia in Umbria, where they were besieged by Octavian and his generals. Starvation forced Lucius and his army to surrender early in 40. While Lucius was undoubtedly pardoned, there is uncertainty about the fate of the Perusines.[33] Appian asserts that though Octavian executed all but one of the town councillors, he spared those citizens who appealed to him; however, a deranged Perusine burnt the city down before he could plunder it. Dio claims that the city was deliberately burnt, that most of the citizens were killed, and that 300 knights and many senators were sacrificed on the

---

[29] Appian, *B.Civ.* 5.12.   [30] Osgood 2006: 143.

[31] *Epist.* 2.2.51–2. Cf. the presentation of Ofellus in *Sat.* 2.2.

[32] On 1 January 42 the senate had confirmed the deification of his adoptive father Julius Caesar and he was given the title 'son of a god' on coinage probably from 40–39. For non-Romans in the East Octavian allowed precincts to be consecrated to himself. For his policy in this respect, see Dio 51.20.6–7.

[33] App. *B.Civ.* 5.48–9, Dio 48.14.3–6.

altar of Divus Julius; the same figure of 300 (knights and senators) is mentioned by Suetonius (*Aug.* 15), whose report adds that it happened on the Ides of March. This siege is the episode Propertius recalled in 1.21–2, some ten years later, as we saw at the start of the section. Osgood writes that the 'image of an unburied corpse lying on the dusty hills … may be the most chilling in all the literature of civil war'.[34]

The fact that Octavian's ruthlessness had seen through the programme of confiscation and resettlement had put him on a level with Antony as a political and military figure; relations between them continued to deteriorate. In 40 it looked as if another civil war would break out. But when the forces of both triumvirs gathered at Brundisium, they parleyed with each other, making clear their reluctance to fight.[35] Two prominent figures, Maecenas acting for Octavian and Asinius Pollio acting for Antony, brokered a treaty. To cement the peace, Antony married Octavian's sister Octavia. (Fulvia, and Octavia's husband, had just died.) The triumvirs repartitioned their spheres of power, Octavian being allocated most of the West, Antony the East, and Lepidus Africa. Vergil celebrated the peace in his fourth Eclogue, asserting that a new golden age would begin with Pollio's consulship (40). Pollio was a key player in the literary world; and the same was true of Maecenas, at least within the next couple of years. Born into an equestrian family, he claimed descent from the Etruscan king Lars Porsenna. He gathered round him poets of considerable talent, in some cases men of genius such as Vergil and Horace. A remarkable Satire by the latter (1.5) tells how he and Vergil accompanied Maecenas on another diplomatic mission to Antony. The heady optimism of Vergil's Eclogue was not to find immediate fulfilment: the years that followed the confiscations were to prove as dangerous as those that they succeeded.

Sextus Pompeius, the son of Caesar's opponent Pompey the Great, was the surviving leader of the republican cause. Some of those conquered at Philippi fled to him, soon to be joined by victims of the confiscations.[36] To represent him as a pirate is to succumb to

---

[34] Osgood 2006: 170–1. Augustus omits Perusia from his *Res Gestae*: presumably this was not an episode he wished to be memorialized.

[35] App. *B.Civ.* 5.57, 59, 64.   [36] App. *B.Civ.* 4.85.

Octavian's propaganda, but it was easy enough for the latter to play up the piratical aspect of his raids on the Italian coast and his disruption of the grain trade,[37] which caused serious hardship in Rome. The triumvirs came to terms with Sextus in the treaty of Misenum in 39, but though this saw the end of the proscriptions, it did not solve the Pompeius problem in the long term. In 37 Agrippa, Octavian's trusted general, created an inland harbour (the Portus Julius) near Naples in order to train a new navy to deal with him. In an extraordinary feat of engineering, Lake Avernus was joined with the Lucrine Lake by a canal, and a breakwater was built on the coast.[38] The following year Octavian, Agrippa, and Lepidus defeated Sextus in a campaign that ended off Naulochus in Sicily on 3 September.[39] The senate voted that a golden statue of Octavian should be set up on a column with the inscription 'He established peace, long disturbed by discord, by land and sea.'[40] After Naulochus, Octavian forced Lepidus to leave the triumvirate.[41] It was now just him and Antony.

In *Antony and Cleopatra* Shakespeare suggests, with acute historical insight, that the difference in the characters of the two surviving triumvirs was reflected in their Western and Eastern spheres of power, with Octavian evincing a chilling Roman control and Antony an addiction to the decadent luxury of Egypt, though it seems improbable that he was as much under the sway of Cleopatra as Shakespeare portrays him. After all, his relationship with her gave him important military and financial support. The divergent personalities of these two Romans are reflected in their self-identification with gods, Octavian with the rational harmonious Apollo,[42] Antony with Hercules and later Dionysus;[43] though both of these were bringers of civilization, the former had served as the slave of the Eastern queen Omphale and the latter was wedded to the pleasure principle.[44] It became more and more clear that the two men could not coexist.

[37] Flor. 2.18.2.

[38] See e.g. Verg. *Geo.* 2.161–4 (and Prop. 3.22.28 n.); Strabo 5.4.5.

[39] App. *B.Civ.* 5.118–22, Dio 49.8.4–11.1.

[40] App. *B.Civ.* 5.130. Cf. Prop. 3.11.72.

[41] App. *B.Civ.* 5.123–26, Pelling 1996: 10.

[42] Suet. *Aug.* 70.1, Zanker 1988: 48–53, Osgood 2006: 237–9, Miller 2009: 15–30.

[43] Dio 48.39.2, Zanker 1988: 45–7, Osgood 2006: 240–1.

[44] For the contrast between Antony's and Octavian's gods in visual art, see Pelling 1996: 43–4.

Antony's task was to bring a greater level of stability to the East. The main problem, one that he was never to solve, was Parthia.[45] His intention was to realize Caesar's ambition, cut short by his assassination, to take revenge for Crassus' defeat at Carrhae in 53 and to regain the standards which had been lost there. However, despite the successes of his general Ventidius, he suffered disastrous setbacks, even managing to lose more standards.[46]

Meanwhile there was disorder in Italy, gangs of bandits roaming the country openly armed with swords.[47] This proved an opportunity for Octavian: in what Osgood refers to as his 'crackdown on crime' the bandits seem to have been dealt with[48] and some kind of police force was established in Rome. Furthermore he found a peaceful way of settling some 20,000 veterans after the defeat of Sextus Pompeius; the catastrophic destabilization caused by the confiscations was not repeated.[49] And, since grain could now arrive from Sicily, Rome was properly fed.

Most famously, the process now began by which Octavian turned Rome, previously a city of brick, into one of marble.[50] Octavian himself and his and Antony's supporters erected and rebuilt temples on a sensational scale.[51] There must have been a strong sense of renewal throughout the city. Among Octavian's most famous buildings were the Temple of Apollo (dedicated in 28), the great family Mausoleum (28), and the Theatre of Marcellus (13). (Marcellus, Octavian's nephew and son-in-law, was the first person to be interred in the Mausoleum.) The most important of the public works of the late thirties were those of Octavian's right-hand man Agrippa, who transformed Rome's water supply system.[52] In 34 he paid for repairs to the Aqua Marcia aqueduct and ensured that it supplied areas of the city which had formerly been inadequately served. In his

[45] Cf. Prop. 3.4. In general see A. N. Sherwin-White, *Roman Foreign Policy in the East: 168 BC–AD 1* (London, 1984), esp. 307–21; G. C. Sampson, *The Defeat of Rome: Crassus, Carrhae, and the Invasion of the East* (Barnsley, 2008).
[46] Dio 49.44.2, 53.33.2.   [47] Suet. *Aug.* 32.1.
[48] App. *B.Civ.* 5.132; cf. Suet. *Aug.* 32.1–2, Dio 49.15.1, Pelling 1996: 37, Osgood 2006: 324.
[49] App. *B.Civ.* 5.129, Dio 49.14.
[50] Suet. *Aug.* 28.3; cf. Dio 56.30.3, Augustus, *Res Gestae* 19–21.
[51] Zanker 1988: 65–77, Purcell, *CAH* 10, 2nd edn (1996), 782–9.
[52] H. Evans, 'Agrippa's water plan', *AJA* 86 (1982), 401–11.

aedileship in 33 he repaired the Aqua Appia and the Aqua Anio Vetus aqueducts.[53] In a channel on top of the Aqua Marcia he built an entirely new stream of water into the city named the Aqua Julia in honour of Octavian (as we have noted, his full name was Gaius Julius Caesar Octavianus). Pliny tells us that in his aedileship 'he built 700 cisterns, 500 fountains as well, 130 distribution tanks, many of them magnificently decorated' (*Nat.* 36.121). In addition he drained, cleaned and restored the city's sewer system. He gave a face-lift to Rome's public baths, establishing free admission.[54] In view of the fact that Rome had had no new aqueduct for 100 years and the four that had existed were 'almost in a state of collapse' (Front. *Aq.* 9), the expenditure and labour organized by Agrippa must have transformed conditions in the city.

Antony was responsible for the Eastern provinces, and there he stayed, but his absence from Italy enabled Octavian to promulgate lethal propaganda against him. It is true that his marriage with Octavia had broken down in 37 and that he was having a lasting affair with Cleopatra. But was it also true, as Dio claims (49.41.1–4), that he gave away Roman provinces to her children by Caesar and himself?[55] Just as damaging was the fiction which circulated in Italy that, if he conquered Octavian, Antony would present Rome to Cleopatra and make Alexandria the centre of the empire.[56] From the speech that Dio puts into Octavian's mouth on the eve of the inevitable battle (50.24.6–7), we get some impression of the tone of the propaganda: the contemptible and cowardly Egyptians worship reptiles and other beasts, and, worst of all, are slaves to a woman.

When Octavian declared war on Cleopatra in 32, he was doubtless aiming to obfuscate the truth that he was launching a civil war.[57] Certainly Vergil, in a great propagandist passage of the *Aeneid*, presents the conflict as a clash between Egypt and Rome (8.678–713). In point of fact, however, the two consuls as well as a significant number of senators had fled to Antony. And Horace in his ninth

---

[53] Plin. *Nat.* 36.121, Front. *Aq.* 9.   [54] Plin. *Nat.* 36.121.

[55] For the gaudy but largely decorative show of the Donations at Alexandria, see Pelling 1996: 42–3.

[56] Dio 50.4.1,5.4; cf. Hor. *Odes* 1.37.6–12, Prop. 3.11.31–2, Ov. *Met.* 15.826–28, Flor. 2.21.2. For the propaganda war as a whole, see Pelling 1996: 40–1.

[57] But see *contra* Woodman 1983 on Vell. Pat. 2.82.4.

Epode scornfully points us to the Roman soldiers who, he asserts, are the slaves of an Egyptian woman and her eunuchs (11–16). Octavian and Agrippa defeated the combined forces of Antony and Cleopatra in a somewhat anticlimactic encounter at Actium (on the west coast of Greece) in 31. It is arguable that Antony and Cleopatra won the battle.[58] However, they certainly lost the war, and the following year they committed suicide in Egypt. Octavian, who had pursued them there, had become the undisputed master of the Roman world, and he could now make the claim that the whole of Italy had supported him (*Res Gestae* 25.2). A great deal was made in 29 BC of the closing of the Gates of War in the shrine of Janus, signifying peace throughout the Roman world: this had apparently not happened since 235. Perhaps the golden age forecast in Vergil's fourth Eclogue had at last arrived.

In 29, after a period of mopping-up operations in various areas while Maecenas remained in tight control at Rome, Octavian eventually returned to Italy. He was later to assert that by the consent of everybody he had power over everything (*Res Gestae* 34.1). On arrival he held a three-day triumph, the first day for the Dalmatian campaign which had preceded the final reckoning with Antony, the second for Actium, and the third for Egypt, which was now his personal possession. This is not the place to analyse the arrangements through which Octavian became emperor in all but name: he was called *princeps* (first citizen). When on 16 January 27 he changed his name to Augustus, he made use of a word with strong religious associations. In one of history's most remarkable exercises of political spin, he had since the mid-thirties been attempting—with considerable success—to render obsolete his ruthless and blood-stained image as the young triumvir and to reinvent himself as the pious father of the fatherland (*pater patriae*), a title he actually assumed in 2 BC. His domination certainly brought an end to the horrors of civil war and gave Italy and the Roman world the stability for which everybody must have longed. But peace and stability came at a price. A hundred years later Tacitus asserted (*Ann.* 1.4), with hyperbole* but with truth, that 'the state had been completely transformed. There was no trace anywhere of the old free Roman

[58] Pelling 1996: 59.

character. Equality no longer meant anything. Everybody was at the emperor's beck and call.'

Augustus ruled till AD 14 and the fundamental stability which he brought to Rome and its empire was to continue long after his death. Not everybody was content, however, and there were conspiracies against him spanning his whole reign.[59] How did the poets of the period feel? Maecenas' protégés and friends Vergil and Horace certainly wrote in support of the regime, but their attitude can at times be disconcertingly hard to read. The current standard reading of the *Aeneid* is heavily influenced by the so-called 'Harvard School' of scholars in the USA in the 1950s and 60s[60] who felt that the poem has two voices, 'a public voice of triumph and a private voice of regret'.[61] Many readers find that the optimism attendant on the Roman mission is offset, perhaps overwhelmed, by the poem's acknowledgement of the horror and suffering which it caused.

Some claim that Augustan poets cannot have expressed attitudes subversive of the regime: it would have been impossible to get away with it under an autocracy. One answer is that they didn't always manage to do so. Augustus withdrew his friendship from the love elegist Cornelius Gallus,[62] who then committed suicide in 26. Though the reasons behind his forfeiting Augustus' *amicitia* were almost certainly political—Gallus was the governor of the emperor's private province of Egypt—his poetry was not enough to save him. Then much later, in AD 8, Ovid was banished from Rome, partly, it seems, for political reasons, but also because his *Ars Amatoria* was seen by Augustus as corrosive of his moral legislation. If the others spoke out, it was not going to be loud and bold.[63]

---

[59] Suet. *Aug.* 19.1, Dio 54.15.1. For the conspiracy by Fannius Caepio and Murena in 22, see Dio 54.3.4–8, Vell. Pat. 2.91.2.

[60] S. J. Harrison in Harrison (ed.), *Oxford Readings in Vergil's* Aeneid (Oxford, 1990), 5–6.

[61] A. Parry, 'The two voices of Virgil's *Aeneid*', *Arion* 2–4 (1963), 66–80, quotation p. 79.

[62] See p. 5, and n. 6, for the poems P. addresses to him in Book 1.

[63] For discussion of the analogous issues attending the interpretation of the twentieth-century Russian composer Dmitri Shostakovich, see J. Morwood, *Virgil: a Poet in Augustan Rome* (Cambridge, 2008), 2.

3. PROPERTIUS, 'LIBER II' AND THE
AUGUSTAN REGIME

How does the history matter to the reader of Propertius? In the first place, we should return to the remarkable fact that in a book published in 29 BC (or thereabouts) 1.21–2 draw attention to the committed opposition of his relative to Octavian in the Perusine War over a decade earlier. The young Caesar is now in control of the Roman world, but the elegist still associates his name with disorder and death. It is against this background that we should read the references to Maecenas and Caesar in the later books. Book 2 begins by addressing the readership at large (O), before turning, in the manner of a Horace or a Vergil,[64] to Maecenas (2.1.17–45):

> quod mihi si tantum, Maecenas, fata dedissent,
>   ut possem heroas ducere in arma manus,
> non ego Titanas canerem, non ...
> bellaque resque tui memorarem Caesaris, et tu   25
>   Caesare sub magno cura secunda fores.
> nam quotiens Mutinam aut, ciuilia busta, Philippos
>   aut canerem Siculae classica bella fugae,
> euersosque focos antiquae gentis Etruscae,
>   et Ptolemaeei litora capta Phari,   30
> aut canerem Aegyptum et Nilum, cum tractus in urbem
>   septem captiuis debilis ibat aquis,
> et regum auratis circumdata colla catenis,
>   Actiaque in Sacra currere rostra Via,
> te mea Musa illis semper contexeret armis,   35
>   et sumpta et posita pace fidele caput.   36
> sed neque Phlegraeos Iouis Enceladique tumultus   39
>   intonat angusto pectore Callimachus,   40
> nec mea conueniunt duro praecordia uersu
>   Caesaris in Phrygios condere nomen auos.
> nauita de uentis, de tauris narrat arator;
>   enumerat miles uulnera, pastor oues;
> nos contra angusto uersamus proelia lecto.   45

---

[64] *Satires* 1.1.1, *Epod.* 1.4, *Odes* 1.1.1; Verg. *Geo.* 1.2, 2.41, 3.41, 4.2.

But, Maecenas, if the fates had given me so much that I could lead heroic hands to arms, I would not sing Titans, not <*mythology or Greek or earlier Roman history*>: I would record the wars and actions of your Caesar, and you would be my second concern, just behind mighty Caesar. For as often as I was singing Mutina, or Philippi, burial place of citizens, or the naval wars involving rout off Sicily, and the overturned hearths of the ancient Etruscan race [i.e. the Perusine War], and the capture of the shore of the Ptolemaic Pharos, [30] or Egypt and Nile, when he was going feebly, dragged into the city, his seven waters captured, and the necks of kings encircled by gilded chains and the beaks [of ships] from Actium running on the Via Sacra, my Muse would always weave you into those arms, a faithful individual at the taking up and at the putting down of peace.

But neither does narrow-chested Callimachus thunder the Phlegraean uproar of Jupiter and Enceladus, [40] nor does my heart suit the composition of Caesar's name back to his Phrygian ancestors in epic verse. A sailor talks about winds, a ploughman about oxen; a soldier (re-)counts wounds, a herdsman sheep; we on the other hand engage in [*and* versify] battles on our narrow bed.

Though the argument concentrates on the poet's inability to write of anything but his love, this is in effect a *recusatio**, a refusal to compose a panegyrical epic, such as Maecenas would wish. Though readers have taken this as an acknowledgement of Maecenas' patronage, there is no sign here that gifts have been given. The summary of poetry P. might have written if he could contains some unfortunate details: amid the victories of Octavian, Perusia appears again, recalling the last two poems of the previous book; and in the reference to Philippi we are forcefully reminded that all the battles referred to here occurred in civil wars (*ciuilia busta*, 27). The elegy ends by putting on the lips of the man who has been asking for an epic a quintessentially elegiac pentameter (2.1.71–8):

> quandocumque igitur uitam me Fata reposcent,
>   et breue in exiguo marmore nomen ero,
> Maecenas, nostrae spes inuidiosa iuuentae,
>   et uitae et morti gloria iusta meae,
> si te forte meo ducet uia proxima busto,   75
>   esseda caelatis siste Britanna iugis,
> taliaque illacrimans mutae iace uerba fauillae:
>   'Huic misero fatum dura puella fuit.'

Therefore, whenever the Fates demand life back from me, and I am a brief name on a small piece of marble, Maecenas, envied hope of our youth, just glory for my life and death, if by chance the route close to my tomb carries you, bring to a halt your British chariot with its carved yoke, and weeping cast such words as these to the mute ash: 'A hard-hearted girl was the destiny [*or* the death] of this poor soul.'

One area where we know of opposition to Augustus is in the reforms aimed at strengthening and encouraging marriage. Suetonius, *Aug.* 34 reports:

> He revised the laws and enacted some new ones, for example one about luxury, and on adultery and sexual behaviour, on electoral bribery, and on marriage for senators and knights. This last law he had framed rather more severely than the others, and he was unable to carry it in view of the demonstrations of those opposed to it, except by removing and softening some of the penalties, granting a three-year delay before it came into force and increasing the rewards.[65]

An early law of just this kind is mentioned in 2.7 (we have no other evidence for it): P. celebrates the abrogation of the law, which might have forced him to get married (and thus abandon 'Cynthia'), and does so in terms that imply the existence as early as 28 of the kind of arguments with which Augustus will be concerned, in particular the need to keep the birth-rate high among Roman citizens in order to maintain a supply of soldiers and officers for the army. He grants that Caesar is great (*at magnus Caesar*, 5); but that greatness is limited to one sphere (*sed magnus Caesar in armis*); in matters of love military victories count for nothing (*deuictae gentes nil in amore ualent*, 6). The attempted interference is treated with scorn. Moreover, the importance that Augustus attached to his policies on marriage gives a keen edge to elegy 3.12, for there P. examines the conflict between the emphasis given to marriage and the regime's foreign policy, always pushing out the boundaries of the empire, and thus requiring Roman soldiers and magistrates to spend their lives far from Italy. In 3.12 (and again in 4.3) it is not an elegist and his mistress who are separated by foreign travel, but husband and wife: he goes to war, she is left at home, desolate.

---

[65] Those married and with children were granted rights, especially of inheritance, not available to others. Further reference to opposition is found in Dio 54.16, 56.1–10.

Caesar appears again in 2.10 (**P**), directly addressed this time, as *Auguste*. The poem apparently lacks its opening, the first extant words being *sed tempus lustrare aliis Helicona choreis* [but it is time to traverse Helicon with different dances]. The new style, P. goes on to reveal, will feature *tumultus* and *bella* (7, 8), since his *puella* is written.[66] He urges his Muses to gather their strength and begins to sing grandly of military victories over Parthia, India, Arabia (11–16). But then he desists, and puts the project off to some future moment: this brief promise is all he can offer—and the final word of the poem is *Amor*. The tone of this poem will depend on what follows; if we find that the programme is changed, that the closing reference to *Amor* was a farewell, that Caesar's victories begin to play a major part, then we will find sincerity here, and a real change of attitude. But we do not: this plays out on a larger scale the move in 2.7.5 from *at magnus Caesar* to *sed magnus Caesar in armis*: brief acceptance of Caesar's greatness in fighting successful wars is followed by a reassertion of the poet's interest, in *Amor* not *Arma*.

The issue is complicated by the nature of 'Book 2'.[67] As transmitted, it is, at 1,362 verses, almost 300 lines longer than any other Augustan poetry book.[68] There are, moreover, many places where scholars have reasonably suspected *lacunae**, and certain series of couplets seem to be mere fragments of poems (e.g. 2.3.45–4.22; 11; 17.1–18.38; 2.30.1–22[69]); it is easy to imagine that a few hundred lines have been lost from two original books of between, say, 800 and 1000. And this possibility is raised to a high level of probability by the

[66] Here we see a striking instance of the equation of Cynthia and the elegiac book, as discussed by Wyke 2002: 46–77.

[67] On the division of 'Book 2', see Heyworth, *PLLS* 8 (1995), 165–85 (with references to earlier discussions, of which the most important is O. Skutsch, 'The Second Book of Propertius', *HSCPh* 79 (1975), 229–33; Lyne 2007: 184–210 and 227–50; Günther 1997: 6–14; C. E. Murgia, 'The division of Propertius 2', *MD* 45 (2000), 147–242.

[68] Hor. *Sat.* 2 has 1,083 verses.

[69] The canonical numeration is based neither on a probable reconstruction of the division into elegies nor on the divisions marked in any manuscript (which are apparently due to medieval conjecture for P. as for other poets such as Catullus, Horace, and Ovid whose work involves discrete poems collected into books); this can be particularly unhelpful in 'Book 2'. It is important that readers do not take the numeration to indicate the status of groups of verses, but use it simply to refer to individual verses or groups of verses.

mention of three books as part of P.'s imminent funeral cortège at 2.13.25–6:

> sat mea sat magna est si tres sint pompa libelli,
> quos ego Persephonae maxima dona feram.

Large enough is my funeral procession, if there are to be three little books in it, for me to bear to Persephone as the greatest gifts.

The *tres libelli* in context must refer to the poet's own work; and this implies that the third book is now begun (*liber alter*[70] at 2.3.4 having marked the early stages of the second book). It looks as though 2.10 was part of the signing off from the original second book (perhaps even the very end), while 2.13 works very well as the start of a book: structurally it has similarities to 2.1, and the first fourteen lines (**Q**) make statements about the origin, purpose and potential audience of his poetry, using the symbolism of earlier poetic programmes* to make their point.[71] If 2.10 is a promise of what P. will write next time he takes up his stylus and begins a book (more elevated poetry, epic based on Caesar's forthcoming victory over the Parthians), the opening hexameter of 2.13 seems to be fulfilling the promise:

> Non tot Achaemeniis armatur Itura sagittis
> spicula quot nostro pectore fixit Amor.

Ituraea is not armed with so many Persian shafts as Love has fixed arrows in my breast.

The military vocabulary, the epithet *Achaemeniis,* and *Itura* (or whatever Eastern place-name lies below the transmitted *etrusca*) recall his promise to sing of victories in the East; but *Amor* in the pentameter reduces the epic pretension to a fleeting simile, and reasserts the elegiac and erotic nature of the poet's work.[72]

---

[70] The use of *liber alter,* together with the similarity of subject matter (Cynthia's dominance in particular), shows that it is misguided to give the title 'Monobiblos' to Book 1, as some do: a *monobiblos* is a work complete in a single volume, whereas P. stresses the continuities in his poetry. (Martial must be referring to a specific edition when he uses the expression *Monobiblos Properti* in the title to 14.189.)

[71] See L. P. Wilkinson, 'The continuity of Propertius 2.13', *CR* 16 (1966), 141–4, and Heyworth, *Mnemosyne* 45 (1992), 45–59: Callimachean* motifs are prominent.

[72] Further links are: 2.13.3–4 with 2.10.25–6; 2.13.11 with 2.34.57, 59; 2.13.16 with 2.34.18. As the final poem of the book, 2.34 moves from the territory of love elegy into literary history and thus mirrors the pattern of 2.13 at the start.

It has been widely accepted that 'Book 2' is an amalgamation of two original books, with material lost in lacunae*. Moreover, given the length of 2B (952 verses + lacunae from the start of 2.13) and its incoherence, there remains a strong case for suspecting that elements transmitted as part of 2B did not originally stand there. And the length of 2A (380 + *lacunae* to the end of 2.10) further suggests that some of the later material originally belonged here. It seems likely then that the fragment 2.11 once stood near the end of 2A, where it could mark a (temporary) dismissal of the beloved, and the couplets that apparently refer to the reception of Book 1[73] could also come from the original second book, e.g. 2.24.1–2:

> 'sic loqueris, cum sis iam noto fabula libro
> et tua sit toto Cynthia lecta foro?'

'Do you speak so, although you are a byword since your book became known, and your Cynthia is read all over the forum?'

Still, there is much that is speculative about such a thesis, and what we call 'Book 2' has a general programme of developing the relationship between the poet and his Cynthia against the backgrounds of contemporary politics, as we have seen, and the poetic tradition. So Callimachus, who is present only through allusion* in Book 1, is named at 2.1.40 (cited above): he did not have the capacity to write grand epic; nor does Propertius. But the Greek elegist is evoked already in the opening couplets (2.1.1–4):

> Quaeritis unde mihi totiens scribantur amores,
> unde meus ueniat mollis in ora liber.
> non haec Calliope, non haec mihi cantat Apollo:
> ingenium nobis ipsa puella facit.

You ask how it happens that so often I write of love affairs, how my book comes in elegiac form on to people's lips. It is not Calliope who sings this for me, nor Apollo: it is my girl herself who creates my poetic talent.

The second couplet responds directly to Callimachus's accounts of his inspiration in the *Aetia* (fr. 1.21–8 [B]; and in the encounter with the Muses that follows), but at the same time asserts the Latin elegist's novelty and difference. *totiens* in the first verse evokes

---

[73] Note the singular *libro* in the citation. The other such couplet is 2.20.21–2.

Πολλάκι [often], the first word of the *Aetia*, and draws attention to the way that the second book reprises *amores*, the theme of the first. So it should be little surprise that 2.1–9 describe the poet's inability to live without Cynthia and the pain of living with her, her notoriety and waywardness, her interest in other men and in material gain, the uniqueness of her gifts, and the utter commitment of the poet's love. Elegy 2.13, the apparent start of the original third book, is followed by two poems that celebrate first a reunion with Cynthia and then a night in bed with her: such a way of life does not lead to the horrors of civil war (2.15.41–8: Actium is mentioned in 46). Other poems deal with ageing (2.18.5–20) and cosmetics (2.18.23–30), with Cynthia's infidelity (2.16A, B, 2.21) and his (2.22 A, B, 2.23), and with her departure to the countryside (2.19) or by sea (2.26B)—in each case the poet follows. He dreams that she is ship-wrecked and drowning, and he cannot save her (2.26A), and has a dreamlike encounter with a group of Cupids, who arrest and take him home (2.29A). He describes a life-threatening illness, and Cynthia's recovery when he prays for her (2.28). He bemoans her enthusiasm for making a public exhibition of herself in the towns of Latium (2.31–2)—why not stay in Rome, especially now the portico of the temple of Apollo has been opened on the Palatine? He complains about the chastity required of the devotees of Isis (2.33A) and about Cynthia's ability to drink and ignore him (2.33B).

In 2.34, P. addresses a friend, given the Greek pseudonym Lynceus, who has in a moment of drunkenness tried to seduce Cynthia, and this despite his being a poet of high philosophical seriousness. The wish to educate in the ways of love gradually asserts itself over the anger with which the poem begins, and the poem goes on to give advice on what is suitable for a writer who is interested in love (as all men are: 2.34.24): Lynceus should not write ethics (27–8) or natural philosophy (51–4), nor epic (39–40) or tragedy (41), but elegy in imitation of Callimachus and Philitas (31–2) and Propertius himself, whose reward is to rule over symposia, amidst a crowd of girls (57).[74] He enjoys this role; it is Vergil's task to write the *Aeneid*, a greater (but not necessarily better) work than the *Iliad*. But Vergil also wrote the *Georgics* and more notably the *Eclogues*, a work concerned, in P.'s

---

[74] Verses 51–66 are cited in the appendix as item R.

description (67–76), with love: so too Varro wrote of Leucadia, Catullus of Lesbia, Calvus of Quintilia, Gallus of Lycoris—and Propertius' Cynthia will live on too, if Fama gives him a place among his predecessors (2.34.93–4: the final couplet):

> Cynthia quin uiuet uersu laudata Properti,
>   hos inter si me ponere Fama uolet.

4. BOOK 3

By the time he began Book 3, Propertius' relationship with Cynthia and his role as lover and poet were thus firmly established and fully explored. From this well-grounded elegiac stance he now makes raids into a variety of new territories: compact versions of earlier texts, such as the Homeric epics (1, 12), Ennius' *Annales* (3), and a tragedy (15); a hymn to Bacchus (17); social commentary on travel for profit and for war (4, 5, 7, 12), on luxury (13), nudity (15), and relations between the sexes (11, 19); he explores the breadth of Rome's empire, and the advantages and disadvantages it brings. The opening sequence defines his poetic and political intentions more precisely than anything he had written previously; and the closing sequence revisits material from Book 1 and in other ways marks the movement towards the farewell to Cynthia in the final poem. And amid these developments continuity is maintained by a number of poems that could well have appeared in earlier books: in poem 6 a slave, Lygdamus, serves as go-between when Propertius and Cynthia have fallen out; in 8 the two of them have fought; 3.10 celebrates her birthday; and 3.16 shows the poet reacting to an imperious demand that he come at once, even at night, to see her at Tibur, some twenty miles from Rome.

Exposition of individual poems we leave to the commentary, but it may be useful to discuss here some aspects of the book's style, structure, diction and themes. In the section on versification (pp. 41–2), we shall mention the use of the vocative to provide metrical flexibility; but even in this book, which has far fewer whole poems constructed as conversations than does Book 1, use of the second person is common. In the first poem for example, the initial *Callimachi manes et Coi sacra Philitae* (maintained by verbs as far as line 6) is followed in verse 13 by a second person addressed (implicitly) to *scriptores*, by the vocatives *Roma* (15) and *Pegasides* (i.e. 'Muses', 19), with a second person of the reader in between (*quod pace legas*, 17). Verses 25–30 are a rhetorical question (thus implying an audience); and in 31–2 we have a paired address to *Ilion* and *Troia*. Elegy 3.2 addresses Polyphemus in 7, and any girl celebrated by the poet in 17–18. In 3.3 the poet addresses *Alba* (3) and *Pan* (30); and is himself addressed by Apollo in 15–24, and by Calliope in 39–50. A succession of vocatives gives particular liveliness to 3.4: *Quiris* (3), *prorae*, and *armigeri*, serving to imply the army as a whole (7–8), *Mars* and the fires of Vesta (11), *Venus* (19). And so on in the poems that follow, with the second person regularly appearing in initial couplets (3.6, 8, 9, 12, 14, 17, 20, 22, 24), even when the addressee does not dominate the poem as a whole (3.7.1 *pecunia*; 11.1 *quid mirare*; 13.1 *quaeritis*; 19.1 *a te*). In short, Propertian elegy is a conversational mode.

Structure and Sequence

Attempts to find an architectural structure to Book 3 akin to that discerned by some in Book 1 and in Vergil's *Eclogues*[75] have been largely unavailing.[76] On the other hand there have been good discussions of sequences of poems, in particular the opening five,[77] 3.12–14,[78] and the closing run;[79] this seems a more helpful way to

[75] e.g. O. Skutsch, 'The structure of the Propertian Monobiblos', *CPh* 58 (1963), 238–9, and E. Courtney, 'The structure of Propertius Book I and some textual consequences', *Phoenix* 22 (1968), 250–8; and, for the *Eclogues*, P. Maury, 'Le secret de Virgile et l'architecture des *Bucoliques*', *Lettres d'Humanité* 3 (1944), 71–147, O. Skutsch, 'Symmetry and sense in the *Eclogues*', *HSCPh* 73 (1969), 153–69, largely debunked by N. Rudd, *Lines of Enquiry* (Cambridge, 1976), 119–44, and in D. West's review of Rudd's book, *CR* 28 (1978), 76–8; see also G. O. Hutchinson, 'Propertius and the unity of the book', *JRS* 74 (1984), 99–106.

[76] For one such see A. Woolley, 'The structure of Propertius Book 3', *BICS* 14 (1967), 80–3.

[77] F. Solmsen, *CPh* 43 (1948), 105–9; Nethercut, *AJPh* 91 (1970), 385–407; D. P. Harmon, *Studies in Latin Literature and Roman History* (ed. C. Deroux, 1; 1979), 317–34; Butrica, *ICS* 21 (1996), 131–9.

[78] Nethercut, *CPh* 65 (1970), 99–102; Jacobson, *ICS* 1 (1976), 161–4.

[79] Courtney, *Phoenix* 24 (1970), 48–53; Jacobson, *ICS* 1 (1976), 164–73; Putnam, *Arethusa* 13 (1980), 105–10.

think about structural aspects of the book—how is the reading of each poem affected by its place within the context? This is an issue we have tried to direct attention towards in the commentary, though we realize much more could be said. Poems 1–2 assert P.'s continuing commitment to elegy and the immortal fame that can result from it, which is equal to what a Homer can gain; we therefore have a clear pointer to the outcome of the dream in 3.3. But there is conflict between the advice of Apollo and Calliope in 3.3, that he is suited to elegy, not epic, and the start of 3.4, describing Augustus' plans to attack Parthia. That war is presented in 3.4, and again in 3.5, as motivated by greed, and marginal to the poet's concerns and future plans. Elegy 3.6 then confirms the elegiac stance, by returning us to an account of a temporary separation from Cynthia; and 3.7 confirms the dangers of travel and greed by giving a graphic account of a youth who left Rome to seek his fortune in the East, with disastrous consequences. The poem addressed to Maecenas (3.9) is sandwiched between two further pieces of erotic elegy, 3.8, celebrating a lovers' fight, and 3.10, celebrating a birthday. The latter is then succeeded by 3.11, the poem on the subservience of even the greatest heroes to female command: like Propertius were Jason, Achilles, Hercules, Antony—but not Augustus. Again, however, 3.12 brings a striking change of approach: an attack on Postumus for abandoning his wife to seek wealth through service in the army facing the Parthians, i.e. for acting in accordance with the interests and purposes of the _princeps_ (except to the extent that Augustus wants to promote marriage). Looking East is a persistent aspect in this sequence: after Semiramis and Cleopatra in 3.11, we have the misadventures of Postumus in 12, Eastern luxuries and _suttee_ performed by Indian wives in 13, and nakedness of Spartan girls exercising in 14.

The final poem of the book is a farewell to Cynthia that recalls 1.1 in its reference to the attempts of a Thessalian witch and family friends to cure him of his love (3.24.9–10 n.). Each of the preceding sequence has some strongly closural element: 23 reports the loss of the writing tablets that have carried the exchange of messages (and, implicitly, the elegies themselves), and the final couplet reworks the final line of Hor., _Sat._ 1. Poem 21 presents the poet about to leave Rome to travel to Athens, a journey he has refused to undertake at 1.6.13 because it would mean separation from Cynthia; and 22 addresses for the first time since Book 1 the Tullus with whom he has failed to make that eastward journey, and urges him to return to Rome, in a counterpoint to P.'s own movement. It is in 3.20 that the run of closing poems seems to begin in earnest: what could better express alienation from Cynthia than an attempt to seduce another? However, Courtney (*Phoenix* 24 (1970), 48–51) pointed out that 3.17 is already an attempt to escape from love, through wine rather than travel or the taking of a new lover. And reminiscence of Book 1, and 1.1 in particular, is significant at moments in 3.15 (esp. 3–4), where we find that Lycinna, not Cynthia, was actually his first love, and even in 3.10, where verse 15 recalls Cynthia's first capture of his eyes. As often, it is impossible to say where the ending begins.[80]

Some poems point to the closure of the Cynthia collection by glancing ahead to themes of Book 4.[81] Whereas Book 3 has a tendency to look out to the empire, 4 will bring us back to Rome. This is signalled by the summoning of Tullus from abroad; 4.1.1 will immediately show that, at least as a poet, P. has not gone ahead with his departure for Athens. In their concern with mythical narrative, poems such as 3.15 (Antiope) and 19 (various lustful women from myth) look towards 4.4, 9 and 10; and, as a poem on Marcellus, a member of the imperial household, 3.18 is followed by 4.11 on Cornelia, Augustus' step-daughter. The selective summaries of *Iliad* (3.1.25–30) and *Odyssey* (3.12.23–37) will be succeeded in 4 by two poems (7 and 8) that model themselves on scenes from the Homeric epics. And 3.12 also prepares the way for 4.3, Arethusa's letter to her husband Lycotas, absent at wars in the East.

Some Imagery, Themes, and Words

Book 3 has a greater range of reference and of generic and stylistic affiliation than the previous books. The commentary attempts to

---

[80] An even more extraordinary example of an ending that begins early comes in the *Aeneid*, where the word *finis* ('end') occurs 9 times in Book 1 (but only once in Book 12), including the pointed sequence at 199 *dabit deus his quoque finem*, 223 *et iam finis erat*, 241 *quem das finem, rex magne, laborum*, 279 *imperium sine fine dedi*.

[81] For more on Book 4, including citation of 4.1.1, see pp. 342–4.

guide readers through this breadth in the notes on individual couplets, and, where appropriate, in the paragraphs introducing poems.
The index will also guide readers to topics for which we might
otherwise have found space here. The best accounts of P.'s diction
and of his imagery are in German (Tränkle 1960, Riesenweber 2007
respectively), though much can be gleaned from the commentaries
(including Shackleton Bailey's *Propertiana*) and from what is said by
way of comparison in R. Maltby, 'Tibullus and the language of Latin
elegy', *PBA* 93 (1999), 377–98. As Maltby says (377), 'It is Propertius
whose verbal exuberance and mythological complexity mark him out
from the others.' Myth is prominent in fewer poems of Book 3 than 1
(see pp. 2–4); but verbal exuberance is much in evidence, poems
developing through complex combinations of metonymy* and metaphor. Four phrases from 3.20 may illustrate the dynamism of P.'s
diction.[82] The words *pectus amore terat* (6) mix the physical *terat*
('may rub') with the apparently abstract *amore*; this can, however, be
taken as 'darling', just as *pectus* could be the physical 'chest' as well as
the emotional 'heart'. *OLD* places *cedent* (19) under meaning 5 '(of
periods of time) to pass': with *multae horae* as subject, this is clearly
valid; but the addition of the dative *meis sermonibus* implies the sense
'allow room for' (cf. *OLD* 8, 16). In verse 17 *constringet pignora signo*,
the pledges are abstract, and if we take the signet ring as physical,
constringet ('will bind') must be metaphorical. Shortly after, in *uincitur foedere lectus* (21), the bed is a physical symbol, a metonym* of
the couple's love; the verb ('is bound') is again metaphorical, but this
time the binding is done by the abstract *foedus*.

One important source of imagery, and a model for the rapid
succession of one image by another, such as we can see in parts of
3.1, 3, 9, 24, is the prologue to Callimachus' *Aetia* (B; along with his
other metapoetic* writings). This tradition was explored at length by
both Wimmel 1960 and Kambylis 1965; again there is nothing in
English which covers the ground so thoroughly. From Callimachus
and his imitators P. takes the metapoetic images of small v large, thin
v fat, light v heavy, refined v braying; of water (n.b. C: the sea, large

---

[82] See also 3.20.2 n. for the bold imagery of that line (two striking metonymies*
juxtaposed).

rivers, small streams, the pure fountain;[83] a drink to be contrasted with the wine imbibed by those who seek rough-and-ready inspiration rather than exquisite artistry); of *uiae*, the journeys, on boats, on foot (3.1.6; 15.25–8; 21.21–4) or in a chariot (3.1.11–14; 3.18; 9.58), and the paths along which men travel, whether broad and crowded or narrow and new (*Aet.* 1.25–8 [**B**]: cf. 3.1.14–18; 16.30). Some have argued that P. has a visual or painterly imagination (e.g. Boucher 1965: 41–64). It is true that he mentions painters (1.2.22; other artists too in 3.9.9–16), and engages with their art (e.g. 2.3.41–4; 6.27–36; 12), but Skutsch (*CQ* 23 (1973), 322–3) was able to show that even in 2.12 the language functions through concepts rather than visual images. The quickly and subtly shifting images in the programmatic* poems also point to the primacy of words in the Propertian imagination.

One characteristic of Propertian diction is the repeated use of loaded words with contrary force.[84] For example, *cura* is regularly used in Books 1 and 2 to mean the emotion 'love' (1.1.36, 8.1), or to refer to Cynthia herself, as his 'love' (2.25.1, 34.9). But we also find the senses 'care' and 'source of anxiety', the latter most strikingly at 2.16.1, when it is applied to a rival, the *praetor* returning from Illyria: *maxima praeda tibi, maxima cura mihi* [the greatest source of gain for you, of anxiety for me]. Within Book 3, the noun is used for the troubles caused by money (3.7.3), and with the epithet *molesta* to condemn hair-dressing (3.14.28). When it is used in connexion with love, it is now only as something the poet wishes to be rid of: Bacchus' wine potentially provides a *curarum medicina* at 3.17.4, and at 3.21.3 *cura puellae* is something that grows with constant gazing—which P. will avoid by travelling to Greece. There is similar complexity to the use of the pair *mollis* and *durus*. As we note on 3.1.19–20, there is a recurring antithesis between *durus*, used of epic (or tragedy) or the masculine, and *mollis*, of elegy or the feminine.[85]

---

[83] E.g. 3.1.3–6; 3.1–6, 23–4, 32, 45–6; 5.11–14; 7; 9.35–6; 15.31–4; 21.1–20.

[84] This should not be taken to imply that such plays are not found in other poets too: cf. Vergil's use of *cura* at *Ecl.* 10.22, *Geo.* 2.433, 4.345, *Aen.* 1.227, 1.261, 4.1.

[85] Further examples of the antithesis at 3.11.20, 15.29; cf. also 3.3.18 *mollia prata*; 3.5.2 *proelia dura*.

But like others who reject love (2.30.13, 32.47), the elegiac mistress can also be *dura* (1.7.6, 17.16 *quamuis dura, tamen rara puella fuit* [although hard-hearted, yet she was a girl in a million]; 2.1.78) and so as a consequence is the life lived by the elegiac lover (1.6.36, 1.7.8). Within Book 3, the *mollitia* of the shade on Helicon (3.3.1) seems to deceive the poet into thinking that he can drink directly from the epic fountain by which he lies, and the epithet *mollia* at 3.9.57, emphasized by being cast first in the couplet, asserts the elegiac nature of the reins Maecenas is urged to take up, though that might seem at odds with the (in fact unrealistic) expectation that he will drive the chariot on an epic path.

Another word that contributes to the generic complexity of the text is *mora* (together with the whole concept of delay). In the first couplet of 1.12, *mora* is an alternative for *desidia*, something of which conventional morality firmly disapproves:

> Quid mihi desidiae non cessas fingere crimen,
>   quod faciat nobis Cynthia[86], Roma, moram?

Why don't you cease inventing a charge of sloth against me, on the grounds that Cynthia is causing us a distraction, Rome?

At the same time it is a state P. longs for, as he is currently estranged from Cynthia (3–14). Moreover, between *Roma* and *mora(m)* we hear *amor*, a third anagram,[87] and one glossed by *Cynthia*, the preceding word (and cf. *amores*, 5). Elsewhere too *mora* refers to time spent with a girl ('dalliance' rather than 'delay', e.g. at 1.1.35, 3.44, 8.1), and it has a flavour of pleasure particularly at 2.15.6, where it refers to teasing delay during sexual play, and 10, where the couple's kisses are prolonged. In 3.1.7 *a ualeat, Phoebum quicumque moratur in armis*, the verb suggests the length and the tedium of epic. The lack of movement it implies leads to the lightly contrasting *eat* (8) and the metaphor of poetic movement that builds up thereafter. Both the verb and the noun (and synonyms such as *cunctari*) are regularly used to comment on a slow narrative pace: e.g. Hor. *Sat.*

---

[86] A conjecture for the transmitted *conscia*, but the only plausible solution to the problems of the transmitted text: see *Cynthia, ad loc.*

[87] Itself juxtaposed with *mora* at 1.3.44, 13.6.

1.1.13.[88] Thus *mora*, with which he has been charged at 1.12.2, is here thrown in the teeth of those who write on war as well as those who wage it. In such a context *mora* deserves the elegist's disapproval.[89] At 3.3.19–20, on the other hand, Apollo reveals that the Propertian book is written to be 'tossed on a stool for a girl to read when she is waiting for her man': without the man's delay in coming the book does not get read, and the girl does not prepare herself properly for the erotic encounter.[90] On the other hand, in 3.14.21–8, the attraction of Spartan society is that there is no problem of access or delay, no need to outwit a husband; attractive as that may be, it leaves no function for Propertian elegy—if lovers are always together there is no time for reading, no need for the comus* or the tricking of *austeri uiri* (3.3.50, echoed at 3.14.24). In short, elegiac *amor* requires *mora*.

5. METRE, SCANSION, AND VERSIFICATION

Quantity

The scansion of Latin verse of the classical period is quantitative, not based on speech stress as in English. Syllables are either light or heavy, regardless of where the speech stress falls in each word.

(a) All syllables which contain a long vowel or a diphthong are heavy, e.g. both syllables in each of *cautē, Paetī, cārās*. For the purposes of scansion heavy syllables are marked with a macron –, light syllables with the symbol ◡. This convention sometimes results in a syllable containing a short vowel being marked with a macron; see below.

---

[88] Followed by *deducam* to hurry the climax; cf. Ov. *Met.* 2.105–6; 3.225; 8.549, 652; 10.659–80.

[89] At 3.16.2 it is Cynthia who disapproves of delay, telling him to come at once (*missa ... mora*); similarly 3.23.12. In 3.20 the sun is urged not to delay (12), whereas the moon's lingering is just what the poet wants, once night comes (14).

[90] As Katherine van Schaik pointed out to us.

(b) If a short vowel is followed by two consonants whether in the same or in different words, the syllable is heavy, e.g.:

> dīcĭtĕ, quō părĭtēr cārmēn tĕnŭāstĭs ĭn āntrō? [3.1.5]

In this line the syllables underlined are heavy although in each case the vowel is—and should be pronounced—short. When the consonants are in different words, one of them will almost always be at the end of the first and the other at the start of the second, but very rarely they are both in the second word (this happens in Homer too) as in:

> iūră dără̆rē stătŭās īntĕr ĕt ārmă Mără̆rī [3.11.46][91]

(c) Exceptions to rule (b)

(i) if a short vowel is followed by a combination of mute (*p, t, c, b, d, g*) and liquid (*r* and less commonly *l*), the syllable may be scanned either light or heavy, depending on whether the syllable is treated as dividing between or before the pair of consonants, e.g. *pāt-rĭs* (3.3.29) and *sāc-ră* (3.1.1), but *pă-trēs* (3.11.32), *dŭ-plĭcī* (3.1.22), and *uŏlŭ-crēs*:

> ēt Vĕnĕrīs dŏmĭnāē uŏlŭ-crēs, mĕă tūrbă, cŏlūmbāē [3.3.31]

(ii) in Homer metrical necessity can cause a short consonant to remain short even when it comes before two consonants which are not mute and liquid. P. does this occasionally:

> Īdāēūm Sĭmŏēntă Iŏuīs cūm prōlĕ Scămāndrō[92] [3.1.27]

If P. wants to use the word *Scamander* at all, the metrical demands of elegiac couplets mean that he will have to precede it with a short syllable. However, a long syllable could stand perfectly well before *spēctāstī* in the following case: he makes the choice to have a syllable which scans short in front of the initial two consonants:

> brācchĭă spēctāstī sācrīs ādmōrsă cŏlūbrīs [3.11.53]

Similarly in 3.11.67, 19.21.

---

[91] See *Cynthia* 165–6.

[92] This is a conjecture by Wolff, but an extremely probable one. Homer has the word 12 times in the *Iliad*, e.g. 5.36.

(d) *h* has no metrical value; it does not count as a consonant.
qu functions as a single consonant.
x and *z* both count as double consonants (= *cs*, *ds*).

(e) The second *i* in *mihi* and *tibi* can be short (commonly) or long
(3.3.17; 6.19; 8.40; 9.31; 10.11; 13.45; 16.23; 19.2; 20.16; 21.5, 16, 34; 23.9;
25.3). Also variable is the *i* in the pronominal genitive ending -*ius*: thus it is
short in *illĭŭs* at 3.6.10, but long in *īstīŭs* at 4.5.58.

Elision (and Prodelision)

A final open vowel (i.e. a vowel at the end of a word) followed by a vowel at
the start of the next word is elided (as in French *c'est*, but in Latin the elision
is not marked):

  prīmŭs ĕg(o) īngrĕdĭōr pūrō dē fōntĕ săcērdōs [3.1.3]

The final *o* of *ego* elides before the *i* of *ingredior*. *h*, having no metrical value,
does not stop elision:

  flūmĭnăqu(e) Haēmŏnĭō cōmmĭnŭs īssĕ uĭrō [3.1.26]

The *e* of *que* elides before *(H)aemonio*.
  For the purposes of reading Latin, the best advice is not to pronounce the
elided vowel unless it makes a vital contribution to the meaning.
  More surprisingly, a final syllable ending −*m* elides before a following
vowel, e.g.:

  ēt mēc(um) īn cūrrū pāruī uēctāntŭr Ămōrēs [3.1.11]

When reading, do not pronounce the elided syllable fully but nasalize the
vowel (Allen 1989: 31).
  A vowel before *est* (or *es*) is liable to *prodelision*, i.e. the *e* of *est* disappears,
not the vowel at the end of the word before, e.g.:

  tūtă sŭb ēxĭgŭō flūmĭnĕ nōstră mŏrā (e)st [3.9.36]

Types of elision may be classified in order of ascending gravity: (a) short
vowels (of which that in *que* is especially easily lost); (b) vowels + final *m*;
(c) long vowels; (d) diphthongs.[93]

---

[93] For details, see Platnauer 73–8.

The elegiac couplet

This consists of a hexameter followed by a pentameter.

$$1 \quad 2 \quad 3 \quad\quad 4 \quad 5 \quad 6$$
$$-\underline{\smile\smile} \mid -\underline{\smile\smile} \mid - \parallel \underline{\smile\smile} \mid -\underline{\smile\smile} \mid -\underline{\smile\smile} \mid -\underline{\smile}$$

$$1 \quad\quad 2 \quad\quad\quad 3 \quad\quad 4$$
$$-\underline{\smile\smile} \mid -\underline{\smile\smile} \mid - \parallel -\smile\smile \mid -\smile\smile \mid \underline{\smile}$$

The *hexameter* consists of six feet, the first five of them basically dactylic in pattern ($-\smile\smile$). However, a spondee ($--$) may be substituted for a dactyl in any of the first four feet; the fifth foot is nearly always a dactyl and the sixth foot is always a spondee or trochee ($-\smile$). Book 3 contains one hexameter with a fifth-foot spondee (often called a 'spondeiazon'[94]); as in all bar one of the Propertian instances found in other books this involves a Greek word:

īnfēlīx Ăquĭlō, rāptāē tĭmŏr Ōrīthȳīaē [3.7.13]

There is usually a strong caesura (lit. 'a cutting'), a break between words after the first long syllable of the foot, in the middle of the third foot, e.g.:

Cāllĭmăchī mānēs // ēt Cōī sācră Phīlītāē [3.1.1]

The *pentameter* consists of the first two and a half feet of a hexameter (i.e. as far as the third foot caesura), followed by the same again, but without variation in the second half of the line, which always contains two dactyls. (As in the hexameter the final syllable can be long or short.)

īn uēstrūm, quāēsō, // mē sĭnĭt(e) īrĕ nĕmŭs [3.1.2]

M. Platnauer, *Latin Elegiac Verse* (Cambridge, 1951) offers a very helpful account of how the elegiac couplet is handled by Propertius, Tibullus and Ovid, and serves as a backgound to the more detailed observations that follow.

Caesurae (i.e. word-breaks in the middle of a foot)

As has been said, in the hexameter the main caesura nearly always comes after the first syllable of the third foot (3s: s = 'strong', as opposed to w =

---

[94] Cf. Cicero, *Att.* 7.2.1.

'weak', where the caesura follows a light syllable). Where this is missing, P. usually has a caesura after the first syllable of the fourth (4s) or the second foot (2s), and mainly both; thus in Book 3 there are fifty-four lines lacking a strong caesura in the third foot; twenty-six have the sequence 2s, 3w, 4s; and a further fourteen have 2s, 4s without a true caesura in the third foot, e.g. 3.15.29 (where the conjunction *et* strictly belongs with what follows). There are six verses where the only strong caesura in the middle feet is in the fourth foot (3.2.3, 6.39, 7.57, 11.33, 14.7, 21.7), and two with only 2s (3.5.39, 22.9). The following six are more unusual:[95]

1 /   2   /   3   /   4   / 5   / 6

Dēïphŏbŭmqu(e) Hĕlĕnūmqu(e) ēt Pūly̆dămāntŏs ĭn ārmīs [3.1.29]

Elision at 2s and 3s; no caesura at all until 5w: with 3w also in 27 and 31 there seems to be a concerted effort to imitate Homeric patterns here.

1 / 2   / 3 / 4 /   5   / 6

ōrgĭă Mūsār(um) ēt Sīlēnī pātrĭs ĭmāgō [3.3.29]

No true caesura until 5w; that in 3 follows *et*.

1 /   2   /   3   / 4 /   5   /   6

tēlă fŭgācĭs ĕqu(i) ēt brācātī mīlĭtĭs ārcūs [3.4.17]

Caesurae at 1w, 2w, and after *et* at 3s.

1 /   2   /   3   /   4 /   5   /   6

nōn mē mōrĭbŭs īllă, sĕd hērbīs īmprŏbă uīcĭt [3.6.25]

Caesurae only at 1s and 3w.

1   /   2   /   3   / 4 /   5   /   6

āut ĭn ămōrĕ dŏlērĕ uŏl(o) āut āudīrĕ dŏlēntĕm [3.8.23]

Caesurae at 2w, 3w and after *aut* at 1s, 4s.

1   /   2   /   3   / 4 /   5   /   6

āut spătĭ(a) ānnōr(um) ēt lōng(a) īntēruāllă prŏfūndī [3.21.31]

No true caesura until 5w; those at 1s and 3s follow *aut* and *et*.

---

[95] In general there is in P. a higher proportion of unusual lines than in Tibullus and Ovid: he shows a greater willingness to experiment (but some oddities may be the result of textual corruption).

In the pentameter there is a word break at the half-way point save where *que* is elided at 3.22.10.

Elision in Elegy

Elisions are found rarely or not at all in certain places in the second half of both lines: see Platnauer 1951: 85–6 on the fifth and sixth feet of hexameters and 87–90 on pentameters.

Hiatus

Hiatus is the 'gaping' that occurs when an open vowel is not elided before another vowel. It is regularly found after (but not before) exclamations, e.g. *o* in the phrase *o utinam* (1.3.39, 4.4.51 etc.), though this happens not to occur in Book 3. Otherwise the only secure instance in the whole corpus* comes at 3.7.49:

> aut thyio thalamō a͞ut Oricia terebintho

Some Oddities of Scansion

3.5.7 *Prometheō*, 41 *Phinēī*, 6.36 *e͞adem* (q.v.); 19.13 *Enipeō*; 23.6 *e͞aͤdem* are all examples of synizesis* (where two vowels within a word coalesce into a single long syllable).

3.9.35 *findŏ*: the shortened -*o* is first found here in a verb with a long penultimate syllable. The shortening of -*o* in a verb with a short penult, such as *uolo* at 2.10.9, begins to emerge in Catullus (e.g. 6.16).

3.19.12 *ābiēgnaͤe*: the *i* is treated as a consonant.

3.23.11 *fuĕrunt*; 3.24.20 *excidĕrunt*: the form with light *e* is a licence frequently used by the poets (and often corrupted by their scribes into the pluperfect or future perfect, as has happened in both these cases).

Start of the Hexameter

Though spondees are freely used as the alternative to dactyls in the first four feet of the hexameter and the first two feet of the pentameter, at the start of the line poets often prefer a dactyl (and they try to avoid opening with a word that forms a spondee in itself). This can be illustrated by the use of *neque* rather than *nec* after an opening monosyllable, e.g. at 3.2.19:[96]

---

[96] There is an analogous preference for *nihil* over *nil* in the same position, as at 2.6.39.

nām nĕquĕ pyramidum sumptus ad sidera ducti,

and by the introduction of *ego* after first person verbs, as in 3.21.24:

scānd(am) ĕgŏ Theseae bracchia longa uiae.

One striking effect is the occasional use of polysyllabic Greek names that fill the opening two and half feet of the line: 3.3.2 *Bĕllĕrŏphōntēī*, 3.14.14 *Thērmōdōntĭācīs* (also 1.20.6 *Thĭŏdāmāntēŏ*; 4.9.1 *Āmphĭtrў̄ōnĭădēs* [cf. Cat. 68.112, Verg. *Aen.* 8.103]).

Ending of the Hexameter

The final word of the hexameter is almost always trisyllabic or disyllabic (sometimes two monosyllables together, as with *et tu* at 3.1.31). (Prodelided *est* and *es* are freely added to the final word, as at 3.7.1; 3.9.59.) The major group of exceptions involve four- or five-syllable Greek words or other manifestations of Greek rhythm (e.g. in the case of *spondeiazontes*: see p. 36). Thus the two examples in Book 3 are 3.7.49 (also with hiatus at the caesura):

nec thyio thalamo aut Ōrĭcĭā tĕrĕbīnthō

and the *spondeiazon* 3.7.13 (as always, the fourth foot is dactylic):

infelix Aquilo, rāptāē tĭmŏr Ōrīthȳīāē.

While there are inevitably some clashes in the first four feet of a hexameter between the way the words are pronounced and the way they are accented by the rhythm of the line, these restrictions on the final feet ensure that the hexameter usually ends with the two in harmony. (See section on Reading, p. 43.)

Ending of the Pentameter

After his first book, P. moves towards the usage familiar from Tibullus, where non-disyllabic words are rare at the end of the pentameter.[97] Polysyllabic endings in Book 3: 3.3.28 *pūmĭcĭbŭs*; 3.4.10 *hīstŏrĭāē*; (3.7.22 *Ăthămāntĭădāē*); 3.11.72 *Iŏnĭŏ*; 3.12.30 *Lāmpĕtĭē*; 3.13.24 *Pēnĕlŏpē*; 3.13.30 *călăthōs*; 3.14.2 *gȳmnăsĭī*; 3.14.8 *pāncrătĭŏ*; 3.19.10 *nĕquĭtĭāē*; 3.20.28

[97] Ovid goes further and has only disyllabic words here, until poetry belonging certainly (*ex Ponto*) or apparently (*Fasti, Heroides* 16–21) to the period of exile.

hīstŏrĭāe; 3.21.20 hīstŏrĭāe; 3.23.20 ĕphēmĕrĭdăs. (Prodelided *est* and *es* are freely added to the final word, as at 3.16.18.)

Since the metre will inevitably lay a certain stress on the final syllable while the word stress in disyllabic words will fall on the penultimate syllable, there is regularly a discord at the end of a pentameter. (See section on Reading, p. 43.)

The final word of the pentameter is usually a noun or verb; otherwise mainly a pronoun or possessive (i.e. *mĕŭs* etc.); parts of *nŏuŭs* appear a number of times (3.19.16, 20.16, 22.14), other adjectives when predicative or otherwise emphatic (3.7.72 *ĭnērs*; 3.9.38 *părī*; 3.13.56 *pĭō*; 3.25.2 *lŏquāx*); the adverb *măgĭs* is found at 3.19.2, *hĕrī* at 3.23.12.

Internal Rhyme

Both in hexameters and in pentameters P., like the other elegists, freely uses internal rhyme between the pre-caesural word (usually an adjective) and the final word of the line (usually a noun). Normally the words are in agreement or in parallel; both are found at 3.12.31–2, e.g.:

> et thalamum Aeaeae // flentis fugisse puellae,
> totque hiemis noctes // totque natasse dies.

Word Order

The previous item has illustrated one basic element of word order in Augustan poetry: the common separation of adjective and noun. Platnauer (1951: 97–103) usefully analyses the flexibility that this gives the elegists in the placement of prepositions. When governing a phrase *inter* regularly comes either first (*inter seros... nepotes*, 3.1.35) or second (*cognatos inter... rogos*, 3.7.10); likewise *in*, but when a monosyllable comes second it normally comes immediately before the noun (*Gallica... in arma*, 3.13.54). Rare are instances where the preposition is not adjacent to any part of the phrase it governs, and we may properly call 3.4.18 an example of hyperbaton* (i.e. dislocation of words):

> et subter captos arma sedere duces

subter governs *arma* here, not *captos... duces*.

Postponement* of conjunctions is another standard part of poetic style in P.'s day. It can be used to help make the verse scan or feel rhythmically effective (e.g. by enabling the poet to have a dactyl in the first foot). Here is a list (we hope tolerably complete) of the instances in Book 3 (asterisks indicate postponement to later than second position):

at: 5.14

aut: 2.24; 3.45; 18.28; 21.27, 24.10

cum: 7.40; 9.41; 15.31; 18.5*; 21.19*, 23.18

cur: 5.32*, 36*

et: 3.12; 5.24, 34, 38; 6.16*, 18, 33; 8.2; 9.22, 33, 52, 53 (?); 10.6, 20, 30;
    11.25, 26, 44; 12.2; 13.8, 37; 14.6; 17.24; 18.10; 21.18; 22.3; 23.10

qua: 3.2; 16.3; 21.22; 22.2

quam: 20.20

quamuis: 19.28*

qui (and other parts of the relative pronoun): *qui* 9.2*; 11.29; 12.14;
    15.36*; 16.11; 18.31*; *quae* 5.31; 11.57; 19.11*; 22.4*; *quem* 11.48,
    20.2*; *quod* 1.21, 4.20, 17.9; *cui* 7.42; 11.15; *quorum* 13.26; *quis** 16.12*

quicumque: 1.7

quis? 16.19; *quem?* 15.22

ne: 12.10*; 16.25

nec: 9.8; 10.10*; 22.28*, 35

neque: 14.28

neu: 12.12*

si: 2.10*, 17; 5.39*, 40*; 6.35, 41; 8.13*, 39, [25*]; 11.38; 23.21

ubi: 10.19

ut: 2.2; 7.54, 11.12

and the enclitics* -*ne*: 6.12*; 16.5*

    -*que*: 21.16*; 25.15

Alternative Forms, Number, and Case

Metrical flexibility is provided by the alternative endings (a) in passive and
deponent forms of the second person singular of the present indicative,
present subjunctive, future indicative: -*ārĕ* for -*ărĭs*, -*ērĕ* for -*ērĭs*, -*bĕrĕ* for
-*bĕrĭs*; and (b) of the third person plural of the perfect indicative active: -*ērĕ*
for -*ērūnt*.

(a) *uectabere* 3.39, *uehere* 5.14, *mirare* 11.1, *tueare* 13.36, *patiare* 25.15,
quererе 25.4;

(b) *meruere* 4.21, *tremuere* 5.33, *fregere* 7.39, *ualuere* 7.42, *coiere* 7.54,
fuere 7.14, *crepuere* 10.4, *accepere* 11.52, *cecidere* 12.14, *nocuere* 12.24, *dedere*
13.34, *concrepuere* 18.6, *periere* 23.1, 2, *mansere* 23.9, *promeruere* 23.10,
tetigere 24.15, *coiere* 24.19.

Propertius also makes use of the collective singular*, and poetic plurals
(on which see e.g. 3.9.30, 3.16.21 nn.). Proper names and other nouns

are sometimes put in the vocative, partly for reasons of metrical convenience, especially in the second half of the pentameter (3.5.6 n.).

The Shaping of the Couplet

Within couplets short sentences often stand in parallel, structure being
provided by anaphora* or polyptoton*, as in 3.20.7–8:

> **est** tibi forma potens, **sunt** castae Pallados artes,
> splendidaque a docto fama refulget auo.

That is a tricolon*, as is 3.6.15–16, but with the second clause spilling over
into the pentameter:

> **tristis** erat domus, et **tristes** sua pensa ministrae
> carpebant, medio nebat et ipsa loco.

At other times the hexameter has a single clause of which the pentameter is
then a restatement or variant, e.g. 3.8.23–4:

> **aut** in amore **dolere** uolo **aut** audire **dol**entem,
> **siue** meas lacrimas **siue** uidere tuas.

Given the balance within each line, as well as the revised statement in the
pentameter of the point made in the hexameter, this can be seen as classically
elegiac in shape, just as it is in expression, with the concentration on the pain
of love and the mutual emotion of the pair of lovers. The balanced phrasing
of the pentameter encourages the reader to supply *uidere* in the first half and
lacrimas in the second (sometimes called ἀπὸ κοινοῦ construction [= 'in
common']); so too at 3.14.18 *hic uictor pugnis, ille futurus equis*; 3.21.9–10
Cynthia...quantum [i.e. *iuerit*] *oculis, animo tam procul ibit Amor*, where the
antithetical *oculis* and *animo* are juxtaposed, while *Cynthia* and *Amor* are set
as far apart as possible. A more difficult instance at 3.19.17–20 has apparently been corrupted by the manuscript tradition: *referam* from 17 has to be
supplied in 19, and *facinus* (or an alternative noun from 19) in 17.

For the definition of the so-called 'golden line', see Glossary.

The Couplet as Unit of Composition

The elegiac couplet is normally end-stopped in Latin. Even in longer sentences and lists, the couplet remains the basic unit into which the thought
falls (e.g. 3.2.11–16, 19–22; 3.5.25–46). A particularly extended sentence
occurs at 3.3.1–14, with carry-over of sense in 1–4, and from 6 to 7.

Three cases where there is a pause in the course of a couplet stronger than between the couplets come at 3.11.47–50 (a striking enjambment* in 49), 3.15.35–8, 3.16.27–30.

Reading

Learning how to scan helps in accurate reading of Latin verse (and prose too, in time); reading aloud often makes the text easier to understand—one begins to see and hear how the words fit together, the regular links for example between the adjective before or after the caesura and the noun at the end of the line. The verse should be read using the natural pronunciation of the Latin words, with the stress normally on the penultimate syllable when that is heavy (*habére, Iugúrtha*) and in disyllabic words (*iúgum*), and on the previous one when the penultimate syllable is light (*cónsule, Mário*). The rhythm of the elegiac couplets may be left to look after itself; it will still come across.

There is sometimes a marked clash between the speech stress (accent) and the underlying verse stress (ictus: underlined). For example 3.16.9:

peccáram sémel, et tótum sum púlsus in ánnum.

Here the clashes in all the first four feet, together with the sequence of *m*s, seem to reflect the poet's unhappy memory of the breakdown of his relationship.

Hidden Quantities

Most modern dictionaries and grammars mark all long vowels, including 'hidden quantities', i.e. the length of vowels before two or more consonants. They will usually scan long, but must be pronounced according to their natural lengths. Some circumstances that cause a vowel to be naturally long before more than one consonant are:

- if they come before *ns, nf, nct, nx* (e.g. *īnfāns*)
- if they occur in most *x* and *ps* perfects (e.g. *rēxi, tēxi, scrīpsi, sūmpsi*)
- if they come before the verbal suffix *sc* (e.g. *crēsco, quiēsco, obliuīscor*).

There are many other instances of naturally long hidden quantities. A good outline is given in Allen 1989, chapter 3 (p. 75 contains a particularly valuable list of miscellaneous hidden quantities).

6. TEXT AND TRANSMISSION

Propertius wrote and published Book 3 in the second half of the 20s BC. For the next millennium and a half all substantial copies were made by scribes and interested readers laboriously writing out, line by line, or couplet by couplet, what they saw in the existing manuscript in front of them. Our earliest evidence for the text is a single couplet (3.16.13–14) written on a wall in Pompeii; that was perhaps a work of memory. But for the bulk of the text we rely on medieval manuscripts, the earliest of them (N) written in northern France in the twelfth century. There is one thirteenth-century manuscript (A), of which only the first two quires (gatherings of parchment leaves) now survive (as far as 2.1.62); given that this (and its descendants) is correct where N is corrupt, we can be certain that A is independent of N. The one MS from the fourteenth century (F) has been shown to be a grandchild of A in its original, complete form. Finally there are over 140 manuscripts from the fifteenth and early sixteenth centuries. Of these some are cousins of F, to be used in the absence of A; and others have been shown to have independent access to the archetype, that is the latest common ancestor of the tradition, likely to have been a copy written in the tenth century or later.[98]

In the meantime the text had been much corrupted: even the more conservative of modern editors accept several hundred conjectural changes of reading. Conscientious medieval and Renaissance scribes typically make something of the order of a hundred fresh errors in writing the 4,000 or so lines of Propertius; those working with less care or knowledge can easily make two or three times this number. Some of these errors may be corrected by readers looking at another manuscript or simply deducing what should have been written, but such attempted corrections may themselves be wrong. There is no reason to think that the process was significantly different in antiquity. We have little idea how many copies stood between the archetype and Propertius' autograph; but it would be optimistic to think fewer than a dozen. Moreover, the longer we imagine to have passed between each copying the greater the chance of physical damage to the exemplar and

---

[98] Working out the familial relationships is a complicated and controversial task, based on reconstructing what the author is likely to have written, and making deductions based on the kinds of errors and changes scribes and readers make in MSS. Though more is said later in the section, this not the place for a full exposition: see Butrica 1984, and the preface to Heyworth's OCT; and for a sensible account of the issues in general, M. L. West, *Textual Criticism and Editorial Technique* (Stuttgart, 1973).

the greater the unfamiliarity of the script and conventions for abbreviation. Readers should not be surprised therefore to find that the text printed in the Oxford Classical Text and again here contains a large number of conjectures (i.e. suggestions made by scholars since the fifteenth century).[99]

Errors occur in manuscripts for a large number of reasons, more than one of which may be operative at any moment. Anyone who writes a text that is above a few lines in length makes mistakes, whether he is the author or a scribe reproducing the material of another: such corruption is fundamentally psychological, a function of the human incapacity for sustained attention and coordination of mind and hand. Since scribes usually know well the language of the text they are writing, they are more likely to replace one word with another than to make a mistake over a single letter and thus produce a nonsense-word: *fingere* becomes *findere* rather than *singere* or *fnigere*. Adjacent forms are repeatedly confused, e.g. moods and tenses of verbs, cases of nouns. Scribes write anagrams (e.g. *integras* for *et nigras* at 3.5.23), replace words with synonyms (and antonyms* too); they write twice what should occur once (dittography*) and once what should occur twice (haplography). At times, one word is substituted for another of the same metrical pattern (e.g. dactylic substitution, especially in the fifth foot of the hexameter, where *tempora, pectora, munere, numine* often interchange, and iambic substitution at the end of the pentameter: see 3.6.30, 14.28). The ends of lines are vulnerable though failures of memory, but also because on the right-hand page of any opening (the 'recto') they are most liable to be damaged; likewise the initial letters on the 'verso' (the left-hand page). Moreover, the first letter of the verse was written separately in many manuscripts, often in colour, and perhaps without reference to the exemplar. Hence the validity of Kenney's Law, 'that any monosyllable at the start of the verse may have arisen from any other', relevant for 3.24.6.[100] Mistakes are made in writing letters pronounced the same, and in reading letter forms that look alike (especially easy in the case of 'minims', the minimal strokes from which many letters are made up, of which there are ten in 'minim' itself). The context often has an effect, with one word assimilated to another nearby in meaning or in form.[101] Words change places, and so do part of words (cf. spoonerism). Lines and couplets are omitted, especially where

---

[99] For further discussion, see Goold, *HSCPh* 71 (1966), 59–106; Butrica, *CQ* 47 (1997), 176–208; Günther 1997. We twice give capitals to words that do not have them in the OCT: *Pecunia* (3.7.1) and *Palatia* (3.9.49).

[100] Cf. *CQ* 8 (1958), 65. We may note 1.9.4 *et*] *quod* C; 2.7.15 *quod*] *et* F; 2.26.18 *qui*] *quam* N: *quod* FL: *et* C; 3.8.18 *has*] *nam* Π; 4.4.53 *te*] *et* C; Juv. 13.65 *hoc*] *ut* Φ.

[101] E.g. *nocturnis* at 3.10.23 has been infected by *nox* two lines earlier, and *intecta* at 3.12.7 by *tectus*, the following word.

some similarity in phrasing makes it easy for the scribe's eye to skip (see the effect of *caput* at 3.10.16, 18); if the missing material is restored in the margin, it may not find its way to its proper home in any subsequent copy (see 3.15 intro.). But material is often inserted from the margin, even though it may have been written there not as a correction, but for some other purpose, e.g. as a parallel (3.25.13–14). Glosses* too may replace the original text if they happen to scan correctly (3.22.13, apparently). Awareness of these phenomena lies behind any claim in the commentary that a particular conjecture has 'palaeographical plausibility'.

Besides trying to preserve what is rightly transmitted and to restore what has been corrupted, the editor of a classical text has to use the most helpful punctuation and orthography. There is no reason to think that Propertius differentiated between lower and upper case, in particular as a means of marking proper nouns;[102] but modern readers expect this, and it confuses if we abandon the convention. This enforces an inauthentic distinction between *amor* and *Amor*, e.g. (see 3.21.2 n.). Modern punctuation is different from that of the Augustan age; but for Augustan books we have little evidence (the Gallus fragment* and what can be surmised from inscriptions); again current usage is the guide for most editors. Though we do not know how P. marked the beginning and end of elegies, we can be sure he did so in some way. This information was apparently lost in the course of transmission, as happened in the case of a number of poets whose books break into separate poems (e.g. Catullus, Horace, and Ovid); the divisions indicated in the manuscripts are conjectural restorations, and there are many errors of omission and commission across the whole corpus*. Book 3 is less problematic in this regard than the other books, but even here the numeration leads us astray in one case, implying the division of 3.24 into '3.24' and '3.25'.[103]

These are the manuscripts on which the text here is based (Roman capitals being used for extant manuscripts, Greek for hypothetical ones):

N: Wolfenbüttel Gudianus 224: the so-called 'Neapolitanus' (it was once in Naples). Written in northern France in the twelfth century.

(A: Leiden, Voss. lat. O.38. Written in northern France c.1230–60. Only extant as far as 2.1.62, so not directly relevant for Book 3.)

Π: lost MS copied from A in 1333 by or for Petrarch, and the ancestor of FLP.

---

[102] He probably expected his text to be read in capitals, like the Gallus papyrus [F].
[103] So e.g. Barber and Camps.

F: Florence, Bibl. Laur. plut. 36,49. Written *c.*1380 for Coluccio Salutati.

L: Oxford, Bodleian Holkham misc. 36 (only extant from 2.21.3). Written in northern Italy in 1421.

P: Paris, Bibl. Nat. lat. 7989. Written, apparently in Florence, in 1423.

Λ: lost MS brought to Italy by Poggio Bracciolini in 1423, and sent to Niccolò Niccoli in Florence in 1427; the ancestor of T and S directly, and through lost intermediaries of JKW, MUR, C.

T: Vatican, Vat. lat. 3273. Written in 1427 by Panormita when he was visiting Florence.

S: Munich, Univ. Cim. 22. Written *c.*1460–70 by Jacopo Bracciolini, son of Poggio.

Γ ('gamma'): lost manuscript; the latest common ancestor of JKW.

J: Parma, Palatinus Parm. 140. Written in Florence *c.*1430–45.

K: Wroclaw, Univ. Akc. 1948 KN 197. Written in Padua in 1469.

W: Vatican, Capponianus 196. Written in Italy *c.*1450–75.

Υ ('hypsilon'): lost manuscript; the latest common ancestor of MUR

M: Paris, Bibl. Nat. lat. 8233. Written in Florence in 1465.

U: Vatican, Urbinas lat. 641. Written in Florence *c.*1465–70.

R: Cologny-Genève, Bodmer 141. Written in Florence in 1466.

C: Rome, Casanatense 15. Written *c.*1470 by Pomponio Leto.

As the earliest extant manuscript, N is necessarily independent of the others; its value is also shown when it fails to include the demonstrably false supplements found in the later manuscripts at 3.1.27, 5.39, 11.58, and in verses such as 3.6.22, 8.19, where it is closer to the original text than ΠΛ, but with readings that can hardly be conjectures as they do not make Latinate sense in themselves. The descendants of Λ form the branch that makes the smallest contribution to the text: at least one of their ancestors must have been a very careless copy, and F itself, the oldest of the three, is full of new errors. But their independence is shown by avoidance of N's errors (mainly ignored in the brief apparatus given here); there are also one or two places in Book 3 where they have an apparently correct reading lost in the other two branches (3.11.25, 23.20), though it is possible that these are due to slips that happened to coincide with the truth.

If manuscripts only ever contained one reading, any deviation would be a mistake in copying, and it would generally[104] be possible to work out the transmitted reading by setting a plurality of independent descendants against the single branch, which would be the one in error. However, it is rare for medieval copies not to contain variants (perhaps copied from the exemplar, or another copy, or else conjectured by a reader). We have already noticed that the other manuscripts share supplements not found in N: this does not show common descent, for the supplements may have been added after the N branch was copied from the archetype, or have been present but ignored by the scribe. A place where the presence of variants in the archetype is clear comes at 3.5.35:

plaustra Boötes] flamma boon *N*: flamma palustra *Π*

It looks very much as though *flamma boon* (or something like it) stood in the text of the archetype. But a reader, perhaps systematically checking against the exemplar, has spotted the error *flamma* for *plaustra* (the words are of similar shape, and *igne* follows in the pentameter), and written the correction above the line. To N comes simply the base text (or a slight corruption of it); the Π branch has taken *plaustra* to be a correction of the nonsensical *boon* (or whatever longer form was in the archetype); but altered it to a form that scans (cf. *paluster*, 'marshy'). Here the third group of manuscripts show their value, choosing the correct pair of words from the three that stood in the archetype:

plaustra bootes *SC*: plaustra boetes *T (with* boone[*in the outside margin)*: plaustra boones *MUR*: palustra boetes *JKW*[105]

What is striking is not so much that the group offers the correct reading,[106] either in the original orthography (*bootes*), or the medieval (*boetes*); but that four of them transmit the nonsensical *boones*, thus shown to be the original of N's *boon*. The *Λ* group has a number of other true readings that are unlikely to be conjectural (e.g. 3.5.6, 10.17); they regularly avoid the errors of N on the one hand and of FLP on the other; and they can be linked to Poggio Bracciolini's bringing to Italy of a new Propertian manuscript; 3.5.35 effectively completes the argument for their independence from the two earlier branches.

---

[104] 'Generally', because occasionally two copyists will coincide in making a mistake.

[105] Here, as elsewhere, this group has been influenced by the Π reading.

[106] An intelligent humanist might have conjectured this on the basis of Sen. *Ag.* 70 (*uersat plaustra Bootes*) and *Med.* 315.

The following abbreviations and Latin expressions appear in the *apparatus criticus*, the list of variants in and deviations from the manuscripts given after (or, in other editions, below) the text:

ante 45 = *ante* 45 <*transposuit*> (i.e. the lines were transposed to a position before 45 by the scholar named)

apud = 'in the text of' (i.e. 'when cited by')

de N incertum (i.e. N cannot be read, or it has an abbreviation of which the interpretation is uncertain)

del. = *deleuit*: deleted (i.e. the line or word was deleted by the scholar named)

inscr. = <*uersus in muro Pompeiano*> *inscripti* (i.e. 3.16.13–14 as written on a wall in Pompeii, *CIL* 4.1950)

inter se mut. = *inter se mutauit* (i.e. the named scholar exchanged the position of the two lines)

lac. = *lacunam* <*posuit*> (i.e. a lacuna* was postulated by the scholar named)

om. = *omittit*: omits (i.e. the line or word is omitted by the named manuscript(s))

post 12 = *post* 12 <*transposuit*> (i.e. the lines were transposed to a position after 12 by the scholar named)

uel similia = 'or similar things' (used as a short cut where there are minor variations in the MSS)

Λ (the Greek capital 'lambda') = all the related manuscripts TSJKWMURC

λ (the lower case 'lambda') = one or more (but not all) of the related manuscripts TSJKWMURC

Π (the Greek capital 'pi') = all the related manuscripts FLP

π (the lower case 'pi') = one or two of the related manuscripts FLP

Ω (the Greek capital 'omega') = the archetype, the latest common ancestor of the extant manuscripts

ς ('stigma', i.e. a symbol used for the combination 'sigma' + 'tau') = an apparently conjectural reading found in a manuscript or a fifteenth-century edition

Because the text of Propertius is notoriously corrupt, as well as the *apparatus criticus* we have given more space to discussion of textual problems than is normal in a commentary of this sort. We believe it is important for students to be aware from early on that the text is uncertain, that repeated copying by fallible scribes and guesswork by fallible editors lies behind what they are reading. One of the authors of this book tried in *Cynthia: a Companion to the Text of Propertius* (Oxford, 2007) to give a reasoned account of the choices made in the Oxford text published in the same year, and readers are encouraged to look in that commentary for more evidence, argument, and bibliography. As the preface of *Cynthia* says, 'no text is definitive'; we hope that readers of this volume too may be moved to propose alternative readings as well as alternative interpretations.

7. GLOSSARY

adjurative: making an earnest or formal appeal: 3.17.19.[107]

adynata: things that can never happen, cited in order to emphasize the unlikelihood of something else: 3.19.5–10.

aetiology (**aetiological**): the study or description of the origins of peoples, places, creatures, customs: 3.11.45.

agon: a formal dispute or debate between two characters, frequent in ancient drama (e.g. those between Theseus and the Herald in Euripides, *Supplices* 399–584; the 'Better Argument' and the 'Worse Argument' in Aristophanes, *Clouds* 889–1112; Hippolytus and the Nurse in Seneca, *Phaedra* 435–579): 3.15 intro.

allusion: an indirect but significant reference to another text: 3.20.18.

amoebaean: referring to passages in poetry in which couplets or longer groups of lines are assigned to two speakers (or sets of speakers) alternately: 3.6 intro.

anaphora: the repetition of a word or phrase in two or more successive clauses: 3.5.1, 13.49.

antonym: a term of opposite meaning to another: 3.21.34.

apopompe: a prayer in which the speaker wishes on others what he wants to avoid himself: 3.8.20.

apostrophe: address of a character within a narrative (from which the writer 'turns away'): 3.15 intro.

apotropaic: lit. 'turning aside', used of magic that directs something unpleasant against an alternative victim: 3.24.9.

apposition: the placing of a noun or phrase alongside another in the same case, without grammatical connexion; sometimes one noun is 'enclosed' within a phrase with which it agrees (3.3.31, 19.22).

aretalogy: a list of the powers (ἀρεταί) of a god: 3.17 intro.

---

[107] References are to notes in the commentary.

asseveration: an assertion backed up by formal language, such as an oath, a wish, or a prayer: 3.15.1.

asyndeton: the omission of conjunctions (such as 'and' or 'but') where these words might occur: 3.11.45–6, 13.49–50.

beatitude: e.g. 'happy the one who...': 3.13.15, 20.9; and n.b. 20.3.

Callimachean(ism): the literary aesthetic (privileging the small-scale, the artful and the learned) associated with the poet Callimachus, prominent in the literary circles of Alexandria in the third century BC, and with his followers in Greek and Latin. Usefully discussed in Hunter 2006, esp. 1–6, 141–6.

chiasmus (chiastic): phrasing where the order of the second half reverses that of the first: 3.2.12.

cletic: adjective applied to hymns that summon a deity: 3.17 intro.

comus (comastic): a practice prominent in Greek and then Latin poetry of passing through the streets after a symposium to visit the house of friends or (especially) loved ones; the comasts will usually be drunk and garlanded. See also paraclausithyron*.

corpus: 'body' of text, the works collected under an author's name: 3.5.14, 21.7.

correption: in metre, the shortening of a long vowel or diphthong at the end of a word when the next word starts with a vowel: 3.11.17 (*Omphale in*).

dactylic: the metrical pattern $-\cup\cup$: 3.23.18. **Dactylic verse** is poetry written using this pattern, i.e. (dactylic) hexameters (the usual metre of epic, didactic, pastoral and satire) and elegiac couplets.

diatribe: 3.13 intro.

disjunctiveness: 3.7.19–20.

dittography: writing twice what should be written once: 3.20.13.

enclitic: a short word attached to the end of another word, e.g. *-ne*: 3.6.12. (In an English translation enclitics are usually rendered before the word to which they are attached.)

enclosure: the existence of links between the start and finish of a poem: 3.14.34.

enjambment (enjambed): the running over of the final word(s) of a sentence from one line, or couplet, of poetry into another: 3.3.13–14 n. (with reference to 18–20).

epexegetic: explanatory: 3.11.64.

epicedion: a funeral poem: 3.18 intro.

ethnography (ethnographical): the description of races and peoples with their customs: 3.13 intro.

exemplum (plural *exempla*): mythological or historical example(s) cited to illustrate a scene or an argument: 3.11 intro., 7–8.

fragments (abbreviated as 'fr.'): portions of a text now mainly lost; these survive sometimes as a result of papyrus* finds, sometimes through citations by other authors: 3.1.1, 5.3–4.

gigantomachy: the battle fought between the gods and the giants: 3.9 synopsis.

gloss: an explanatory word or phrase, especially as added by a scribe to a manuscript: 3.19.19.

gnomē (gnomic): pointed generalization: 3.16.13–14.

golden line: consisting of two adjectives and two nouns with a verb in the middle: the first adjective agrees with the first noun, the second with the second: 3.15.14. See e.g. Wilkinson 1963: 215–16 (he goes on to define a 'silver' and a 'bronze' pattern).

Hellenistic: referring to the period of Greek culture between the death of Alexander in 323 BC and ending either with the sack of Corinth in 146 or with the death of Cleopatra in 30 BC.

hendiadys: 'one' object or idea expressed 'by two' nouns: 3.12.25, 27; 3.14.33, 3.17.37.

homoearchon: referring to words, lines or clauses with the same beginnings: 3.7.51–6; **homoeomeson**: referring to words, lines or clauses that are identical in the middle: 3.7 intro.; **homoeoteleuton**: referring to words, lines or clauses with the same endings: 3.11.57–8, 24.9–10. All three of these frequently result in the omission of text when it is being copied. Homoeoteleuton between adjacent words is allowed by P. (as by some other poets) only within quite strict limits: see Shackleton Bailey 1994.

hyperbaton: unorthodox word order: see p. 41.

hyperbole: the use of exaggerated terms, not be taken literally: 3.12.38.

iambic: a metrical unit having one light (short) syllable followed by one heavy (long) syllable ($\cup -$): 3.6.9.

iconography: visual representation of any kind: 3.17.2.

interstice: a gap between portions of texts, such as two poems: 3.15 intro.

intertext: a text with which the text in question has a link, not necessarily of a kind intended by the author: 3.4 intro., 5.39–46, 6.25–30. **Intertextuality** is the nature or the exploration of such links.

lacuna (lacunose): a missing portion in a piece of text: 3.6.3–4, 22.6.

metapoetic: discussing the nature of poetry: 3.1 intro.

metonym (metonymy): a word associated with someone or something used in place of that person or thing (e.g. 'the Crown' for 'the Queen'): 3.3.21. This is fundamental to Latin poetic style; P. uses *limen* ('threshold': 3.24.29 = 25.9) for example to imply the hardships of the locked out lover. A significant group of metonyms in Latin comes in the use of the names of divinities, e.g. *Bacchus* for wine: 3.17.6. Cf. also synecdoche*.

neoteric: a modern term (derived from Cicero, *Att.* 7.2.1) referring to the 'modern' poets of the middle of the first century BC such as Catullus, Calvus, and Cinna.

onomatopoeia: the phenomenon through which the sound of a word or a phrase suggests its sense: 3.14.6.

oxymoron: the juxtaposition of two words of contradictory meaning to emphasize the contradiction: e.g. 'bitter sweet': 3.5.34, 10.25.

papyrus (plural *papyri*): ancient 'paper', made from the papyrus plant; many fragments, occasionally complete rolls, have been found since the late nineteenth century, and have provided texts that had previously been lost: 3.1 intro., 3.1.8.

paraclausithyron: a poem set 'at the locked door' of the poet's beloved, often the culmination of a comus*: 3.24.30 (= 25.10).

paradoxography: the collection of marvels from geography, biology and anthropology: 3.13 intro.

parataxis (**paratactic**): the juxtaposition of logically related clauses or sentences without the use of subordinating conjunctions: 3.6.1–2.

pejorative: used in a depreciatory way: 3.7.72.

periphrasis (plural *periphrases*): circumlocution, e.g. using a phrase where a single noun might suffice: 3.21.23.

personification: the representation of an idea or thing as having human characteristics: 3.11.51, 13.2, 15.4.

pleonasm: the use of words that reinforce but do not change the sense: 3.15.34.

polyptoton: the repetition of a word in different forms or cases: 3.5.1, 7.33, 17 intro.

postponement, postponed: the placing of conjunctions (and interrogatives) that normally begin clauses at a second or subsequent position; see pp. 40–1 for a list of examples.

preterite: past, i.e. the so-called 'perfect' tense of Latin in historic sequence, where *feci* means 'I did', not 'I have done'.

priamel: statements about other people or things that throw emphasis on the climactic statement about the central figure: 3.2 intro., 3.9.1.

programmatic: announcing or implying the style and content of the literary work that follows: 3.1 intro.

proleptic: the use of an adjective before it actually becomes applicable: 3.6.3, 14.27.

propempticon (plural *propemptica*): a poem written to mark a departure: 3.4 intro.

recusatio: 'refusal', used by modern scholars to describe a poet's declining to write an epic or a poem of praise: 3.9 intro.

semantic: relating to the meanings of words: 3.23.14.

singular, collective: referring to the use of a singular noun to denote a whole group: 3.5.36, 12.3.

sphragis: a passage in which a poet identifies himself, especially at the beginning and end of a poem or a collection: 3.23.24.

syllepsis: an expression in which the same verb is used in two different senses, usually literal and metaphorical (contrast zeugma*): 3.9.23–4, 20.5.

synaesthesia: a blending or confusion of different kinds of sense impression: 3.2.2.

syncope (syncopated): the compression of a word into a shorter form: 3.1.5, 28, 30.

synecdoche: the part for the whole (a subset of metonymy*): 3.1.16, 24.15.

synizesis: where two vowels within a word coalesce into a single long syllable: 3.6.36, 19.13.

tautology: repetition of the same notion in different words: 3.11.17, 3.17.7–8.

tricolon: a series of three parallel phrases.

trope: the use of words in senses beyond their literal meaning, especially applied to groups of interconnected metaphors: 3.8 intro.

zeugma: a figure of speech in which a verb or adjective is applied to two nouns, though it is properly applicable to only one of them: 3.7.29 (cf. *Aen.* 2.780).

Also worth noting are the following conventions, illustrated by examples that occur in the commentary:

[Tibullus] or [Tib.]: square brackets are used to indicate that a work edited under the name of an author is not actually by him, as is the case with what is known as '[Tibullus] 3'.

Annales fr. 1 Skutsch: for authors (such as Ennius) whose fragments* are collected together under different numerations, the numbering used is indicated with the name of the editor (sometimes in abbreviated form, eg. 'Sk.')

8. PARAPHRASE, BIBLIOGRAPHY, IMAGES, AND MAPS

An English version of the printed text was published in *Cynthia* (565–86); we have made use of this for the translations used to convey the sense of individual couplets and phrases. Before each poem we have given a paraphrase; this is at points close enough to the Latin to help as an interpretation of the original phrasing.

On the whole we have restricted the bibliography provided to items in English, but we have cited both in the introduction and the commentary some important items in German, Italian, and French. In the commentary to each poem we append 'additional' items, i.e. those we think helpful that have not been mentioned in the course of the commentary. Works of broader importance and those that are referred to more than once appear in the bibliography at the end.

At one stage we had intended to include (besides the maps that follow) some other images; but in the end we preferred to use the space for text, and came more easily to this decision because so many images are easily found on the Internet (which is also a source of information on topics or words that we have not explained): we encourage those interested to search for images such as the following:

'Cephisodotus' (statue of Eirene with Plutus): 3.5 5–6
'cataphract': 3.12.12
'Dirce'(Farnese bull): 3.15.37–8
'Tivoli Falls' (photographs and paintings of the Villa Gregoriana waterfall): 3.16.4
'Ariadne and Bacchus' (Titian's painting): 3.17.7–8
'treading grapes': 3.17.17–18.

The maps include the majority of the most important geographical features mentioned in Book 3, and should help the reader who wishes, e.g., to trace the planned journey to Athens in 3.21. They illustrate the extent to which the book looks East.

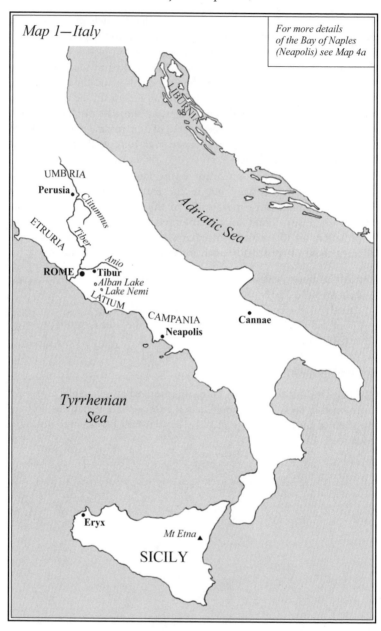

Map 1

Map 2—Greece

THRACE

Oricos   THESSALY

▲ Pindus

Pelion ▲   Aegean Sea

Nicopolis
Actium
LEUCAS
ITHACA   Parnassus   EUBOEA
                Delphi ●   ▲
                     BOEOTIA
                        ▲ Helicon
                        ▲ Cithaeron   Rocks of
                Megara ●   Caphereus
                Corinth ● ● ● ATHENS
Olympia   Mycenae ●   Piraeus
   ●
         ARCADIA
                Eurotas
         Sparta ●   NAXOS
         Taygetus ▲

                Cape
                Malea
   Taenarus ●

                                    DIA
                                 CRETE

Map 2

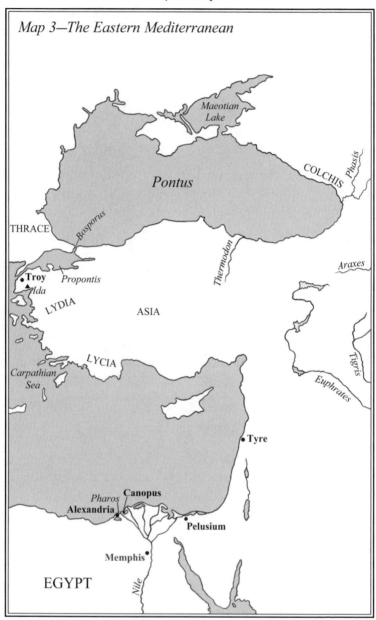

Map 3—The Eastern Mediterranean

Map 3

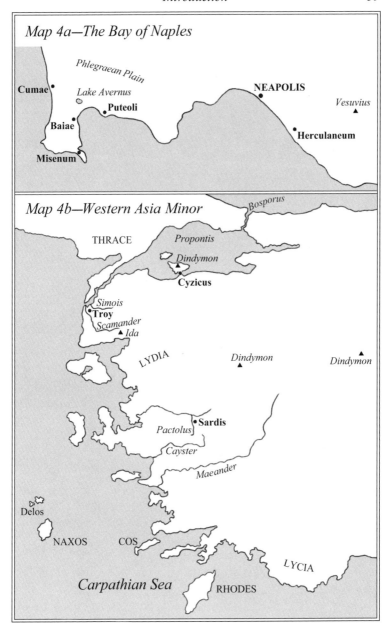

Map 4

PROPERTIUS, BOOK 3

3.1

CALLIMACHI manes et Coi sacra Philitae,
  in uestrum, quaeso, me sinite ire nemus.
primus ego ingredior puro de fonte sacerdos
  Itala per Graios orgia ferre choros.
dicite, quo pariter carmen tenuastis in antro?   5
  quoue pede ingressi? quamue bibistis aquam?
a ualeat, Phoebum quicumque moratur in armis.
  exactus tenui pumice uersus eat.
quo me Fama leuat terra sublimis, et a me
  nata coronatis Musa triumphat equis,   10
et mecum in curru parui uectantur Amores,
  scriptorumque meas turba secuta rotas.
quid frustra immissis mecum certatis habenis?
  non datur ad Musas currere lata uia.
multi, Roma, tuas laudes annalibus addent,   15
  qui finem imperii Bactra futura canent;
sed, quod pace legas, opus hoc de monte Sororum
  detulit intacta pagina nostra uia.
mollia, Pegasides, date uestro serta poetae:
  non faciet capiti dura corona meo.   20
at mihi quod uiuo detraxerit inuida turba,
  post obitum duplici faenore reddet honos.
omnia post obitum fingit maiora uetustas;
  maius ab exsequiis nomen in ora uenit.
nam quis equo pulsas abiegno nosceret arces?   25
  fluminaque Haemonio comminus isse uiro,
Idaeum Simoenta Iouis cum prole Scamandro?
  Hectora per campos ter maculasse rotas?
Deiphobumque Helenumque et Pulydamantos in armis
  qualemcumque Parim uix sua nosset humus.   30
exiguo sermone fores nunc, Ilion, et tu,
  Troia bis Oetaei numine capta dei.

necnon ille tui casus memorator Homerus
  posteritate suum crescere sensit opus;
meque inter seros laudabit Roma nepotes: 35
  illum post cineres auguror ipse diem.
ne mea contempto lapis indicet ossa sepulchro
  prouisum est Lycio uota probante deo.

3.2

CARMINIS interea nostri redeamus in orbem
  gaudeat ut solito tacta puella sono.
Orphea detinuisse feras et concita dicunt
  flumina Threicia sustinuisse lyra;
saxa Cithaeronis Thebanam agitata per artem   5
  sponte sua in muri membra coisse ferunt;
quin etiam, Polypheme, fera Galatea sub Aetna
  ad tua rorantes carmina flexit equos:
miremur, nobis et Baccho et Apolline dextro,
  turba puellarum si mea uerba colit?   10
quod non Taenariis domus est mihi fulta columnis,
  nec camera auratas inter eburna trabes,
nec mea Phaeacas aequant pomaria siluas,
  non operosa rigat Marcius antra liquor;
at Musae comites, et carmina cara legenti,   15
  et defessa choris Calliopea meis.
fortunata meo si qua es celebrata libello:
  carmina erunt formae tot monumenta tuae.
nam neque pyramidum sumptus ad sidera ducti,
  nec Iouis Elei caelum imitata domus,   20
nec Mausolei diues fortuna sepulchri   '
  mortis ab extrema condicione uacant.
aut illis flamma aut imber subducet honores,
  annorum aut tacito pondere uicta ruent.
at non ingenio quaesitum nomen ab aeuo   25
  excidet: ingenio stat sine morte decus.

3.3

Visus eram molli recubans Heliconis in umbra,
    Bellerophontei qua fluit umor equi,
reges, Alba, tuos et regum facta tuorum,
    tantum operis, neruis hiscere posse meis;
paruaque iam magnis admoram fontibus ora   5
    unde pater sitiens Ennius ante bibit
et cecinit Curios fratres et Horatia pila
    regiaque Aemilia uecta tropaea rate,
uictricesque moras Fabii pugnamque sinistram
    Cannensem et uersos ad pia uota deos,   10
Hannibalemque Lares Romana sede fugantes,
    anseris et tutum uoce fuisse Iouem;
cum me Castalia speculans ex arbore Phoebus
    sic ait aurata nixus ad antra lyra:
'quid tibi cum tali, demens, est flumine? quis te   15
    carminis heroi tangere iussit opus?
non hinc ulla tibi speranda est fama, Properti:
    mollia sunt paruis prata terenda rotis,
ut tuus in scamno iactetur saepe libellus
    quem legat exspectans sola puella uirum.   20
cur tua praescriptos euecta est pagina gyros?
    non est ingenii cumba grauanda tui.
alter remus aquas, alter tibi radat harenas;
    tutus eris: medio maxima turba mari est.'
dixerat et plectro sedem mihi monstrat eburno   25
    qua noua muscoso semita facta solo est.
hic erat affixis uiridis spelunca lapillis,
    pendebantque cauis tympana pumicibus,
orgia Musarum et Sileni patris imago
    fictilis et calami, Pan Tegeaee, tui;   30
et Veneris dominae uolucres, mea turba, columbae
    tingunt Gorgoneo punica rostra lacu;
diuersaeque nouem sortitae iura Puellae
    exercent teneras in sua dona manus:
haec hederas legit in thyrsos, haec carmina neruis   35
    aptat, at illa manu texit utraque rosam.

e quarum numero me contigit una dearum
    (ut reor a facie, Calliopea fuit):
'contentus niueis semper uectabere cycnis,
    nec te fortis equi ducet ad arma sonus.   40
ne tibi sit rauco praeconia classica cornu
    flare, nec Aonium tingere Marte nemus;
aut quibus in campis Mariano proelia signo
    stent et Teutonicas Roma refringat opes;
barbarus aut Suebo perfusus sanguine Rhenus   45
    saucia maerenti corpora uectet aqua.
quippe coronatos alienum ad limen amantis
    nocturnaeque canes ebria signa morae,
ut per te clausas sciat excantare puellas
    qui uolet austeros arte ferire uiros.'   50
talia Calliope, lymphisque a fonte petitis
    ora Philitea nostra rigauit aqua.

3.4

ARMA deus Caesar dites meditatur ad Indos,
    et freta gemmiferi findere classe maris.
magna, Quiris, merces: parat ultima terra triumphos;
    Tigris et Euphrates sub tua iura fluent;
sera, sed Ausoniis ueniet prouincia uirgis;   5
    assuescent Latio Partha tropaea Ioui.
ite agite; expertae bello, date lintea, prorae;
    ad solitum, armigeri, ducite munus equos.
omina fausta cano: Crassos clademque piate.
    ite et Romanae consulite historiae.   10
Mars pater, et sanctae fatalia lumina Vestae,
    ante meos obitus sit precor illa dies
qua uideam spoliis oneratos Caesaris axes,   13
    < . . . . >
tela fugacis equi et bracati militis arcus,   17
    et subter captos arma sedere duces,   18
< . . . . >
    ad uulgi plausus saepe resistere equos;   14

inque sinu carae nixus spectare puellae 15
    incipiam et titulis oppida capta legam. 16
ipsa tuam serua prolem, Venus: hoc sit in aeuum 19
    cernis ab Aenea quod superesse caput. 20
praeda sit haec illis quorum meruere labores:
    mi sat erit Sacra plaudere posse Via.

3.5

PACIS Amor deus est; pacem ueneramur amantes.
    stant mihi cum domina proelia dura mea;
nec tamen inuiso uictus mihi carpitur auro,
    nec bibit e gemma diuite nostra sitis,
nec mihi mille iugis Campania pinguis aratur, 5
    nec mixta aera paro clade, Corinthe, tua.
o prima infelix fingenti terra Prometheo!
    ille parum caute pectoris egit opus;
corpora disponens mentem non uidit in arto:
    recta animi primum debuit esse uia. 10
nunc maris incauti uento iactamur, et hostem
    quaerimus, atque armis nectimus arma noua.
haud ullas portabis opes Acherontis ad undas;
    nudus at inferna, stulte, uehere rate.
uictor cum uicto pariter miscetur in umbris: 15
    consule cum Mario, capte Iugurtha, sedes;
Lydus Dulichio non distat Croesus ab Iro.
    optima mors carpta quae uenit ante die.
me iuuat in prima coluisse Helicona iuuenta
    Musarumque choris implicuisse manus; 20
me iuuat et multo mentem uincire Lyaeo
    et caput in uerna semper habere rosa.
atque ubi iam Venerem grauis interceperit aetas
    sparserit et nigras alba senecta comas,
tum mihi naturae libeat perdiscere mores, 25
    quis deus hanc mundi temperet arte domum;
qua uenit exoriens, qua decidit; unde coactis
    cornibus in plenum menstrua luna redit;

unde salo superant uenti; quid flamine captet
    Eurus; et in nubes unde perennis aqua;   30
si uentura dies mundi quae subruat arcem;
    purpureus pluuias cur bibit arcus aquas;
aut cur Perrhaebi tremuere cacumina Pindi,
    solis et atratis luxerit orbis equis;
cur serus uersare boues et plaustra Bootes;   35
    Pleïadum spisso cur coit igne chorus;
curue suos fines altum non exeat aequor,
    plenus et in partes quattuor annus eat;
sub terris si iura deum et tormenta reorum;   39
    num rota, num scopuli, num sitis inter aquas,   42
aut Alcmaeoniae furiae aut ieiunia Phinei;   41
    Tisiphones atro si furit angue caput;   40
num tribus infernum custodit faucibus antrum   43
    Cerberus, et Tityo iugera pauca nouem;
an ficta in miseras descendit fabula gentes   45
    et timor haud ultra quam rogus esse potest.
exitus hic uitae superest mihi; uos quibus arma
    grata magis, Crassi signa referte domum.

3.6

Dic mihi de nostra quae sensti uera puella:
    sic tibi sint dominae, Lygdame, dempta iuga.   2
omnis enim debet sine uano nuntius esse,   5
    maioremque metu seruus habere fidem.
nunc mihi, si qua tenes, ab origine dicere prima
    incipe: suspensis auribus ista bibam.
sic illam incomptis uidisti flere capillis?
    illius ex oculis multa cadebat aqua?   10
nec speculum in strato uidisti, Lygdame, lecto?
    ornabat niueas nullane gemma manus?   12
num me laetitia tumefactum fallis inani,   3
    haec referens quae me credere uelle putas?   4
<'..............................>
    <..........................>

et maestam teneris uestem pendere lacertis, 13
  scriniaque ad lecti clausa iacere pedes.
tristis erat domus, et tristes sua pensa ministrae 15
  carpebant, medio nebat et ipsa loco,
umidaque impressa siccabat lumina lana,
  rettulit et querulo iurgia uestra sono:
"haec te teste mihi promissa est, Lygdame, merces?
  est poena et seruo rumpere teste fidem. 20
ille potest nullo miseram me linquere facto,
  et qualem nolo dicere habere domi?
gaudet me uacuo solam tabescere lecto?
  si placet, insultet, Lygdame, morte mea.
non me moribus illa, sed herbis improba uicit: 25
  staminea rhombi ducitur ille rota;
illum turgentis sanie portenta rubetae
  et lecta exsucis anguibus ossa trahunt,
et strigis inuentae per busta recentia plumae
  raptaque funesto lanea uitta toro. 30
si non uana cadunt mea somnia, Lygdame, testor,
  poena erit ante meos sera sed ampla pedes:
putris et in uacuo texetur aranea lecto:
  noctibus illorum dormiet ipsa Venus."'
quae tibi si ueris animis est questa puella, 35
  hac eadem rursus, Lygdame, curre uia,
et mea cum multis lacrimis mandata reporta:
  iram, non fraudes, esse in amore meo.
me quoque consimili impositum torrerier igni
  iurabo, bis sex integer ipse dies. 40
quod mihi si tanto felix concordia bello
  exstiterit, per me, Lygdame, liber eris.

3.7

ERGO sollicitae tu causa, Pecunia, uitae es.
  per te immaturum mortis adimus iter;
tu uitiis hominum crudelia pabula praebes;
  semina curarum de capite orta tuo.

tu Paetum ad Pharios tendentem lintea portus   5
    obruis insano terque quaterque mari.
nam, dum te sequitur, primo miser excidit aeuo,
    et noua longinquis piscibus esca natat.   8
ite, rates curuas et leti texite causas: 29
    ista per humanas mors uenit acta manus.   30
terra parum fuerat; fatis adiecimus undas:
    fortunae miseras auximus arte uias.
ancora te teneat quem non tenuere Penates?
    quid meritum dicas cui sua terra parum est?
uentorum est quodcumque paras: haud ulla carina   35
    consenuit; fallit portus et ipse fidem.   36
nam tibi nocturnis ad saxa ligata procellis   19
    omnia detrito uincula fune cadunt.   20
natura insidians pontum substrauit auaris: 37
    ut tibi succedat uix semel esse potest.
saxa triumphales fregere Capherea puppes,
    naufraga cum uasto Graecia tracta salo est.   40
paulatim socium iacturam fleuit Vlixes,
    in mare cui soliti non ualuere doli.   42
nunc tulit et Paetus stridorem audire procellae   47
    et duro teneras laedere fune manus;
nec thyio thalamo aut Oricia terebintho
    effultum est pluma uersicolore caput: 50
hunc paruo ferri uidit nox improba ligno,   53
    et miser inuisam traxit hiatus aquam;   52
huic fluctus uiuo radicitus abstulit ungues: 51
    Paetus ut occideret, tot coiere mala.   54
flens tamen extremis dedit haec mandata querelis,   55
    cum moribunda niger clauderet ora liquor:
'di maris Aegaei et quos sunt penes aequora uenti
    et quaecumque meum degrauat unda caput,
quo rapitis miseros primae lanuginis annos?
    attulimus longas in freta uestra comas.   60
a miser alcyonum scopulis affligar acutis!
    in me caeruleo fuscina sumpta deo est.
at saltem Italiae regionibus euehat aestus:
    hoc de me sat erit si modo matris erit.   64
Paete, quid aetatem numeras? quid cara natanti   17
    mater in ore tibi est? non habet unda deos.'   18

subtrahit haec fantem torta uertigine fluctus; 65
    ultimaque haec Paeto uoxque diesque fuit. 66
quod si contentus patrio boue uerteret agros, 43
    uerbaque duxisset pondus habere mea,
uiueret ante suos dulcis conuiua Penates, 45
    pauper, at in terra nil nisi fleret opes. 46
o centum aequoreae Nereo genitore puellae, 67
    et tu materno tacta dolore Theti,
uos decuit lasso supponere bracchia mento:
    non poterat uestras ille grauare manus. 70
infelix Aquilo, raptae timor Orithyiae, 13
    quae spolia ex illo tanta fuere tibi?
aut quidnam fracta gaudes, Neptune, carina? 15
    portabat sanctos alueus ille uiros. 16
    < . . . . >
       < . . . . >
sed tua nunc uolucres astant super ossa marinae, 11
    nunc tibi, pro tumulo Carpathium omne mare est, 12
et mater non iusta piae dare debita terrae 9
    nec pote cognatos inter humare rogos. 10
reddite corpus, aquae: posita est in gurgite uita; 25
    Paetum sponte tua, uilis harena, tegas;
et, quotiens Paeti transibit nauta sepulchrum,
    dicat: 'et audaci tu timor esse potes.' 28
at tu, saeue Aquilo, numquam mea uela uidebis: 71
    ante fores dominae condar oportet iners.

[sunt Agamemnonias testantia litora curas, 21
    quae notat Argynni poena Athamantiadae.
hoc iuuene amisso classem non soluit Atrides,
    pro qua mactata est Iphigenia mora.]

3.8

Dvlcis ad hesternas fuerat mihi rixa lucernas
    uocis et insanae tot maledicta tuae. 2
tu uero nostros audax inuade capillos 5
    et mea formosis unguibus ora nota,

tu minitare oculos subiecta exurere flamma;
    fac mea rescisso pectora nuda sinu!   8
cum furibunda mero mensam propellis et in me   3
    proicis insana cymbia plena manu,   4
nimirum ueri dantur mihi signa caloris: 9
    nam sine amore graui femina nulla dolet.   10
quae mulier rabida iactat conuicia lingua,
    haec Veneris magnae uoluitur ante pedes;
custodum grege si circa se stipat euntem,
    seu sequitur medias Maenas ut icta uias,
seu timidam crebro dementia somnia terrent,   15
    seu miseram in tabula picta puella mouet,
his ego tormentis animi sum uerus haruspex;
    has didici certo saepe in amore notas.
non est certa fides quam non in iurgia uertas:
    hostibus eueniat lenta puella meis.   20
in morso aequales uideant mea uulnera collo:
    me doceat liuor mecum habuisse meam.
aut in amore dolere uolo aut audire dolentem,
    siue meas lacrimas siue uidere tuas.   24
odi ego quos numquam pungunt suspiria somnos;   27
    semper in irata pallidus esse uelim.
dulcior ignis erat Paridi, cum Graia per arma
    Tyndaridi poterat gaudia ferre suae: 30
dum uincunt Danai, dum restat Dardanus Hector,
    ille Helenae in gremio maxima bella gerit.
aut tecum aut pro te mihi cum riualibus arma
    semper erunt: in te pax mihi nulla placet.   34
at tibi, qui nostro nexisti retia lecto,   37
    sit socer aeternum nec sine matre domus!
cui nunc si qua data est furandae copia noctis,
    offensa illa mihi, non tibi amica, dedit.   40

[tecta superciliis si quando uerba remittis,   25
    aut tua cum digitis scripta silenda notas]   26

[gaude, quod nulla est aeque formosa: doleres,   35
    si qua foret: nunc sis iure superba licet.]   36

3.9

MAECENAS, eques Etrusco de sanguine regum,
    intra fortunam qui cupis esse tuam,
quid me scribendi tam uastum mittis in aequor?
    non sunt apta meae grandia uela rati.
turpe est quod nequeas capiti committere pondus   5
    et pressum inflexo mox dare terga genu.
omnia non pariter neruis sunt omnibus apta,
    palma nec haec ex quo ducitur illa iugo.
gloria Lysippo est animosa effingere signa;
    exactis Calamis se mihi iactat equis.   10
in Veneris tabula summam sibi ponit Apelles;
    Parrhasius parua uindicat arte iocum.
argumenta magis sunt Mentoris addita formae;
    at Myos exiguum flectit acanthus iter.
Phidiacus signo se Iuppiter ornat eburno;   15
    Praxitelen propria uendit ab urbe lapis.
est quibus Eleae concurrit palma quadrigae;
    est quibus in celeres gloria nata pedes;
hic satus ad pacem, hic castrensibus utilis armis:
    naturae sequitur semina quisque suae.   20
tu, cum Romano dominas in honore secures   23
    et liceat medio ponere iura foro,
uel tibi Medorum pugnaces ire per arcus,   25
    atque onerare tuam fixa per arma domum,
et tibi ad effectum uires det Caesar, et omni
    tempore tam faciles insinuentur opes,
parcis et in tenues humilem te colligis umbras;
    uelorum plenos subtrahis ipse sinus.   30
crede mihi, magnos aequabunt ista Camillos
    iudicia, et uenies tu quoque in ora uirum,
Caesaris et famae uestigia iuncta tenebis:
    Maecenatis erunt uera tropaea fides.   34
at tua, Maecenas, uitae praecepta recepi,   21
    cogor et exemplis te superare tuis.   22
non ego uelifera tumidum mare findo carina: 35
    tuta sub exiguo flumine nostra mora est.

non flebo in cineres arcem sedisse tepentes
    Cadmi nec septem proelia clade pari;
nec referam Scaeas et Pergama, Apollinis arces,
    et Danaum decimo uere redisse rates,   40
moenia cum Graio Neptunia pressit aratro
    uictor Palladiae ligneus artis equus.
inter Callimachi sat erit placuisse libellos
    et cecinisse modis, Coe poeta, tuis.
haec urant pueros, haec urant scripta puellas,   45
    meque deum clament et mihi sacra ferant.   46
mollia tu coeptae fautor cape lora iuuentae,   57
    dexteraque immissis da mihi signa rotis;   58
te duce uel Iouis arma canam caeloque minantem   47
    Coeum et Phlegraeis Oromedonta iugis;
celsaque Romanis decerpta Palatia tauris
    ordiar et caeso moenia firma Remo,   50
eductosque pares siluestri ex ubere reges,
    crescat et ingenium sub tua iussa meum;
prosequar et currus utroque ab litore ouantes,
    Parthorum astutae tela remissa fugae,
claustraque Pelusi Romano subruta ferro,   55
    Antonique graues in sua fata manus.   56
nunc mihi, Maecenas, laudes concedis, et a te est   59
    quod ferar in partes ipse fuisse tuas.   60

3.10

MIRABAR quidnam risissent mane Camenae
    ante meum stantes sole rubente torum.
natalis nostrae signum misere puellae
    et manibus faustos ter crepuere sonos.
transeat hic sine nube dies, stent aëre uenti,   5
    ponat et in sicco molliter unda minas.
aspiciam nullos hodierna luce dolentes,
    et Niobae lacrimas supprimat ipse lapis;
alcyonum positis requiescant ora querelis,
    increpet absumptum nec sua mater Ityn.   10

tuque, o cara mihi, felicibus edita pennis,
    surge et praesentes iusta precare deos.
ac primum pura somnum tibi discute lympha,
    et nitidas presso pollice finge comas.
dein qua primum oculos cepisti ueste Properti   15
    indue, nec uacuum flore relinque caput,
et pete, qua polles, ut sit tibi forma perennis,
    inque meum semper stent tua regna caput.
inde coronatas ubi ture piaueris aras
    luxerit et tota flamma secunda domo,   20
sit mensae ratio noxque inter pocula surgat
    et crocino nares murreus ungat onyx;
tibia continuis succumbat rauca choreis;
    adsint nequitiae libera uerba tuae,
dulciaque ingratos adimant conuicia somnos;   25
    publica uicinae perstrepat aura uiae.
sint sortes nobis talorum interprete iactu
    quem grauius pennis uerberet ille puer.
cum fuerit multis exacta trientibus hora,
    noctis et instituet sacra ministra Venus,   30
annua soluamus thalamo sollemnia nostro,
    natalisque tui sic peragamus iter.

3.11

Qvid mirare meam si uersat femina uitam
    et trahit addictum sub sua iura uirum,
criminaque ignaui capitis mihi turpia fingis,
    quod nequeam fracto rumpere uincla iugo?   4
ista ego praeterita iactaui uerba iuuenta: 7
    tu nunc exemplo disce timere meo.
Colchis flagrantes adamantina sub iuga tauros
    egit et armifera proelia seuit humo,   10
custodisque feros clausit serpentis hiatus
    iret ut Aesonias aurea lana domos.
ausa ferox ab equo quondam oppugnare sagittis
    Maeotis Danaum Penthesilea rates;

aurea cui postquam nudauit cassida frontem,   15
    uicit uictorem candida forma uirum.
quin etiam in tantum formae processit honorem
    Lydia Gygaeo tincta puella lacu
ut qui pacato statuisset in orbe columnas
    tam dura traheret mollia pensa manu.   20
Persarum statuit Babylona Semiramis urbem
    et solidum cocto sustulit aggere opus
ut duo in aduersum mitti per moenia currus
    nec possent tacto stringere ab axe latus.
duxit et Euphraten medium quam condidit arcis,   25
    iussit et imperio subdere Bactra caput.
nam quid ego heroas, quid raptem in crimina diuos?
    (Iuppiter infamat seque suamque domum.)
quid, modo qui nostris opprobria nexerit armis
    et famulos inter femina trita suos?   30
coniugii obsceni pretium Romana poposcit
    moenia et addictos in sua regna patres.
noxia Alexandria dolis aptissima tellus;
    et, totiens nostro Memphi cruenta malo,
tres tua Pompeio detraxit harena triumphos.   35
    tollet nulla dies hanc tibi, Roma, notam;
issent Phlegraeo melius quam ibi funera campo,
    uel sua si socero colla daturus erat.
scilicet, incesti meretrix regina Canopi,
    una Philippei sanguinis usta nota,   40
ausa Ioui nostro es latrantem opponere Anubin,
    et Tiberim Nili cogere ferre minas,
Romanamque tubam crepitanti pellere sistro,
    baridos et contis rostra Liburna sequi,
foedaque Tarpeio conopia tendere saxo,   45
    iura dare statuas inter et arma Mari.
quid nunc Tarquinii fractas iuuat esse secures,
    nomine quem simili uita superba notat,
si mulier patienda fuit? cane, Roma, triumphum
    et longum Augusto salua precare diem.   50
fugisti tamen in timidi uaga flumina Nili;
    accepere tuae Romula uincla manus.

bracchia spectasti sacris admorsa colubris,
  et trahere occultum membra soporis iter.
'non hoc, Roma, fui tanto tibi ciue uerenda:'   55
  dixerat assiduo lingua sepulta mero.
septem urbs alta iugis, toti quae praesidet orbi,   57
  <.........................>
haec di condiderant, haec di quoque moenia seruant: 65
  uix timeat saluo Caesare Roma Iouem.
nunc ubi Scipiadae classes, ubi signa Camilli,
  aut modo Pompeia, Bospore, capta manu?   68
Hannibalis spolia et uicti <fera tela> Syphacis   59
  et Pyrrhi ad nostros gloria fracta pedes?   60
Curtius expletis statuit monumenta lacunis;
  admisso Decius proelia rupit equo;
Coclitis abscissos testatur semita pontes;
  est cui cognomen coruus habere dedit.   64
Leucadius uersas acies memorabit Apollo: 69
  tantum operis belli sustulit una dies.   70
at tu, siue petes portus seu, nauita, linques,
  Caesaris in toto sis memor Ionio.

[uenturam melius praesagit nauita mortem,   5
  uulneribus didicit miles habere metum.]   6

3.12

POSTUME, plorantem potuisti linquere Gallam,
  miles et Augusti fortia signa sequi?
tantine ulla fuit spoliati gloria Parthi,
  ne faceres Galla multa rogante tua?
si fas est, omnes pariter pereatis auari   5
  et quisquis fido praetulit arma toro.
tu tamen immunda tectus, uesane, lacerna
  potabis galea fessus Araxis aquam.
illa quidem interea fama tabescet inani,
  haec tua ne uirtus fiat amara tibi,   10
neue tua Medae laetentur caede sagittae,
  ferreus armato neu cataphractus equo,

neue aliquid de te flendum referatur in urna:
    sic redeunt illis qui cecidere locis.
ter quater in casta felix, o Postume, Galla: 15
    moribus his alia coniuge dignus eras.
quid faciet nullo munita puella marito
    cum sit luxuriae Roma magistra suae?
sed securus eas: Gallam non munera uincent,
    duritiaeque tuae non erit illa memor.   20
nam quocumque die saluum te fata remittent,
    pendebit collo Galla pudica tuo.
Postumus alter erit miranda coniuge Vlixes:
    non illi longae tot nocuere morae,
castra decem annorum, et Ciconum mors, Ismara capta,   25
    exustaeque tuae nox, Polypheme, genae,
et Circae fraudes, lotosque herbaeque tenaces,
    Scyllaque et alterna saeua Charybdis aqua,
Lampeties Ithacis ueribus mugisse iuuencos
    (pauerat hos Phoebo filia Lampetie),   30
et thalamum Aeaeae flentis fugisse puellae,
    totque hiemis noctes totque natasse dies,
nigrantesque domos animarum intrasse silentum,
    Sirenum surdo remige adisse lyras,
et ueteres arcus leto renouasse procorum,   35
    errorisque sui sic statuisse modum;
nec frustra, quia casta domi persederat uxor.
    uincit Penelopes Aelia Galla fidem.

3.13

QVAERITIS unde auidis nox sit pretiosa puellis
    et Venere exhaustae damna querantur opes.
certa quidem tantis causa et manifesta ruinis:
    luxuriae nimium libera facta uia est.
Inda cauis aurum mittit formica metallis   5
    et uenit e Rubro concha Erycina salo,
et Tyros ostrinos praebet Cadmea colores,
    cinnamon et culti messor odoris Arabs:

haec etiam clausas expugnant arma puellas,
 quaeque gerunt fastus, Icarioti, tuos.   10
matrona incedit census induta nepotum
 et spolia opprobrii nostra per ora trahit.
nulla est poscendi, nulla est reuerentia dandi,
 aut, si qua est, pretio tollitur ipsa mora.
felix Eois lex funeris illa maritis,   15
 quos Aurora suis rubra colorat aquis.
namque ubi mortifero iacta est fax ultima lecto,
 uxorum fusis stat pia turba comis,
et certamen habent leti, quae uiua sequatur
 coniugium: pudor est non licuisse mori. 20
gaudent uictrices et flammae pectora praebent,
 imponuntque suis ora perusta uiris.
hoc genus infidum nuptarum, hic nulla puella
 nec fida Euadne nec pia Penelope.
felix agrestum quondam pacata iuuentus 25
 diuitiae quorum messis et arbor erant.
illis munus erant decussa Cydonia ramo,
 et dare puniceis plena canistra rubis,
nunc uiolas tondere manu, nunc mixta referre
 lilia uimineos lucida per calathos,   30
et portare suis uestitas frondibus uuas
 aut uariam plumae uersicoloris auem.
his tum blanditiis furtiua per antra puellae
 oscula siluicolis empta dedere uiris.
hinnulei pellis iunctos operibat amantes, 35
 altaque natiuo creuerat herba toro,
pinus et incumbens lentis circumdabat umbras. 37
   < . . . . >
corniger Arcadii uacuam pastoris in aulam 39
 dux aries saturas ipse reduxit oues.   40
< . . . . >
 nec fuerat nudas poena uidere deas;   38
dique deaeque omnes quibus est tutela per agros 41
 praebebant dextris uerba benigna focis:
'et leporem, quicumque uenis, uenaberis, hospes,
 et si forte meo tramite quaeris auem;

et me Pana tibi comitem de rupe uocato,   45
    siue petes calamo praemia, siue cane.'
at nunc desertis cessant sacraria lucis:
    aurum omnes uicta iam pietate colunt.
auro pulsa fides, auro uenalia iura,
    aurum lex sequitur, mox sine lege pudor.   50
torrida sacrilegum testantur limina Brennum
    dum petit intonsi Pythia regna dei:
at mons laurigero concussus uertice diras
    Gallica Parnasus sparsit in arma niues.
te scelus accepto Thracis Polymestoris auro   55
    nutrit in hospitio non, Polydore, pio.
tu quoque ut auratos gereres, Eriphyla, lacertos
    delapsis nusquam est Amphiaraus equis.
proloquar (atque utinam patriae sim falsus haruspex!):
    frangitur ipsa suis Roma superba bonis.   60
certa loquor, sed nulla fides: nempe Ilia quondam
    uerax Pergamei Maenas habenda mali;
sola Parim Phrygiae fatum componere, sola
    fallacem Troiae serpere dixit equum.
ille furor patriae fuit utilis, ille parenti;   65
    experta est ueros irrita lingua deos.

3.14

MVLTA tuae, Sparte, miramur iura palaestrae,
    sed mage uirginei tot bona gymnasii,
quod non infames exercet corpore ludos
    inter luctantes nuda puella uiros,
cum pila ueloces flectit per inania iactus,   5
    increpat et uersi clauis adunca trochi,
puluerulentaque ad extremas stat femina metas,
    et patitur duro uulnera pancratio;
nunc ligat ad caestum gaudentia bracchia loris,
    missile nunc disci pondus in orbe rotat;   10
gyrum pulsat equis, niueum latus ense reuincit,
    uirgineumque cauo protegit aere caput,

qualis Amazonidum nudatis bellica mammis
   Thermodontiacis turma uagatur agris.
et modo Taygeti, crines aspersa pruina,   15
   sectatur patrios per iuga longa canes;
<et modo . . . . >
   < . . . . >
qualis et Eurotae Pollux et Castor harenis
   hic uictor pugnis, ille futurus equis,
inter quos Helene nudis capere arma papillis
   fertur nec fratres erubuisse deos.   20
lex igitur Spartana uetat secedere amantes
   et licet in triuiis ad latus esse suae;
nec timor est ulli clausae tutela puellae,
   nec grauis austeri poena cauenda uiri:
nullo praemisso de rebus tute loquaris   25
   ipse tuis: longae nulla repulsa morae.
nec Tyriae uestes errantia lumina fallunt,
   est neque odoratae cura molesta comae.
at nostra ingenti uadit circumdata turba,
   nec digitum angusta est inseruisse uia,   30
nec quae sint faciles nec quae dent uerba roganti
   inuenias: caecum uersat amator iter.
quod si iura fores pugnasque imitata Laconum,
   carior hoc esses tu mihi, Roma, bono.

3.15

Vt mihi praetexti pudor est releuatus amictus
   et data libertas noscere Amoris iter,
illa rudes animos per noctes conscia primas   5
   imbuit, heu nullis capta Lycinna datis.
tertius (haud multo minus est) iam ducitur annus:
   uix memini nobis uerba coisse decem.
cuncta tuus sepeliuit amor, nec femina post te
   ulla dedit collo dulcia uincla meo.   10
fabula nulla tuas de nobis concitet aures;   45
   te solam et lignis funeris ustus amem: 46

sic ego non ullos iam norim in amore tumultus   1
    nec ueniat sine te nox uigilanda mihi.   2
at tu non meritam parcas uexare Lycinnam: 43
    nescit uestra ruens ira referre pedem.   44
testis erit Dirce, tam uero crimine saeua   11
    Nycteos Antiopen accubuisse Lyco.
a quotiens pulchros uulsit regina capillos,
    molliaque immites fixit in ora manus.
a quotiens famulam pensis onerauit iniquis   15
    et caput in dura ponere iussit humo.
saepe illam immundis passa est habitare tenebris;
    uilem ieiunae saepe negauit aquam.
Iuppiter, Antiopae nusquam succurris habenti
    tot mala? corrumpit dura catena manus.   20
si deus es, tibi turpe tuam seruire puellam:
    inuocet Antiope quem nisi uincta Iouem?
sola tamen, quaecumque aderant in corpore uires,
    regales manicas rupit utraque manu.
inde Cithaeronis timido pede currit in arces;   25
    nox erat et sparso triste cubile gelu.
saepe uago Asopi sonitu permota fluentis
    credebat dominae pone uenire pedes.
et durum Zethum et lacrimis Amphiona mollem
    experta est stabulis mater abacta suis.   30
ac ueluti, magnos cum ponunt aequora motus,
    Eurus et aduersus desinit ire Noto,
litore subtractae sonitus rarescit harenae,
    sic cadit inflexo lapsa puella genu.
sera tamen, pietas; natis est cognitus error.   35
    digne Iouis natos qui tueare senex,
tu reddis pueris matrem; puerique trahendam
    uinxerunt Dircen sub trucis ora bouis.
Antiope, cognosce Iouem: tibi gloria; Dirce
    ducitur in multis mortem obitura locis.   40
prata cruentantur Zethi, uictorque canebat
    paeana Amphion rupe, Aracynthe, tua.   42

3.16

Nox media, et dominae mihi uenit epistula nostrae:
    Tibure me missa iussit adesse mora,
candida qua geminas ostendunt culmina turres
    et cadit in patulos nympha Aniena lacus.
quid faciam? obductis committam mene tenebris,   5
    ut timeam audaces in mea membra manus?
at si haec distulero nostro mandata timore,
    nocturno fletus saeuior hoste mihi.
peccaram semel, et totum sum pulsus in annum:
    in me mansuetas non habet illa manus.   10
nec tamen est quisquam sacros qui laedat amantes;
    Scironis media quis licet ire uia.
quisquis amator erit, Scythicis licet ambulet oris,
    nemo adeo ut feriat barbarus esse uolet.   14
sanguine tam paruo quis enim spargatur amantis   19
    improbus? ecce suis it comes ipsa Venus;   20
luna ministrat iter; demonstrant astra salebras;   15
    ipse Amor accensas concutit ante faces;
saeua canum rabies morsus auertit hiantes:
    huic generi quouis tempore tuta uia est.   18
quod si certa meos sequerentur funera casus,   21
    talis mors pretio uel sit emenda mihi.
afferet haec unguenta mihi sertisque sepulchrum
    ornabit, custos ad mea busta sedens.
di faciant mea ne terra locet ossa frequenti   25
    qua facit assiduo tramite uulgus iter.
post mortem tumuli sic infamantur amantum.
    me tegat arborea deuia terra coma,
aut humer ignotae cumulis uallatus harenae.
    non iuuat in media nomen habere uia.   30

3.17

Nvnc, o Bacche, tuis humiles aduoluimur aris:
    da mihi pacato uela secunda, pater.   2

te quoque enim non esse rudem testatur amoris   7
    lyncibus ad caelum uecta Ariadna tuis.   8
tu potes insanae Veneris compescere flatus,   3
    curarumque tuo fit medicina mero.
per te iunguntur, per te soluuntur amantes: 5
    tu uitium ex animo dilue, Bacche, meo.   6
hoc mihi quod ueteres custodit in ossibus ignes   9
    funera sanabunt aut tua uina malum.   10
semper enim uacuos nox sobria torquet amantes;
    spesque timorque animum uersat utroque modo.
quod si, Bacche, tuis per feruida tempora donis
    accersitus erit somnus in ossa mea,
ipse seram colles pangamque ex ordine uites,   15
    quas carpant nullae me uigilante ferae.
dum modo purpureo spument mihi dolia musto
    et noua pressantes inquinet uua pedes,
quod superest uitae per te et tua cornua uiuam,
    uirtutisque tuae, Bacche, poeta ferar.   20
dicam ego maternos Aetnaeo fulmine partus,
    Indica Nysaeis arma fugata choris,
uesanumque noua nequiquam in uite Lycurgum,
    Pentheos et triplici funera grata gregi,
curuaque Tyrrhenos delphinum corpora nautas   25
    in uada pampinea desiluisse rate,
et tibi per mediam bene olentia flumina Diam,
    unde tuum potant Naxia turba merum.
candida laxatis onerabo colla corymbis;
    cinget Bassaricas Lydia mitra comas;   30
leuis odorato ceruix manabit oliuo,
    et feries nudos ueste fluente pedes;
mollia Dircaeae pulsabunt tympana Thebae;
    capripedes calamo Panes hiante canent;
uertice turrigero iuxta dea magna Cybebe   35
    tundet ad Idaeos cymbala rauca choros;
ante fores templi cratere antistes et auro
    libabit, fundens in tua sacra merum.
haec ego non humili referam memoranda coturno,
    qualis Pindarico spiritus ore tonat: 40

tu modo seruitio uacuum me siste superbo,
    atque hoc sollicitum uince sopore caput.

3.18

CLAVSVS ab umbroso qua ludit pontus Auerno,
    fumida<que exundant> stagna tepentis aquae,
qua iacet Euboica tubicen Troianus harena,
    et sonat Herculeo structa labore uia,
hic olim, <Hesperias> dexter cum quaereret urbes,   5
    cymbala Thebano concrepuere deo.
at nunc, inuisae magno cum crimine Baiae,
    quis deus in uestra constitit hostis aqua?
< . . . . >
    < . . . . >
his pressus Stygias uultum demisit in undas,
    errat et inferno spiritus ille lacu.   10
quid genus aut uirtus aut optima profuit illi
    mater, et amplexum Caesaris esse focos?
aut modo tam pleno fluitantia uela theatro,
    et per maturas omnia gesta manus?
occidit, et misero steterat uicesimus annus: 15
    tot bona tam paruo clausit in orbe dies.
i nunc, tolle animos et tecum finge triumphos,
    stantiaque in plausum tota theatra iuuent;
Attalicas supera uestes, atque omnia conchis
    gemmea sint Indis: ignibus ista dabis.   20
sed tamen huc omnes, huc primus et ultimus ordo:
    est mala sed cunctis ista terenda uia;
exoranda canis tria sunt latrantia colla,
    scandenda est torui publica cumba senis.
ille licet ferro cautus se condat et aere,   25
    mors tamen inclusum protrahit inde caput.
Nirea non facies, non uis exemit Achillem,
    Croesum aut Pactoli quas parit umor opes.   28
at tibi nauta pias hominum qui traicit umbras   31
    hac animae portet corpus inane suae

    qua Siculae uictor telluris Claudius et qua
        Caesar ab humana cessit in astra uia.

    [hic olim ignaros luctus populauit Achiuos,   29
        Atridae magno cum stetit alter amor.]   30

3.19

OBICITVR totiens a te mihi nostra libido.
    crede mihi, uobis imperat ista magis.
uos, ubi contempti rupistis frena pudoris,
    nescitis captae mentis habere modum.
flamma per incensas citius sedetur aristas,   5
    fluminaque ad fontis sint reditura caput,
et placidum Syrtes portum, et bona litora nautis
    praebeat hospitio saeua Malea suo,
quam possit uestros quisquam reprehendere cursus
    et rabidae stimulos frangere nequitiae.   10
testis Cretaei fastus quae passa iuuenci
    induit abiegnae cornua falsa bouis;
testis Thessalico flagrans Salmonis Enipeo
    quae uoluit liquido tota subire deo;   14
nam quid Medeae referam, quo tempore matris   17
    iram natorum caede piauit amor,
quidue <tuum facinus>, propter quam tota Mycenis
    infamis stupro stat Pelopea domus?   20
crimen et illa fuit patria succensa senecta,   15
    arboris in frondes condita Myrrha nouae,   16
tuque o Minoa uenumdata Scylla figura   21
    tondens purpuream regna paterna comam.
hanc igitur dotem uirgo desponderat hosti:
    Nise, tuas portas fraude reclusit Amor.
at uos, innuptae, felicius urite taedas: 25
    pendet Cretaea tracta puella rate.
non tamen immerito Minos sedet arbiter Orci:
    uictor erat quamuis, aequus in hoste fuit.

3.20

CREDIS eum iam posse tuae meminisse figurae
    uidisti a lecto quem dare uela tuo?
durus qui lucro potuit mutare puellam.
    tantine ut lacrimes Africa tota fuit?
at tu, stulta, deos, tu fingis inania uerba;   5
    forsitan ille alio pectus amore terat.
est tibi forma potens, sunt castae Pallados artes,
    splendidaque a docto fama refulget auo.
fortunata domus, modo sit tibi fidus amicus;
    fidus ero: in nostros curre, puella, toros.   10
tu quoque, qui aestiuos spatiosius exigis ignes,
    Phoebe, moraturae contrahe lucis iter;
nox mihi prima uenit: primae da tempora nocti.
    longius in primo, luna, morare toro.   14
quam multae ante meis cedent sermonibus horae   19
    dulcia quam nobis concitet arma Venus!   20
foedera sunt ponenda prius signandaque iura   15
    et scribenda mihi lex in amore nouo.
haec Amor ipse suo constringet pignora signo,
    testis sidereae torta corona deae.   18
namque ubi non certo uincitur foedere lectus,   21
    non habet ultores nox uigilata deos,
et quibus imposuit soluit mox uincla libido:
    contineant nobis omina prima fidem.
ergo qui tacta sic foedera ruperit ara,   25
    pollueritque nouo sacra marita toro,
illi sint quicumque solent in amore dolores
    et caput argutae praebeat historiae,
nec flenti dominae patefiant nocte fenestrae:
    semper amet, fructu semper amoris egens.   30

3.21

MAGNVM iter ad doctas proficisci cogor Athenas
    ut me longa graui soluat Amore uia.

crescit enim assidue spectando cura puellae;
    ipse alimenta sibi maxima praebet Amor.
omnia sunt temptata mihi quacumque fugari   5
    possit: at exsomnis me premit usque deus.
bis tamen aut semel admittit, cum saepe negarit;
    seu uenit, extremo dormit amicta toro.
unum erit auxilium: mutatis Cynthia terris
    quantum oculis, animo tam procul ibit Amor.   10
nunc agite, o socii, propellite in aequora nauem,
    remorumque pares ducite sorte uices;
iungiteque extremo felicia lintea malo:
    iam liquidum nautis aura secundat iter.
Romanae turres et uos ualeatis amici,   15
    qualiscumque mihi tuque, puella, uale.
ergo ego nunc rudis Hadriaci uehar aequoris hospes,
    cogar et undisonos nunc prece adire deos.
deinde per Ionium uectus cum fessa Lechaei
    sedarit placida uela phaselus aqua,   20
quod superest, sufferre, pedes, properate laborem
    isthmos qua terris arcet utrumque mare.
inde ubi Piraei capient me litora portus,
    scandam ego Theseae bracchia longa uiae.
illic in spatiis animum emendare Platonis   25
    incipiam, aut hortis, docte Epicure, tuis;
persequar aut studium linguae, Demosthenis arma,
    libaboque tuos, munde Menandre, sales;
aut certe tabulae capient mea lumina pictae,
    siue ebore exactae seu magis aere manus.   30
aut spatia annorum et longa interualla profundi
    lenibunt tacito uulnera nostra sinu;
seu moriar, fato, non turpi fractus amore;
    atque erit illa mihi mortis honesta dies.

3.22

Frigida tam multos placuit tibi Cyzicus annos,
    Tulle, Propontiaca qua fluit isthmos aqua

Dindymis et sacra fabricata e uite Cybebe
    raptorisque tulit quae uia Ditis equos?
si te forte iuuant Helles Athamantidos urbes,   5
    < .... >
siue et olorigeri uisenda est ora Caystri   15
    et quae serpentes temperat unda uias;   16
< .... >
    et desiderio, Tulle, mouere meo.   6
tu licet aspicias caelum omne Atlanta gerentem,
    sectaque Persea Phorcidos ora manu,
Geryonae stabula et luctantum in puluere signa
    Herculis Antaeique Hesperidumque choros;   10
tuque tuo Colchum propellas remige Phasim
    Peliacaeque trabis totum iter ipse legas,
qua rudis immissa natat inter saxa columba
    in faciem prorae pinus adacta nouae;   14
omnia Romanae cedent miracula terrae: 17
    natura hic posuit quicquid ubique fuit.
armis apta magis tellus quam commoda noxae,
    Famam, Roma, tuae non pudet historiae.   20
nam quantum ferro tantum pietate potentes
    stamus: uictrices temperat ira manus.
hic, Anio Tiburne, fluis, Clitumnus ab Vmbro
    tramite, et aeternum Marcius umor opus,
Albanus lacus, et foliis Nemorensis abundans,   25
    potaque Pollucis nympha salubris equo.
at non squamoso labuntur uentre cerastae,
    Itala portentis nec furit unda nouis;
non hic Andromedae resonant pro matre catenae,
    nec tremis Ausonias, Phoebe fugate, dapes;   30
nec cuiquam absentes arserunt in caput ignes,
    exitium nato matre mouente suo;
Penthea non saeuae uenantur in arbore Bacchae,
    nec soluit Danaas subdita cerua rates;
cornua nec ualuit curuare in paelice Iuno   35
    aut faciem turpi dedecorare boue;   36
haec tibi, Tulle, parens, haec est pulcherrima sedes,   39
    hic tibi pro digna gente petendus honos,   40

hic tibi ad eloquium ciues, hic ampla nepotum
    spes, et uenturae coniugis aptus amor.

[arboreasque cruces Sinis, et non hospita Grais   37
    saxa, et curuatas in sua fata trabes.]

3.23

ERGO tam doctae nobis periere tabellae,
    scripta quibus pariter tot periere bona!
has quondam nostris manibus detriuerat usus,
    qui non signatas iussit habere fidem.
illae iam sine me norant placare puellas   5
    atque eaedem sine me uerba diserta loqui;
non illas fixum caras effecerat aurum:
    uulgari buxo sordida cera fuit.
qualescumque, mihi semper mansere fideles,
    semper et effectus promeruere bonos.   10
forsitan haec illis fuerunt mandata tabellis:
    'irascor quoniam es, lente, moratus heri:
an tibi nescioquae uisa est formosior? an tu
    non bene de nobis crimina ficta iacis?'
aut dixit: 'uenies hodie, cessabimus una: 15
    hospitium tota nocte parauit Amor;'
et quaecumque uolens reperit non stulta puella,
    garrula cum blandis ducitur hora iocis.
me miserum, his aliquis rationem scribit auarus
    et ponit duras inter ephemeridas!   20
quas si quis mihi rettulerit, donabitur auro:
    quis pro diuitiis ligna retenta uelit?
i puer, et citus haec aliqua propone columna,
    et dominum Esquiliis scribe habitare tuum.

3.24

FALSA est ista tuae, mulier, fiducia formae,
    olim elegis nimium facta superba meis.

noster amor tales tribuit tibi, Cynthia, laudes:
    uersibus insignem te pudet esse meis.
mixtam te uaria laudaui saepe figura,   5
    cum quod non esses esse putaret Amor;
et color est totiens roseo collatus Eoo,
    cum tibi quaesitus candor in ore foret.   8
haec ego nunc ferro, nunc igne coactus, et ipsa   11
    naufragus Aegaea uerba loquebar aqua.
correptus saeuo Veneris torrebar aeno;
    uinctus eram uersas in mea terga manus.   14
quod mihi non patrii poterant auertere amici,   9
    eluere aut uasto Thessala saga mari.   10
ecce coronatae portum tetigere carinae;   15
    traiectae Syrtes, ancora iacta mihi est.
nunc demum uasto fessi resipiscimus aestu,
    uulneraque ad sanum nunc coiere mea.
Mens Bona, si qua dea es, tua me in sacraria dono:
    exciderunt surdo tot mea uota Ioui.   20
risus eram positis inter conuiuia mensis   25.1
    et de me poterat quilibet esse loquax.
quinque tibi potui seruire fideliter annos:
    ungue meam morso saepe querere fidem.
nil moueor lacrimis; ista sum captus ab arte;   25.5
    semper ad insidias, Cynthia, flere soles.
flebo ego discedens, sed fletum iniuria uincit:
    tu bene conueniens non sinis ire iugum.
limina iam nostris ualeant lacrimantia uerbis
    nec tamen irata ianua fracta manu.   25.10
at te celatis aetas grauis urgeat annis
    et ueniat formae ruga sinistra tuae;   25.12
exclusa inque uicem fastus patiare superbos,   25.15
    et quae fecisti facta queraris anus.
has tibi fatales cecinit mea pagina diras:
    euentum formae disce timere tuae.

[uellere tum cupias albos a stirpe capillos   25.13
    a speculo rugas increpitante tibi.]

Apparatus Criticus

3.1.11 curru π: currum NπΛ   13 immissis *Auratus*: missis Ω
mecum π: in me NπΛ   22 reddet Λ: reddit NΠ   honos
ς: onus Ω   25 arces ς: artes Ω   27 cum prole Scamandro
Wolff: om. N: cunabula parui ΠΛ   29 pulydamantos *Postgate*: puli
ledamantes *uel similia* Ω

3.2.2 ut ς: in Ω   5 Thebanam *Heinsius*: thebas Ω   6 in muri
λ: in numeri Nπλ   16 et ΠΛ: om. N: nec *Baehrens*   17 es ς:
est Ω   24 tacito *van Eldik*: ictu Ω

3.3.5 iam *Guyetus*: tam Ω   17 hinc ς: hic Ω   21 praescriptos
euecta...gyros *Lipsius*: praescripto seuecta...gyro Ω   26 qua
ΠΛ: quo N   29 orgia *Heinsius*: ergo Ω   33 iura ς:
rura Ω   41 ne *Passerat*: nil Ω   42 flare *Fruterius*:
flere Ω   48 morae *Heyworth*: fugae Ω

3.4.3 Quiris *Wistrand*: uiri Ω   8 ad *van Eldik*: et Ω   equos *Baeh-*
rens: equi Ω   11 sanctae *Postgate*: sacrae Ω   13, *lac.*, 17–18,
lac., 14 *Heyworth*   22 mi ς: me Ω

3.5.3 uictus *Giardina*: pectus Ω   6 mixta *Ruhnken*: miser Ω
aera Λ: aere N: ire Π   9 in arto *Housman*: in arte Ω   11
incauti *Alton*: in tantum Ω   14 at inferna...rate *Schrader*: ad
infernas...rates Ω   15 uicto *Willis*: uictis Ω   miscetur in
Housman: miscebitur Ω   18 carpta *Baehrens*: parca Ω   ante
Helm: acta *uel* apta Ω   21 iuuat πλ: iuuet Nπλ   24 sparserit
et nigras λ: sparserit&integras λ: sparserit et integras Nλ: sparsit et
integras Π   27 decidit *Hutchinson*: deficit Ω   31 si ς: sit Ω
arcem ς: arces NΛ: artes π   35 plaustra bootes λ: plaustra
boones λ: flamma boon N: flamma palustra Π   39 si ς: sint Ω
reorum *Housman*: om. N: gigantum ΠΛ   42, 40 *inter se mut.*
Housman

3.6.1 sensti *Butrica*: sensit Ω   6 metu *Muretus*: timens Ω   9 sic
illam *Havet*: sicut eam ΠΛ: si eam N   11 in *Heinsius*:

om. Ω   3–4 *et lac. post* 12 *Heyworth*   3 num λ: non *N*:
dum *ΠΛ*   13 et *Keil*: ac Ω   18 uestra *Gruppe*:
nostra Ω   20 poena et *Shackleton Bailey*: poenae Ω   22 et
qualem *N*: aequalem *ΠΛ*   nolo *Palmer*: nullo *N*: nulla *ΠΛ*   domi
Heinsius: domo Ω   27 sanie *Heinsius*: ranae Ω   28 exsucis
Burman: exsectis Ω   29 recentia *Heinsius*: iacentia Ω   30
rapta *Heyworth*: cincta Ω   toro *Heinsius*: uiro Ω   31 cadunt ς:
canunt Ω   39 torrerier *Palmerius*: torquerier Ω   40 ipse
Housman: esse Ω

3.7.29 curuas *Passerat*: curuae Ω   33 quem λ: quam *ΠΛ*: *de*
N incertum   19–20 *post* 36 *Housman*   21–4 *del. Willymott*
42 soliti ς: soli Ω   43–6 *post* 66 *Heyworth*   47 nunc *Barber*:
non Ω   et *Heyworth*: haec λ: hoc πλ: hunc πλ: *de N incertum*   49 nec
Heyworth: sed Ω   50 effultum ς: et fultum Ω   53 *et* 51 *inter se*
mut. Fischer   57 et *Voss*: *om.* Ω   60 comas *Oudendorp*:
manus Ω   17–18 *post* 64 *Vivona*   66 que haec ς: quae Ω
46 nisi ς: ubi Ω   fleret opes *Baehrens*: flere potest   Ω
68 tacta ς: tracta Ω   13–16 *post* 70 *Postgate*   *lac.,* 11–12,
9–10 *ante* 25 *Heyworth*   25–8 *ante* 71 *Carutti*   25
aquae *Damsté*: humo Ω   est *N*: que *ΠΛ*   [22 quae π: qua
NπΛ   Athamantiadae *Hertzberg*: minantis aquae Ω]

3.8.3–4 *post* 8 *Heyworth*   3 cum ς: cur Ω   11 rabida *Scaliger*:
grauida Ω   12 haec *Livineius*: et Ω   13 grege si *Butrica*:
gregi λ: gregis λ: que gregi λ: gregibus *NΠλ*   19 in iurgia
N: iniuria *ΠΛ*   uertas *Vahlen*: uersat *NπΛ*: uertat π   25–6
del. Dorvillius   27 quos ς: quae Ω   28 irata *Guyetus*:
iratam Ω   29 Graia *Palmerius*: grata Ω   31 Dardanus
Heinsius: barbarus Ω   35–6 *del. Burman*   37 nexisti
apud Priscian. (GLK *2.536.15*), *Diomed.* (GLK *1.369.22*): tendisti Ω
40 offensa ς: offensam Ω

3.9.7 neruis *Palmer*: rerum Ω   8 palma ς: flamma Ω   haec ex quo
Sandstroem: ex aequo Ω   illa ς: ulla Ω   11 ponit λ: poscit *Nπ*: posita
π: *om.* λ   12 iocum *Lachmann*: locum Ω   14 at ς: ad Ω
Myos ς: miros *πΛ*: nuros π: muros *N*   16 uendit ab *Barber*:
uindicat Ω   17 contingit *Vannini*: concurrit Ω   21–2 *post*
34 *Heyworth*   23 tu cum *Heyworth*: cum tibi Ω   25 arcus
Helvetius: hostes Ω   35 *om. N*   36 tuta ς: tota Ω   37
tepentes *Heyworth*: paternos Ω   38 septem *Lipsius*: semper Ω

44 Coe *ς*: dure *Ω*   45 urant…urant *ς*:   curant…curant *Ω*
57–8 *ante* 47 *Heyworth*   57 mollia *Broukhusius*: mollis *Ω*
fautor *Λ*: faustor *Π*: factor *N*   52 crescat *Camps*: crescet *Ω*   55
claustra *Palmerius*: castra *Ω*   59 nunc *Heyworth*: hoc *Ω*

3.10.1 risissent *Passerat*: misissent *Ω*   6 ponat *Colucius*: ponet *Ω*
minas *Colucius*: minax *Ω*   12 praesentes *ς*: poscentes *Ω*
17–18 *om.* *Nλ*   17 polles *Λ*: pelles *Π*   21 surgat *Cornelissen*:
currat *Ω*   23 continuis *Housman*: nocturnis *Ω*   24 adsint
Heyworth: et sint *Ω*   25 conuicia *Broukhusius*: conuiuia *Ω*
26 perstrepat *Colucius*: perstrepet *Ω*   27 sint sortes *Sandbach*: sit
sors et *Ω*   28 grauius *Guyetus*: grauibus *Ω*

3.11.5–6 *del. Georg*   10 armifera *Livineius*: armigera *Ω*   17
quin etiam *Heinsius*: Omphale *uel simile Ω*   22 et…sustulit
Giardina: ut…tolleret *Ω*   23 ut *ς*: et *Ω*   mitti *Tyrrell*: missi *Ω*
25 quam *Π*: qua *NΛ*   26 subdere *Burman sen.*: surgere *Ω*
27 crimina *ς*: crimine *Ω*   29 qui *Baehrens*: quae *Ω*   nexerit *ς*:
uexerit *Ω*   31 coniugii *Passerat*: coniugis *Ω*   35 tua *Hoeufft*:
ubi *Nλ*: tibi *Πλ*   37 quam ibi *Heyworth*: tibi *Ω*   38 sua…
erat *Butrica*: tua…eras *Ω*   40 Philippei sanguinis usta *Heyworth*:
Philippeo sanguine adusta *Ω*   41 es *Heyworth*: *om.* *NπΛ*: est *π*
49 cane *Camps*: cape *Ω*   51 uaga *λ*: uada *NΠλ*   53
spectasti *Markland*: spectaui *Ω*   55 fui *ς*: fuit *Ω*   56
dixerat *Housman*: dixit et *Ω*   57 toti *Colucius*: toto *Ω*
58 *om. N*: femineas timuit territa Marte minas *uel sim. Λ*: femineas
territa Marte minas *uel sim. Π*: stat non humana deicienda manu
Sandbach, e.g.   65–8 *ante* 59 *Housman*   59 <fera tela>
Heyworth, e.g.: monumenta *Ω*   62 admisso Decius *Scaliger*: at
(ac *π*) Decius misso *Ω*   64 est *ς*: et *Ω*

3.12.7 immunda *Heyworth*: intecta *Ω*   12 armato *Broukhusius*:
aurato *Ω*   14 sic redeunt *λ*: si credunt *Nλ*: si credent
Πλ   17 marito *Heinsius*: timore *Ω*   18 suae *ς*: tuae *Ω*
25 mors *ς*: mons *Ω*   capta *Fontein*: calpe *uel* talpe *Ω*   26 nox
Higt: mox *Ω*   28 alterna…aqua *Camps*: alternas…aquas *Ω*
saeua *Faltin*: scissa *Ω*   34 lyras *Heyworth*: lacus *Nλ*: latreus
Πλ   35 leto *ς*: lecto *Ω*   38 Penelopes Aelia *Gulielmius*:
penelope laelia *Ω* (delia *λ*)

3.13.2 Venere ς: Venerem *Ω*   8 culti messor *Fontein*: multi
pastor *Ω*   9 puellas *Markland*: pudicas *Ω*   10 gerunt
Scioppius: terunt *Ω*   15 illa *Markland*: una *Ω*   16 aquis ς:
equis *Ω*   21 gaudent *Stephanus*: ardent *Ω*   30 uimineos
Fruterius: uirgineos *Ω*   32 uersicoloris *πλ*: uiricoloris *Nπλ*
35 hinnulei *Scaliger*: atque hinuli *uel* humili *Ω*   iunctos *Shackleton Bailey*:
totos *Ω*   37 lentis *Baehrens*: lentas *NπΛ*: laetas *π*   *lac.*, 39–40,
lac. post 37 *posuit Heyworth*   39 Arcadii *Hertzberg*: atque dei *Ω*
42 dextris *Heyworth*: uestris *Ω*   53 laurigero ς: aurigero *Ω*
55 te ς: et *NΠλ*   59 falsus ς: uerus *Ω*   61 nempe *Housman*:
neque enim *Ω*   62 Pergamei... mali *Housman*: Pergameis... malis *Ω*
64 Troiae *Shackleton Bailey*: patriae *Ω*

3.14.3 ludos *Auratus*: laudes *Ω*   5 flectit *Heyworth*: fallit *Ω*
inania *Cornelissen*: bracchia *Ω*   14 turma *Gulielmius*: turba *Ω*
uagatur *Heinsius*: lauatur *Ω*   agris *Heinsius*: aquis *Ω*   *post* 16
lacunam Richmond   17 harenis ς: habenis *NΛ*: athenis *Π*
23 est ulli *Broukhusius*: aut ulla est *NπΛ*   28 comae *Canter*:
domi *Ω*   31 faciles ς: facies *Ω*   dent uerba *Enk*: sint uerba *Ω*
roganti *Burman sen.*: rogandi *ΠΛ*: rogand *N*

3.15.3 praetexti *N*: praetexta *ΠΛ*   releuatus *Fontein*: uelatus *Ω*   amictus
π: amicus *NπΛ*   7 iam *Postgate*: cum *Ω*   45–6 *post* 10 *Fischer*,
1–2 *Heyworth*, 43–4 *Vulpius*   13 uulsit *Titius*: ussit *NΠλ*: iussit *λ*
14 immites ς: immittens *Ω*   21 deus es ς: deus est *Ω*   22
uincta *π*: uicta *NπΛ*   27 uago *λ*: uaga *NΠλ*   30 stabulis ς:
tabulis *Ω*   32 et *Keil*: *om. λ*: sub *N*: in *Πλ*   aduersus *λ*: aduersos
ΠΛ: aduerso *Nλ*   noto *N*: notos *ΠΛ*   33 subtractae *Richardson*:
sic tacito *Ω*   40 obitura *Heinsius*: habitura *Ω*   41 prata ς: parta *Ω*

3.16.2 Tibure *λ*: tiburi *NΠ*   12 quis licet *Watt*: si licet *Πλ*: scilicet
N   13–14 = CIL *4.1950 (inscr. Pomp.)*   13 Scythicis]
Scythiae *inscr.*   ambulet *inscr.*, *Λπ*: ambulat *Nπ*   14 adeo *inscr.*:
deo *Ω*   feriat *inscr.*: noceat *Ω*   19–20 *post* 14 *Struchtmeyer*
20 ecce suis *Fischer*: exclusis *Ω*   it *Dorvillius*: fit *Ω*   16 concutit
Francius: percutit *Ω*   23 haec ς: huc *Ω*   25 ne ς: nec *Ω*
29 humer *λ*: humeri *Nλ*: humor *Πλ*

3.17.7–8 *ante* 3 *Heyworth*   7 amoris *Burman*: in astris *Ω*   3
flatus *Camps*: fastus *Ω*   12 animum ς: animo *Ω*   15–16
colles...uites/ quas *Guyetus*: uites...colles/ quos *Ω*   17 spument

ϛ: numen *uel similia* Ω   24 et triplici...gregi *Heyworth*: in
triplices...greges Ω   27 Diam ϛ: naxon Ω   29 onerabo
ϛ: onerato Ω   30 cinget ϛ: cingit Ω   36 tundet *Canter*:
fundet Ω   37 cratere ϛ: crater Ω   antistes et *Heinsius*:
antistitis Ω   38 libabit *Foster*: libatum Ω

3.18.2 fumida *Scaliger*: humida Ω   que exundant *Heyworth, e.g.*:
Baiarum Ω   3 Euboica...Troianus *Heinsius*: et Troiae...
Misenus Ω   5 olim Hesperias *Heyworth, e.g.*: ubi mortales Ω
ante 9 *lac. Guyetus*   10 inferno *Housman*: in uestro *uel* nostro Ω
14 maturas *Barber*: maternas Ω   19–20 conchis ... Indis
Housman: magnis...ludis Ω   24 torui λ: torci πλ: torti π: troci N
29–30 *del. Scaliger*   31 traicit *Paley*: traicis Ω   32 hac
Guyetus: huc Ω   portet ϛ: portent Ω   suae *Heinsius*: tuae Ω

3.19.10 rabidae ϛ: rapidae Ω   15–16 *post* 20 *Postgate*   19
tuum facinus *Housman, e.g.*: Clytaemestrae Ω   22 purpuream...
comam *Markland*: purpurea...coma Ω   27–8 *ante* 25 *Housman*

3.20.4 tantine ut lacrimes *Heinsius*: tantisne in lacrimis Ω
13 da...nocti *Palmer*: date...noctis Ω   19–20 *ante* 15 *Lachmann*
17 constringet ϛ: constringit *NΛ*: confringit *Π*   22 uigilata
Palmer: uigila N: uigilanda *ΛΠ*   23 mox ϛ: nox Ω   25
tacta sic...ara *Housman*: pactas in...aras Ω

3.21.6 exsomnis *Barber*: ex omni Ω   usque *Heinsius*: ipse Ω
7 bis *Cornelissen*: uix Ω   admittit ϛ: amittit Ω   8 amicta
Scaliger: amica Ω   11 aequora π: aequore *NπΛ*   25 in
Heyworth: uel Ω   spatiis *Broukhusius*: studiis Ω   28 libabo *Suringar*: librorum Ω   munde *Kuinoel*: docte Ω   31 et *Scaliger*:
aut Ω

3.22.2 qua ϛ: quae Ω   3 Dindymis *Unger*: Dindymus Ω   e uite
Haupt: inuenta Ω   4 quae ϛ: qua Ω   5 iuuant ϛ: iuuat Ω
5, *lac.*, 15–16, *lac.*, 6 *Heyworth*   15 siue et *Heyworth*: et (at π, aut π)
si qua Ω   olorigeri ϛ: orige Ω   16 quae *Palmer*: qua Ω
serpentes *Hubbard*: septenas Ω   13 immissa *Heyworth*: Argoa Ω
23 fluis ϛ: flues Ω   25 foliis...abundans *Housman*: socii...ab
unda Ω   28 furit ϛ: fuit Ω   unda ϛ: una Ω   36 boue ϛ:
boui Ω   37–8 *del. Knoche*

3.23.6 atque eaedem *Heinsius*: et quaedam Ω   11 fuerunt λ: fuerant
ΠΛ: fuerint Nλ   14 bene ς: bona Ω   15 dixit π: dixi NπΛ
cessabimus ς: cessauimus Ω   17 uolens ς: dolens Ω   18
iocis ς: dolis Ω   19 auarus ς: auari Ω   20 duras Π:
diras NΛ   22 ligna ς: signa Ω

3.24.2 elegis *Schrader*: oculis Ω   6 cum *Dousa*: ut Ω   9–10
post 14 *Tremenheere*   11 nunc...nunc *Heyworth*: non...non Ω
12 loquebar *Heyworth*: fatebor Ω   10 eluere πλ: fluere Nπλ
19 dea es ς: deo est Ω   20 exciderunt ς: exciderant Ω
3.25.6 ad insidias *Baehrens*: ab insidiis Ω   13–14 *del. Heyworth*

Commentary

3.1

1–6: Spirits of the Greek poets Callimachus and Philitas, give me poetic inspiration. I am the first to draw on a pure source in treating Italian subjects in the Greek manner. What kind of poetry did you write? 7–20: I am no poet of warfare. What makes my poetry celebrated is its polish. I sing of love, outclassing my rivals. The Muses have inspired me to write what can be read at a time of peace. 21–40: Though I am a victim of envious detraction, I shall win posthumous glory. 25–34: It is Homer that has given the Trojan war its great fame and his fame has grown too. 35–8: Apollo has granted that I shall be celebrated at Rome after my death.

This opening poem is both metapoetic* (it discusses the nature of poetry) and programmatic* (it suggests some themes and approaches of the book which it launches). Elegy is treated as something of religious power, carefully wrought, sublime, select and fit to be read in peacetime. It avoids military themes, but Propertius expects to share with Homer posthumous fame; the six-verse evocation of the *Iliad* looks ahead to versions of other works, notably the *Odyssey* at 3.12.24–36 and the tragedy *Antiope* in 3.15.

Though we lack the majority of the work of Callimachus and Philitas, the two Greek elegists addressed at the start (and also important in 3.3), we can see that the poem draws in significant ways on other models too, of which a number are included in the Appendix:

D: Lucretius 1.117–19: cf. verses 3, 17–20.
E: Lucretius 4.1–5 [= 1.926–30]: cf. verses 3–6, 17–20.
K: Vergil, *Georgics* 2.173–6: see esp. 3–6. This comes from the end of the so-called *laudes Italiae*, to which 3.22 responds.
L: Vergil, *Georgics* 3.8–18: see esp. 3, 9–12, 17–18.
M: Horace, *Odes* 3.30: see esp. 4, 34.

Besides these the most important influence is the prologue to the third book of Callimachus' *Aetia*, a papyrus* of which was discovered in the 1970s, relevant for 3–6, 17–20. This is too fragmentary to quote here; but see R. F. Thomas, 'Callimachus, the *Victoria Berenices*, and Roman poetry', *CQ* 33 (1983), 92–113 (esp. 101–3). Other passages of Callimachus (see **B, C**) are cited in the notes on 3, 8, 10, 14, 21, 38.

Something of the poem's humorous tone is captured in the mischievous version with which Ezra Pound begins *Homage to Sextus Propertius*, e.g. 'Annalists will continue to record Roman reputations, ... | And expound the distentions of Empire, | But for something to read in normal circumstances? | For a few pages brought down from the forked hill unsullied? | I ask a wreath which will not crush my head.' [= 15–20]

1–2 Callimachi: see Index. Like *Cynthia* at 1.1.1 the name is arrestingly placed at the very start of the book.   **Coi sacra Philitae:** 'poetic rites of Coan Philitas'. Philitas of Cos (a Greek island off the south-west coast of what is now Turkey: Map 4b) was the first of the Hellenistic* scholar-poets, an elegist of the generation before Callimachus (with whom he is regularly paired: 2.34.31–2; 3.9.43–4; Quintilian 10.1.58); only tiny fragments* of his poetry now survive (see Spanoudakis 2002). The names of the two poets are balanced against each other at either end of the line.   **sacra:** lit. 'sacred rites'. For poetry described as *sacra* see *OLD sacrum* 3e. Vergil, *Geo.* 2.475–6, has *Musae | quarum sacra fero*. Reading the poetry of Callimachus or Philitas or writing poetry in imitation of them is an act of worship. But there is also evidence that great poets, like heroes, were given shrines and sacrifices.   **nemus:** i.e. the grove haunted by the poets' presence and from which they drew their inspiration: cf. 2.13.4 (**Q**); Hor. *Odes* 1.1.30, *Epist.* 2.2.77 *scriptorum chorus omnis amat nemus et fugit urbem* [the whole chorus of authors loves the wood and avoids the city], Tac. *Dial.* 12; and the wood where Elegia and Tragoedia compete for Ovid's attention in *Amores* 3.1.

3–4 primus ego ... ingredior ... sacerdos: 'I am the first (Italian) priest to begin...', lit. 'I first, a priest, begin'. For the poet as a priest of the Muses or of Apollo, cf. 4.6.1–10 and Horace, *Odes* 3.1.3 *Musarum sacerdos. ingredior* + inf. = 'I begin (to)', *OLD* 4c; cf. Verg. *Geo.* 2.175 (**K**). Note the stress on beginning, which suits the opening of a book (cf. 1.1.1 *Cynthia prima*). **puro de fonte**: construe with *ferre*. The water that the priest brings from the spring of the Muses is pure, symbolizing the refined perfection of the poetry: cf. Apollo's words at Callimachus, *Hymn to Apollo* 110–12: 'The water that the bees bring to Deo...comes up clean and pure from a holy spring.' For the water of inspiration which poets drink, cf. 6 and 3.3.5, 51–2, 4.6.4; Lucretius 4.2 (E); Hor. *Odes* 1.26.6; N.B. Crowther, 'Water and wine as symbols of inspiration', *Mnemosyne* 32 (1979), 1–11. The springs of the Muses go back to Hesiod, *Theogony* 5 (A); and the notions of opening them up afresh or drinking from the pure source can be traced back at least as far as Ennius (15 n.): see Hinds 1998, 52–5. **Italos per Graios orgia ferre choros**: 'to carry Italian sacraments to the accompaniment of Greek music', i.e. to treat Italian subjects in the Greek manner. The word *orgia* means 'mystic emblems' and reinforces the idea of the sacred status of both the poet and poetry that is so important in this poem. *choros* refers to singing and dancing and here conveys the metres and music of Greek poetry. Claims to be the pioneer poet in treating Roman subjects in the Greek style were made earlier by Vergil at *Geo.* 2.175–6 and by Horace at *Odes* 3.30.13–14. It is in each case a playful rather than a justified assertion: Hinds (1998: 56–63) shows how the similar claim to be the first to import the Greek Muses to Latin goes back again to Ennius, who was, however, already anticipated by the earliest known Latin poets Livius and Naevius.

5–6 quo...carmen tenuastis in antro?: 'in what glen did you refine your song?' *tenuastis* (*tenuauistis* in syncope*) is a metaphor from spinning (cf. Hor. *Epist.* 2.1.225): 'did you spin your verse fine' in the Callimachean* manner (8 n.). *antrum* can mean either a cave or a glen. It is used of a haunt of Apollo and the Muses: cf. 3.3.14, and Cairns 2006: 131–6. **pariter**: 'together' or 'side by side', referring to Callimachus and Philitas, or perhaps even 'in pairs', referring to the form of the elegiac couplet. **quo...pede ingressi?**: understand *estis*: 'with what foot did you begin?' There are two meanings here: 'how did you enter?'; and 'with what metre (metrical *foot*) did you begin?' Poets love to pun on *pes*, and attached epithets often provide a reflection on style: in 1.1.4 the victorious

Cupid imposes his feet (i.e. elegiac couplets) on P.; at Cat. 63.2 *citato...pede* comments on the fast pace of the galliambic metre; and at Ov. *Am.* 3.1.8 the nymph Elegia has one *pes* (leg, but implying line) longer than the other. The verb *ingredior* is repeated from 3, the echo stressing the similarity between P. and his models. **quamue bibistis aquam**: different springs bring different inspiration at 76–84 of the Hellenistic* poem *Epitaphios Bionis* (Homer drank from Hippocrene and wrote the *Iliad*; Bion from Arethusa, and wrote bucolic); cf. also 2.10.25–6 (**P**), Hor. *Epist.* 1.3.10 *Pindarici fontis*. The enclitic* *-ue* ('or') can be used, as it is twice in this line, of alternative statements or questions that do not rule each other out. We have here variants on a single question.

7–8 How does this couplet fit into its context? One solution is to regard it as an oracular response from the shrine of Callimachus and Philitas: it provides a tangential answer to the questions posed in 5–6. The speaker may be the spirits of his poetic predecessors, or perhaps the poet himself: the *uates* drinks the water and is inspired.   **a ualeat, Phoebum quicumque moratur in armis**: 'Ah, farewell to any who keeps Phoebus long under arms', i.e. any poet who uses his inspiration (Phoebus Apollo being the god of poetic inspiration) to write epic poetry about warfare. The verb *moratur* suggests the length and tedium of epic: by using a derivative of *mora* (see pp. 32–3) P. casts at his poetic rivals the charge laid against him at 1.12.2.   **exactus tenui pumice**: 'completed by (the polishing of) a fine pumice stone'. Pumice was used for smoothing the surface of the papyrus* scrolls on which poetry was written. P. alludes to Cat. 1.1–2 *Cui dono lepidum nouum libellum | arido modo pumice expolitum?* [to whom do I present the charming new book, freshly polished off with dry pumice?], but *uersus* makes the sense explicitly metaphorical. As well as describing the pumice, the adjective *tenuis* refers to the sort of poetry P. wishes to write: perfectly finished and slimmed down. In the Prologue to his *Aetia* (**B**) Callimachus wrote that Apollo had told him to fatten the beast he offered to the gods but to keep his style lean (fr. 1.23–4), and the Latin poets find a variety of ways to imitate the conceit: cf. esp. Verg. *Ecl.* 6.3–5 (**I**).   **exactus...eat**: P. likes to make adjectives dynamic by attaching them to the verb *ire* (e.g. 2.7.16 *non mihi sat magnus Castoris iret equus* [Castor's horse would not go big enough for me]); 'let the verse flow' makes for a contrast with the lack of movement in *moratur* and in the Horatian phrase evoked by *exactus*: *Odes* 3.30.1 *Exegi monumentum aere perennius* (**M**).

9–10 quo: 'by means of which (poetry)', i.e. 'owing to that style of poetry'.   **sublimis:** agrees with Fama ('sublime Fame'), but its literal meaning 'on high' is in harmony with the idea of elevation in these lines. Fame lifts the poet up and his Muse rides in triumph in a chariot: for the combination of images cf. *Geo.* 3.8–18 (**L**). **terrā:** ablative, 'from the earth'.   **a me nata...Musa:** 'the Muse, born from me [*or* my daughter]', i.e. his poetry: cf. Callimachus, *Aetia* fr. 1.19–20 'do not expect a loud-resounding song *to be born from me*'. The combination of this with the Roman triumph imagery is the first of many examples of the technique advertised in verse 4.

11–12 mecum: the poet has replaced the Muse as the *triumphator*. **parui:** emphasizes the small-scale.   **Amores:** the little Cupids, or Amoretti, ride with him because he composes love poetry (often called *Amores*, like Ovid's first collection). These boys accompany him like the children of a real-life *triumphator* (Livy 45.40.8; Tacitus, *Annals* 2.41.3).   **secuta:** supply *uectatur*. We have moved to the image of a chariot race: the crowd of poets following him, his inferior imitators, drive, but cannot compete—this image continues in 13–14. Note the contemptuous hissing of the *ss* in this line and the next.

13–14 immissis...habenis: lit. 'the reins having been slackened', i.e. 'giving rein to your horses'.   **non datur ad Musas currere lata via:** 'to run to the Muses no broad path is given'. P.'s rivals cannot overtake him because he travels on so narrow a track. At *Aetia* fr. 1.25–8 Callimachus bids the poet drive his chariot on unworn paths, even if they are narrower than the tracks shared with others.

15–16 annalibus: 'to the annals', 'to the record of history'. There is a glance here at the *Annals* of Ennius (239–169 BC), the first great Roman poet. This was a narrative poem in fifteen books (later expanded to eighteen) telling the history of the Roman people in chronological order. Others too wrote verse *Annales*, such as Volusius, whose work Catullus condemned as *cacata carta* ('shitty sheets', 36.1).

Vergil had distinguished himself from such poetasters, *Ecl.* 6.6–7 *namque super tibi erunt qui dicere laudes,* | *Vare, tuas cupiant et tristia condere bella* [for there will be more than enough eager to utter your praise, Varus, and to compose grim wars]. An assurance that others will write the required encomium is a common element in the *recusatio**, cf. Hor. *Odes* 1.6.1–2, 4.2.33–4.   **qui finem imperii Bactra futura canent:** 'who will sing that Bactra will be the limit of the empire': *Bactra* is n. pl.; understand *esse* with *futura*. The many poets of line 15 will encourage warfare: cf. e.g. Hor. *Odes* 3.5.2–4 *praesens diuus habebitur | Augustus adiectis Britannis | imperio grauibusque Persis* [Augustus will be regarded as a god once the Britons and the formidable Persians have been added to the empire]. Bactra was a province in the Parthian empire and is here intended to convey the whole of that empire (synecdoche*). On Roman relations with the Parthians see the intro to 3.4. It is clear that this poem was written before 20 BC, when Augustus reached a peaceful settlement with these long-term rivals. The bloodless negotiations would not have proved a suitable theme for epic warfare.

17–18 quod pace legas: 'something to read in peacetime', anticipating *opus hoc.* Note the subjunctive expressing purpose: 'for you to read'.   **de monte Sororum:** i.e. from Mount Helicon (3.3.1), where the Muses (the Sisters) dwell (and instruct the poet) already in Hesiod's *Theogony* (A).   **intactā ... uiā:** ablative of the route, referring to P.'s originality (14 n.). For the sentiment and some of the wording, cf. Lucr. 1.117–18 and 4.1–2 (D, E); Verg. *Geo.* 3.11, 40–1 *siluas saltusque sequamur | intactos* (L), 291–3.   **pagina:** see 3.3.21 n.

19–20 mollia: 'soft' because the garland is the reward for elegiac, not 'hard' epic poetry (cf. *dura corona*). P. has a recurring antithesis between *durus*, used of epic or tragedy, and *mollis*, of elegy: cf. 2.1.2 (O), 41 and 2.34.42, 44.   **Pegasides:** the Muses, so called because of their association with Hippocrene, the spring on Mount Helicon which first welled up when struck by the hoof of Pegasus, the hero Bellerophon's winged horse (Aratus 216–24; Ov. *Met.* 5.256–68).   **non faciet:** 'will not suit, do for': *facere* + dat. is used instead of the far more common *facere ad* + acc. The construction is probably taken from colloquial speech (cf. Tränkle 65).

21–2 at: as often, marks a change of direction.   **detraxerit:** *detrahere* is regularly used of disparagement in speech (*OLD* 8), but here with the dative of disadvantage *mihi* and the banking image in the pentameter, it belongs as much with *OLD* 7 'to remove something from somebody'.   **inuida turba:** both Envy (*Hymn to Apollo* 105–13; *Epigram* 21.4 Pf) and the crowd (*Ep.* 28) are terms of Callimachean* disapprobation (fr. 1.17 'Begone, you baneful race of Jealousy' combines the two dislikes); P. himself had attacked *Liuor* at 1.8.29. *turba* is contemptuously repeated from line 12.   **duplici faenore reddet honos:** 'glory will repay it double'. *duplice faenore* means 'with a hundred percent increase': cf. Plin. *Nat.* 18.162; Plautus, *Menaechmi* 546.

23–4 omnia...fingit maiora uetustas: 'antiquity makes everything greater'. *uetustas* refers to 'an age to come, when the present shall be a distant past' (Postgate): cf. Verg. *Aen.* 10.792, Ov. *Tr.* 5.9.8. **ab:** 'after'.

25–32 To illustrate his point that time is what dissipates envy and creates glory, P. works a playful variation on the theme 'who would have heard of Troy, if Homer had not sung?' that we find e.g. at Theocritus 16.48–50. P. implies an unexpected protasis: 'who would have heard of Troy (and Homer too), if the war had only just happened?' (For a further variation see Ov. *Ars* 3.413–14 *quis nosset Homerum,* | *Ilias aeternum si latuisset opus?* [who would know Homer, if the everlasting work, the *Iliad*, had stayed hidden?]; cf. also Dido at *Aen.* 1.565.) Verses 26–30 are intensely evocative of the *Iliad*, in style (esp. 29) and in content, recalling the climactic narrative of books 21–2. But Troy's fall (32–3) was only foreshadowed (e.g. 4.164–5, 24.728–9) and not told in the *Iliad*, the poem that maintains the fame of the war, and the tale of the wooden horse (25) is not mentioned there at all; both appear in brief narratives in the *Odyssey* (in the indirect speech of Demodocus after the invitation by Odysseus at 8.492–520, and from Helen at 4.271–89), and at greater length in the so-called 'cyclic' epics, the Little Iliad and the Sack of Troy, also attributed to Homer by some in antiquity: for these see West 2003.

25–7 equo pulsas abiegno nosceret arces: 'would learn that towers were battered by a wooden horse': supply *esse* with *pulsas*. There was a tradition that the wooden horse was used as a battering ram: cf. Plin. *Nat.* 7.202, Pausanias 1.23.8. P.'s language evokes this rationalist view without supporting it; he may be saying simply that the stratagem of the Trojan horse led to the sack of Troy.   **fluminaque Haemonio comminus isse uiro,** | **Idaeum Simoenta Iouis cum prole Scamandro:** 'and that rivers, Idaean Simois and Jupiter's offspring Scamander, came to grips with the hero from Thessaly'. Simois and Scamander are the rivers of Troy. At *Il.* 21.305–7 the latter calls on the former to help him overwhelm Achilles, the hero from Thessaly (= *Haemonia*). *Simoënta* is a Greek accusative. According to Homer (*Il.* 4.475, 12.19–22) the river flows from the range of Mount Ida (hence *Idaeum*). Scamander, also called Xanthus (the gods' name for him), is described as the offspring of Zeus (= Roman Jupiter) at *Il.* 21.2. *cum prole Scamandro* is an emendation made by G. Wolff. The oldest manuscript N omits the words and the later MSS have *cunabula parui*, a nonsensical attempt to mend the metre. On the scansion of *prole* before the double consonant of *Scamandro*, see p. 34.

28–30 Hectora: a Greek accusative: the word order suggests that it is the subject of the infinitive but the better meaning may result from taking it as the object and *rotas* as the subject: see on *maculasse*. We might have expected a conjunction to link this line to the previous one, but P. often has asyndeton* in his lists: in Book 3 at 4.17; 9.54; 12.29, 34; 17.22; 22.9, 25.   **maculasse** = *maculauisse* (syncope*). If Hector is its subject, *maculo* will mean 'bespatter' (with blood); if he is the object, it will mean 'befoul'. In *Iliad* 22, Achilles, after killing Hector, perforates his heels, ties his corpse to the back of his chariot and drags him back to the Greek camp. What is referred to by P. here is Achilles' obsessive behaviour later. He would repeatedly get up at night, retie the corpse to the chariot and drag it 'three times' (*ter*) round the tomb of his dead friend Patroclus whom Hector had killed (*Il.* 24.15–16).   **Deiphobumque Helenumque:** sons of Priam (as is Paris) and Trojan leaders in the *Iliad*. Line 29 has a very Homeric flavour, with its repeated -*que* and four dactyls. **Pulydamantos in armis** | **qualemcumque Parim:** 'Paris, that sorry figure [lit. 'Paris, of whatever character (he was)'], in the armour of Pulydamas': *Pūlydamantos* is a Greek genitive. The standard English spelling is Polydamas, but in dactylic* poetry the first syllable has to be treated as long, so Homer gives the name as Πουλυδάμας, 'which transliterates into Latin as *Pulydamas*. The son of Panthous, he was the counsellor of Hector, who in the *Iliad* twice takes his advice and twice rejects it, the second time with catastrophic results (18.254–83, cf. 22.100). If the reading is correct, P. has in mind here an episode in which Pulydamas lends his armour to Paris—just as the latter's brother Lycaon had lent him his corselet (*Il.* 3.333). Obscure variants and conflations of mythological characters were the delight of Alexandrian poets, and in this avowedly Callimachean* poem it would not be surprising to find P. playing the scholarly game. The manuscripts give variants of *Pulydamantes*, which would mean 'heroes such as Pulydamas'. However, we would need to print the Greek form *Pulydamantas* to get an accusative plural that scans; but this would still leave the awkwardness of having a plural in the middle of a list of singular names, an intruder amid the sons of Priam, and a lack of conjunction before *Parim*. To read the Greek accusative *Pulydamanta* and follow it with an *et* would lead to good sense, but the change is greater and elisions are very rare in the fifth foot of a hexameter.   **uix sua nosset** (= *nouisset*: syncope*) **humus**: 'their own (patch of) earth would scarcely know'. The names earlier in the couplet are the object of the verb. *suus* is regularly used in poetry to refer to a noun other than the subject, especially where that noun is the dominant notion.

31–2 exiguo sermone: 'a matter for few words', lit. 'with little speech': descriptive ablative.   **Ilion … Troia**: if there is a meaningful distinction between the two names, Ilium is the city and Troia the country (Servius on Verg. *Aen.* 3.3), though it is often the name of the city too. The point may be that the place is so famous that it bears two equally familiar names.   **bis Oetaei numine capta dei**: Hercules ended his mortal life by being cremated in a pyre on Mount Oeta in north-east Greece. He was subsequently deified. He took Troy twice, the first time in person when its king Laomedon refused to pay him the promised reward for killing a sea monster (*Il.* 5.640–51), the second time when, after his death, his bow was wielded by Philoctetes (Sophocles, *Phil.* 1439–40).

33–4 ille tui casus memorator Homerus: 'Homer, the great recorder of your fall'.   **posteritate:** 'through the passing of time': ablative of means, as at Tac. *Ann.* 3.19.2. There is an echo of Horace, *Odes* 3.30.7–8 *postera | crescam laude.* The pentameter presents a pointed ambiguity: Homer's work grows as time passes, in fame, but also in size. This fits the addition of non-Iliadic material to the Iliadic core in 26–30 (see 25–32 n.).

35–6 inter seros nepotes: 'amongst its distant generations'. **post cineres:** 'after (I am reduced to) ashes'.   **auguror:** 'I prophesy'; cf. *sacerdos* (3).

37–8 ne mea contempto lapis indicet ossa sepulchro | prouisum est: 'it has been provided for that the tombstone will not mark my bones as lying in a neglected grave'. *prouideo ne* + subj. is regular Latin for 'I see to it that … not'. On the poet's tomb, see 3.16.21–30.   **Lycio … deo:** Apollo. The epithet *Lycius* was used by Callimachus at *Aetia* fr. 1.22. The approval of Apollo ensures the success of P.'s poetry and thus the cultivation of his tomb by generations to come—just as he cultivates the grove of Callimachus and Philitas at the start of the poem.

Additional bibliography: Woodman, *CQ* 48 (1998), 568–9; Newman 1997: 229–37; Hunter 2006: 7–16; Keith 2008: 77–9; Miller 2009: 314–18.

3.2

1–2: Let us return to the usual topics so that my girl may rejoice in my poetry. 3–10: Mythology gives us examples of the power of song. Is it surprising if my poetry makes me popular among the girls? 11–18: I may not be wealthy but my poetic talent makes you, my girlfriend, fortunate in being celebrated by me. 19–26: The wonders of the world will perish but a poet can confer true immortality.

While the previous poem has invoked the poetic doctrine of Callimachus and his symbolism to celebrate Propertius' attainment of immortality as a poet, 3.2 deals with his success in a more personal

way, as the singer of his girlfriend. The two poems are closely related
and will be read together, even if we do not follow those editors who
run them together without a break. (For the arguments here, see
Heyworth 2007: 285–7.)

After the initial couplet, the elegy proceeds through a sequence of
priamels* (i.e. statements about others that throw emphasis on the
climactic statement about the central figure, here P. himself): 3–10,
11–16, 19–26.

1–2 Interea: 'but now'. For this use of the word denoting a change of
theme and a new beginning, cf. *OLD* c; *Aen.* 5.1, 10.1,
11.1.   **orbem:** 'cycle', i.e. the topics through which poetry
revolves: cf. 3.3.21. The Cynthia cycle will end at the end of the
book: for this implication in *orbis*, cf. 3.18.16. Another metaphorical
use of the word comes at Juv. 5.20–1 of the client's 'round' of social
calls.   **ut:** postponed* and introducing a purpose clause: 'so
that (my) girl'.   **solito puella tacta sono:** the 'familiar sound'
in which his girl is to rejoice is that of his love poetry. For the
confusion of different senses (synaesthesia*), cf. e.g. Lucretius
1.643–4 *quae belle tangere possunt aures* ('things that can touch the
ears prettily').

3–4 detinuisse: 'restrained', 'kept fixed to the spot': cf. Tib. 1.8.20,
Mart. 14.166.2 *detinuit…feras*, Stat. *Silu.* 5.5.63 *flumina detineas.*
sustinuisse: 'stopped'. The repetition of compounds of *teneo* in the
perfect infinitive emphasizes the fact that Orpheus brings nature to
a standstill. The music of Orpheus held nature and wild beasts
spellbound, as well as moving what was normally immovable (esp.
trees and the gods of death); poets refer to these powers in passages
that reflect on poetry's own seductiveness, such as Ap. *Arg.* 1.23–34
(cf. 1.494–515), Verg. *Ecl.* 6.27–30, *Geo.* 4.467–84, Ov. *Met.* 10.40–8,
11.1–2; and in an earlier Propertian programme at 2.13.5–6 (**Q**).
Orpheus holds up rivers also at Hor. *Odes* 1.12.9–10 *arte materna
rapidos morantem fluminum lapsus* [delaying the flowing of swift
rivers with the art his mother (Calliope) gave him], and Phaedrus
3.*prol.*59 *qui saxa cantu mouit et domuit feras | Hebrique tenuit
impetus dulci mora* [who moved rocks with his singing and tamed
wild beasts and held the rushing of the river Hebrus with pleasant
delay].

5–6 saxa . . . coisse ferunt: *ferunt* here = 'they say', with accusative +
infinitive.   **Cithaeronis:** Cithaeron is a mountain range near
Thebes.   **Thebanam agitata per artem:** 'put in motion by the
Theban's art'. The Theban is Amphion, the music of whose lyre
caused the stones to form the walls of Thebes: cf. Euripides, fr.
223.90–5 (*Antiope*), Ap. *Arg.* 1.735–41. The reference anticipates
the role of Amphion in 3.15.   **sponte sua:** i.e. without the
use of force.   **in muri membra coisse:** 'to come together into
the form (lit. 'limbs', 'components') of a wall'.

7–8 quin etiam: 'what is more', 'yes, and', marking the climax of this
group: the one-eyed Cyclops Polyphemus who dwells on the bleak
slopes of Etna and yet seduces the sea-nymph Galatea. His songs
feature in Theocritus, *Idylls* 6, 11. In *Idyll* 6 the love is teasingly
requited (see Hunter's commentary), and even in 11 his poetry is
credited with providing a relief or cure, as in Callimachus' response
(*Ep.* 46 Pf. = *Anth. Pal.* 12.150). Perhaps following another source (cf.
in art *LIMC* V Addenda 'Galateia' 37–9; and in later Greek texts
Lucian 78.1; Nonnus 40.555–7), P. turns this into a story of success,
the music of the pipe attracting Galatea from the sea. The chariot and
horses regularly attributed to sea gods (Poseidon at *Il.* 13.23–31,
Neptune at *Aen.* 1.147–56) are here passed on to the sea-nymph.
They are dewy (**rorantes**) because of the spray they throw up as they
skim the sea.   **ferā:** the landscape of the 'wild' volcano Etna
characterizes its inhabitant. The adjective is used of mountains and
the like at Verg. *Ecl.* 5.28, Ov. *Tr.* 1.8.40.

  It may be significant that Polyphemus' love for Galatea was regularly presented as hopeless and resulting in the death of her lover Acis
(Ov. *Met.* 13.750–897). Orpheus lost his wife, and his music was
ultimately unsuccessful in regaining her (Verg. *Geo.* 4.467–84, Ov.
Met. 10.16–77). Cithaeron and Thebes also bring a note of ill-omen:
both the city and the mountain frequently feature as the site of fatal
action in tragedies such as Sophocles' *Oedipus the King*, Euripides'
Bacchae and *Antiope* (cf. 3.15). These references to the overmastering
power of music seem to subvert themselves.

9–10 miremur . . . si: deliberative subjunctive introducing indirect
question ('are we to feel surprise if?').   **nobis et Baccho et
Apolline dextro:** 'seeing that both Bacchus and Apollo give me (lit. 'us')

their favour': ablative absolute with the verb 'to be' understood: cf. *Caesare duce.* Apollo, player of the lyre (2.31.6, 16), and Bacchus, god of drama and wild inspiration (2.30.38), are both patrons of poets, and both will appear in Book 3, Apollo in 3.3.13–26 giving instruction on the limits of elegy, Bacchus in 3.17, as god of wine, a potential source of forgetfulness and a new direction. They are paired again at 4.6.76 *Bacche, soles Phoebo fertilis esse tuo* [Bacchus (i.e. wine), you are usually fertile for your brother Phoebus].   **dextro:** since this agrees with the two nouns *Baccho* and *Apolline,* one might expect a plural adjective, but that would have been confusing in view of the plural *nobis,* and Latin as easily makes an adjective agree with the nearest of a sequence of nouns.   **turba:** P. moves away from two familiar positions: previously he has sought the attention of Cynthia alone (1.7.11, 2.13.11–14 [**Q**]; but note the move in this direction at 2.34.57 *ut regnem mixtas inter conuiua puellas* [**R**]), and the *turba* has been condemned (3.1.21 n.).

11–12 quod: the basic meaning is 'as for the fact that', but in conjunction with *at* ('yet') in 15, it has a concessive force ('although'). **Taenariis … columnis:** i.e. columns made of the black marble from Taenarus in Sparta: cf. Plin. *Nat.* 36.135.   **est mihi:** possessive dative, = 'I have'.   **fulta:** from *fulcio* = I support.   **nec camera auratas inter eburna trabes:** 'and no ivory ceiling with gilded beams': i.e. the roof is vaulted, with ivory panels intersected by beams. *inter* governs *auratas trabes*: on the word order, see p. 40. The line has a fine chiastic* structure (noun, adj., prep. adj. noun), and, as Camps' commentary suggests, 'the word order helps to convey the alternation of materials in the coffering of the roof'. Vergil draws a similar contrast between a luxurious and a fulfilled way of life at *Geo.* 2.461–74, and his phrasing *si non … at* is used in Ovid's imitation of our passage at *Am.* 1.3.7–14; cf. also Lucr. 2.24–33, Hor. *Odes* 2.18, 3.1.17–48, Tib. 1.1. Wealth, and the evils suffered and caused by those who seek it, are subjects much discussed later in the book (4.1–3, 13; 5.1–17; 7.1–8, 43–6; 12.3–6, 17–18; 13.1–14).

13 Phaeacas … siluas: the reference is to the idealized garden of Alcinous, king of the island of Phaeacia, described at Hom. *Od.* 7.112–32.   **pomaria:** 'orchards'. The Latin proverb *Alcinoo* *poma dare* ('to give fruit to Alcinous') has the same meaning as our 'coals to Newcastle'. For tree plantations as a sign of wealth, see 1.14.5–6, Hor. *Odes* 3.1.9–10 *est ut uiro uir latius ordinet arbusta sulcis* [it is the case that one man lines up trees in furrows more broadly than another].

14 Marcius liquor: water from the *aqua Marcia* (3.22.24 n.), the aqueduct built to bring water to Rome by Q. Marcius Rex, who was praetor in 144 and 143 BC. A remarkable feat of engineering, it passed (mainly underground) from the Sabine hills near Tibur (modern Tivoli). In time Rome came to be served by eleven aqueducts which brought about 1.2 million cubic metres of water a day to its million or so inhabitants. Water could be fed into private houses at a price; it would be extravagant to use the excellent drinking water of the *aqua Marcia* for fountains.   **operosa antra:** 'artificial grottoes': cf. 3.3.27–30 n. Such *nymphaea* are prominent among the archaeological remains, e.g. in the so-called 'Auditorium' of Maecenas on the Esquiline, and at the end of the Canopus at Hadrian's Villa.

15–16 carmina cara legenti: 'poems dear to the reader'. The dative is common after *carus* (*OLD* 2b, 3b).   **et defessa ... Calliopea:** *Calliopea* is a variant for Calliope, the chief of the Muses, and the only one named by P. To say that she is exhausted with the poet's dances has been seen by some as less than flattering to his work, and *nec* has been suggested as a substitute for *et*, causing Calliope to be 'not tired', i.e. 'tireless'. But *et* is surely unproblematic: the Muse's assiduous involvement with the poet is stressed (cf. 1.3.5 *assiduis Edonis fessa choreis*). Calliope converses with Callimachus in fr. 7.22. P. will meet the Muses in 3.3, where Calliope speaks for them all, and 3.10.

17–18 fortunata meo si qua es celebrata libello: 'fortunate you are, whoever have been celebrated in my book': *es* functions twice. The indefinite *si qua* takes us far from the *Cynthia* of 1.1.1. *libellus* can be used as a metrically convenient alternative to *liber,* but here as often the diminutive force remains: the little book contains many monuments (18), and even the Wonders of the World (19–21).   **carmina erunt formae tot monumenta tuae:** 'my every poem will be a monument to your beauty' (*quot* being understood with *carmina:* 'as many songs, so many monuments') or 'my poems will be so many monuments to your beauty'.

19–20 neque: P. (like Ovid) prefers *neque* to *nec* when it gives him a dactyl* in the first foot (cf. p. 38–9); otherwise he uses it almost exclusively before vowels.   **pyramidum sumptūs:** 'the costly pyramids' (lit. 'the expenses of the pyramids'). The pyramids; the temple of Jupiter at Olympia (20); and the Mausoleum (21), the great tomb built for King Mausolus of Halicarnassus by his widow Artemisia in the fourth century BC, were three of the seven Wonders of the ancient World.   **Iouis Elei... domus:** the temple of Zeus (Jupiter) at Olympia in Elis in southern Greece was built between about 470 and 456 BC.   **caelum imitata:** it was like the heavens in its size; as a home of Zeus; and, most pointedly, in the form and decoration of its ceiling, which was possibly vaulted and certainly embossed, that is *caelatum*. Etymological play between *caelum* and *caelo* is very frequent in the Augustan poets, e.g. Verg. *Ecl.* 3.37 *caelatum diuini opus Alcimedontis* (the cups are 'the engraved' [but also 'heavenly'] 'work of the divine artist Alcimedon'); Ov. *Fast.* 2.79 *caelatum stellis Delphina* [the Dolphin (the constellation) embossed with stars]; Manilius 5.288–9 *sculpentem... sanctis laquearia templis | condentemque nouum caelum per tecta Tonantis* [a man who engraves vaulted ceilings in holy temples and creates a new heaven in the Thunderer's halls]. G. M. Sargeaunt (*CR* 39 (1925), 19) argued that 'the ceiling... was painted blue and picked out with stars... according to Greek custom'.

21–2 Mausolei diues fortuna sepulcri: lit. 'the rich fortune of the tomb of Mausolus'. As in 19 the extravagance of the language suits the richness of the buildings described.   **mortis ab extrema condicione uacant:** 'is free from the final state of death'. One might have expected a singular verb, but there are three subjects, even if they are linked by 'neither... nor', and the first of those is plural.

23–4 illis: dative of disadvantage ('will remove glories *from them*'). **tacito:** van Eldik's emendation for the unsatisfactory *ictu. tacitus* is used of the passage of time by Ovid (*Fast.* 1.65, 6.771; *Trist.* 4.10.27).   **annorum... pondere:** Old age is often figured as weighed down (*OLD* s.v. *pondus* 5c, *grauis* 7b); this case is unusual in not referring to human beings. For the thought in lines 18–26, compare Horace, *Odes* 3.30.1–6 (**M:** n.b. *monumentum, pyramidum, imber, diruere, annorum*), and Cicero on Julius Caesar at *Marc.* 11–12: 'This feat is so great that time will bring an end to your trophies and monuments (for there is nothing made by the labour of hands that old age does not destroy and consume), yet this justice and clemency of yours will flourish more and more every day.'

25–6 ingenio quaesitum nomen: 'the name acquired by the poet's talent'.   **ab aeuo**: 'in all eternity', lit. 'by (the working of) the passage of time'.   **excidet**: 'will perish'.   **stat**: 'persists, stands firm': cf. Ennius's famous phrase *moribus antiquis res stat Romana uirisque* [the Roman state stands firm on ancient traditions and men]. The Roman woman had no chance of winning military or political glory; but with a poet for lover she could yet win immortality greater than monuments.   **decus**: 'beauty' or 'distinction'. Shakespeare begins his sonnet 65 with the question:

> Since brass, nor stone, nor earth, nor boundless sea,
> But sad mortality o'ersways their power,
> How with this rage shall beauty hold a plea,
> Whose action is no stronger than a flower?

He concludes with the hope 'That in black ink my love may still shine bright'.

Additional bibliography: J. F. Miller, *TAPhA* 113 (1983), 289–99; G. Mader, *CJ* 88 (1993), 321–40; Newman 1997: 237–42.

3.3

1–12: I had dreamt that I was relaxing on Mount Helicon where Hippocrene flows, with the strength to produce a poem on the Alban kings, and had put my lips to the fountain from where Ennius drank and sang various stories from the Annales, *when Apollo spied me from a tree and said: (15–24:) 'What are you doing touching the river of epic song? This is not to be the source of your fame. You must write elegy, so your book can be there for a girl to read when waiting for her man. You must not overburden your boat or head for the ocean.' 25–36: Apollo pointed out the new path to the Muses' grotto, decorated and hung with symbols of gods and music. Venus' doves drank from a pool of Hippocrene's water, and the Muses were busy with various tasks, making thyrsi or garlands or playing music. 37–50: One of them, Calliope, touched me and said: 'You shall be drawn by swans, not led to arms by a warhorse. Do not blast martial alarums or tell of bloody victories over German tribes. You shall sing of the locked out lover so that a man may trick stern husbands with your help and charm out girls.' 51–2: She wet my lips with the water from the elegiac spring.*

From Hesiod on, poets encounter gods and muses in the wild, and they receive inspiration in dreams: this poem sets itself in a long and glorious tradition. Helpful preparation would be to read through the passages in the Appendix, especially items A–E, G–J. The central model is the opening of Callimachus' *Aetia*, which has the poet receiving advice from Apollo in the proem (**B**), and then a dream encounter with the Muses set on Helicon, in the place where they had previously met Hesiod (fr. 2.1–2; cf. **A**):

> ποιμένι μῆλα νέμοντι παρ' ἴχνιον ὀξέος ἵππου
> Ἡσιόδωι Μουσέων ἑσμὸς ὅτ' ἠντίασεν

When the flock of the Muses met Hesiod the shepherd pasturing his sheep by the footprint of the swift horse [Pegasus], . . .

Hesiod's initiation is evoked by other Hellenistic* poets, such as Theocritus (*Idyll* 7.91–3):

> πολλὰ μὲν ἄλλα
> Νύμφαι κἠμὲ δίδαξαν ἀν' ὤρεα βουκολέοντα
> ἐσθλά, τά που καὶ Ζηνὸς ἐπὶ θρόνον ἄγαγε φάμα.

Many other songs the Nymphs taught me too, when I was herding on the mountains, good ones, which report has brought even to the throne of Zeus, I think.

The programmatic* dream is brought into Latin poetry by Ennius (239–169 BC) at the start of his *Annales*. In this patriotic epic he told the history of Rome from before the foundation to his own day (6–12): he launched the poem by telling of a dream in which Homer appeared and announced that, through the transmigration of souls, Ennius was his reincarnation. We have many allusions* to the passage (see esp. Lucretius 1.117–26, **D**), but of the text tiny disconnected fragments* (Skutsch 1985, fr. 1–3, and nn.):

Musae, quae pedibus magnum pulsatis Olympum
] somno leni placidoque reuinctus
] uisus Homerus adesse poeta

...you Muses, who pound great Olympus with your feet... \<when I was\>
bound in calm and gentle sleep... the poet Homer seemed to appear

Propertius himself produced other dream narratives. In 2.26A he
gives us an account of Cynthia shipwrecked that has details of
extraordinary realism: he is absorbed in her desperation but
distanced from it, eager to help but unable to do so, and when he
eventually dives off a cliff (19–20), he wakes up and the poem ends.
This is very different from the typical epic dream, where the sleeper
in bed is visited by a god or a ghost with a message (*Il.* 23.62–101
Patroclus appears to Achilles, imitated by P. in 4.7; *Od.* 6.15–40
Athena, disguised, to Nausicaa; *Aen.* 3.146–78 the Penates to Aeneas).
In 3.3 too the dreamer is active, travelling through a shifting landscape created from the poetry he is involved with and meeting figures
who are important in his waking life.

The poem has an especially rich and evocative collection of the
imagery of poetic inspiration. In 13–26 Apollo speaks to the poet as
he does in the proem to the *Aetia* (fr. 1.21–8) and Vergil's Sixth
Eclogue (3–5), followed by Calliope, as representative of the Muses
(37–52), who instructed Hesiod at the start of the *Theogony* and
Callimachus in *Aetia* 1–2. The two speakers implicitly answer the
questions posed to Callimachus and Philitas in 3.1.1–6. Water features throughout, in the form of Hippocrene, as a source of epic
(1–12) or elegy (31–2, 51–2), a large river (15–17, 45–6), and the epic
sea (22–4). There are cameo appearances by the chariot (18) and the
path (26), by horses (2, 21, 40) and birds (12, 31–2, 39), and by
groves (13, 42) and caves (14, 27–8). The landscape of such scenes
responds to the fact that Hesiod was herding in the *Theogony* and
owes much to pastoral (e.g. Theoc. *Id.* 1; Verg. *Ecl.* 1, 10), and
something to the lost elegies of Gallus (see Ross 1975: 20–36, 71–4,
85–99; Cairns 2006: 110–43). P. has found inspiration in similar
territory already at 2.13.3–6 (**Q**), 3.1.1–6, 2.30.25–7:

libeat tibi, Cynthia, mecum
rorida muscosis antra tenere iugis.
illic aspicies scopulis haerere Sorores.

May it please you, Cynthia, to occupy with me dewy caves on mossy ridges. There you will see the Sisters [i.e. the Muses] clinging to the rocks.

As well as a rejection of epic, we should find here an exploration of the potential of elegy. The poem proceeds through a rapid sequence of oppositions, often elemental in nature, such as we might expect from epic: mountain and spring (1–2), rustic and domestic (18–20), land and sea (23–4), nature and art (27–30), plain and river (43–6), and foreign and domestic (43–50). The elegist moves between both parts of a pair (23–4) or is figured by doves and swans (31–2, 39), and perhaps the flying horse Pegasus too.

1–2 Visus eram: lit. 'I had seemed to', i.e. 'I had dreamt that I'. This recalls instances in two other dream poems, the opening *Vidi* of 2.26A, and *uisa est* at 4.7.3 (cf. e.g. *Aen.* 2.271); grammatically it looks forward to *posse* in 4 ('that I had the power to'). The pluperfect tense leads into the sequence with *admoram* (5; = *admoueram*) and the inverted *cum* in 13.   **molli recubans Heliconis in umbra:** this echoes the start of Vergil's pastoral collection, the *Eclogues* (**H**), where Tityrus is presented *recubans* (1.1) and *lentus in umbra*. Vergil's terms *siluestrem* and *tenui* are replaced by the elegiac *molli*: the scene is at odds with the work proposed in 3–4. Pausanias gives a tourist's guide to Helicon at 9.28–31.   **umor equi:** see 3.1.19 n. on Hippocrene, the spring on Mount Helicon made by a blow from the hoof of Bellerophon's horse Pegasus. There is a potentially comic, deflating element here, however, since *umor* can refer to urine (*OLD* 2a).

3–4 Alba: the town in the hills south-east of Rome which Ascanius, the son of Aeneas, the founder of the Roman nation, had built and at which their descendants ruled until Romulus founded Rome. In his comment on *Ecl.* 6.3 (**I**), the 4th-century commentator Servius claims that Vergil refers in the phrase *reges et proelia* either to the *Aeneid* or to the *gesta regum Albanorum, quae coepta omisit nominum asperitate deterritus* [the acts of the Alban kings, a work he began but abandoned, discouraged by the harshness of the names]. P. is an even less likely author of such a work; perhaps there was a shared joke about unlikely topics, or perhaps P.'s playful fantasy here has infected the Vergilian scholarship. Though there are lists of the kings in Livy 1.3 and Ov. *Fast.*

4.41–54, 'no one ever seriously projected an epic on the kings of Alba, a dim line of shadows invented to fill a chronological gap' (Hubbard, 79, n. 1). The vocative here suits elegy (pp. 26–7), and shows P.'s unfitness for the projected narrative; the repetitive flatness of *reges . . . et regum facta tuorum* evokes historical style. **tantum operis:** 'so great a work', an allusion* to Livy, *praef.* 13 (Woodman, *CQ* 48 (1998), 568–9; cf. also 3.11.70), in apposition* to *reges . . . et regum facta. opus* is used again, by Apollo, at 16.   **hiscere:** 'to utter' (*OLD* 2b). But the main meaning of the word is 'gape'. The hint of comedy (2 n.) continues: P. opens his mouth as wide as possible to sing of the kings and their deeds—and nothing comes out.   **neruis . . . meis:** either 'with my strength' or 'to the accompaniment of my strings', or both. *neruus* means both a sinew (3.9.7) and the string of a musical instrument (35).

5–6 parua . . . ora: the phrase gapes apart to enclose the whole line, including the contrasting *magnis fontibus*.   **iam:** his lips are already positioned to drink, perhaps already drinking as the poem tells epic tales from Ennius, so Apollo's intervention will be in the nick of time.   **pater Ennius:** see intro., 3.1.15 n. *pater* is a respectful title often used for gods (29, 3.17.2 n.); here it also brings out Ennius's role as the early father figure of Latin poetry.

7–12 A disorderly account of Ennius' *Annales*: verse 7 recalls an episode from the reign of Rome's third king, Tullus Hostilius, which comes from Ennius' second book, and 8 evokes the war that ended with the conquest of Macedon (171–67 BC), which must have been dealt with in the closing Book 18. Even the account of the Second Punic War (218–201BC) in verses 9–11 places the *uictrices morae* before the disastrous battle of Cannae; and Hannibal's threat to Rome belongs after the invasion of the Gauls (390 BC) to which the story of the Capitoline geese belongs (but see 12 n.).

7–8 Curios fratres: these must be the three Curiatii brothers who fought the three Horatii on behalf of their cities, Rome and Alba, a famous episode narrated by Livy (1.24–6; he acknowledges that it is uncertain which brothers represented which city). Only here in extant texts are they referred to as *Cŭrĭī* but *Cūrĭātĭī* will not scan in dactylic* verse, and Skutsch (on fr. 123) suggests that the short

form originated in Ennius' hexameters.   **Horatia pila:** in
context this must be accusative, and thus neuter plural, meaning
either the victors' weapons or those of the conquered set up as a
trophy; but P. is playing, for elsewhere (Livy 1.26.10; Dion. Hal.
3.22.9) *Horatia pila* is a feminine singular referring to the column
set up as a monument.   **regiăque Aemiliă uectă tropaeă
rate:** 'and the royal trophies carried on the boat of Aemilius'.
Though this apparently refers to the triumph in 167 BC of Aemilius
Paullus after his conquest of Perseus, king of Macedon, and his
shipping of the immense booty up the Tiber (Livy 45.35.3 *regia
naue ingentis magnitudinis ... ornata Macedonicis spoliis* [in a royal
ship of huge size adorned with Macedonian spoils]), Ennius can
hardly have recounted this episode, for Cicero (who knew Roman
history and the *Annales*) believed he died in 169 BC (*Brut.* 78, *Sen.*
14). Another Aemilius, Regillus, defeated Antiochus, king of Syria,
in a sea battle at Myonnesus in 190 BC, but that brought no famous
booty. We know very little about the final book of the *Annales*
(even whether it was finished), but there seems room for Ennius to
have begun an account of the Third Macedonian War, in which
case P. evokes the closing topic by describing what would have
made a fittingly triumphant ending if Ennius had lived to write
it: we may compare his creative accounts of Vergil's *Eclogues*
(2.34.67–76), the *Iliad* (3.1.25–30) and the *Odyssey* (3.12.24–36).

9–12 uictricesque moras Fabii: Quintus Fabius Maximus was given
the title *Cunctator* ('Delayer') because his tactics of putting off any
battle had weakened Hannibal's forces and given Rome a vital breathing space in the Second Punic War. Ennius wrote of him (*Ann.* 363):
unus homo nobis cunctando restituit rem [one man restored our state
by delaying].   **sinistram:** 'ill-omened'. The reference is to the
battle of Cannae in 216 BC, where Hannibal inflicted on the Romans
the most severe defeat they had known; our sources talk of 70,000
killed. After the disaster Rome seemed to be at Hannibal's mercy,
but (as 10 reveals) the gods paid attention to the pious offerings
(*ad pia uota*), i.e. the Romans' public supplications (Livy 23.11).
Lares: the gods that protect the home (hence *sede*: see *OLD* s.v.
sedes 4–5), or, as here, the whole settlement of Rome (cf. Ov. *Fast.*
5.129–42). Hannibal came close to the walls of Rome in 211 before

turning back; a shrine was set up on the spot to Rediculus ('the going away god'), perhaps treated by Ennius, or by P. here, as equivalent to the *Lares* (Skutsch 1985: 471).   **anseris**: the cackling of the sacred geese woke Manlius and saved the temple of Jupiter on the Capitol from being captured by the Gauls in 390 or 387 (Livy 5.47; Polybius 1.6.2). This too may be a creative misreading of Ennius, who seems to have the Gauls killing the guards (fr. 227–8), and to have narrated the episode as a flashback during the Second Punic War. The unlovely sound of the goose is given poetic point by Vergil at *Ecl.* 9.36 *argutos inter strepere anser olores* [to cackle like a goose amid tuneful swans].   **et**: postponed*. There is a list of instances of postponed *et* and other conjunctions on pp. 40–1.

13–14 Castalia speculans ex arbore: the Castalian spring was located not on Mount Helicon but on Mount Parnassus, close to Apollo's sanctuary at Delphi; visitors would purify themselves in its waters. It is a source of poetic inspiration at Verg. *Geo.* 3.293, Ov. *Am.* 1.15.36, and Martial will later call the Muses *Castalides sorores* (4.14.1). The logic of P.'s dream causes the spring's Apolline associations to take precedence over geography.   **arbore**: lit. 'tree', here perhaps a collective singular* = 'grove'.   **ad antra**: 'by the cave' or 'grotto': 3.1.5 n. The evocation of the poetic landscape is more important than the precise feature. The poet's dream of epic utterance has been expressed in an appropriately long sentence (1–14; cf. 3.12.24–36); it ends here with Apollo's interruption. Though this speech will extend the sentence for a further ten lines, only one of the couplets is enjambed* (18), and generally the style becomes elegiac.   **aurata ... lyra**: Apollo's lyre and bow are described as 'golden' or 'gilded' at Call. *Hymn* 2.32–4; Ennius, *trag.* 34–5 Warmington.

15–16 quid tibi cum: 'what is your business with . . . ?' The structure is a very common and informal idiom (Plaut. *Aul.* 631; *Men.* 323, 369; Cic. *Cael.* 33), used frequently by Ovid (e.g. *Met.* 1.456 *quid ... tibi, lasciue puer, cum fortibus armis?* [what is your business with arms of war, mischievous boy (Cupid)]).   **flumine**: the metaphor of the river evokes the strong flow of epic poetry (*carminis heroi*): cf. Call. *Hymn* 2.108–9 (C); Hor. *Odes* 4.2.5–8. As in the *Aetia* prologue, the imagery will swiftly change.

17–18 mollia sunt paruis prata terenda rotis: 'soft meadows are to be worn down by small wheels'. For the word *mollis*, repeated from 1, see 3.1.19 n. The small wheels are those of P.'s light poetic chariot; for such imagery cf. 3.1.11, 3.9.58; Call. *Aet.* fr. 1.27 (B); Verg. *Geo.* 3.18 (L); Ov. *Ars* 1.40 *haec erit admissa meta terenda rota* [this will be the final turning post to be scraped by my speeding chariot], 1.264 *imparibus uecta Thalia rotis* [Thalia travelling on unequal wheels (i.e. the elegiac couplet)].

19–20 ut tuus in scamno iactetur saepe libellus: 'so that your book may often be tossed [*or* displayed] on a stool'. The girl will pick the *libellus* up from the stool and possibly sit down on it to read. *iactetur* looks like an act of dismissal (*OLD* 3), but such a verb of motion would not normally be followed by *in* + ablative, and it is possible we should understand it as 'shown off' (*OLD* 12); in any case the pentameter renders the description positive. Horace, *Epist.* 1.20 envisages an equally vivid, but even less grand future for his book, neglected and ending up as a school text. Though *libellus* does not necessarily have a diminutive force (*Cynthia* 1.9.13), it does in this Callimachean* and feminine context.   **quem legat exspectans sola puella uirum:** the relative with the subjunctive expresses purpose: 'for a girl to read, while she is alone, waiting for her [*or* a] man'. *uir* can mean 'husband' (*OLD* 2a), but is more likely here to mean 'lover' (2b). The book will pass the time, but also prepare the reader for an erotic encounter; if we understand *iactetur* to mean 'be displayed', it will signal her receptiveness. Elsewhere P. imagines a readership of male lovers (49–50; 1.7.23–4)—and Cynthia.

21–4 praescriptos euecta est ... gyros: '... been carried out of its prescribed circuits'. For *euehor* + acc. see *OLD* 2b. *praescriptos gyros* refers to the precise turns required of the horse (Verg. *Geo.* 3.115; Ov. *Ars* 3.384 [cited on 3.14.6], Tac. *Germ.* 6.3) rather than the ring where they were trained (3.14.11). For horses used to symbolize poetic progress, see 3.9.57–8 n.   **pagina** ('column'; more loosely 'page') is a synecdoche* for the papyrus* roll as a whole, and thus a metonym* for poetry.   **cumba:** 'a small boat' or 'skiff', appropriate for P.'s lighter talent. The image of poetry as a voyage goes back to Pindar (*Nem.* 3.27), and was developed by Latin poets in the light of Callimachus' use of bodies of water to symbolize larger and purer poetry at the

end of his Hymn to Apollo (**C**). Cf. in particular Verg. *Geo.* 2.39–45 (**J**);
Hor. *Odes* 3.29.57–64; Ov. *Rem.* 811–12; 3.17.2 n.   **non est ...
grauanda**: 'is not to be overloaded': for Callimachean* rejection of the
weighty, see *Aet.* fr. 1.35–6 (**B**); 1.9.9, 2.10.9 (**P**); Ov. *Am.* 1.1.1 *Arma
graui numero* [arms in epic metre].   **alter remus aquas, alter
tibi radat harenas**: the two oars brilliantly evoke the two verses of the
elegiac couplet, the hexameter out to sea, the pentameter manipulated
with a shorter stroke closer to shore: cf. the personification* Elegia
at Ov. *Am.* 3.1.8 *pes illi longior alter erat* [she had one longer leg],
and *alternus* used to suggest the couplet at 1.9.24, 1.10.10; Ov. *Her.*
15.5 *alterna carmina, Trist.* 3.1.11 *alterno uersu. tibi* is possessive
dative ('your oar' or 'for you').   **turba**: in context the most
obvious meaning is 'commotion', i.e. 'rough water': by staying close
to the shore P. will escape the danger of storms (3.9.3, 35). But there
is an additional implication that mid sea (i.e. grand epic) is where
the greatest 'crowd' of poets sails: a Callimachean should avoid the
throng (3.1.12–14).

25–6 plectro ... eburno: a suitably musical pointer for the lyre-playing
Apollo to use.   **noua**: reflecting the novelty of P.'s poetry: cf.
Cat. 1.1 *nouum libellum*; Ov. *Am.* 1.1.14 *opus nouum*, 17 *noua pagina*;
Met. 1.1 *In noua fert animus.*   **semita**: the word was derived
from *semi-iter* ('half-road': Varro, *Ling. Lat.* 5.35) and thus implies an
appropriate narrowness: cf. Call. fr. 1.25–8 (**B**) and 3.1.18 n.; and
contrast the complaint of Manilius, writing some thirty years later
(2.50): *omnis ad accessus Heliconos semita trita est* [every path to the
approaches of Helicon is worn away].

27–30 affixis ... lapillis: lit. 'with pebbles having been fixed on', i.e.
'with an adornment of pebbles'. Such grottoes constructed of pumice
are mentioned by Plin. *Nat.* 36.154; Ov. *Met.* 3.157–60, 8.562–4: the
confusion of nature and artifice was found appealing, and suits the
home of the Muses.   **pendebantque cauis tympana pumici-
bus**: 'and drums hanging from the hollow pumice'. The phrasing
varies Verg. *Geo.* 4.374 *pendentia pumice tecta* [buildings hanging
with pumice] and Lucr. 6.195 *speluncas ... saxis pendentibus structas*
[caves built with overhanging rocks]. *cauis* could imply the hollow-
ness that makes pumice light, or perhaps that the rocks are overhanging. On pumice see also 3.1.8 n. *tympana* are 'small drums'

associated with the ecstatic worship of Cybebe (3.17.35 n.) and Bacchus (3.17.33): festivals, the Dionysia in Athens and the Megalensia in Rome, associate each deity with drama, but 29 and 35 continue the evocation of Bacchus here. **Sileni patris imago fictilis:** 'an earthenware image of father Silenus'. Terracotta was used for the adornments of Roman temples before imported marble became common. Silenus was an elderly, drunken and animalistic inhabitant of the wild, the teacher and attendant of Bacchus. His combination of mischief, lewdness, wisdom and musical skill is well illustrated by Vergil's Sixth Eclogue. **Pan Tĕgĕaēĕ:** 'Arcadian Pan'. Pan was a pastoral god from Arcadia, in which lay the town of Tegea. Half-man and half-goat, he played the pan pipes (*calami*: 3.17.34 n.); the sound of *Tegeaee* may be intended to evoke the sound of the pipes (cf. *Ecl.* 1.1 *Tityre tu*).

31–2 mea turba: 'my (sort of) crowd'. Doves are symbols of Venus and the love poet identifies with them. *mea* gives approval to this *turba* in contrast to that in 24. The phrase is in apposition* to *uolucres columbae*, about which it provides further information. Such enclosed appositions are a regular feature of Latin poetic style from Verg. *Ecl.* 1.57 (*raucae, mea cura, palumbes*) on: see J. B. Solodow, *HSCPh* 90 (1986), 129–53. **punica rostra:** *punica rostra* could mean 'the beaks of Carthaginian ships' (i.e. projections from bows used in ramming other ships), suitable matter for annalistic epic (Nethercut, *AJPh* 91 (1970), 393), but here they are transformed into the 'red beaks' of doves. **Gorgoneo...lacu:** Pegasus sprang from the blood of the Gorgon Medusa's severed neck, and so, through this more recherché (and monstrous) epithet, we are back with the water from Hippocrene, the spring of 1–6, not now *magni fontes* fit to inspire epic, but a pool where doves can drink (cf. 2.10.26 [**P**], Hor. *Odes* 4.2.27–32).

33–6 diuersae nouem: 'nine in different parts' of the cave (we might think of a grotto in garden, with nine statues artfully distributed; Hunter 2006: 31–2 compares *Daphnis & Chloe* 1.4); but the force of *diuersae* also carries over to the different duties. **sortitae iura Puellae:** 'Maidens allotted their own areas of jurisdiction'. The nine Maidens are of course the Muses. Modern iconography* allocates a specific genre to each (with Clio the Muse of history, Thalia of comedy, Calliope of epic, and so on), but there is little ancient justification for these: though Thalia tends to be associated with light poetry (Verg. *Ecl.* 6.2; she is *lasciua* at Stat. *Silu.* 2.1.116 and 5.3.98), Calliope, the oldest and grandest sister, who often speaks for the rest, is the only Muse named by P. (6 times)—she thus has a claim to be the Muse of elegy. The main motivation for ancient authors in allocating roles is etymological: see in general Plato, *Phaedrus* 259c–d; on *Erato* Ap. *Arg.* 3.1–5 and Ov. *Fast.* 4.195–6.   **in sua dona:** '(to produce) their particular gifts', with the implication that they will be giving these to their aficionados (so Bacchus at 3.17.13).   **legit:** 'picks', but playing on 'reads' (3.22.12 n.), another activity appropriate for a Muse.   **in thyrsos:** 'for thyrsi'. These were fennel rods tipped with pine cones carried by the followers of Bacchus, god of wine, but also of drama.   **haec carmina neruis aptat:** 'another harmonizes songs to her strings', i.e. of her lyre (implying lyric). But see also 4 n.: each Muse works in the sphere for which her abilities suit her, i.e. her 'strengths'.   **manu ... utraque:** 'with either hand'. The epithet perhaps hints at elegy (cf. 23), a metre in which rose garlands often feature (both in Greek epigram and Latin elegy).   **rosam:** a collective singular*, often used of flowers (as at 3.5.22). The Muse is making garlands, perhaps for symposia (cf. 47 n.; 2.15.51–2, 2.33.37).

37–8 contigit: here and at 52 the Muse touches him and moistens his lips, in contrast to 5 and 16, where the poet tries to be active in 'touching' the epic spring. Ovid uses *contigit* similarly at *Fast.* 4.16, where Venus touches the poet with myrtle.   **una dearum** recalls Verg. *Ecl.* 6.64–5 *Gallum... Aonas in montes ut duxerit una Sororum* [how one of the Sisters led Gallus up into the Aonian mountains], and possibly the passage of Gallus which Vergil was imitating. **Calliopea:** see 33, 3.2.16 nn. P. works out her identity because hers is the name that implies a 'beautiful face' (κάλλος 'beauty'; ὄψ, ὀπός 'face' or 'voice': for the ambiguity cf. *ora*, 52).

39–40 contentus as at 3.7.43 implies a willingness to accept restraint, not to aim for excess.   **semper** asserts that he will never move away from erotic poetry.   **uectabere cycnis:** 'you will be carried by swans' (like Ovid at *Ars* 3.809–10). From a Muse a prediction is also an instruction: as often the future has the effect of an imperative (3.23.15 n.). The chariot on which Venus rides is drawn by swans: cf. Hor. *Odes.* 3.28.13–15 *quae... Paphon iunctis uisit oloribus* [who visits Paphos with yoked swans], 4.1.10; Ov. *Met.* 10.708. Swans were also famous for the beauty of their (dying) song (a point implied by the contrast with the *equi sonus* in 40).   **fortis equi:** i.e. a war horse. The phrase recalls a related context in Lucretius (3.6–8):

> quid enim contendat hirundo
> *cycnis*, aut quidnam tremulis facere artubus haedi
> consimile in cursu possint et *fortis equi* vis?

For why would a swallow compete with swans, or what could kids with trembling limbs do in a race comparable with the might of a strong horse?

P. recombines two of Lucretius' creatures in imitation of the cicada/ ass antithesis at Call. *Aet.* fr. 1.29–32 (**B**).   **ad arma:** i.e. to epic; as at 3.1.7, 3.4.1, 3.5.47 P. exploits the first word of the *Aeneid.* **sonus** evokes *sonipes* ('foot-sounder'), the epic word for a horse, used by Vergil in vividly cacophonous verses such as 4.135 and 11.599–600 *fremit aequore toto* | *insultans sonipes et pressis pugnat habenis* [the foot-sounding horse snorts, prancing all over the plain, and fights the restricted reins].

41–2 ne tibi sit: 'let it be no concern of yours'. With infinitives following, the expression is more idiomatic than the transmitted *nil tibi sit.*   **rauco praeconia classica cornu** | **flare:** 'to blow martial alarms on a noisy trumpet': Calliope herself mimics the cacophony of battle scenes. But the puzzle she sets for the reader does not seem very epic: *classicus* is used as an adjective meaning (among other things) 'naval' or 'military', and *classicum* as a noun, meaning 'trumpet' or 'trumpet blast'; *praeconius* = 'connected with a *praeco* (public crier)', *praeconium* = 'a public proclamation'. Is the sense then 'military proclamations' or 'public trumpet blasts'? Or perhaps (*OLD classicus*, 3) 'trumpeted proclamations'?   **Aonium...nemus:** Aonia is the area of Boeotia around Mount Helicon (Verg. *Ecl.* 6.65 [37 n.], *Geo.* 3.11 [**L**]): the geographical reference is thus to the grove inhabited by the Muses (cf. 1), and the meaning is 'poetry'.   **tingere:** 'to wet' or 'dye'; *Marte* thus implies 'the blood of war': cf. 45–6, and contrast 32.

43–6 quibus in campis: introducing an indirect question: '(let it be no concern of yours) <to tell> on what plains . . .'   **Mariano signo:** 'under Marius' standard': Marius established the eagle as the legionary standard (Plin. *Nat.* 10.16). He defeated the Teutones at Aquae Sextiae and the Cimbri at Vercellae in 102 and 101 BC respectively.   **proelia . . . stent:** 'battle lines are formed'. **aut:** postponed*. The indirect question continues, with 'how' or 'where' understood.   **Suebo:** the Suebi, a German tribe, crossed the Rhine and were defeated by C. Carrinas, a victory marked on the first day of Augustus's triple triumph in 29 BC (Dio Cassius 51.21.5–6).   **perfusus sanguine Rhenus | saucia maerenti corpora uectet aqua:** Calliope—and Propertius—have sounded an epic note, at least briefly, using grimly martial diction and foreign names that illustrate Rome's power (cf. Hor. *Sat.* 1.10.36–7: **G**). The blood-stained water of the barbarian river makes a striking contrast with the pool of 32 (though *Gorgoneo* evokes blood there too). But we may notice that the pentameter, in moving on to the grief of the river, returns us to a traditional motif of elegy. C. Powell Frost, *AJPh* 112 (1991), 251–9, finds significant links with Vergil's picture of the Nile welcoming those vanquished at the battle of Actium to its embrace (*Aen.* 8.711–13).

47–50 quippe: apparently 'in fact', 'to be sure', confirming the assertion (as at 4.1.33), rather than explanatory ('for').   **coronatos:** this marks the scene as comastic*: having been at a symposium the lovers have headed out into the streets still wearing their garlands, with the intention of visiting the beloved, gaining access if possible, or at least singing a serenade. The *comus* is a vital part of ancient love poetry from the time of archaic Greek lyric (Alcaeus 178 Page), e.g. in comedy (Plautus, *Curculio* 1–160), epigram (*Anth. Pal.* 5.167, 213), pastoral (Theocritus, *Idyll* 3), elegy (Ov. *Am.* 1.6) and Horace's *Odes* (1.25, 3.10). In passing P. has emphasized the closure of the door and the hardness of the threshold (1.5.20; 1.4.22); elsewhere he concentrates on his drunkenness (1.3, 2.29A); most memorably he puts an account

---

of the practice in the mouth of a door (1.16), including some details that are echoed here (1.16.7–8; *nocturnis* appears in 5):

> et mihi non desunt turpes pendere corollae,
>   semper et exclusi signa iacere faces.

and foul garlands do not fail to hang on me and torches constantly to lie as signs of the excluded lover.

nocturnae ... canes ebria signa morae: 'you shall sing the drunken symbols of a night-time's dalliance', i.e. the garlands themselves (left hanging on the door in *Anth. Pal.* 5.145, 191; Lucr. 4.1177–8), wine-flasks and torches (Tib. 1.2.1; Chariton 1.3.2), perhaps even copies of the serenade. The transmitted *signa fugae* does not lead on to the lover's success in the next couplet and fails to describe a typical scene, whereas the conjecture *signa morae* matches 1.16.7–8 (above), and is parodied by Ovid at *Am.* 1.6.70, where he says to the garland he leaves behind *temporis absumpti tam male testis eris* [you will be a witness to time so badly wasted]: see *CQ* 36 (1986), 202–3.   **per te clausas sciat excantare puellas**: 'thanks to you he may know how to charm out girls locked in'. The subject is provided by the relative clause in the next line, 'the man who ...'. *excantare* evokes the persuasive singing of the elegiac poet. *clausae puellae* will return at 3.13.9, 3.14.23 (with an *austerus uir* in 24).   **uolet**: note the future: lovers will benefit from the sort of poetry P. will continue to write. **ferire**: lit. 'to strike', but the context, especially *arte*, shows it here means 'to trick' (*OLD* 9b; 4.5.44).

51–2 talia Calliope: 'things like this Calliope (said)'.   **ora**: 'face', but implying also 'mouth' (which utters the poetry). At *Aetia* fr. 7.13–14 it is his elegies that Callimachus asks the Muses to anoint.   **Philitea ... aqua**: 'the water Philitas drank', rather than the *magni fontes* from which Ennius took his inspiration (2–6), though this still seems to be Hippocrene (32 n.). For Philitas, see 3.1.1 n.; there is likely to be widespread allusion* to his poetry in 3.3, as there is to that of Callimachus, but in the absence of all bar the meagrest fragments* we can only speculate (see e.g. E. L. Bowie, *CQ* 35 (1985), 83–4).

Additional bibliography: J. F. Miller, 'Ennius and the elegists', *ICS* 8 (1983), 277–95 (at 277–83).

3.4

1–6: Caesar is planning a military expedition in the East. The rewards are great: Parthia will become a Roman province, and its trophies will stand in a Roman temple. 7–10: Come on; set sail, ships; squires, lead out horses. The omens are favourable: make amends for the defeat of the Crassi. 11–16 (incl. 17–18): Mars and Vesta, may the day come on which I see Caesar's triumph, leaning on the bosom of my girl. 19–20: Protect your offspring, Venus: he is descended from Aeneas. 21–2: A triumph for those who have earned it; enough for me to applaud on the Sacred Way.

The Roman province of Syria (annexed by Pompey in 64 BC) was made insecure by the dominance of the Parthian empire to the east; extending power beyond the Euphrates into Mesopotamia was a long-term goal of the Romans. As part of his agreement with Pompey and Julius Caesar, the wealthy dynast Crassus was allotted the province, and set off in 55 BC with the intention of leading an expedition against the Parthians. His army was decisively beaten at Carrhae in the desert beyond the Euphrates in 53; among the thousands killed were Crassus and his son; thousands more were taken prisoner and legionary standards lost. Vengeance and the recovery of the standards now became a powerful motive in Roman foreign policy. Campaigns mounted by Antony resulted in the loss of further standards. The public pressures are well illustrated by Horace, *Odes* 3.5.1–8:

> Caelo tonantem credidimus Iouem
> regnare: praesens diuus habebitur
>   Augustus adiectis Britannis
>   imperio grauibusque Persis.
> milesne Crassi coniuge barbara   5
> turpis maritus uixit et hostium
>   (pro saecula[1] inuersique mores!)
>   consenuit socerorum in armis?

[1] *saecula* Cornelissen: *curia* MSS.

We have come to believe that Jupiter who thunders rules in heaven; Augustus will be regarded as a god on earth once the Britons and the formidable Persians have been added to the empire. Has the soldier of Crassus lived to be disgraced by a barbarian wife, and grown old in the armour of enemy fathers-in-law (oh, the degeneration of times and behaviour)?

Note also *Odes* 1.12.53–4 *seu Parthos Latio imminentes | egerit iusto domitos triumpho* [or if with a just triumph he drives into servitude the Parthians threatening Latium]; 1.35.30–2 *iuuenum recens | examen Eois timendum | partibus Oceanoque rubro* [a fresh swarm of youth to be feared in Eastern parts and the Indian Ocean]; 3.2.3–4 *Parthos feroces | uexet eques metuendus hasta* [let him as a knight harry the fierce Parthians, causing fear with his lance]. P. himself made a similar pronouncement in his aborted move to Augustan panegyric at 2.10.13–16 (**P**).

The standards were eventually returned in 20 BC, through a negotiated settlement (we are not told what gold or promises changed hands). The event is celebrated in the depiction at the centre of the breastplate on the statue of Augustus found at Prima Porta near Rome, and by Horace at *Odes* 4.15.4–8, with scant regard for historical accuracy:

> tua, Caesar, aetas
> fruges et agris rettulit uberes
> et signa nostro restituit Ioui
> derepta Parthorum superbis
> postibus.

Your era, Caesar, has brought back abundant crops to the fields and has restored to our Jupiter the standards snatched down from the proud doorposts of the Parthians.

P. attributes similar sentiments to an unnamed poet at 4.6.79–84.

Other passages that describe triumphs at length are to be found at Verg. *Geo.* 3.10–25 (imagined: Caesar, and Vergil, over the Greek East), *Aen.* 8.714–28 (real: Augustus's triple triumph), Hor. *Odes* 4.2.33–52 (apparently never achieved: Augustus over the Sygambri); Ov. *Am.* 1.2.23–52 (imaginary: Cupid over Ovid), *Ars* 1.177–228 (never achieved: Gaius over the Parthians); *Tristia* 4.2 (never achieved: Tiberius in Germany); similarly *ex Ponto* 2.1 and 3.4. A number of the Ovidian passages imitate this poem, e.g. *Tristia* 4.2.19–20, 53–4:

> ergo omnis populus *po*terit *spectare* triumphos,
>   cumque *du*cum *titulis oppida capta leg*et...
> ipse sono *plau*suque simul fremituque fauentum[2]
>   quadriiugos cernes *saepe resistere equos.*

So the whole people will be able to watch the triumph and will read the names of captured towns along with their leaders... You yourself amid the noise and the applause too and the cheers of supporters will often see the horses pulling your chariot come to a halt.

All of these passages make use of panegyrical material; but the tone varies significantly, depending on the context or the poet's general approach, the details of the rhetoric, and in particular how the poet sets himself within the triumph: it is funny when Ovid is the imaginary victim in *Am.* 1.2 and poignant when he stresses his enforced absence as an exile in *Tristia* 4.2; Horace joins in as one of the crowd at *Odes* 4.2.45–52, whereas P. is a mere spectator set in contrast to the soldiers in the procession. For discussion, see G. K. Galinsky, 'The triumph theme in the Augustan elegy', *WSt* 3 (1969), 75–105; S. J. Heyworth, *PCPhS* 41 (1995), 145–9; and for a brilliant exposé of the mythical element even in historical accounts, see M. Beard, *The Roman Triumph* (Cambridge, MA, 2007).

Book 1 has two *propemptica*, poems in which P. bids others farewell as they head off for a distant part of the empire: in 1.8A he addresses Cynthia, and persuades her to stay with him in Rome (as 1.8B then shows); 1.6 (**N**) is more like 3.4, and a significant intertext*. In sending Tullus off as part of his uncle's cohort, he contrasts his life of love with his addressee's interest in *militia* and *imperium*.

Elegy 3.3 has shown the poet being given firm instructions by Apollo, then by Calliope to avoid epic and continue with love elegy; it should be a surprise to the reader that 3.4 describes preparations for war and looks ahead to a triumph. The tone is thus immediately complex.

1–2 Arma deus Caesar: this plays on the opening words of the *Aeneid*: *Arma uirumque* (where 'the man' is Augustus' putative ancestor Aeneas: cf. 19–20); a response comes in 3.5.1 *Pacis Amor deus est.*

Augustus has been *Diui Filius* since the deification of Julius in 44, and received divine honours in the East after Actium; in poetry he is treated as inevitably becoming divine as early as *Geo.* 1.24–42 and he is equated with Pollux, Hercules and Bacchus at *Odes* 3.3.11–12. But the bluntness of the title *deus* is striking here. P. has himself been a triumphator at 3.1.9–12; so too he will see himself as potentially divine at 3.9.46. **meditatur** ('is planning') is followed by a direct object *arma* ('warfare') and the infinitive *findere* ('to cleave'). **Indos**: 'Indians' may stand, as often, for distant eastern peoples; but there was contact, political (Aug. *Res Gestae* 31.1, Dio 54.9.8) and through trade (Plin. *Nat.* 6.101). Cairns (2006, 405) points out that mention of India puts Caesar alongside Bacchus and Alexander. **dites | gemmiferi**: together the two epithets imply that the emphasis on wealth is not merely conventional. The theme is maintained by *magna merces* (3), *spoliis* (13), *praeda* (21), and its significance brought out in the prolonged rejection of riches in favour of a life of peace and love in the opening 22 verses of 3.5.

3–4 Quiris: 'Roman citizen': a collective address. The word is normally found in the plural, and not elsewhere in the vocative singular, so this is a bold conjecture (by Wistrand) for the transmitted *uiri*; but it supplies perfectly what the context needs: a singular address to lead on to *tua iura* in the pentameter. Ovid uses a vocative in the collective singular* in his imitation at *Ars* 1.179 *Parthe, dabis poenas; Crassi, gaudete, sepulti* [Parthian, you will be punished; Crassi, rejoice where you lie buried]. **Tigris et Euphrates**: as the most significant feature rivers often symbolize populated territory in ancient poetry (n.b. the prominence of the Nile, Euphrates and other rivers on the shield of Aeneas: *Aen.* 8.711–13, 726–8). The Euphrates formed the eastern boundary of Syria, and runs down from the mountains south of the Black Sea all the way to the Persian Gulf, roughly parallel to the Tigris, on the bank of which stood the main Parthian capital Ctesiphon. But Parthian territory extended a long way east, even to northern India (cf. 1).

5 sera, sed . . . ueniet: P. likes to give emphasis to the main point by placing such qualifying adjectives before *sed*: cf. 3.18.22 *est mala, sed . . . terenda uia*; 4.1.98, 4.8.32. **ueniet prouincia**: the land between Tigris and Euphrates will come as a province:

for the singular cf. Livy 5.12.6 *Volsci prouincia euenerat.*
Ausoniis . . . uirgis: dative of advantage: 'for Italian fasces <to
control>'; the *uirgae* are the sticks carried by the lictors who
attended on Roman magistrates.

6 assuescent Latio Partha tropaea Ioui: 'Parthian trophies will get
used to Roman Jupiter' (or 'to the Italian climate', which Jove
signifies as the sky god). *Partha tropaea* are symbols of a Parthian
defeat to be placed in turn in Roman temples. The text assumes an
unspoken 'as our trophies have been growing accustomed to their
gods'. For the turning of the tables, see 4.6.79–80.

7–8 Ships and cavalry briefly sum up the expedition.   **ite
agite**: 'come on, act', implying impatience, almost 'come on, get on
with it'.   **expertae bello**: like *solitum* in the pentameter this
conveys the experience in war that Augustus's forces have acquired in
the campaigns of the 30s and early 20s.   **date lintea, prorae**:
for boats setting their own sails, we may compare Ovid, *Heroides*
16.122 *cum uellent nostrae iam dare uela rates.*   **ad solitum,
armigeri, ducite munus equos**: 'Squires, lead the horses to their
customary duty': *armigeri* provides the vocative to match *prorae*. As
at *Aen.* 10.858 *equum duci iubet*, the leading out of the horse marks
the start of the movement into hostilities.

9–10 Crassos clademque: it is a striking irony that the words that
follow *omina fausta cano* are this ill-omened hendiadys*: 'the disaster
of the Crassi' (see intro.).   **Romanae consulite historiae**:
consulere with the dative has the sense 'look after the interests of':
Carrhae is a stain on Roman history that must be removed. The
Gallus fragment* (**F**) provides an intertext* (note the placing of the
words, especially the quadrisyllabic close to the pentameter): *maxima
Romanae pars eris historiae* (Hollis 145.3).

11 Mars pater et sanctae fatalia lumina Vestae: P. appeals to two
aspects of Rome's origin: the father of its founder Romulus, and the
fires brought by Aeneas from Troy, with which the city's fate is bound
up. Postgate's conjecture *sanctae* is preferred to the transmitted *sacrae*
because the latter is only used as an epithet for deities in the metrically distinctive form *sacer.*

12 ante meos obitus sit precor illa dies: 'I pray that before my death may be that day . . .'. *ut* is frequently omitted in indirect wishes, as in English we can say 'May that day be before my death, I pray'. The plural *meos obitus* avoids the elision that would make *meum obitum* unmetrical. For a similar wish in a similar context, cf. 2.10.20 (**P**).

13–18 These verses describe the typical features of a triumph that he expects to see as a spectator: carts burdened with spoils, weapons and armour taken from the defeated enemy, subdued enemy generals, an applauding crowd. It is clear that 17–18 have been displaced in the manuscript tradition: the objects need to be governed by a verb of seeing, and the couplet 13–14 is both truncated in itself and problematic because of the asyndeton* in 14 (a feature P. allows in lists, but not in pairs). The text printed supposes that four lines were omitted, beginning with a pentameter, but that when the omission was made good by a reader checking against the exemplar or another text only the complete couplet in the middle was restored: the lost lines might have given detail of Caesar's appearance and more on the crowd. As often in Propertian lists the construction is varied: a single verb has as its object both nouns (17), participial phrases (13), and noun clauses (accusatives + infinitives in 18, 14); cf. 3.12.25–36 (in apposition* to *morae*, the subject), 3.18.21–8.

13 axes: 'axles', but frequently used by synecdoche* for the whole chariot or cart (*OLD* 1b).

17 tela fugacis equi et bracati militis arcus: 'the weapons of the fleeing horse' are probably to be identified with 'the bows of the trousered soldier': the Parthians' light-armed archers turned round to shoot at the enemy while riding in the opposite direction: cf. 3.9.54.

18 On the word order, see p. 40.

15–16 P. returns from the general picture to himself; he will enjoy the spectacle, at first at least (n.b. *incipiam*), leaning on Cynthia's bosom. Ovid turns the scene into didactic advice for the would-be lover at *Ars* 1.177–228.   **legam:** Despite being a poet, he will read not his own laudatory poems, but, as any spectator might, the *tituli* on

132   *A Commentary on Propertius, Book 3*

the triumphal carts identifying captured towns (cf. Plin. *Nat.* 5.36–7). *legam* also occurs in Gallus' lines addressed to Caesar (**F**).

19–20 The scene with the lovers leads on to a prayer to Venus. However, *ipsa* sets her against Mars and Vesta, and the prayer asks for immortality for Augustus, not merely a propitious life (*ante meos obitus etc.*) for P.: the descendant of Aeneas is opposed to the protégé of Cupid. **hoc sit in aeuum | cernis ab Aenea quod superesse caput**: either 'may there exist for ever this life [*OLD caput* 4; *or* this individual (*OLD* 7)] that you see descends from Aeneas' or 'may there exist for this age the individual that you see descends from Aeneas'. As elsewhere, a conjunction is postponed* to the second half of the pentameter.

21–2 The implicit contrast between P. (**mi**) and those involved in the campaign (**illis quorum meruere labores**) is made sharper: he does not seek booty (cf. 1–2); the extent of his labour will be to applaud as the triumph passes along the Via Sacra towards the Capitol. *meruere* (= *meruerunt*) stands here for the future perfect.

Additional bibliography: L. P. Wilkinson, in *Studi in onore di L.Castiglioni* (2 vols., Florence, 1960), 1091–103; Williams 1968: 431–3; M. C. J. Putnam, *ZPE* 39 (1980), 49–56.

3.5

1–6: Love is a god of peace. I have battles with my mistress, but I do not eat off golden plates or drink from jewelled goblets; I don't have a thousand pairs of oxen, nor do I buy Corinthian bronzes. 7–10: It was unfortunate when Prometheus was forming earth into human shape: he carelessly arranged the body before the mind and ran low on intelligence. 11–12: As a result we are tossed at sea by the winds, we seek enemies, we attach new wars to old. 13–18: Fool, you will not take your riches to the Underworld. There the conqueror sits beside the defeated, the rich man by the beggar. Death comes best when life has been enjoyed first. 19–22: It is my pleasure to have danced with the Muses in my youth, to drink heavily and ever to have a garland of roses. 23–46: When old age cuts off the time for love-making, then it

would please me to learn about natural phenomena and the truth or
falsehood of beliefs concerning the underworld. 47–8: This is how I
shall end my life; you to whom arms are a greater delight may bring
home the standards of Crassus.

This poem continues some of the themes of its predecessor (seeking wealth through warfare, and the poet's distance from such goals), and some have thought them a single unit. However, one is concerned with Augustus's proposed expedition, the other with the poet's future; 3.4 has a strong ending (n.b. the closural *sat* in 22), which is matched by the final couplet of 3.5, just as the opening words in each are set in contrast.

Readers of 3.5 also need to be aware of 2.10, an apparently fragmentary piece from the end of the original second book (**P**; and see p. 23). This looks ahead to a new beginning—time to change genre: 'I shall sing wars, since my girl is written' (8). He goes on to describe the political situation in the East as the threat of Augustan might is realized (see 3.4 intro.), and promises to become a great poet of Roman expansion (2.10.19–20). However, in 2.13 he returns to addressing Cynthia once more, and war in the East serves only to provide imagery that enhances his commitment to love (2.13.1–2: **Q**): Parthian arrows are not so numerous as those which Amor has shot into his heart. He envisages the funeral that his current rejection by Cynthia brings near, and in terms like those to be found again at 3.5.3–6 rejects any exhibition of wealth, e.g. 2.13.21–2:

> nec *mihi* tunc fulcro sternatur lectus eburno,
>   *nec* sit in Attalico mors mea nixa toro.

Let no ivory-footed bier be draped for me, nor my corpse rest on a couch of golden cloth.

In addressing Cynthia he re-establishes their love, however, and the poems that follow 2.13 return to exploration of the relationship with no attempt to write Augustan panegyric.

It might seem that 3.4 was a return to the promised poetry on Eastern expansion; but P. has represented himself in 15–16 as a lover and a reader, not a poet. And in 3.5 he offers a quite different programme for his old age: not epic or panegyric, but natural philosophy (and even that is not presented as imminent). The final couplet hammers the point home, as he sharply contrasts himself with those who take pleasure in *arma*.

1 Pacis Amor deus est: 'Love is a god of peace.' The genitive indicates the area in which the god's power operates: cf. Woodcock §85.I(c). **pacem ueneramur amantes:** hymnic style is used to describe the deity: anaphora* at the start of each clause (*Pacis/pacem*) with polyptoton* (variation of ending) also in *Amor/amantes*. The balance identifies the god strongly with his followers, and this is reinforced by the pun in *ueneramur*: what else would lovers do than imitate Venus?

2–6 The sequence of thought is a complex one, not least because the pentameter for once moves away from the sense of the hexameter (already repeated) and introduces a strikingly new thought: P. grants in 2 that he regularly has epic battles with his mistress; but (*tamen*) he goes on to claim in 3–6 that he is neither avaricious nor wealthy. Verse 2 establishes a paradox: the peace of Amor involves battles; 3–6 show that what it avoids is greed and luxury. Thus a redefinition of *pax* is realized. This is striking because Peace is often associated with Wealth (e.g. in the statue by Cephisodotus mentioned by Pausanias in his travellers' guide to Greek art, 9.16.2; more generally at Hor. *Epist.* 1.12.25–9, *Carmen Saeculare* 57–60, and in the Augustan iconography* culminating in the Ara Pacis); the redefinition matches the way the openings of 3.4 and 3.5 have dissociated Augustus from Pax (a link discussed, e.g., by Galinsky 1996: 148).

2 stant: 'endure', 'persist' (*OLD* 17). (Many have printed Livineius' *sat*, with the sense 'I have battles hard enough with my mistress'. But this renders the *tamen* of 3 impossible to construe, and further changes would be necessary.)   **dura:** frequently used by P. to mark what is epic, as opposed to elegiac (often signified by *mollis*); but at times the mistress too can be *dura* ('hard-hearted').

3–4 The two lines together make an allusion* to one of the few extant fragments* of Varius, *de Morte* (148 Hollis = 2 Courtney): *incubet ut Tyriis atque ex solido bibat auro* [so he may lie on Tyrian cloth and drink from solid gold]: Vergil reworks this at *Geo.* 2.506–7, and other allusions are reported by Macrobius in *Ecl.* 8

and *Aen.* 6.   **nec tamen inuiso uictus mihi carpitur auro:**
'and yet my food is not snatched from hateful gold'. Giardina's
brilliant conjecture *uictus* for *pectus* avoids the awkward ellipse in
'nor is my heart plucked at by <desire for> hateful gold', and
matches the hexameter neatly with the reference to drinking in the
pentameter. He compares Seneca, *Thyestes* 452–3 *tutusque mensa
capitur angusta cibus;* | *uenenum in auro bibitur* [food is taken
safely from a narrow table; poison is drunk in a gold goblet], and
Statius, *Thebaid* 1.149–50 *nec cura mero committere gemmas* |
atque aurum uiolare cibis [nor was it a concern to entrust jewels
to wine and to spoil gold with foods]. *mihi* could be read as
possessive dative with *uictus* (as in the translation, and in 5) or
as dative of the agent with *carpitur* ('picked by me').   **nec
bibit e gemma diuite nostra sitis:** 'nor does my thirst drink from a
rich gem': see 3 n., and cf. *Geo.* 2.506 *ut gemma bibat.* In these
phrases *gemma* is presumably a synecdoche* ('a jewelled cup', as
auro in 3 = 'a plate of gold'), but there is a heightening of the
rejected ostentation in the implication that a jewel might be big
enough to drink from (cf. Cic. *Verr.* 2.4.62). For the move from
mihi to *noster*, see 3.16.1 n.

5 **mille iugis:** 'by a thousand yokes', i.e. two thousand oxen.
Campania is used as an example of land-owning wealth at Tib.
1.9.33 and Ov. *ex Ponto* 4.15.17; see also the encomia of the region
by Pliny, at *Nat.* 3.40–2, 60.

6 **mixta aera . . . clade, Corinthe, tua:** according to legend quantities
of gold, silver and copper were melted together, by chance, during the
burning of Corinth when it was captured by the Romans under
Mummius in 144 BC; thus was created an alloy of enormous value
(Plin. *Nat.* 34.6, though he goes on to deny the story in the next
paragraph). The conjecture *mixta* is thus apt in sense and grammar
('mixed by your destruction'), whereas the transmitted *miser*
is pointless ('nor, unhappy, do I . . .').   **paro:** here 'I acquire',
not 'I prepare' (P. is not thinking of becoming a metal-worker).
Corinthe: the vocative is metrically convenient in the second half of
the pentameter (cf. 14, 16; 3.3.30; 3.11.34, 68; 3.12.26; 3.13.56; 3.15.42;
3.21.26, 28; 3.22.30), but it adds poignancy in giving life to the

defeated city; and that has an edge in a poem that sets the poet in
opposition to Rome's imperial adventures: cf. Servius Sulpicius' observations in his letter to Cicero (*Fam.* 4.5.4) about Corinth and other
cities nearby that had flourished once and now lay in ruins, all (though
he does not say so) through Roman aggression.

7–18 Reflections on greed lead the poet to the thought that this is
man's primeval flaw; it leads to travel, warfare, and, by implication,
early death—and all for nothing: folly has blinded men's minds so
that they do not see that wealth never survives life's end.

7–10 'O primeval earth, unsuccessful for the creator Prometheus! He
did his work on the intellect with insufficient care. Arranging the body,
he did not see that the brain was in short supply: the path of the mind
ought to have been set straight first.' P. adopts the myth that Prometheus, one of the Titans, the previous generation to the Olympian
gods, was responsible for the creation of mankind (so too Horace at
Odes 1.16.13–16, cited below). His name in Greek implies 'fore-
thought', and poets regularly describe him in terms that make this
appropriate: Hesiod, *Theogony* 511; Cat. 64.294 *sollerti corde*; Hor.
Odes 2.18.35 *callidum*. But, as at [Aeschylus,] *Prometheus Bound* 85,
this Prometheus does not live up to his name and acts *parum caute*, like
his brother Epimetheus ('Afterthought') in the version told in Plato,
Protagoras 321.   **pectoris**: the ancients regularly sited intelligence in the chest: *OLD* 3b.   **mentem non uidit in arto**: the
fact that the mind was not given priority is responsible for its deficiency. Cf. Hor. *Odes* 1.16.13–16 (explaining the human propensity to
anger): *fertur Prometheus addere principi | limo coactus particulam
undique | desectam et insani leonis | uim stomacho apposuisse nostro*
[it is said that Prometheus was compelled to add to the original mud a
portion cut from anywhere and that he put the violence of a maddened
lion in our belly]: 'Prometheus was, it seems, driven to desperate
expedients by the scarcity of raw materials' (Nisbet & Hubbard on v.
14). *in arto* is Housman's conjecture for *in arte*, which contributes
nothing but confusion to the context. For the phrasing compare
Tacitus, *Hist.* 3.13 *in arto commeatum* ('food in short supply').

11–12 nunc has an adversative sense, as often, setting what actually is
against what might be the case. Because of Prometheus' mistake

'unwary of the sea we are driven here and there by the wind', i.e. our greed endangers our lives when we seek wealth through trade (so Paetus in 3.7) or conquest (so Caesar in 3.4). Sea travel is repeatedly presented as a transgression of mankind's boundaries: Aratus, *Phaen.* 110–11; Hor. *Odes* 1.3; Tib. 1.3.35–50. **armis nectimus arma noua**: cf. Lucretius 5.1202 *uotis nectere uota* ('to link vows with vows').

13–14 haud ullas: emphatic, 'not any'. **Acherontis ad undas** = *Aeneid* 6.295. Acheron is one of the rivers of the Under-world, sometimes used for the whole place by synecdoche*, but here the approach to the river prepares for the ferry crossing in the pentameter. **nudus at inferna . . . uehere rate**: the phrasing was imitated by the poet who wrote 3.3.10 in the Tibullian corpus*: *nudus Lethaea cogerer ire rate* [naked I would be compelled to travel on the Lethe ferry (i.e. Charon's boat)]. *at* (postponed*) sets up a contrast between the negatively phrased hexameter and the positive pentameter: 'you will carry no goods, but will be transported naked'. *uehēre* = *ueheris*: see p. 41. **stulte**: At 3.1023, in a passage that lies behind verses 39–46 (n.), Lucretius describes the Underworld as *stultorum uita*, the 'life of fools'; by using the adjective here P. characterizes all who expect to go on this journey as misguided.

15–18 This vision of the Underworld is distinct from that used in 4.7 and 11, e.g., or *Aen.* 6, or Tib. 1.3, and more like *Od.* 11 in having the shades of the dead existing as a grimly undifferentiated mass. For the sentiment cf. *Anth. Pal.* 7.538: 'This man was Manes once when he was alive; now he is dead he has power equal to the great Darius.' On the text of 15 and 18 see Goold, *HSCPh* 71 (1966), 79–81.

15–16 uictor cum uicto: the text sets the two contrasting figures side by side, as again in the next two lines. **miscetur** implies the intermingling of those who were quite separate in life, but also the mixing of one man's ashes with another. **consule cum Mario, capte Iugurtha**: Marius, the first of the great Roman dynasts of the late Republic, came to ascendancy through his victory in Rome's long war (112–105 BC) against Jugurtha, king of Numidia in North Africa. They had previously been comrades, serving under

Scipio Aemilianus at the siege of Numantia. Jugurtha was paraded in Marius' triumph, then strangled; whereas the Roman, despite a period of exile, remained a major figure in Roman politics till his death in 86 BC, the year of his seventh consulship, his opponents having been butchered on his return to the city.

17 Lydus Dulichio non distat Croesus ab Iro: in life Croesus (sixth-century King of Lydia, and famously rich: see 3.18.28) was distant from Irus (beggar in the palace of Odysseus, who responds to his abuse with a thrashing in *Od.* 18) in time, geography, race and wealth. Herodotus (1.30–4) tells the story of the visit to Croesus by Solon, the Athenian statesman and poet, who refuses to call his host 'happy' until he has reached his life's end: the point there is that the king will suffer much misfortune and lose his kingdom. P. displays him after death, no better off than a disgusting beggar. Irus lives on Ithaca, regularly identified with Dulichia by Roman poets (2.21.13; Verg. *Ecl.* 6.76).

18 'that death is best which comes when [*or* if] life has been enjoyed first': *carpta die* is an ablative absolute with a temporal or conditional sense. The phrase *carpere diem* (literally 'to pluck the day', an image drawn from picking fruit) occurs at Hor. *Odes* 1.11.8: the whole collection lays much emphasis on the enjoyment of life while there is still time: see e.g. R. Ancona, *Time and the Erotic in Horace's* Odes (Durham, NC, 1994). The lifestyle Horace has in mind is what P. goes on to depict in verses 19–22; and he does so in a context which stresses the inevitability of ageing and death.

19–46 P. sets the partying that gives him pleasure now (19–22), and since his early youth (19), against what he would take pleasure in once he grows old and grey (23–4), the study of natural philosophy (25–46). Old age lies ahead, and his wishes for it are marked with a suitably uncertain subjunctive (*libeat*, 25) in contrast to the indicative *iuuat* in 19, 21 (the manuscript evidence in itself favours *iuuet* in 21). G. B. Conte, *CQ* 50 (2000), 307–10, explores the allusion* to Lucretius 4.1–5 (E): Lucretius' garland is metaphorical and poetic, P.'s that of a lover and symposiast; Lucretius teaches how to liberate the mind from the snares of religion (*religionum animum nodis exsoluere*, 4.7), P. delights in the binding of his own mind with wine.

19–20 coluisse...implicuisse: the elegists employ the perfect infinitive as a metrically useful alternative to the present (e.g. *implicare* will not fit in dactylic* verse), but here the reference may be to the past, reminiscing about becoming a poet (just as Callimachus at *Aetia* fr. 1.21–2 [B] talks of first setting the writing tablet on his knee). **Helicona:** the mountain where the Muses danced and instructed Hesiod (*Theogony* 1–34: A); Callimachus met them there too in his dream in *Aetia* 1 (B), as did P. himself in 3.3 (see 3.3.1 n. and intro.); for reference to dancing cf. 3.2.16 and 2.10.1 *tempus lustrare aliis Helicona choreis* (P).

21–2 et: 'also'.   **uincire Lyaeo:** 'to bind with the Loosening god [i.e. wine]'. Poets often pun on this name of Bacchus: e.g. 3.17.5–6, Hor. *Epod.* 9.37–8 *curam metumque Caesaris rerum iuuat | dulci Lyaeo soluere* [it pleases to resolve with the sweet Loosener my concern and anxiety for the affairs of Caesar], *Odes* 1.7.22–3; Tib. 1.7.40.   **caput in uerna semper habere rosa:** Guests at a symposium wore garlands; P. sees himself *always* in such a role. In addition *uerna* further associates him with youth, for which spring is a conventional image (*OLD* s.v. *uer* 1b).

23–4 interceperit...sparserit: future perfects: the coming of old age is in the future, but it will have manifested itself already (*iam*) before P. changes his way of life. He does not specify whether he sees the abandonment of love (*Venerem*: a common metonym*) as likely to be due to physical, psychological, or social causes (the last for Tibullus at 1.1.71).   **grauis...aetas:** the epithet is frequently applied to those who are weighed down by years (Hor. *Satires* 1.1.4, e.g.), but also to troubles that weigh victims down (and cf. 3.3.22 n.). **nigras alba senecta comas:** white old age appears appropriately in the middle of the black hair (cf. e.g. Ov. *Trist.* 4.8.2).

25–46 In apposition* to *naturae mores* ('the habits of nature') comes a long sequence of indirect questions, mainly on natural phenomena, but culminating in questions about the nature of the afterlife. Natural philosophy is the subject of Lucretius' *de Rerum Natura*; astronomy that of Aratus' *Phaenomena*, and Cicero's translation of it. Such study is considered by later poets, usually to reject it as too difficult (*Geo.* 2.475–82, 490–2: astronomy, eclipses, earthquakes, tides and tidal waves, the seasons; *rerum causae* and the afterlife) or unsuitable (Tib. 2.4.17–18); Statius sees it as a prospect for his recently deceased father (*Siluae* 5.3.19–23). For illuminating discussion, see Innes, *CQ* 29 (1979), 165–71; A. la Penna, 'Towards a history of the poetic catalogue of philosophical themes', in S. J. Harrison (ed.), *Homage to Horace* (Oxford, 1995), 314–28. It is an especially striking commitment from the poet who has told Lynceus that natural philosophy is of no use to the lover (2.34.51–4):

> harum nulla solet rationem quaerere mundi,
>   nec cur frenatis luna laboret equis,
> nec si post Stygias aliquid restabimus undas,
>   nec si consulto fulmina missa tonent.

None of these girls is in the habit of seeking an explanation of the universe, nor why the moon labours with her horses curbed, nor if we continue to exist as something beyond the waters of the Styx, nor if crashing thunder-bolts are sent deliberately.

He himself is a better model (55–9): *aspice me... | ut regnem mixtas inter conuiua puellas | ... | me iuuat hesternis positum languere corollis* [Look at me,...how I am king at the symposium amid a group of girls...It pleases me to languish settled on yesterday's garlands]. The repetition of *me iuuat* in 19, 21 helps point to the inversion. When we bear in mind the misleading announcement of 2.10, anything but Augustan panegyric seems to be the promise. So it should not surprise the reader that we shall have no further examination in P.'s poetry of most of the questions posed here; though Book 4 will have much to say on the afterlife, e.g. *Sunt aliquid manes* [4.7.1: The dead have some existence], the mode is mythical and biographical, not philosophical. We should wonder at the tone of the catalogue, and how that is affected by its extraordinary length: at the very least it throws enormous weight on the poem's concluding couplet.

25–26 naturae...mores: 'nature's behaviour'. *mores* may seem a surprising word to apply to nature, but compare *Geo.* 1.51–2, where it fits the capriciousness of weather: *uentos et uarium caeli praediscere morem / cura sit* [let it be your concern to learn in advance the winds and the varying behaviour of the weather] and Vitruvius 4.2.6 *omnia...a ueris naturae deducta moribus* [everything derived from the true practices of

nature].   **quis deus hanc mundi temperet arte domum:**
'which god artfully governs this house of the world': an odd and
oddly phrased question, possibly corrupt: *arte* contributes little to
the sense; and *hanc* limits the control to the adjacent part of the
universe, whether the earth or Europe. But above all the identity of
the controller of the universe (or whatever the predicate means) is not
a philosophical question: when Ovid says at *Am.* 3.10.21 *sideream
mundi qui temperat arcem* [the being who governs the starry vault of
heaven], he means Jupiter, and so does Horace at *Odes* 1.12.14–16
(*qui...mundum temperat*). The closest parallel is *quis deus* at Stat.
Silu. 5.3.20 (a passage that imitates this), but the lack of predicate
leaves that question far more open. The oddity may mean that P. is
deliberately implying his inadequacy for the task ahead.

27–8 Questions are posed about some of the most obvious phenomena (cf. the similar placing of Lucretius 1.128 *solis lunaeque meatus*
at the head of a list): the route taken by the sun in rising and setting,
and then 'how it comes about that' (*unde*) the moon returns to the
full, its horns brought together (*OLD cogo* 6b). But one may observe
the path of the setting sun without scientific investigation.
qua uenit: P. freely uses indicative as well as the normal subjunctive
in indirect questions: eleven times in this catalogue against six
subjunctives. *qua* = *qua uia* ('by what route').   **exoriens:** a
substantive here, = 'the rising sun', as *exoriens* at *Elegiae in Maecena-
tem* 56, *oriens* at *Geo.* 1.250, and Ov. *Fast.* 1.653 (where the *oriens*
also sets).   **decidit:** 'sets', Hutchinson's conjecture for *deficit*
('suffers an eclipse', which duplicates 34).

29–30 unde: in each case both 'how it comes about that' (the winds
prevail at sea/water is constantly available for the clouds), and 'from
where', to match *quid captet* ('what does Eurus aim for') and *in nubes*
('<comes> into the clouds').

31 si here and at 39 introduces an indirect question, just like 'if' for
'whether' in English: see 40, and *OLD* 13. (In both cases it has been
corrupted to *sit*; the verb is needed less than the conjunction.) The
end of the universe was discussed both by Epicureans (e.g. Lucretius
5.96 *ruet moles et machina mundi* [the mass and system of the world
will fall into ruin] and by Stoics (alternating destruction by water and

fire: Seneca, *Nat. Quaest.* 3.27–8).   **mundi ... arcem**: in the light of Lucretius' phrase perhaps 'the stronghold that protects the universe' (*OLD arx* 3) rather than 'the height of heaven' (*OLD* 6).

32 purpureus: 'radiant' (*OLD* 3a).   **bibit arcus aquas**: the rainbow was envisaged as drinking up water that would fall as rain: *Geo.* 1.380–1, Tib. 1.4.44.

33–4 Perrhaebi tremuere cacumina Pindi: Pindus is one of the mountain ranges of northern Greece, to the west of Thessaly (of which Perrhaebia is the northern part): Map 2. The perfect implies reference to a past event; we do not know what, though Herodotus speculates about the part played by earthquakes in creating the geography of Thessaly at 7.129. P. adds specificity in developing Vergil's *unde tremor terris* (*Geo.* 2.479).   **luxerit** is a pun. The form is the perfect subjunctive from either *lucere* or *lugere*: in the former case it yields an oxymoron*, the sun in eclipse shining 'with black-draped horses'; in the latter it explains the darkness of the eclipse—the god is in mourning (presumably for his son Phaëthon, as at Ov. *Met.* 2.381–5).

35 serus uersare boues et plaustra Bootes: Bootes is a large constellation, visible for ten months of the year in the northern hemisphere. From Homer (*Od.* 5.272) on he was therefore described as 'late' or 'slow' to set or to move the wagon he was depicted as driving in the star-charts (also known as the Plough or Great Bear): so esp. Aratus, *Phaen.* 581–4 'It takes four signs of the Zodiac together to receive Bootes' setting. When he is sated with daylight, he occupies more than half of the passing night in the loosing of his oxen, in the season when he begins setting as the sun goes down' (Kidd's translation). The question might be thought one of literary interpretation—how to interpret Homer's phrase 'late setting'? For the use of the infinitive with the adjective *serus*, see the general discussion of Woodcock 1985 (§26). As in 31 (and again in 39, 42, 41, 44) *sit* (or *sint*) is to be supplied.

36 'why the chorus of the Pleiades collects together with dense-packed flames' (*igne* is collective singular*, like *angue* in 40). The Pleiades form the most prominent star-cluster, usually identified as the family of Atlas and Maia. Aratus mentions the absence of one of a canonical seven daughters (*Phaen.* 257–8), and Ovid at *Fast.* 4.169–78 suggests mythological explanations—Merope ashamed that she married only the mortal Sisyphus or Electra hiding her eyes from the sight of Troy's ruin.

37–8 The couplet reprises the sequence at *Geo.* 2.479–82, where Vergil hopes that the Muses may reveal the cause of the swelling and sinking back of the high seas (*maria alta*) and the reasons why winter suns set early and the nights are prolonged (2.481–2 are repeated, along with similar material, in the song of Iopas at *Aen.* 1.745–6).

39–46 Lucretius presents as one of his central purposes the exposure of the stories told about the afterlife as fanciful myth: since the soul dies with the body there is no need to fear posthumous punishment. Book 3's demonstration of the mortality of the soul leads at 978–1023 to a rationalist's reading of the myths of Tantalus, Tityos, Sisyphus, the Danaides, and (more briefly) Cerberus and the Furies. P. responds as Vergil himself did in the description of Tartarus at *Aen.* 6.562–627, by generalizing some conventional punishments (42) and adding new figures (41). Though he questions the reality of the stories (as Vergil does too when he has Aeneas exit through the Gates of Ivory, the gate of false dreams, at 6.893–9), there is pointedly little that recalls Lucretius in diction or style here. However, similar material must have been treated in the lost *de Morte* of Vergil's Epicurean friend Varius Rufus (3–4 n.), and if this had survived it might have been a more significant intertext*.

40–2 Housman's transposition of the pentameters is a big improvement: the *tormenta* of 39 are immediately exemplified by the familiar punishments of Ixion (spun on a burning wheel), Sisyphus and Tantalus (stood in a pool he cannot drink), then the Propertian novelties of 41, with *aut...aut* providing variation on the repeated *num*, and *sint* understood throughout.   **scopuli:** The plural perhaps combines references to the boulder Sisyphus pushes and the crag he fails to push it over; but we might take the oddity as encouragement to think of punished sinners more generally. Thus in *Aeneid* 6 Vergil makes plural those who roll rocks, those who spin on wheels (616–17), and (if we read *quos* in 602) those threatened by crags.   **aut Alcmaeoniae furiae aut ieiunia Phinei:** P. transfers to the Underworld the madness of Alcmaeon, pursued by Furies for killing his mother, and the hunger of Phineus, punished (for revealing too much in his prophecies) by the bird-like Harpies, who foul his food every time he tries to eat (Apollonius, *Argonautica* 2.178–300). The Furies are regularly found in the Underworld (e.g. Lucretius 3.1011), and save for the balance with *ieiunia* one might think of printing *Furiae* with a capital; the Harpy Celaeno describes herself to Aeneas as *Furiarum maxima* (*Aen.* 3.252), and at *Aen.* 6.605–6 we see the *Furiarum maxima* stopping sinners in Tartarus from eating. Again the study seems to be close reading of poetry rather than philosophy.   **Tisiphones:** Greek genitive. Tisiphone is one of the Furies (n.b. *furit*), and she is represented as having snakes instead of hair also at Tib. 1.3.69, Ov. *Met.* 4.474–83.

43–4 Multiple heads are a traditional feature of Cerberus, the guard dog of the Underworld (see West on *Theog.* 312, where he has fifty; more often two, in art, or three, e.g. in Latin 3.18.23 n., Cic. *Tusc. Disp.* 1.10 [a passage on the features of hell that one might fear], *Geo.* 4.483), as are the nine *iugera* over which Tityos' bulk spread (*Od.* 11.577; Lucr. 3.988–9; Tib. 1.3.75); this is approximately 6 acres, but still 'too few' (*OLD paucus* 1c) for the giant.

45–6 in miseras descendit fabula gentes: P. perhaps exploits Lucretius' image of mankind lying oppressed beneath the towering figure of *religio* (1.62–5), which is responsible for the false stories.

47–8 P. opposes his own future (the study of philosophy, or at least a poetic pastiche of philosophy) to that of the warmongers, and of those who in preferring *arma* prefer the *Aeneid* (3.4.1 n.). There is intense disdain here.   **Crassi:** printed as a genitive of Crassus, and thus an echo of 3.4.9; but in contemporary script and punctuation it will not have been distinguished from the vocative plural *crassi*: 'bring home standards, thickheads' (cf. 14 n.).

Additional bibliography: E. Courtney, *BICS* 16 (1969), 70–2; Stahl 195–205; G. Mader, *WSt* 116 (2003), 115–34; Cairns 2006: 345–7.

3.6

1–2, 5–8: Tell me the truth about our mistress, Lygdamus (messengers should be truthful, slaves especially). I'll drink in your news. 9–12, 3–4: Was she weeping? Did she show no concern for her appearance? Don't just tell me what you think I want to hear. 13–18: '<I tell you truly that... > and that she was wearing funereal clothing. Everything about the house was sad; her slaves girls were spinning, she was sewing. She kept drying her eyes, and told the story of your quarrel. 19–24: "Is this what he promised, Lygdamus (even a slave must tell the truth)? Could he leave me for no reason, and for a woman of that kind? Does it please him that I'm wasting away? 25–30: She has not got the better of me through her character, but with magic. 31–4: If my dreams are true, he will be punished at my feet. Let there be spider's webs woven on his bed, and Venus herself sleep when they are together." ' 35–40: If this is what she said, Lygdamus, run straight back and tell her that I have been angry, not deceitful. I'll swear that I've been in similar pain and celibate for twelve days. 41–2: If there is peace after such a war, as far as I'm concerned, you'll be free.

Seruitium amoris ('the slavery of love') is a key element in Propertius' love poetry from the start. Already in the first poem (1.1.21) he talks about his beloved as *domina* ('mistress'). The usage goes back to Lucilius fr. 730 M; Catullus has only the synonym *era* (at 68.136); *domina* itself appears with this sense in the Gallus fragment* (**F:** fr. 4.2). In a society supported by the labour and attention of slaves, this is no dead metaphor. In 1.1, for example, P. goes on to imagine the torture Cynthia might inflict on him (1.1.27), but acknowledges the imagery by using the word *libertas* in the following line:

> fortiter et ferrum saeuos patiemur et ignes,
> sit modo libertas quae uelit ira loqui.

Boldly I shall suffer iron and fierce fire, if only I have the freedom to say what my passion would wish.

domina is thereafter a regular way of denoting the beloved and the affair is called *seruitium*, both being appropriately used in contexts that talk of the poet's fear (1.3.17, 2.17.17) or Cynthia's severity

(1.5.19, 1.7.6, 1.17.15), but also with a less loaded tone (1.4.4, 2.3.10, 42, 2.9.45). At 2.13.36 the poet's role as a 'slave of one love' encapsulates his nature for his future epitaph. In 1.16 the beloved is the mistress at one and the same time of the door and the poet (1.16.9, 17, 28, 47); here in 3.6 (as again in 4.8) the presence of a real[3] slave allows a similar angle to be developed more fully. The image is also explored in Tibullus and Ovid. For extended discussion see R. O. A. M. Lyne, '*Seruitium amoris*', *CQ* 29 (1979), 117–30 = 2007: 85–100 (written before the discovery of the Gallus fragment).

The structure of this poem is an unusual (and controversial) one. It begins with the poet interrogating his slave Lygdamus about how Cynthia was behaving when he went to her house. After line 12 the questions stop, and the description of the household becomes more detailed, including as direct speech in verses 19–34 Cynthia's complaints (which confirm the reader's suspicions that the pair are currently at odds). It looks very much as though this portion of the poem should be attributed to Lygdamus himself: as the accusative and infinitive clauses in 13–14 lack a governing verb, the absence of a short passage is in any case very probable. Once Lygdamus has fulfilled P.'s hopes that Cynthia is feeling the separation as strongly as he, he responds by instructing him to take a further message and to effect a reconciliation. Though a large proportion of the corpus* can be read as conversational, in no other poem do we get a direct response from the addressee. Similar structures may, however, be found in Greek epigram (*Anth. Pal.* 7.524 [= Call. *Epig.* 13 Pf.], 5.46 [= Philodemus 20 Sider]), Catullus 67, Hor. *Epod.* 17, *Odes* 3.9 (which has links with formal amoebaean*), and some of the second book of *Satires* (also known as *Sermones*, 'Conversations'). Speech is attributed to specified individuals in a number of places, but always as the whole of a poem (1.16, 1.21, 4.1B, 4.2, 4.11) or in a narrative style (e.g. when Cynthia speaks at 1.3.35–46, 2.29.31–8, 4.7.13–94). As the poem presents both P. and Lygdamus as slaves of Cynthia, the interweaving of their voices might be taken as a reflection of their similarity; but the direct citation of Lygdamus might alternatively be seen as implying the master's power over the voice of his slave.

---

[3] 'real' here means 'proper', not 'actual' in opposition to 'fictional'. It would be foolish to assert where Lygdamus lies on the spectrum between 'entirely invented' and 'entirely true'.

The dramatic structure enhances the closeness to a scene from Terence's *Heauton Timorumenos* ('The Self-Tormentor'), 267–309, in which Syrus explains to Clinias, his young master's friend, how he found his beloved Antiphila living sombrely while Clinias has been away. Note how 285–8, *texentem telam studiose ipsam offendimus,* | *mediocriter uestitam ueste lugubri* | *(eius anuis causa opinor quae erat mortua),* | *sine auro* [we found her weaving carefully at her loom, modestly wearing mourning clothes (I assume for the sake of the old woman who had died), and no gold], are imitated in 9–16.

1–2 Dic mihi: the conversational form is immediately conveyed by the imperative.   **nostra ... puella:** Though we could translate this 'my girl', the involvement of slaves in the affairs of the masters gives Lygdamus an interest too: *OLD noster* 3a.   **sensti:** contracted from *sensisti.* This is a conjecture; the manuscript tradition has the anagram *sentis,* which would ask for an opinion ('what you reckon'), not a report ('what you perceived').   **sic tibi sint ... dempta iuga:** 'so may the yoke be taken off you'. *tibi* is dative of disadvantage. 'As you tell me the truth' is implied as the lead-in to *sic,* but the construction is paratactic*, i.e. two clauses of which one might be subordinated to the other are placed 'side by side' without a subordinating conjunction: similar are 1.21.5–6, Hor. *Odes* 1.3.1–8, Tib. 2.5.121, 2.6.30, Ov. *Am.* 1.6.25, *Her.* 16.282.   **Lygdame:** the slave appears here for the first time; subsequently in 4.7 (where he is accused by the dead Cynthia of having poisoned her: 35–6) and 4.8 (where he assists at his master's party with Phyllis and Teïa [37–8], and P. promises Cynthia that he will sell him [67–81]). The name appears later of the 'I' figure in poems 3.1–6 attached to the works of Tibullus: see F. Navarro Antolín, *Lygdamus: Corpus Tibullianum III.1–6* (Leiden, 1996), 3–20. A possible link with λύγδην ('with sobs') makes it an appropriate name for an elegiac character (18 n.). **dominae:** this could imply that Lygdamus is Cynthia's slave; but he is certainly not in 4.8. Rather then we should see the wish for his freedom from his *domina* as a piece of playfulness: as P. is a slave to Cynthia, so his slave is her slave too.

5–6 A pair of *sententiae* (moral generalizations): it is not surprising that the hexameter is found in the thirteenth-century florilegium (Vatican, Reg. Lat. 2120) that contains Propertian verses. After *omnis* *nuntius* the *-que* in 6 introduces the implication 'and a slave in particular'.   **sine uano:** 'without falseness': though there is no exact parallel for this, the neuter *uanum* is common in adverbial phrases. **metu:** 'out of fear' (causal ablative): a correction of the transmitted *timens*, which would either introduce an odd limitation of *seruus* or have to be read in an unidiomatic way with a causal force.

7–8 si qua tenes: 'if you retain any details <in your mind>' (*OLD teneo* 24).   **ab origine... prima:** the phrase has a grand formality to it, at odds with the context: more typical are instances such as Lucretius 5.548 *pariter prima concepta ab origine mundi* ('the earth was 'conceived along <with the air> from the very beginning of the universe'); Verg. *Aen.* 1.753–4 *a prima dic, hospes, origine nobis | insidias...Danaum* [from the very beginning, guest, tell us the story of the Greek trick], *Geo.* 4.286; Ovid, *Met.* 1.3.   **ista:** 'your words': an instance that makes the second-person force of *iste* especially clear. **suspensis auribus... bibam:** 'I shall drink in with anxious ears', lit. 'with ears held poised': the physical sense introduces a slightly comic tone, as in Statius, *Siluae* 5.2.58 *bibe talia pronis | auribus* [drink in such things with eager (*lit.* inclining) ears]; Cic. *Att.* 2.14.1 *sitientes aures* ('thirsty ears'). Cf. also Hor. *Odes* 2.13.32 *bibit aure uulgus*; Ov. *Trist.* 3.5.14.

9–11 As often in modern languages, it is tone rather than the presence of an interrogative that shows the sentences to be questions (so too at 19, 21–3; 3.2.9–10, 3.7.33, 3.12.1–2, 3.15.19–20, 3.20.1–2, 3.22.1–4).   **sic** looks ahead to *incomptis...flere capillis* [Is that how you saw her, weeping, her hair unmade?]. Uncombed hair is a regular sign of female distress: so Calypso, at 1.15.11, sad at the departure of Ulysses, or Ariadne at Ov. *Fast.* 3.470, complaining about the infidelity of Bacchus.   **illam:** a conjecture, where the MSS (though in disagreement) point rather to *sicine eam*. However, it would be unwise to base on so uncertain a foundation what would be the poet's sole use of *eam*, especially with *illius* following in the pentameter. Use of *is* is very limited in elegy. For the emphatic repetition *illam... illius*, cf. e.g. 3.23.5–7.

11–12 Just as the imagined Cynthia does not have her hair combed, so she does not have a mirror on hand to check her appearance, or any

jewelled rings on her fingers.   **lecto:** beds become a major
motif of the poem (cf. 14, 23, 33).   **niueas...manus:** snow-
white skin is regularly presented as an attractive feature in a world
where slaves and the poor worked in the sun. It is found of the elegiac
mistress, for example, at Tib. 1.5.66, Ov. *Am.* 2.16.29, 3.2.42, 3.3.6,
3.7.8 *bracchia Sithonia candidiora niue* [arms whiter than Thracian
snow].   **nullane:** the question enclitic* -*ne* is delayed to give a
short syllable in the second half of the pentameter.

3–4 are misplaced by the tradition, it seems: *dic* (1) and *dicere... incipe*
(7–8) are first requests for information, and thus in conflict with the
substance of this couplet, where P. reacts suspiciously to news already
delivered. Housman placed it after 8, but it is simpler to assume one
dislocation and place it in the lacuna* before 13 (see intro.). Lygdamus's speech will have begun in a lost couplet, the change of speaker
no doubt clearly marked by an address or at least a *uidi* responding to
uidisti (11).

3 **tumefactum** is proleptic*, i.e. it results from the action of the verb:
'surely you are not deceiving me and so puffing me up with baseless
delight'. The question implies that P. is reacting to Lygdamus' assent
with joy—an ironic reaction to the picture of mournful distress.

13–14 **et:** the synonym *ac* is transmitted but P. elsewhere uses it only
in set phrases (*ac ueluti, ac primum*).   **maestam...uestem
pendere:** as verse 9 recalls one part of the description of Calypso, so
this reprises *maesta* (1.15.11). The dress is presumably such as might
have been worn for a funeral; *pendere* implies that it does not hug the
body suggestively. The accusative + infinitive depends on a verb lost
in the lacuna* (e.g. 'I tell you').   **teneris:** 'youthful' or 'delicate'.   **scrinia:** these have been taken as boxes for holding
perfume or cosmetics, but the word is also regularly used for con-
tainers for book-rolls: the affair is poetically as well as socially
dormant.

15–16 The classic depiction of the Roman matron in the absence of
her husband has her in a sombre household, busy working with her
maids: so Antiphila (see intro.) and Lucretia at Livy 1.57.9 *nocte sera
deditam lanae inter lucubrantes ancillas in medio aedium sedentem
inueniunt* [they find her busy with her wool, sitting in the middle of

the house amid slave-girls working in lamp-light] (similarly Ov. *Fast.* 2.741–58); so Cynthia describes her evenings at 1.3.39–46, Arethusa hers at 4.3.33–42; and so Tibullus hopes to find Delia when he returns home (1.3.83–8).   **tristis..., tristes..., ipsa**: the anaphora* suggests that *tristis* applies to Cynthia too.   **pensa...carpebant**: 'they were plucking at their stints of wool' i.e. preparing portions of wool to be spun down for thread: Fordyce (1961) gives a helpful account on Cat. 64.311 ff.

17–18 Cynthia perhaps puts on a show (cf. Ulysses's tears at Ov. *Met.* 13.132–3); the use of a golden line* might support the sense of artfulness.   **querulo**: *queri* and its derivatives are frequent markers of elegy, which typically involves complaint about death or love (cf. Horace's description at *Ars poetica* 75: *uersibus inpariter iunctis querimonia* [complaints in verses unequally paired (i.e. elegiac couplets)]; 1.16.39, 1.18.29), and P. uses them to mark Cynthia's speech (cf. 35 *questa*; 1.3.43 *querebar*; 4.7.95 *querula...sub lite*).   **iurgia**: 'quarrels' (1.3.18, and esp. 3.8.19), though the reported words deal with the breach in general rather than a specific argument.

19 haec...mihi promissa est...merces? She casts herself as an Ariadne figure: *at non haec quondam blanda promissa dedisti | uoce mihi* (Cat. 64.139–40: 'Not these are the promises you once gave me in your persuasive speech'); so too Arethusa at 4.3.11 *haecne marita fides et pacta haec foedera nobis?* [Is this the loyalty of a husband, and this the troth pledged by us?].   **est poena et seruo rumpere teste fidem.** The legal position of slaves as witnesses was different to that of citizens: their first duty was expected to be to their master, and they had to give evidence under torture; but, as Cynthia asserts, even a slave was liable to punishment if found to have committed perjury. *poena et* is Shackleton Bailey's correction of the transmitted *poenae*: it supplies the *et* ('even') required by the rhetoric, and restores the idiom *poena est* + infinitive that P. uses at 3.13.38. In her interest in Lygdamus's legal position and her assertion that it is his duty to show *fides*, Cynthia is like P. (2, 5–6). She returns to legal diction in 31–2 (*testor, poena*); he in 37–40 (*mandata, iurabo*). Each of them repeatedly uses the slave's name, perhaps in an effort to win his favour in the argument.

21–2 nullo…facto: either ablative absolute, 'nothing having been committed' (*OLD facio* 21b), *nullo* standing for *nihilo*, or 'at no misdeed' (*OLD factum* 2b).   **qualem nolo dicere:** 'a woman of such a kind as I am unwilling to mention'. Cynthia implies that the woman she suspects of having taken over the poet's affections is a prostitute, but by using the euphemism she avoids specificity. *nolo* is Palmer's conjecture (*nullo* N: *nulla* ΠΛ); similar phrases occur at Cat. 67.45–6 *quem dicere nolo* | *nomine* ('a man whom I'm unwilling to mention by name'), Lucilius 543–4 Marx.   **habere domi:** a common expression in comedy and prose, but rare in verse after comedy (Verg. *Ecl.* 7.15), it adds to the comic tone: cf. Plautus, *Curculio* 698 (the slave-girl Planesium talking about the *leno* [brothel-keeper] Cappodox) *bene et pudice me domi habuit* [he kept me at his house kindly and chastely], Ter. *Hecyra* 677–8; [Q. Cic.] *Pet.* 8 *amicam quam domi palam habet* [the mistress whom he keeps openly at home].

23–4 Again Cynthia echoes P.'s own phrasing, his pained outburst at 2.8.17–20

> sic igitur prima moriere aetate, Properti;
> sed morere: interitu **gaudeat** illa tuo!
> exagitet nostros manes, sectetur et umbras,
> **insultet**que rogis, calcet et ossa mea!

So then you will die in the first flush of youth, Propertius. Well, die: let her rejoice at your demise; let her harry my ghost, and pursue my shade, and dance on my pyre, and tread on my bones.

The parallel suggests that **morte mea** is to be taken as 'on my corpse'. **gaudet** is followed by an accusative and infinitive expressing the cause of the joy ('rejoice that').

25–30 The new woman is accused of having gained control of the poet by witchcraft, which is evoked by some typical devices and ingredients: compare Ovid's characterization of the *lena* Dipsas at *Am.* 1.8.7–8 *scit bene quid gramen, quid torto concita rhombo* | *licia, quid ualeat uirus amantis equae* [she knows well what power there is in a herb, what in the threads moved swiftly as the rhombus is whirled, what in the secretions of a mare in heat]. An important intertext* is Hor. *Epod.* 5.17–24, a poem in which Canidia starves a boy to death so that she can use his organs in spells designed to regain the love of Varus, seduced by more powerful witchcraft:

> iubet sepulcris caprificos erutas,
> iubet cupressus funebres
> et uncta turpis ova ranae sanguine
> plumamque nocturnae strigis   20
> herbasque quas Iolcos atque Hiberia
> mittit uenenorum ferax,
> et ossa ab ore rapta ieiunae canis
> flammis aduri Colchicis.

She orders wild fig-trees uprooted from tombs, she orders funereal cypress-trees and, drenched in the blood of a foul frog [*or* toad], the eggs and the feather of a nocturnal *strix* (29 n.) and the herbs that are sent by Iolcos and Spain, fertile in poisons, and the bones snatched from the mouth of a starving bitch, all to be burnt in Colchian [= magic] flames.

26 staminea rhombi ... rota: the rhombus is (here at least) a magic wheel, rotated on a string (*stamen*) to draw in the lover (n.b. *ducitur*): cf. the more explicitly 'sympathetic' magic at Theocritus, *Idyll* 2.30–1 ('As this bronze rhombus turns thanks to Aphrodite, so may *he* turn at my door'); Propertius mentions the *rhombus* also at 2.28.35 (where an attempt is being made to ward off Cynthia's illness).

27–8 turgentis sanie portenta rubetae: 'the magic powers of the toad swelling with pus'. For *portenta* cf. Hor. *Epist.* 2.2.209 *nocturnos lemures portentaque Thessala rides?* [do you laugh at nocturnal ghouls and frightening feats of Thessalian magic?]. Pliny mentions the use of a toad to end love (*Nat.* 32.139), but *trahunt* shows that attraction is the purpose here. *sanie* has been replaced in the manuscripts by *ranae* (perhaps a gloss* on *rubetae*, with which it commonly forms a phrase in technical texts): the sense of *turgentis* needs the clarification that the ablative provides. Cf. the 'swelter'd venom' of the toad used by the witches in their charm at *Macbeth* IV.i.8. **lecta exsucis anguibus ossa**: 'bones picked from dried up snakes', contrasting with the toads and moisture in the hexameter. Drying ingredients enhances their flavour and power: cf. Hor. *Epod.* 5.37–8 *exsuca uti medulla et aridum iecur | amoris esset poculum* [so that the dried up marrow and parched liver might be a love potion].

29–30 Objects associated with the recently dead are seen as having particular power in magic: besides *Epod.* 5, cf. Ov. *Ibis* 231–2 (or 233–4) *pannis | a male deserto quos rapuere rogo* [cloths which they snatched from an unfortunately neglected pyre]; Lucan 6.533–5 *ardentiaque ossa | e mediis rapit illa rogis ipsamque parentes | quam tenuere facem* [she snatched burning bones from the middle of pyres and the very torch that parents held]; Apuleius, *Metamorphoses* 2.21.7. **strigis... plumae:** the *strix* is here envisaged as a bird, a 'screech-owl', but the word can also mean a witch (one who transforms herself into such an ill-omened creature). In either form they most frequently appear in the context of death and corpses.   **per busta recentia:** *per* apparently implies a search through a series of tombs; cf. Statius, *Thebaid* 1.183 *Hyanteos inuenit regna per agros* (Cadmus 'found a kingdom among the Boeotian fields'); and especially Juvenal 14.75 *inuenta per deuia rura lacerta* [with lizards found across the trackless countryside], where *lacerta* is shown to be a collective singular*, as *pluma* perhaps is here.   **raptaque funesto lanea uitta toro:** *toro* is 'dative of disadvantage' ('snatched *from* a funeral bier'): cf. 4.3.64 *raptaue odorato carbasa lina duci* [or linen robes snatched from a perfumed general]. *toro* (or possibly *rogo*) has been corrupted to *uiro* in the manuscript tradition: such exchanges are common in the final word of the pentameter (where the scribe is most stretching his memory): so too at 2.9.16 (where *uiduo*, earlier in the line, encourages the corruption, as *uitta* does here). *rapta* is also a conjecture, for *cincta*: the parallelism of the clauses shows that we need a participle describing the witch's action and akin in force to *lecta* and *inuentae*. *dempta* is also possible; but *rapta* is more vivid.

31–2 **si non uana cadunt mea somnia:** 'if my dreams do not turn out false': cf. Plautus, *Miles gloriosus* 381 *mi hau falsum euenit somnium* [my dream has not turned out false], and Cicero, *de Legibus* 2.33 *ex augurum praedictis multa incredibiliter uera cecidisse* [that many of the predictions of the augurs have incredibly turned out true]; *OLD* s.v. *cado* 17b. **poena erit ante meos sera sed ampla pedes:** Cynthia dreams of a return to dominance, with P. the abject slave at her feet: cf. both Lygdamus and P. himself at 4.8.69–72 ('and prostrate he makes a prayer to my guardian angel.... With hands in supplication then at last I sued for peace, when she reluctantly let me touch her feet'), or Hercules cowering at the feet of Omphale and awaiting the lash in *Heroides* 9.81–2.

33 The immediate form of the punishment is vengeance on P. and the supposed new woman: there will be no sexual activity between them. **putris ... aranea**: 'decaying cobweb': the adjective conveys a sense of neglect as much as it describes the cobweb itself. Spiders' webs are used to evoke lack of use also at 2.6.35, Cat. 13.7–8 *Catulli | plenus sacculus est aranearum* [Catullus' purse is full of cobwebs], 68.49; and, most significantly, of the hero's abandoned bed at *Odyssey* 16.34–5.		**noctibus illorum**: ablative of time at which ('on their nights together').		**dormiet ipsa Venus**: if Venus sleeps, the implication is that sleep is the best P. and the girl will manage. For the disengagement of Venus used as a symbol of sexual impotence, cf. Tib. 1.5.39–40 *cum gaudia adirem, | admonuit dominae deseruitque Venus* [when I was approaching delight (i.e. orgasm), Venus reminded me of my mistress and left].

35–6 After the (anti-)climactic 34, **puella** (in the third person) and the address **Lygdame** show that the poet is speaking once again. **ueris animis**: 'sincerely'. There is an illogicality here: even if Cynthia has spoken insincerely there is no need for P. to worry, as she clearly wishes to seem keen for him to apologize and to return to her. Earlier in the poem (1, 5–6, 3–4), he has been concerned about the accuracy of Lygdamus's report and here we might have expected 'If she really said that to you'. But lovers want sincerity.		**eādem**: the first two vowels coalesce into a single long sound (synizesis*) to make the word disyllabic, as the metre requires: cf. 2.8.26 *hoc eōdem ferro*, 4.7.7–8.		**curre**: the poem imitates a comic dialogue with a slave (see intro.); with this instruction P. creates a momentary image of another comic figure, the *seruus currens*, whose concentration on the hurry to deliver his message is such that he ends up delaying it (e.g. Plaut. *Stichus* 274–312, *Curc.* 280–312; Ter. *Phorm.* 177–97, 844–52).

37–8 Earlier Lygdamus has been reporting Cynthia's weeping (9–10, 15–18); now he is instructed to carry 'many tears' along with his message. The parallelism between the lovers is brought out once more; but given that the poet's tears are part of an instructed message, the reader may reasonably wonder whether Cynthia's are

similarly fictional.   **iram, non fraudes, esse in amore meo:**
'that there is anger, not deceit in my love': accusative and infinitive as
object of *reporta*, loosely in apposition* to *mandata*; the construction
seems to carry on in 39 until *iurabo* (40) offers itself to govern the
second indirect statement. The emphasis on *ira* teasingly allies P. with
Achilles, whose anger motivates the action of the *Iliad* from the first
word ($\mu\hat{\eta}\nu\iota\nu$).

39–40 me quoque consimili impositum torrerier igni: the first three
words stress once again the similarity between P. and Cynthia. The
image of love as fire is a commonplace already in Sappho (e.g. fr. 31.10);
it is prominent in Catullus (e.g. 35.15, 45.16, 51.10) and Vergil (*Ecl.*
5.10, *Geo.* 3.244, *Aen.* 4.2), and informs P's diction from 1.1.27 on.
torrerier: the archaic alternative to *torreri* as the passive infinitive is
used only here in Augustan elegy. *torquerier* ('tortured') is transmitted,
but *torquere*, the commoner word, is frequently written by scribes
instead of *torrere*, and 'toasted' maintains the imagery of fire (cf.
3.24.13, 4.9.21, and Tib. 1.4.81). *torrerier* also works better with *impositum*, which evokes a pyre, and marks an allusion* to Lucretius
3.888–90:

> nam si in morte malum est malis morsuque ferarum
> tractari, non inuenio qui non sit acerbum
> *ignibus impositum* calidis *torrescere* flammis.

For if in death it is bad to endure the jaws and bite of wild beasts, I do not see
how it is not bitter to be placed on fires and to roast in hot flames.

Separation from Cynthia makes the flames of love seem like those of
death. *mea morte* (24) has suggested that the feeling is mutual.
iurabo. When Ovid swears his fidelity in the last couplet of *Am.*
2.7, it is immediately followed in the next poem by a revelation that
he was lying. P. leaves the truth entirely open.   **bis sex
integer ipse dies:** 'chaste [*lit.* whole] myself for twice six days':
accusative of time throughout which. It is impossible to fit *dŭŏdĕcim*,
the Latin word for 'twelve', into an elegiac couplet.

41–2 quod (...) si regularly marks a change in direction, and
Propertius uses the phrase to introduce the final thought in a number
of poems, 1.1.37, 2.14.31, 2.26.57, 2.32.61.   **tanto felix**

concordia bello: Both the argument and the peace are elevated to epic level. Concordia was a goddess to whom several temples were dedicated in Rome, usually after civil discord.   **per me...liber eris:** 'as far as I'm concerned, you will be free'—in contrast to P. himself, whose *seruitium* will have been re-established by Lygdamus' aid. Of course, Cynthia may have other ideas, as *per me* allows (cf. 4.8.79–80).

Additional bibliography: Tränkle 1960: 167–8; J. L. Butrica *EMC* 2 (1983), 17–37; J. C. Yardley, *Phoenix* 40 (1986), 198–200.

3.7

1–8: Money, you cause a troubled life, lead to early death, promote human faults and anxieties. You drowned Paetus while he was sailing to Alexandria. Pursuing you, he died young and is food for fish. 29–36, 19–20: Go on, build boats and cause death. We have added the sea to the Fates. Could an anchor hold the man whom his home did not hold? Your profit belongs to the winds; ships are wrecked even in harbour; cables are worn away. 37–42: The sea is a trap for the greedy: a single success is rare. The Greeks who had sacked Troy were wrecked at Caphereus; Ulysses could not trick the sea and lost his comrades. 47–54: Now Paetus has dared to sail; but he did not gain a luxurious life-style. Night saw him carried on a plank, swallowing water, his nails torn out by the waves. 55–64, 17–18: These were his dying words, as he wept: 'Powers of the sea, why are you destroying my youthful innocence? I shall be smashed on the rocks; Neptune is attacking me. May I at least be cast up on the shore of Italy, so my mother may have my corpse. Paetus, why do you count your years or talk of your mother? The sea has no gods.' 65–6: He drowned as he said this. 43–6: But if he were ploughing on his ancestral farm, he would be enjoying life in his own home, poor, but with nothing else to weep over. 67–70: Nereids and Thetis, it would have been right and easy for you to save him. 13–16: North Wind, you had no benefit from despoiling him; Neptune, the men on that boat were holy. <................, Paetus,..................> 11–12, 9–10: Now sea-birds settle on your bones; the sea is your tomb. Your mother cannot *bury you properly among your relatives. 25–8: Return the corpse, waters; sand, cover Paetus; and let the sailor say, passing his tomb, 'You cause fear even to the bold.' 71–2: North Wind, you will never see me at sea: I shall be buried before my mistress's door.*

Among the sepulchral epigrams collected in Book 7 of the Palatine Anthology about eighty concern death at sea (concentrated sequences may be found at 263–79, 282–94, 494–506, 582–7); a further six epigrams occur in the 'Nauagica' (= 'shipwreck poems') in the Posidippus papyrus*. Because of the loss of the body and the lack of burial such deaths arouse special pathos (so too Palinurus at *Aen.* 5.870–1, 6.337–83). Similar motifs appear from epigram to epigram, and many have not survived, so it is hard to be sure of the influence of individual poems, but the importance of the tradition in general is not in doubt. The following are a selection of the motifs shared by 3.7 and these epigrams: (a) general reflection on (i) the folly of trading [1–8, 35–8; *A.P.* 7.586] and (ii) the daring of the sailor [29–38; *A.P.* 7.264.3, 266.2]; (b) the horror of the corpse (i) lost far from home [8, 9–10], (ii) its whereabouts known only to gulls [11–12; *A.P.* 7.285.4, 374.4, 652.5], and (iii) consumed by fish [8]; (c) the stormy conditions that led to the wrecking [6, 53–6, 13]; (d) the dead man's (i) pathetic voice [55–66], and (ii) youthful innocence [7, 59–60, 17, 70, 16; *A.P.* 7.263, 495]; (e) concern for his parents [64, 18, 68, 9]; (f) thoughts of his home or previous life [43–6; *A.P.* 7.286.3–4]; (g) contrast between land and sea [31–4, 25–6; *A.P.* 7.532]; (h) blame cast on sea, winds or deities [57–62, 18, 67–70, 13–16]; (j) warning to others, especially the passing sailor [27–8].

Most of these motifs can be found in the following epigrams, all earlier, which also illustrate the tradition in general. (References have been given above only for the motifs not found here.)

Τὸν χρηστὸν Πύθερμον, ὅπου ποτέ, γαῖα μέλαινα,
  ἴσχεις, ὤλετο γὰρ ψυχροῦ ἐπ' Αἰγόκερω,
κοῦφα περίστειλον· πόντου πάτερ, εἰ δὲ σὺ κεύθεις,
  ἄπληκτον ψιλὴν ἔκθες ἐπ' ἠιόνα
ἐν περιφαινομένωι Κύμης, καὶ τὸν νέκυν, ὡς χρή,
  πατρώιηι, πόντου δέσποτα, γῆι ἀπόδος.

(Posidippus 93 A.–B.)

Noble Pythermus, wherever you have him, dark earth (for he died under chilly Capricorn), cover lightly. But, father of the sea, if you hide him, put him unharmed on the bare shore in Cyme's open bay, and, master of the sea, return the corpse, as is right, to his native land.

Νάξιος οὐκ ἐπὶ γῆς ἔθανεν Λύκος, ἀλλ' ἐνὶ πόντωι
   ναῦν ἅμα καὶ ψυχὴν εἶδεν ἀπολλυμένην,
ἔμπορος Αἰγίνηθεν ὅτ' ἔπλεε· χὠ μὲν ἐν ὑγρῆι
   νεκρός· ἐγὼ δ' ἄλλως οὔνομα τύμβος ἔχων
κηρύσσω πανάληθες ἔπος τόδε· φεῦγε θαλάσσηι
   συμμίσγειν Ἐρίφων, ναυτίλε, δυομένων.

(Anth. Pal. 7.272: Callimachus)

Lycus from Naxos did not die on land, but at sea he saw all at once his ship lost and his life, when he was sailing as a merchant from Aegina. The corpse is in the water. But I, the tomb bearing just his name, proclaim this general truth: 'Avoid tangling with the sea, sailor, at the setting of the Kids.'

Εὔρου με τρηχεῖα καὶ αἰπήεσσα καταιγὶς
   καὶ νὺξ καὶ δνοφερῆς κύματα πανδυσίης
ἔβλαψ' Ὠρίωνος. ἀπώλισθον δὲ βίοιο
   Κάλλαισχρος Λιβυκοῦ μέσσα θέων πελάγευς.
κἀγὼ μὲν πόντωι δινεύμενος, ἰχθύσι κύρμα,
   οἴχημαι· ψεύστης δ' οὗτος ἔπεστι λίθος.

(Anth. Pal. 7.273: Leonidas)

A rough and sudden blast of the East wind, and night, and the waves at the gloomy setting of Orion damaged me. I, Callaeschrus, slipped away from life as I was sailing across the Libyan sea. And whirled in the water myself I have perished, booty for fish. But this stone above is a liar.

Ὦ παρ' ἐμὸν στείχων κενὸν ἠρίον, εἶπον, ὁδῖτα,
   εἰς Χίον εὖτ' ἂν ἵκηι, πατρὶ Μελησαγόρηι,
ὡς ἐμὲ μὲν καὶ νῆα καὶ ἐμπορίην κακὸς Εὖρος
   ὤλεσεν, Εὐίππου δ' αὐτὸ λέλειπτ' ὄνομα.

(Anth. Pal. 7.500: Asclepiades)

O traveller passing my empty tomb, if ever you go to Chios, tell my father Melesagoras that a terrible East wind destroyed me and ship and merchandise, and only the name of Euippus is left.

Φεῦγε θαλάσσια ἔργα, βοῶν δ' ἐπιβάλλευ ἐχέτληι,
   εἴ τί τοι ἡδὺ μακρῆς πείρατ' ἰδεῖν βιοτῆς·
ἠπείρωι γὰρ ἔνεστι μακρὸς βίος· εἰν ἁλὶ δ' οὔ πως
   εὐμαρὲς εἰς πολιὴν ἀνδρὸς ἰδεῖν κεφαλήν.

(Anth. Pal. 7.650: Phalaecus)

Avoid labours at sea, and apply yourself to the ox-plough, if it is a matter of any pleasure to you to see the limits of a long life. For long life lives on land; at sea it is not at all easy to set eyes on a man's grey-haired head.

Some further similarities are picked up in individual notes. Horace's Archytas Ode (1.28) is another Augustan development of themes from *nauagic* epigram.

3.7 provides acute problems for the editor, who has to decide between printing the poem with the couplets in the impossible order in which they are transmitted, or choosing from among a wide range of re-orderings, none of them individually of a high degree of probability. Things are made more complicated by the presence of couplets that seem not to belong here at all; it is also likely that lines have been lost entirely. None of the more radical re-orderings comes with a narrative history. However, it is plausible to assume that, as well as single couplets (or pairs), a sizeable passage was omitted for some reason (e.g. the homoeomeson* *Aquilo* in 13 and 71); rectifying a large gap would have been difficult, and one can picture the use of various margins. A later scribe conscientiously gathered the various marginalia together, placing them in his new text between 8 and 29. The Oxford Classical Text offers two versions of the poem, one conjectural, and the other, in an appendix, as the manuscripts order it; and a justification of the order printed here can be found in *Cynthia* (309–12). Our commentary concentrates on explaining the text as printed.

Some (esp. R. F. Thomas, ' "Drownded in the Tide": the *Nauagika* and some "problems" in Augustan poetry', in B. Acosta-Hughes, E. Kosmetatou, and M. Baumbach (eds.), *Labored in Papyrus Leaves: Perspectives on an Epigram Collection Attributed to Posidippus* (Washington, DC, 2004), 259–75) have suggested that the brokenness of the poem is an attempt to imitate an epigrammatic sequence, but it is the manner of the elegists when they start from epigrammatic foundations to go on to build coherent elegies (e.g. 1.1, 1.16, 4.2); and in any case scarcely one of the sequences into which Thomas divides the poem reads like a complete epigram in itself (perhaps 13–16).

1 Ergo: The inferential conjunction ('And so…') gives a conversational tone to the start of the poem: it is as if P. is reflecting on

some recently delivered news.   **tu** stresses the responsibility
of money for man's condition. It also initiates a sequence of
anaphora* such as we regularly find in hymns (see 3.17 intro.):
tu..., *per te...*, *tu...*, *...tuo, tu...*, *...te* (1–7).   **Pecunia**
appears as a deity also at Hor. *Epist.* 1.6.37, Juvenal 1.113. The attack
on money continues a theme that has surfaced in poems 4 and 5,
and appears again in 13.

2 immaturum mortis adimus iter: 'we enter on a premature path to
death'. For genitive used of the destination after *iter* and similar
words, cf. 2.1.20 *caeli iter*; 1.20.18 *Phasidos uiam*; *Aeneid* 2.387–8
salutis iter. The desire for money not only disturbs the lives people
lead (cf. the picture of rejected contentment in 43–6), it also leads to
death, as Paetus' case vividly illustrates.

3–4 An evocative combination of images. Money provides fodder for
human faults (as if they were animals). The fodder is cruel, because of
the effect it has in making men cruel or in leading them to destruction;
but one might also think of the 'cruel fodder', human flesh, given to the
mares of Diomedes (tamed by Hercules, who feeds their master to
them). With **semina**, the imagery moves to the vegetable, as if *uitia* and
curae were plants growing from the soil of *pecunia*; but **de capite orta
tuo** calls to mind the myth of Athena (a rather different deity) sprout-
ing from the head of Jupiter, fully armed.

5–6 tu Paetum: the poem moves from the general to the particular
(though the use of the present in 6–8 maintains a sense of generalization: this continues to happen, P. seems to say). The name Paetus was
carried by a number of figures of some substance in Roman history
(consuls in 337, 286, 201, 198, 167 BC; an addressee of some of Cicero's
letters [*Fam.* 9.15–26]; the Stoic Paetus Thrasea forced into suicide by
Nero), so there is reason to think the name (and even the death) is real,
like the addressees of Book 1, but in contrast to Panthus (2.21),
Demophoon (2.22), and Lynceus (2.34), Romans with invented
Greek names.   **ad Pharios...portus:** Alexandria (Map 3)
was one of Rome's most important trading partners; the port was
dominated by the lighthouse, or Pharos, one of the Wonders of
the World.   **tendentem lintea:** Paetus is vividly depicted
spreading the sails himself (cf. 48), although the young merchant is

more likely to have left such actions to the sailors. **terque quaterque:** despite the madness of the stormy sea, the waves smash over the victim in order. The repetition in the phrase mimics the repeated action. Cf. also Aeneas's words in the storm at *Aen.* 1.94 (imitating *Od.* 5.306).

7 dum te sequitur: this explains why the responsibility for destroying Paetus is given in 5–6 to *pecunia*. A young man might be expected rather to follows his *puella* (so P. himself at 2.26.30). **primo ... aeuo:** his youth increases the poignancy of the loss.

8 noua longinquis piscibus esca: rather than importing foreign goods to Rome, Paetus has himself become a novel food for faraway fish; moreover, 'he ... reverses the natural order of who should eat whom. ... *noua* accentuates this inversion' (Orlebeke, *CQ* 46 (1996), 422). *esca* is in apposition* to the subject: 'as food' (cf. *Anth. Pal.* 7.273.5, cited above). **natat:** 'floats' (2.15.52, 30.17), but grimly ironic of a body that can no longer swim.

29 ite: the address changes to the plural; without a vocative this refers to readers or mankind in general. *i* and *ite* frequently introduce ironic encouragement to perform some pointless or destructive act (3.18.17 n.). **rates curuas et leti texite causas:** a zeugma*: *texere* is regularly used of the 'weaving' of the timbers of a ship's curved hull, and here gets extended to a second object, 'causes of death', effectively in apposition to the first.

30 ista ... mors: 'that sort of death', *ista* (as often) associating the noun with the second person, the group just addressed. Paetus's death too was brought about by his own action in setting sail for Alexandria.

31 terra parum fuerat; fatis adiecimus undas: 'The land was insufficient: we have added the waves to the fates [i.e. the forces that bring death].' The two opposed elements, land and sea, are forcefully placed either end of the verse. P. freely uses the pluperfect of *esse* in cases where imperfect might seem more natural (so 3.8.1, 13.38). From second person plural we move on to first person for statements about the historical mistakes of mankind in general; in 33–8 a generic second person singular is used to convey vividly the threats faced by an individual traveller. Similar sequences are found in 2.27.1–10 and 3.5.11–14.

32 fortunae miseras auximus arte uias: *miseras* limits 'the paths of fortune' to those appropriate in this context, the grim ones. *arte* ('through our cunning', 'deliberately') is equivalent to *per humanas ... manus* in 30, *auximus* to *adiecimus* in 31. *uias*, though here used of *fortuna*, keeps in mind also the merchant's journeys.

33 ancora te teneat quem non tenuere Penates? 'Would an anchor hold you whom the gods of the hearth did not hold?', i.e. if you weren't restrained from travel by the divinities of your home (and the emotional bonds they evoke), what chance is there that the uncertain strength of an anchor would stop your boat from straying into danger? For the rhetorically powerful polyptoton* *teneat ... tenuere*, compare the passages cited by Wills 1996: 300–1, 304–6.

34 quid meritum dicas cui sua terra parum est? 'What would you say that man deserves for whom his own land is not enough?' The reader supplies a pronoun as the antecedent of *cui*. *terra parum* repeats the phrase from 31, but the addition of the pointed *sua* makes the greed for more a betrayal of homeland.

35–6 uentorum est quodcumque paras: 'whatever you acquire belongs to the winds [*lit.* is of the winds]'.   **haud ulla** = *nulla*.   **consenuit:** the ageing *phaselus* of Cat. 4 is a counter-example (*senet*, 4.26), but that may be a model (J. G. Griffith, *Phoenix* 37 (1983), 123–8).   **fallit portus et ipse fidem:** the interweaving of ideas continues: *portus*, like *ancora* in 33, implies an unavailing expectation of safety; both *et* and *ipse* reinforce the point ('even the very harbour betrays its trust'). For shipwreck or drowning in harbour, cf. 2.25.24 *cum saepe in portu fracta carina natet*; *Anth. Pal.* 7.639.

19–20 nam: the couplet illustrates what might happen to a vessel moored in port, apparently safe. **tibi** expresses the interest of the imagined second person in the events described; best translated as 'your', with *uincula*.   **nocturnis ad saxa ligata procellis | omnia detrito uincula fune cadunt:** 'in the nocturnal gales all the moorings tied to rocks fail [*or* fall] as the cable is worn away'. Position makes it easier to take *nocturnis procellis* as ablative of attendant circumstances with the whole sentence rather than ablative of instrument with *detrito*. The sense shows that despite its placing *ligata* is in agreement with *uincula*, not *saxa*. Though it has a separate presence in the sentence the *funis* is one of the *uincula*: Postgate in the introduction to his *Select Elegies* (lxvii–lxix) called this device 'disjunctiveness'* and rightly saw it as a distinctive characteristic of Propertian style. For *cadunt* compare *OLD* 12 and 7.

37–8 auaris: dative after *insidians* ('laying a trap for the greedy') but also after *substrauit* ('nature has spread out the sea for the greedy'). **ut tibi succedat:** 'that there be success [*OLD* 7b] for you', a noun-clause serving as the subject of *uix semel esse potest* ('can scarcely happen once').

39–54 The inevitability of disaster at sea is illustrated by the wreck of the Greek fleet returning in triumph from Troy (a full account was given later in the speech of Eurybates in Seneca, *Agamemnon* 421–578; more briefly, *Odyssey* 4.492–518, Aeschylus, *Ag.* 648–60, Ov. *Met.* 14.466–74); Ulysses' gradual loss of his comrades, as recounted in *Od.* 9–12, but here attributed to the sea; and finally the death of Paetus, which brings us back to the opening theme.

39–40 saxa ... Capherea: Nauplius took vengeance on the Greek army for their killing of his son Palamedes, victim of a plot by Ulysses and Agamemnon: as they sailed home across the Aegean, he lit beacons on the dangerous promontory Mount Caphereus at the southern end of the island of Euboea, and lured the fleet onto the rocks. **triumphales:** the Greek ships are described as if those of a Roman general returning from foreign conquest. **fregere:** 'wrecked'; third person plural, preterite* of *frangere*, which is the standard verb to express the breaking up of a ship (15; *naufraga*, 40). **uasto ... salo:** 'by [*or* on] the desolate sea', but *uastus* perhaps has an active sense here ('devastating': cf. Lucr. 1.722 *uasta Charybdis*, *Aen.* 3.414 *uasta ruina*, Ov. *Trist.* 1.1.85 *uasta procella*). **Graecia:** the fleet is identified with the whole of Greece, as in a similar context at 4.1.116.

41–2 paulatim socium iacturam: 'the gradual loss of his comrades'. *socium* is the short form of the genitive plural; *paulatim* an adverb attached as if an adjective to the noun *iactura*, which is the more easily done because of the noun's closeness to *iacĕre*.   **in mare:** 'against/in the face of the sea'.   **cui:** possessive dative; the pronoun is postponed*.   **soliti...doli:** Ulysses was known for his cunning and deceit, at Troy, during his long voyages, and when he arrived back in Ithaca. But *Od.* 5.291–332 presents him as entirely at the mercy of the sea and the winds.

47–8 nunc climactically adds Paetus as a recent example to those from the Trojan cycle given in verses 39–42; description of Paetus' fate takes more than a couplet, however.   **et:** 'now *even* Paetus has endured hearing the raging of the storm and damaging his soft hands on hard tackle'. As is brought out by the juxtaposition in the pentameter of **duro** and **teneras**, the young Roman seems an unlikely adventurer: cf. Hor. *Odes* 1.29.   **tulit:** for the force, cf. Ov. *Her.* 5.12 (Oenone to Paris) *seruo nubere nympha tuli* ('a nymph, I endured marrying a slave'); for use in such a context, 1.8.8.

49–50 'But his head has not been pillowed on many-coloured feathers in a chamber of citron-wood or Orician terebinth.' Despite his bravery in facing the hardships of sailing Paetus did not gain the luxuries he had hoped to secure when he set out as a merchant. *nec* serves as equivalent to *sed... non*.   **thȳiō thǎlǎmō aūt Ōrǐcǐā tĕrĕbīnthō:** Though the hiatus between *thalamo* and *aut* is not the only one presented by the Propertian manuscripts, it is probably the only one that is original: the line echoes Verg. *Aen.* 10.136 *inclusum buxo aut Oricia terebintho*, which shares the quadrisyllabic final word, unusual in a Latin hexameter, and is itself modelled on Nicander, *Ther.* 516 πύξου δὲ χροιῆι προσαλίγκιος Ὠρικίοιο ('like the colour of Orician boxwood'). P.'s desire to echo the Vergilian line (or a common ancestor) may be responsible for the spurious balance between *thyio thalamo* (where the timber, 'citrus wood', is given in adjectival form) and *Oricia terebintho* (where the wood is the noun). See Plin. *Nat.* 13.91–102 on the mania for citrus-wood furniture (plus R. Meiggs, *Trees and Timber in the Ancient Mediterranean World* (Oxford, 1982), 286–91), 16.204–5, 231 on 'terebinth', the turpentine tree. Oricos was a port on the coast of Illyria (Map 2), perhaps known as a source of timber; but the main function of the adjective is to mark the

literary allusion*.   **pluma uersicolore**: i.e. transparent
covers filled with feathers of various colours; cf. Cic. *Verr.* 2.5.27
puluinus erat perlucidus Melitensis rosa fartus ('there was a translu-
cent Maltese pillow stuffed with rose petals': Verres rests his head
on the pillow while being carried in an eight-man litter; everything
about his equipage is designed for luxury and ease).

51–6 describe Paetus' sufferings after the wrecking of his ship. The
transmitted order places the tearing out of his nails (51) before the
scene (53) where he is carried (*ferri*) on 'a small plank', thus with
hope of safety (as in *Anth. Pal.* 7.289). A more probable text is given
by Fischer's exchange of the two lines: the homoearchon* *hunc/huic*
gives an explanation for the mistake.

53 nox improba: the dangers of sailing in the dark led ancient
seafarers to beach overnight when they could; it can also add to the
horror of a shipwreck (as in *Anth. Pal.* 7.273, cited above).

52 miser...hiatus: 'the poor man's gaping mouth', lit. 'the wretched
gaping'. Having *hiatus* rather than Paetus as the subject makes the
swallowing seem another external force. The shipwrecked man
drinks the water of the Aegean also at *Anth. Pal.* 7.631.4.

51 huic...uiuo: dative of disadvantage: 'from him while he lived'.
radicitus: lit. 'by the roots'. People drowning damage their fingernails
as they desperately grasp at objects; after death the nails can eventually peel right off as the body putrefies: P. seems to combine the two.

54 Paetus ut occideret, tot coiere mala: *tot* picks up on the preceding
list of misfortunes, and it is best to take the *ut*-clause as expressing
purpose ('in order that Paetus might perish so many evils came
together') rather than consequence ('so many evils came together
that Paetus perished'), which would be more likely to follow the main
clause.

55–6 tamen: despite being overwhelmed by the waves, he yet manages
to speak.   **haec** can refer ahead (3.23.11) as well as back (65).
mandata: P. offers *mandata morituri* (or *mortui*) also at 1.21, 2.1.75–8,
2.13.17–42, 3.16.21–30, 4.7.71–94, 4.11.63–96.   **extremis...
querelis / cum moribunda...clauderet ora liquor**: *extremis, moribunda* and *clauderet* signal before the start that this will be Paetus' last

speech. *querelae* ('complaints') is a pointed marker of elegiac utterance in this sepulchral context (3.6.17–18 n.), but the phrase as a whole recalls Cat. 64.130 *haec extremis maestam dixisse querelis* ('that the unhappy girl said this in her final complaints', introducing a speech that has similarities to this).   **niger:** 'fateful' (*OLD* 7–8) as well as reflecting the darkness of the night sky.

57–8 Roman poets give an orderly rhetorical structure even to speeches delivered in desperate confusion. Paetus' speech begins formally, with an increasing tricolon*, addressing the gods of the Aegean Sea, the winds, and the water. Some of the gods are specified in 67–8, 13–16; 2.26.9–10 adds Castor and Pollux, and Leucothoë, who gives Odysseus her veil at *Od.* 5.333–53. The general address avoids omitting any individual deity who might assist.   **Aegaei et:** for *et* preceded by elision and followed by the caesura, see (in Book 3) 3.29, 4.17, 11.59, 12.25, 15.29, 22.9.   **quos … penes:** 'in the hands of whom'.

59–60 quo rapitis: either 'whither' or 'to what end are you snatching me away?'   **miseros:** as in 52, transferred from Paetus himself (cf. 61).   **primae lanuginis annos:** 'the years of first down', cf. Hom. *Il.* 24.348 (Hermes disguised as a youth at 'the loveliest time of youth'), Lucretius 5.888–9. For the first shave as a marker of the coming of adulthood, cf. also Ovid in his autobiography, *Tristia* 4.10.57–8 'When first I read my youthful poems in public, my beard had been cut twice or perhaps once.' **longas … comas:** The run of thought ('why are you seizing a poor youth?') demands a reference to either youth or innocence as the object of *attulimus. comas* is Oudendorp's conjecture for the transmitted *manus*, long, i.e. uncut, hair being a sign of youth (cf. *intonsus*, e.g. at Ov. *Fast.* 3.409). An alternative approach leaves *manus* and replaces *longas* with an adjective such as *castas* or *puras* (both Francius); but the final word of the couplet is especially liable to replacement by a quite dissimilar noun.

61–2 a miser: 'alas, unhappy I'. Exclamatory *a* is used in a restricted number of combinations by the elegists (see Kershaw, *CPh* 75 (1980), 71–2); though not found otherwise in P. variants of *a miser* appear at Tib. 1.9.3, 2.1.79, Ov. *Her.* 11.110, and Verg. *Geo.*

4.526.   **alcyonum:** these birds were said to have come from the metamorphosis of Alcyone and her shipwrecked husband Ceyx (Ov. *Met.* 11.410–748); they are often associated with Alcyone's mourning (3.10.9, Ov. *Her.* 18.81–2) and with a period of winter calm when they produce their young (Varro, *Ling. Lat.* 7.88; Ov. *Met.* 11.743–8; Plin. *Nat.* 2.125), but also as here with deserted seashores (1.17.2; Varro, *Ling. Lat.* 7.88; Verg. *Geo.* 3.338).   **in me:** 'against me'.   **caeruleo...deo:** dative of the agent with *sumpta*. Neptune, god of the sea, has taken on the colour of his domain, described in a way that makes it appear a reflection of the *caelum* (cf. the play at Ov. *Met.* 2.6–8).   **fuscina** is used for Neptune's characteristic weapon also at *Priapea* 9.4, 20.1, Hyginus, *Fab.* 169. At *Od.* 5.292 Neptune uses his trident against Odysseus; at 4.506–11 (and Sen. *Ag.* 553–6) against the lesser Ajax, whose actions and words have offended Pallas Athena, who incites Neptune to action (Eur. *Tro.* 65–71); P. apparently has the punishment of Ajax in mind, as the phrase *acutis scopulis* in 61 picks up on *scopuloque infixit acuto* (*Aen.* 1.45) at the culmination of Juno's account of these events (the phrase recurs only at *Aen.* 1.144–5, in the scene where Neptune uses his trident to help, not punish, the Trojans). Cf. also 15–16 (below).

63–4 saltem: for *saltem* ('at least') in a wish, cf. 2.3.45, Ov. *Met.* 9.281, and in a similar context at *Tristia* 3.3.32 *morituro parcere, diui,* | *ut saltem patria contumularer humo* [gods, spare one who is about to die, so that I may at least be buried in my homeland].   **Italiae regionibus euehat aestus:** 'let the tide cast me out on the coasts [*lit.* regions] of Italy'. Though the verb is regularly found of water moving boats (*OLD* 1a; normally out to sea) and of exporting goods (*OLD* 1b), there is no usage of *euehere* very close to this; in both the following cases for example the subject is human: Sen. *Dial.* 12.19.4 *corpus eius naufraga euexit;* [Quint.] *Decl. min.* 259.5 *tempore... quo naufragam in litus euexerat;* for the ablative cf. *Aen.* 4.373 *eiectum litore* ('cast up on shore').   **hoc de me sat erit si modo matris erit:** 'this will be enough of [*lit.* from] me, if only it will come to [*lit.* belong to] my mother': cf. 35 for the genitive. In 1.17 P. thinks of Cynthia in the storm, Paetus of his mother.

17–18 were placed after verse 66 by the sixteenth-century editor Scaliger: they respond directly to expressions within Paetus' speech—the emphasis he gives to his youth (59–60), the hopeful reference to his mother (64), his initial address to the gods (57). But the closure of his words is marked by *haec fantem* (65); and it would be odd for the poet to give Paetus the grim assurance *non habet unda deos*, and then to address Thetis and the daughters of Nereus. The couplet is therefore to be placed within the speech, as here: *non habet unda deos* thus closes the speech that begins *di maris Aegaei. Paete:* for despairing self-address, cf. 2.8.17. It was probably a reader's failure to comprehend this device that caused the omission. **quid aetatem numeras? quid cara natanti | mater in ore tibi est?** 'Why do you count your age? Why is your dear mother on your lips as you swim?' For such questioning despair, cf. Cat. 64.164–83 (the abandoned Ariadne); Hor. *Odes* 3.27.34–66 (Europē at sea); Verg. *Aen.* 4.590–606, esp. 595–6, with its self-address: *quid loquor? aut ubi sum? quae mentem insania mutat? | infelix Dido, nunc te facta impia tangunt?* [What am I saying? or where am I? What madness has changed my mind? Unlucky Dido, do impious actions now impinge on you?].

65–6 subtrahit haec fantem torta uertigine fluctus: instead of the orderly *dixit* or *sic fatur* that serve in place of closing inverted commas at the end of speeches in Latin poetry, *subtrahit* drags Paetus down as he speaks, and the line ends with him submerged beneath the wave (cf. 56). When we move to the pentameter, on the other hand, the tone is rather that of an epitaph (as befits the signature verse of elegy): 'this was the final word and day for Paetus'.

43–6 contrast Paetus's prospective life with the death that has been described in 47–66 (n.b. *quod*). The place where the lines are transmitted, after 41–2, makes Ulysses the subject: as it is not true that Ulysses would *still* be dining at his own hearth if he had heeded the poet's words, the dislocation is obvious.

43–4 si contentus patrio boue uerteret agros: a classic picture of Italian self-sufficiency: cf. Hor. *Epod.* 2.1–3 *Beatus ille qui procul negotiis, | … | paterna rura bobus exercet suis* [Happy he who far from business… works his father's estate with his own oxen]: this poem turns out to be concerned with *pecunia* too: see 67–70; *Odes*

1.1.11–18; Tib. 1.1.5–50. The imperfect *uerteret* may surprise us at first (cf. *duxisset* [had considered] in the pentameter), but the point is the continuing possibility of farming: 'if he were contentedly ploughing fields with his father's ox, he would live'.   **uerba … mea:** the moral truths of the first part of the poem, as well as imagined versions of them offered to Paetus himself in the past.

45–6 uiueret ante suos dulcis conuiua Penates: each phrase adds to the delight of what Paetus has lost: he would be living, in his familiar home (cf. 33), enjoying a feast (like the farmer of *Epod.* 2.55–66), and a source of pleasure to his companions (cf. *Epod.* 2.40 *dulces liberos*; Horace to Maecenas at *Epist.* 1.7.12 *dulcis amice*; *Satires* 1.4.135 *dulcis amicis occurram*). The pentameter then qualifies this, briefly, with **pauper**, before that is itself qualified, by **at in terra nil nisi fleret opes.** This returns us to the opening themes, money (1–8) and land versus sea (31–4). *fleret* is set against the real tears of 55 (*flens*). *opes* = '(lack of) wealth', i.e. poverty as at Ov. *Fast.* 3.56 *uestras, Faustule pauper, opes*, 2.302; Calpurnius, *Ecl.* 4.34 *nostras miseratus opes*. It took a brilliant conjecture by the nineteenth-century German scholar Baehrens to restore *fleret opes* in place of the transmitted *flere potest* (a near anagram has produced Latin words, but ones that could mean little in context).

67–70, 13–16 Gods with power over the sea are chastised for their parts in the death of Paetus, first female deities, who might have been expected to show sympathy for the young man, then the North Wind, who carried off the Athenian maiden Orithyia but could hope for no such benefit from seizing Paetus, and Neptune, who punished Ajax (62 n.) and took vengeance on Ulysses for blinding his son Polyphemus.

67–70 Nereo genitore could be ablative of origin, or ablative absolute, its force limited by the position: 'the hundred sea-nymphs with Nereus for their father'.   **centum:** Thirty-three Nereids are named already at *Iliad* 18.39–48 (as coming to share Thetis's grief); fifty (including Thetis) at Hesiod, *Theogony* 243–62; Plato, *Critias* 116E is the first to reach a hundred. Their power to calm storms is mentioned at *Theogony* 252–4, and P. himself has appealed for their aid at 1.17.25–6.   **et** can be used to add a specific member of a group already mentioned ('and in particular').   **tu materno tacta dolore Theti:** Thetis is

absorbed by grief over the future death of Achilles from *Il.* 18.37
on, and she thus often serves as a model for maternal mourning
(Callimachus, *Hymn* 2.20–1); she might thus have aided Paetus out
of fellow feeling with his mother. *Theti* shows the standard vocative
of Greek nouns in *-is*.   **uos decuit:** as goddesses who often
show sympathy for seafarers (in addition to the special case made
to Thetis).   **non poterat uestras ille grauare manus:** weight
is a characteristic of divinity (D. Kovacs *CQ* 48 (1998), 553–6), so
the slight young man should have been no great burden for the
goddesses.

13–14 infelix: 'ill-omened' (*OLD* 2b).   **timor:** 'source of
fear', as in 28.   **Orithȳiae:** dative. As at 1.20.31 the Greek
name allows two related oddities: a spondaic fifth-foot and a quadrisyllabic word to close the line (see p. 39). The story of Orithyia's rape
by Boreas (= Aquilo) is mentioned at 2.26.51, discussed by Plato
(*Phaedrus* 229), and narrated by Ovid (*Met.* 6.683–718).

15–16 fracta... carina: ablative after *gaudes*: 'why do you take pleasure in the broken keel [i.e. shipwreck]?'

11–12, 9–10 Paetus' name comes in the vocative only in 17–18, which
belongs as self-address in his speech. As *tua* and *tibi* in 11–12 refer to
Paetus, it appears that a vocative or a *tu* has been lost, wherever we
place the couplet. Hence the lacuna*. Moreover, *nunc* in 11 and 12
needs a reference to the past against which it can be set; 9–10 is
already giving a picture of conditions after Paetus' death: hence this
further transposition, proposed by Walsh. The lost couplet may have
said something of this kind: 'Paetus, though you were a pious youth,
you hoped to gain wealth through trade.' The sequence has much in
common with *A.P.* 7.652 (Leonidas).

> Ἠχήεσσα θάλασσα, τί τὸν Τιμάρεος οὕτως
>   πλώοντ᾽ οὐ πολλῆι νηὶ Τελευταγόρην,
> ἄγρια χειμήνασα, κατεπρηνώσαο πόντωι
>   σὺν φόρτωι, λάβρον κῦμ᾽ ἐπιχευαμένη;
> χὢ μέν που καύηξιν ἢ ἰχθυβόροις λαρίδεσσι
>   τεθρήνητ᾽ ἄπνους εὑρεῖ ἐπ᾽ αἰγιαλῶι·
> Τιμάρης δὲ κενὸν τέκνου κεκλαυμένον ἀθρῶν
>   τύμβον δακρύει παῖδα Τελευταγόρην.

Roaring sea, why wild and stormy did you send Teleutagoras, the son of Timares, sailing as he was in a small boat, down headlong in the sea, cargo and all, pouring a violent wave over him? And he is I suppose dead on a broad beach, mourned by the terns or fish-eating gulls; and Timares, looking on the lamented empty tomb of his child, weeps for his son Teleutagoras.

The sequence *sed...nunc...*, *et...*, where the first clause describes the corpse at sea, and the second the lack of a proper burial, seems to mimic the pattern of *Anth. Pal.* 7.496.5–6 (attributed to Simonides), and especially 7.271.3–4 (Callimachus):

> Ὤφελε μηδ᾽ ἐγένοντο θοαὶ νέες, οὐ γὰρ ἂν ἡμεῖς
> παῖδα Διοκλείδεω Σώπολιν ἐστένομεν·
> νῦν δ᾽ ὁ μὲν εἰν ἁλί που φέρεται νέκυς · ἀντὶ δ᾽ ἐκείνου
> οὔνομα καὶ κενεὸν σᾶμα παρερχόμεθα.

Would that swift ships had not come into being, for we would not mourn Sopolis, the son of Dioclides. **But now** he is borne a corpse somewhere on the sea; **and** instead of him we pass by a name and an empty tomb.

11–12 uolucres astant super ossa marinae: it would be possible to take *astant super* as 'stop over', as in *Aen.* 4.702 (*Iris*) *supra caput astitit*, but *Heroides* 10.123 suggests that Ovid at least took the sense to be 'stand on': *ossa superstabunt uolucres inhumata marinae.* **pro tumulo:** 'for [*or* as] a tomb'.   **Carpathium omne mare:** the south-eastern corner of the Aegean, between Crete and Rhodes (Map 4b): this is the route by which one might head from the trading port of Delos towards Alexandria. Cf. the phrasing of *Anth. Pal.* 7.285.2 (Glaucus) πᾶσα θαλάσσα τάφος ('all the sea is the tomb').

9–10 iusta is used as a substantive already at Plautus, *Cist.* 176 (*uxori iusta facit*) for 'what is justly given' to the dead, 'dues'. Ovid has it with *dare* and the indirect objects *germanae* ('to her sister': *Fast.* 3.560) and *miseris rogis* ('to the unhappy pyre': *Fast.* 6.492); cf. also Valerius, *Arg.* 5.6 *comiti pia iusta tulit* ('he offered the proper dues to his [dead] comrade'), Martial 10.61.4 *manibus exiguis annua iusta dato* ('give annual offerings to the tiny spirit'). Such passages demonstrate the structure here: **piae...terrae** is dative after *dare* (but also after *debita*, 'owed to'). *terrae* is the earth where a body is buried (as well as the earth from which it is made: cf. 3.5.7). *piae* can be variously interpreted: perhaps 'sacred' (of the ground where the burial occurs), or 'pious' (of the son whose funeral is marked, or, transferred, of the mother's action).   **pote:** the adverb that, with *sum*, forms *possum*; here used, for metrical reasons, without *est* (as at 2.1.46). It is to be taken in both clauses: 'and your mother cannot give ... nor bury ...'   **cognatos inter humare rogos:** *humare* as placed amid the burial places of relatives as Paetus' body is not. There is an echo of Catullus' couplet on his brother's burial near Troy, 68.97–8: *quem nunc tam longe non inter nota sepulcra | nec prope cognatos compositum cineres* [Him now so far away, not amid familiar tombs, nor laid to rest near the ashes of relatives ...].

25–6 aquae ... uilis harena: the double address seeks the least that might be hoped for, the corpse's return to land (the sea having taken Paetus' life) and a natural scattering of sand.   **Paeti:** here, and in 27, P. carefully preserves the name without assuming that it is marked on the grave or known to the passer-by.   **tegas:** the subjunctive is a less demanding alternative to the imperative.

27–8 nauta: The passing traveller is a frequent presence in epigrams, especially sepulchral epigrams, and P. reflects this at 4.2.57, 4.7.84, and especially 2.11.5–6 *et tua transibit contemnens ossa uiator, | nec dicet 'cinis hic docta puella fuit'* [and the traveller will ignore your bones as he passes, and not say, 'This ash was once a poetic girl.']. Cf. also *at tu, nauta* at Hor. *Odes* 1.28.23; *Anth. Pal.* 7.269, 282; and the closural, but otherwise rather different, address of the generic sailor at 3.11.71–2.   **et audaci tu timor esse potes:** 'even to the bold you can be a reason for fear'. The sailor is necessarily foolhardy in setting out to sea, but the grave of a shipwrecked man can still cause him fear, just as the poem is intended to do for the general reader.

71–2 After a strong close for the main theme of the poem (assuming that the placing of 25–8 is correct), P. turns to himself, not just as moralist, his role earlier in the poem, but as love elegist, committed to his mistress's doorstep. He shall never be seen sailing (cf. 1.6; contrast 3.21).   **at tu** marks a closural change of direction also at

3.11.71–2, and apparently 2.16.13, 2.18.19, 2.33.21.   **saeue**
Aquilo varies the address in 13 (*infelix Aquilo*).   **condar**
oportet: 'it is inevitable [*or* right] that I be buried', subjunctive used
as alternative to infinitive after the impersonal verb. *condar* makes a
sharp contrast with Paetus, whose tomb may be only in the sea or
its fish, but with *iners* following ('inactive': used of a *nauita* at 1.8.10)
it also implies the life he will lead all the way through to death
and burial. Thus, in contrast to the other aspirations that
have been attacked, he makes a concise and evocative restatement
of his commitment to Cynthia: it is unending, even in death.
iners is normally a pejorative* word, but P. consistently overturns
conventional values (e.g. 1.6 [**N**], 2.7).

[*21–4*: *There are shores that witness the love* [or *pain*] *of Agamemnon,
known for the punishment of Argynnus. After his loss Agamemnon did
not set sail; Iphigenia was sacrificed for this delay.*

21–2 Athenaeus 13.603d tells the tale thus: 'The story is that Agamemnon loved Argynnus, having seen him swimming in the Cephi-
sus [*there are several rivers of this name*]. When he died in it too (for
he was constantly bathing in this river), he buried him and founded
a shrine to Aphrodite Argynnis [i.e. the Love of Argynnus].' Though
this illustrates the danger of water, it has nothing to do with sailing
or trading for profit, and there is no plausible home for the couplet
in this poem, as has long been recognized. It is possible that an
elegiac version had appeared in Phanocles' *Erotes*, a Hellenistic*
poem on homoerotic affairs of which six fragments* survive: such
a source might have explained *poena*, which remains mysterious, as
does the origin of the couplet.   **Athamantiadae:** Athamas
was Argynnus' ancestor, so this is a plausible correction of the
transmitted *minantis aquae*.

23–4 No other source links Argynnus and the sacrifice of Iphigenia.
Given the baldness of the phrasing, it looks as though an annotator,
largely ignorant of Argynnus and prompted by *litora*, has provided
information on another part of Agamemnon's story.]

Additional bibliography: F. Robertson, *TAPhA* 100 (1969), 377–86;
K. Morsley, *CQ* 25 (1975), 315–18; A. Orlebeke, *CQ* 46 (1996),
416–28.

3.8

1–10: I enjoyed last night's abusive quarrel with you. Do continue your aggressive behaviour towards me; when you throw a table or a goblet, it is a sign of your deep love for me. 11–18: The woman who hurls mad abuse is a subject of Venus: crowds of guards, Maenad-like behaviour, terrifying dreams, jealousy of a picture—any of these is evidence of love. 19–28: Fidelity may be turned to a row: let my enemies have an unemotional girl. Let my friends see love-bites on my neck. I want to feel pain or witness the pain of another. I do not like sleep without sighs, and wish always to love an angry girl. 29–32: The violence of the Trojan War made the love of Paris for Helen sweeter; the greatest battles were in her lap. 33–40: I shall always have fights with you or for you. A curse on my rival: if you are given the chance to steal a night, it will only be because she is angry with me.

The trope* of *militia amoris* in Propertius goes back to his version of Meleager's epigram (*Anth. Pal.* 12.101: p. 1–2) in 1.1.1–4. At times the poet-lover has been the conquering hero (e.g. 1.8.28), with rivals as his enemies (2.8.4, 2.9.51–2). At others, it is Cynthia he fights with (3.5.2); these battles may be violent and angry, or sexual (1.3.16, 3.20.20, 4.8.88). This poem is the poet's most concentrated exploration of the image, and verses 33–4 neatly illustrate how flexible it is, though always valid: 'I shall always have fights either with you, or over you, with rivals: in your case no peace satisfies me.' This is real campaigning for P., and persistently contrasted with the warfare of the Roman state (1.6, 2.7, 2.14.23–4, 3.4–5). *Militia* will be a dominant image for the Ovid of the *Amores* too. He is shot by Cupid's arrow in his first poem, and surrenders to him in the second, which develops into a long account of the god's triumph. The culmination of the trope for Ovid comes in *Am.* 1.9 *Militat omnis amans*, an exploration extended to comic length of the ways in which lover and soldier are alike. For fuller discussion, see P. Murgatroyd, '*Militia amoris* and the Roman elegists', *Latomus* 34 (1975), 59–79, and on Tib. 1.10.53–6; Lyne 1980: 71–8; Maltby on Tib. 1.1.75–6.

The poem also recalls earlier poems such as 2.15, which begins with reminiscences of a delightful sexual encounter, and stresses the presence of a lamp (1–2, 3–6):

> Io me felicem! io nox mihi candida! io tu,
>   lectule deliciis facte beate meis!...   2
> quam multa apposita narramus uerba **lucerna**,   3
>   quantaque sublato lumine **rixa** fuit!
> nam modo nudatis mecum est luctata papillis;   5
>   interdum tunica duxit operta moram.

Hey, lucky me! Hey, night fair to me! Hey you, little bed made happy by my darling.... How many words we nattered with the lamp placed beside us, what a row there was when the light was removed! For now she wrestled with me bare-breasted; at other times she drew out delay covered with her tunic.

Whatever parallels we may find, however, it should not obscure the oddity of a poem that celebrates a physical assault by a lover.

1–2 Dulcis: a striking first word for a poem that discusses a fight between lovers.   **ad hesternas...lucernas:** 'yesterday, by lamplight'. Oil lamps played an important role in ancient lives, and they can be treated as emotionally important witnesses of love-making (e.g. 4.8.85; *Anth. Pal.* 5.7, 8; Ov. *Her.* 18–19, where the failure of Hero's light leads to the drowning of Leander); here, unlike in 2.15, the row is a real fight.   **fuerat** = *erat*: P. often uses the pluperfect of *sum* with the force of the imperfect, as do Tibullus and Ovid (see on 3.7.31; and Platnauer 1951: 112–15 for further examples).   **uocis et insanae tot maledicta tuae:** 'and the repeated abuse from your maddened voice'.

5–8 tu..., tu: pronouns used to introduce imperatives seem to add a touch of politeness.   **uero** reinforces the command (*OLD* 5f); 'do really'.   **audax:** adjective with adverbial force: 'boldly', 'be bold and...'.   **capillos:** for female attacks on hair, cf. 3.15.13; 4.8.61 (cited below).   **formosis:** 'beautiful', 'elegant': there is a lively contrast between the girl's finely manicured hands and the marks they leave on the poet's face.   **notā:** 'mark' (imperative). This recalls the phrasing at 1.6.15–16 (though there the threatened face seems to be Cynthia's own: **N**).   **minitare... exurere:** verbs of threatening can be followed by accusative and future infinitive but when the meaning is 'threaten to' rather than 'threaten that', a present infinitive is also regular: compare in particular Plautus, *Menaechmi* 842 *minatur mihi oculos exurere.*   **oculos sub-iecta exurere flamma**: 'having put flames beneath [them], to burn out my eyes'. The parts of P.'s body threatened by Cynthia are either vulnerable or erotically important: he is captivated by her eyes in 1.1.1 (cf. 3.10.15), and forced to lower his own at 1.1.3, for example; at 2.15.12 he asserts that they 'are leaders in love' (*oculi sunt amore duces*). For the range of details, compare the account of Cynthia's attack when he has been consorting with prostitutes at 4.8.57, 60–6:

> Phyllidos iratos in uultum conicit ungues; . . .
> omnis et insana semita uoce sonat.   60
> illas direptisque comis tunicisque solutis
>   excipit obscurae prima taberna uiae.
> Cynthia gaudet in exuuiis uictrixque recurrit
>   et mea peruersa sauciat ora manu;
> imponitque notam collo morsuque cruentat
>   praecipueque oculos, qui meruere, ferit.

She hurled angry finger-nails at Phyllis's face; . . . and the whole alleyway resounds with maddened cries. With their hair torn and clothes undone they find a refuge in the first tavern on the dark backstreet. Cynthia rejoices in her booty and returns victorious—and wounds my face with a blow from the back of her hand; she marks my neck, and raises blood with a bite, and strikes my eyes in particular (they deserved it).

fac . . . pectora nuda: the nakedness that results when the clothing is torn points to the end for the fight P. has in mind. For *fac nuda*, Fedeli compares 2.18.6 *faceret scissas . . . genas* (= *scinderet*) and 2.30.18 *turpia . . . faceret ora* (= *turparet*).   **sinu**: usually the fold of the toga across the chest. Presumably more informal clothing is referred to here, i.e. the top part of a tunic.

3–4 The couplet is transmitted with *cur* as first word (impossible as it implies a rebuke and a request to desist, which would conflict with the imperatives in 5–8), and after 2, where it makes a feeble adjunct to the first couplet if we simply write *cum* for *cur*. Transposition after 8 avoids the unstylish repetition of *insanae* (2)/*insana* (4) in the same unemphatic position in consecutive pentameters, and provides an appropriate lead-in to verse 9, which is otherwise isolated. The sequence runs from the brief account of last night's fight (1–2), to the request for a repetition (5–8), to generalization about what Cynthia's anger shows (3–4, 9).   **furibunda mero**: 2.33B has shown Cynthia drinking deeply, but (to the poet's eyes) unaffected by it.   **cymbia**: a Greek word (n. pl.) for 'wine-cups'. 2.6.17–18 also describes drinking cups being hurled at a symposium, but there it is lust that provokes the Centaurs to attack the Lapiths.

9–10 caloris: 'of heat', i.e. 'of passion' (*OLD* 6).   **nam sine amore graui femina nulla dolet**: from Cynthia's case, P. moves on to a broader 'truth': any woman showing signs of emotion (*dolet*) must be deeply in love. This is then illustrated by 11–18.

11–12 quae mulier..., | **haec**: 'the woman who..., she'. A similar point about abuse being a sign of love is made by Catullus in poems 92 and 83 (*Lesbia mi praesente uiro mala plurima dicit.* | *... non solum meminit, sed, quae multo acrior est res,* | *irata est* [Lesbia abuses me much in the presence of her husband.... She not only thinks of me, but, a far sharper point, she gets angry]).   **rabida**: 'raving'; a conjecture by the great sixteenth-century scholar Joseph Scaliger for the transmitted *grauida* ('pregnant'), which has been influenced by *graui* immediately above in 10.   **uoluitur**: 'rolls', suggesting abject submission to the goddess, as at 3.17.1.

13–16 The point of these lines is not immediately obvious. However, dreams notoriously afflict lovers (Theoc. 30.22) and in epic they regularly compound or cause desire, e.g. Penelope at *Od.* 18.187–205; Medea at Ap. *Arg.* 3.616–44; Europa in Moschus 2.2–27; Dido at *Aen.* 4.9 *quae me suspensam insomnia terrent* [what dreams excite and terrify me!]; cf. also 4.465–73); P. has described himself as jealous of 'paintings of youths' (*iuuenum pictae facies*, 2.6.9); and the image of the Maenad is repeatedly used of the woman who loses all restraint when she fears the loss of her love (Andromache at *Iliad* 22.460; Cat. 64.61; *Aen.* 4.300–3; Ov. *Ars* 2.379–80, 3.709–10). It looks therefore as though all four verses (including 13) describe *tormenta animi* from which P. can deduce *certus amor* (17–18); an unspecified (and different) *mulier* continues to be the subject in each case. Hubbard, *CQ* 18 (1968), 316 interprets differently, taking 13–16 as subordinate to 11–12: 'we have the prude with her crowd of attendants, the wanton, the neurotic coward, and the sentimentalist, the girl of acute sensibility who cries at a picture'. For her, what they have in common is 'the single symptom of *conuicia*'.   **custodum grege si circa se stipat euntem:** 'if she surrounds herself with a crowd of guards about her as she walks'. *se euntem* is the object of *stipat. circa* is used as an adverb ('round about', intensifying the meaning of *stipat*). The girl is being suspiciously self-protective. **medias ... uias** is the object of *sequitur.* For the sense ('public streets'), see 3.16.30 n.   **Maenas ut icta** = 'like an inspired Maenad', a female follower of Bacchus. The Maenads were active proselytizers for their religion and sang and danced with maximum publicity: cf. Eur. *Bacch.* 68–70. The poet imagines his girl as dead to shamelessness. Vergil portrays his Dido wandering frenziedly through the city (*Aen.* 4.68–9), and Ovid describes the suspicious Procris similarly at *Ars* 3.709–10 *per medias passis furibunda capillis,* | *euolat ut thyrso concita Baccha uias* [maddened, with hair spread, she flies out through the public streets like a Bacchant provoked by the thyrsus].   **timidam ... terrent:** 'terrify (her) in her fear'.

17–18 his ... tormentis animi: 'from these torments of the mind'. By using the symptoms he can recognize as a lover, the poet is a true prophet.   **has didici certo saepe in amore notas:** 'I have learnt that these are often the indications in a case of love that is sure [*or* true].' *notas* resumes the language of *signa* (9; cf. also *doceat*, 22), just as *ueri caloris* is echoed by *uerus haruspex* and *certo in amore.*

19–20 certa fides: 'sure commitment': the phrase reprises *certus amor* of the previous line, and the relative clause then takes us back to the opening verses.   **quam non in iurgia uertas:** 'that you cannot turn to quarrelling': the subjunctive and the second person are generic. Vahlen's neat correction of the manuscript reading *uersat* followed the discovery of *in iurgia* in N, corrupted into *iniuria* in all the later MSS.   **hostibus eueniat:** *apopompe** ('driving away') is common in ancient prayers: the speaker wishes on enemies, or at least those who are distant, what he wishes to avoid himself (e.g. Theognis 351–4, to Poverty; Cat. 63.92–3, to the emasculating goddess Cybele; Hor. *Odes* 1.21.13–16, to Apollo on war and famine).   **lenta:** here 'phlegmatic', 'easy-going': a nice inversion of the point at

2.4.17, where P. prays that any enemy of his may love girls (as
opposed to boys, who are far easier to deal with): *hostis si quis erit
nobis, amet ille puellas.* But *lentus* is one of the words P. uses with
contrary senses (see p. 31): 'indifferent' at 2.14.14, but of loving
behaviour at 2.14.22 ('relaxed', 'lingering'), and 2.3.38 ('stubborn',
of Menelaus).

21–2 aequales: either the poet's friends or his rivals: the word means
'contemporaries'.   **mea uulnera:** here any distinction between
anger and lust seems to disappear: the bites are presumably love bites,
and thus a sign that the girl is passionate, not *lenta*. *mea* is strictly
ambiguous: the bites could be on his neck or on hers; but the context
suggests these are wounds given by Cynthia.   **me doceat liuor
mecum habuisse meam:** 'let bruising prove that I have had my girl with
me'. The bruising could be the result of the love bites, or from the blows
struck: all passion counts the same in this context. For love bites, cf.
4.5.39–40, Tib. 1.6.13–14 *liuor… quem facit impresso mutua dente
uenus* [the bruising that mutual love makes with the pressure of
teeth], Ov. *Am.* 1.7.41, 1.8.98. The repetition *mea… me… mecum…
meam* hammers home the identification between lover and beloved.
For *mea* = 'my girl', cf. 3.14.22 *suae*.

23–4: the definitive statement of P.'s philosophy of love, and life: his
purpose is to experience and express emotion, whether his own or
another's. It is appropriate that the couplet is one of his most
balanced: classically elegiac.   **siue** (= 'or') is used to vary
the expression after *aut… aut* also at 3.21.30.   **tuas:** the
poet apparently resumes the address of Cynthia found in the opening
lines (cf. 33–4); but *tuas* could also refer to the generic lover (the poet
enjoys witnessing the affairs of male friends in 1.9, 10, 13, e.g.).

27–8 odi ego: *ego* is not emphatic, but gives an opening dactyl*
(cf. *dicam ego*, 3.17.21; *scandam ego*, 3.21.24).   **quos numquam pungunt suspiria somnos:** 'the sleep which sighs never punc-
ture'. For the sighing and sleepless lover, cf. 2.22.47 *quanta illum toto
uersant suspiria lecto* [what great sighs send him tossing all over the
bed], 2.25.47 *cum satis una suis insomnia portet ocellis* [since one
woman carries sleepless nights enough in her eyes].   **semper**
can be taken effectively with both *irata* and *pallidus*.   **in irata**

pallidus: 'pale over [i.e. emotionally drained by] an angry woman'. Ovid imitates the usage at *Am.* 3.6.25 *Inachus in Melie . . . pallidus* and *Ars* 1.731–2. In 23–4 and this couplet emotional pain has taken the place of physical pain, but *irata* takes us back to the initial theme.

29–34 After the passage on emotional trauma, the poet reverts to the theme of *militia amoris*, now thinking of fights with rivals (33), and taking Paris as a classic example of a man whose love was enhanced by war.   **ignis**: the fire of love: cf. *caloris*, 9; 1.9.17 *necdum etiam palles, uero nec tangeris igni* [you are not yet even pale, nor are you touched by the real flame].   **Graia per arma**: 'through Greek arms': the Trojan War is the backdrop—and adds piquancy— to Paris' love for Helen, the daughter of Tyndareus (*Tyndaris*) whom he had abducted, thus causing that conflict. If the transmitted *grata per arma* is correct, the meaning is entirely different: 'through pleasing warfare', i.e. that of love; and Helen is putting up a resistance which enhances the pleasure. But this would not introduce the point about rivalry ahead of 33, and the phrasing of the pentameter is harder to explain. The love scene between Helen and Paris and its prelude in the *Iliad* (3.421–48) would be in line with either reading. **dum uincunt Danai, dum restat Dardanus Hector**: this summarizes the action of the *Iliad* in Books 3–7 (where the Greeks have the upper hand) and 8–15 (where the Trojan leader Hector not only 'resists' or 'stands firm', but drives them back to their ships). *Danai* is the Latin version of one of Homer's standard words for 'Greeks'. Dardanus was the first king of Troy, and *Dardanus* is regularly used for 'Trojan'. Latin poets love to set epithets for 'Greek' and 'Trojan' against one another: e.g. 1.19.14 *Argiuis Dardana*; 2.8.32 *Hectorea Dorica*; Ov. *Her.* 8.14 *Danaus Phrygias*; *Ars* 1.686 *Graiaque in Iliacis*; note in particular *Ilias Latina* 743 *Dardanidum Danaumque duces*; *Aen.* 2.71–2, 617–18. If the transmitted *barbarus* is correct, it either refers to the fact that Hector was Asian and would thus have been considered a barbarian by the Greeks, or that he was savage (improbable, as the tradition stresses his humanity).

37–8 at tibi: it turns out that there is a rival, and this explains why Cynthia's show of passion has been so sweet: it confirms (*nunc*, 39) that whatever she has done he alone is in possession of her heart. *at tu* is frequently used to change direction at the end of a poem (3.7.71 n.) **nexisti retia**: 'have woven nets'. There is a fleeting reference to *Od.* 8.273–301 where Hephaestus weaves an invisible net to catch his wife Aphrodite (Venus) in adulterous love with Ares; but the sense is little more than 'you are trying to trick me': cf. 2.32.20 *tendis iners docto retia nota mihi* [I've learnt from experience and know the nets you artlessly stretch for me]. *nexisti* is a perfect form of *necto*, alternative to *nexui*, and the reason why the line is cited by the late-antique grammarians Priscian and Diomedes; the manuscripts of P. have substituted the false form *tendisti* (for *tetendisti*, 'stretched').   **socer**: a father-in-law who is constantly on the watch in case the poet's rival is unfaithful to his wife. **aeternum**: adverbial ('for ever').   **matre**: either the mother of the rival's wife or his own mother, both of whom would disapprove of extra-marital relations on the part of the husband. The father-in-law and the mother are character types from Roman (and Greek) comedy: see J. C. Yardley, *Phoenix* 34 (1980), 255–6, who argues for the comic origin of the theme that 'a physical attack on one's sexual partner constitutes a proof of the attacker's love'. He shows how 'the language of the whole poem is redolent of comedy, with certain words occurring in Propertius only in this poem but repeatedly in Roman comedy (e.g. *maledicta* [2], *inuadere* [5], *minitari* [7], *aequales* [21], *offendere* [40]).' The nature of the curse is thus profoundly apt.

39–40 si qua data est furandae copia noctis: 'if a chance of stealing my night has been granted': the implication is that P. owns nights with Cynthia; any taken by another have been stolen.   **offensa illa mihi, non tibi amica, dedit**: 'she gives it not as your girlfriend but because she is cross with me'. *offensa* is the past participle passive, used with a causal sense. In itself this line is a confident assertion that Cynthia feels nothing for his rival and all for P. himself. But there may well be a note of real surprise here. The poet has put across convincingly the idea that conflict with a spirited girlfriend can add spice to a relationship, and indeed imply that it is a meaningful one, but to console himself thus when she has slept with a rival may seem to smack of comic desperation.

[**25–6** Communicating with eyebrows, writing on table-tops, and signing with fingers feature in Tibullus and Ovid (nods at Tib. 1.8.1, e.g., and cf. also *Iliad* 9.620; writing in wine at Tib. 1.6.19–20; nods and fingers at *Ars* 1.137–8; all three at *Amores* 1.4.19–20, 2.5.17–18, *Her.* 17.81–8), but they belong in contexts where the relationship has to be kept hidden, not in a poem like this where the couple have been fighting openly.]

[**35–6** is another irrelevant couplet: neither other beauties nor Cynthia's arrogance are mentioned elsewhere in the poem. It uses *dolere* of hurt pride or perhaps the pain of abandonment, senses quite different to that in 23, which is rooted in the whole run of thought; and it intrudes between mention of rivals and the specific address in 37.]

Addditional bibliography: Hubbard, *CQ* 18 (1968), 315–16; Wistrand 1977: 61–4; J. L. Butrica, *TAPhA* 111 (1981), 23–30; Heyworth, *CQ* 36 (1986), 203–5.

3.9

1–6: Maecenas, you stay within the limits of your good fortune; why do you send me out into an ocean of writing? Big sails do not suit my boat. It's bad to attempt a load you cannot carry. 7–20: Different people have different spheres of ability, different sources of greatness, as is illustrated by the range of famous artists and Olympic competitors. One man is suited to peace, another to war: each follows his nature. 23–34: You could become a consul or win a triumph over the Parthians; yet you retreat into the shade; you reef your sails. This judgement of yours will win fame like Camillus'; loyalty joins you to Caesar's fame. 21–2, 35–46: I have accepted your precepts and I shall not write a Thebaid or an Iliad but continue with my love elegies in the manner of Callimachus and Philitas. These shall make boys and girls treat me as a god. 57–8, 47–56: Take up the reins of my poetic chariot: with you as guide I should write a gigantomachy* or an epic on Roman history. 59–60: As things are, you grant me praise and bring it about that I am said to be your follower.

This poem is at the heart of a controversial issue: was Maecenas in any serious sense a patron[4] of Propertius, or is 3.9 (and 2.1) a rejection of any approach that had been (or might be) made by Augustus's minister (on whom, see Introduction, pp. 13, 17–20)? In the first place, there is no external evidence for a relationship between the two, as opposed to the cases of Vergil (from the ancient lives and Horace's *Satires*) and Horace (from the ancient life, quoting Maecenas' poetry and the words addressed to Augustus appended to Maecenas' will: 'remember Horatius Flaccus as you remember me'). Secondly, P.'s first announcement of political allegiance comes in the two ten-line epigrams at the end of Book 1 which reveal as a key to his identity that a member of his family died having fought against Caesar in the Perusine War in 42 BC (see Introduction, pp. 8–20). Thirdly, we have no poems of invitation, of teasing, of gratitude (contrast Hor. *Odes* 1.20, 3.8, 3.29; *Epod.* 3 and *Odes* 2.17; *Epod.* 1 and *Odes* 3.16); no passages that accept the patron's advice (*Geo.* 3.40–2); the two poems that mention Maecenas do so only to refuse what he is presented as requesting: Augustan epic. (On the other, 2.1, see Introduction, 19–21.) Given the models that the other poets provide, it thus seems possible to read 2.1 and 3.9 as jaundiced reflections on patronage in the Augustan age. For an account of the poems that starts from the firm belief that Maecenas was P.'s patron, see Cairns 2006: 260–9; for discussions that support the line taken here, see Heyworth, *BICS* 50 (2007), 93–128, esp. 101–8, and Stahl 1985: 162–71 (on 2.1).

The elegy toys with the idea of writing epic but pushes it into an improbable future by making it conditional on Maecenas' leading the way. It is thus a kind of *recusatio**, and revisits themes of 3.1–3, where the notion of epic composition has been rejected on the specific advice of Apollo and Calliope (3.3), as hackneyed and untimely (3.1), and unsuited to the lover (3.2). The introductions to those poems provide background.

1–2 Maecenas: a very Horatian opening; note esp. *Odes* 1.1.1 *Maecenas atauis edite regibus* [Maecenas descended from ancestral

---

[4] On literary patronage, see B. K. Gold (ed.), *Literary and Artistic Patronage in Ancient Rome* (Austin, TX, 1982); Gold 1987; P. White, *Promised Verse: Poets in the Society of Augustan Rome* (Cambridge, MA, 1993).

kings] but Maecenas is addressed also in the opening lines of *Satires* 1.1, *Epod.* 1 and *Epist.* 1.1. Propertius does not put his poem first in the book, but in exploring a range of careers that serve to set off his own role as elegist he reworks the priamel* in *Odes* 1.1, as well as Maecenas' place in the poem: cf. Gold 1982: 112–13.   **eques:** cf. Horace's paradoxical phrase *clare Maecenas eques* ('distinguished knight') at *Odes* 1.20.5. Propertius too has a point: just as Maecenas chooses not to be elevated above the rank of *eques* (cf. 2), so the poet does not wish to rise above the level of love poetry.   **Etrusco de sanguine regum:** for Maecenas' descent from Etruscan kings, besides the opening words to the *Odes*, cf. 3.29.1 *Tyrrhena regum progenies* ('Etruscan offspring of kings').   **intra fortunam ... tuam:** 'within the limits of your (good) fortune' or 'within your station': Maecenas declined to hold any magistracy (Tacitus, *Annals* 3.30), but this did not mean that he was politically inactive. For example, in 31–29 BC he was in charge of Rome and Italy while Octavian was absent: 'no title, only armed power' (R. Syme, *The Augustan Aristocracy* (Oxford, 1986), 272).

3–4: for the imagery of the elegiac poet unable to set out onto the epic sea in his small boat, compare 35–6, 3.3.22–4 n.

5–6 turpe est quod nequeas capiti committere pondus: 'it is shameful to entrust to your head a load which you cannot (bear)': understand *ferre*. The subjunctive *nequeas* is generic. Burdens are still carried on the head in many societies today.   **pressum:** '(when you are) weighed down'.   **mox:** 'subsequently', the basic sense of the word.   **dare terga:** 'give way', 'collapse': for the use of the expression to convey submission rather than (as usual) retreat, cf. Sen. *Oed.* 86 *haud est uirile terga Fortunae dare* ('it is not manly to yield to Fortune').

7 neruis ... omnibus: 'for all sinews', 'for all strengths', with a play on the meaning 'strings': cf. 3.3.4 n. *neruis* is Palmer's emendation for the transmitted *rerum: omnia ... rerum* ('everything in the universe') is not impossible—compare the expression at Hor. *Odes* 2.1.23 (*cuncta terrarum:* 'everything in the world')—but *rerum* detracts from the pithiness of the sentiment.

8 palma nec haec ex quo ducitur illa iugo: 'nor is this palm gained from the same mountain as that one'. The transmitted text is *flamma nec ex aequo ducitur ulla iugo*; but mountain ridges are not 'flat' and 'flame' seems to have no relevance here. For the symbol of success brought down from the artistic mountain, cf. the garland at Lucretius 1.118 (**D**) and P.'s echo of this at 3.1.17–20; also 4.10.3–4:

> magnum iter ascendo, sed dat mihi gloria uires:
> non iuuat e facili lecta corona iugo.

It is a great route I climb, but glory lends me strength: a garland picked on an easy summit gives no pleasure.

The branches of art are symbolized by different mountains: each offers a prize for the successful artist, as the following lines attest.

9–16 The eight artists described in these lines are grouped in pairs according to the general area of prowess: sculpture, painting, work in relief, and sculpture again. In the pentameters 12 and 14 small-scale art is emphasized, but 9–10 shows that contrast between grand and humble is not the main point of the pairs. From works that survive (often in copies) we have a sense of some of the artists, and information about them from the critical accounts of writers such as the Elder Pliny in Books 33–6 of his encyclopedic *Natural History* and Pausanias in his *Description of Greece*. As the notes below show, some of the diction in 11–18 is appropriately artful, with puns and extensions of meaning, but the text is at times in doubt. Ovid imitates the passage at *ex Ponto* 4.1.29–36:

> ut Venus artificis labor est et *gloria* Coi
> aequoreo madidas quae premit imbre comas,
> arcis ut Actaeae uel *eburna* uel aerea custos
> bellica *Phidiaca* stat dea facta manu,
> *uindicat* ut *Calamis* laudem quos fecit *equorum*,
> ut similis uerae uacca Myronis opus,
> sic ego pars rerum non ultima, Sexte, tuarum
> tutelaeque feror munus opusque tuae.

As the labour and glory of the Coan artist [Apelles] is the Venus who presses a rain of sea-water from her damp hair; as the warrior goddess who guards the Attic acropolis stands either of ivory or bronze, made by the hand of Phidias; as Calamis lays claim to the fame of the horses that he made, as the work of Myron is a cow like a real one [cf. 2.31.7–8], so I am not the least part of your creations, Sextus, and I am said to be the gift and work of your protection.

9–10 animosa ... signa: 'life-like [*and* spirited] sculptures'. Lysippus was a fourth-century sculptor from Sicyon, who worked in bronze. Alexander the Great is said to have specified him and the painter Apelles (11) as the only artists allowed to portray him (Hor. *Epist.* 2.1.239–41; cf. Plin. *Nat.* 7.125). His Apoxyomenos (Athlete scraping himself clean) was installed by Agrippa in his Baths in Rome in *c*.20 BC. This is lost, but the marble copy in the Vatican Museum shows Lysippus' commitment to naturalism and ideal proportions.   **exactis**: 'finished', 'perfect'. The fifth-century sculptor Calamis was famous for his chariots and horses (*Nat.* 34.71), and also for engraving cups (*Nat.* 33.156, 34.47), not mentioned here.   **se mihi iactat**: 'vaunts himself in my eyes'.

11–12 summam sibi ponit: 'places the woman who was supreme to him'. Apelles, the most celebrated ancient painter (*Nat.* 35.79–97), can be neatly assimilated to P. himself, in putting his ideal woman on display in his art. At 1.2.22 P. praises the naturalness of his colouring. If *poscit* rather than *ponit* is the correct reading, the meaning will be 'demands supremacy for himself' (cf. Plautus, *Truculentus* 727 *solus summam habet hic apud nos* [he alone has the chief place here at our house]).   **Parrhasius**: a painter of the late fifth century from Ephesus. His work was characterized by a fine attention to detail (*parua ... arte*; cf. *Nat.* 35.67). Art on smaller scale finds an appropriate home in the pentameter (as again in 12).   **uindicat ... iocum**: 'vindicates jesting': for this element in Parrhasius' work see *Nat.* 35.72. *iocum* is Lachmann's emendation: if *locum* is the correct reading, the expression will mean 'claims his place'.

13–14 Mentor and Mys were both silversmiths (*Nat.* 33.154–5), the former of the early fourth century, the latter of the fifth century. **argumenta magis sunt Mentoris addita formae**: 'narrative scenes (*argumenta*—OLD 6b) were poured especially (*magis*: cf. 3.14.2) into Mentor's mould (*formae*—OLD 6b)'.   **Myos** is a Greek genitive; as a common noun the word μῦς means 'mouse', and *exiguum* *iter* plays on this (cf. Ov. *Fast.* 2.574 *qua breuis occultum mus sibi fecit iter* [where the little mouse makes a hidden path for itself]). **acanthus**: a plant whose foliage was used in art for decorative purposes, notably in the capitals of Corinthian columns: cf. Verg. *Ecl.* 3.45, *Aen.* 1.649, Ov. *Met.* 13.701 *summus inaurato crater erat asper acantho* [the top of the mixing bowl was embossed with gilded acanthus].

15 Phidiacus signo se Iuppiter ornat eburno: 'the Jupiter of Phidias adorns himself with an ivory statue'. The Athenian Phidias' gold and ivory statue of Zeus (Roman Jupiter) at Olympia was one of the most famous works of art of the ancient world.   **propria ... ab urbe lapis**: 'stone from his own city': Praxiteles was an Athenian and some of his most celebrated works, which dated from the third quarter of the fourth century, were sculpted in Pentelic marble quarried near the city. His most famous work was the Aphrodite of Cnidos: *Nat.* 36.20–2. This is a work of delicate femininity, and a contrast may be implied with the epic grandeur of Phidias' chryselephantine Zeus.   **uendit ab** is Barber's emendation (for *uindicat*; cf. 12): the verb will mean 'recommends' but there could also be a cynical nod towards the art market: its basic meaning is 'sells' (there is a similar ambiguity at 1.2.4, complaining about Cynthia's exotic clothing and make-up, *teque peregrinis uendere muneribus*: 'and deck yourself out [for sale?] in foreign goods').

17–20 We now turn from the arts to other spheres of human activity. Even at the Olympic games chariot racing and running provide alternative routes to glory; so more broadly do peace and war, a contrast that looks ahead to the presentations of Maecenas and P. himself.   **est quibus Eleae contingit palma quadrigae**: lit. 'there are some to whom comes the palm of the chariot in Elis', i.e. 'there are some who win first prize in the Olympic chariot race': Olympia is in Elis, in the north-western Peloponnese. *est quibus* = ἔστιν οἷς ('there are those to whom', 'for some'). As he turns to the Olympic games, P. uses a Greek expression unique in Latin poetry, but evoking an important intertext*, Hor. *Odes* 1.1.3–4 *sunt quos curriculo puluerem Olympicum | collegisse iuuat* [there are those whom it pleases to collect Olympic dust in a chariot].   **quibus in celeres gloria nata pedes**: 'for whose swift feet glory was created': there is no doubt also a suggestion that their running ability is innate

(cf. *naturae semina* in 20).   **hic satus** ('born', lit. 'sown')
ad pacem, hic castrensibus utilis armis: The contrast in this line is
given very strong emphasis by the fact that a neat balance is denied us.
The caesura falls not at the comma, but after *hic* since the *em* of *pacem*
elides. As so often in Roman life, war impinges on peace.

21–34 At 7 the poet has begun his argument that every man is not
fitted to finding fame in every field: many succeed in achieving
greatness (9–19) by following their natural inclinations (20). In 23–
30 he explores Maecenas' nature (his humility, and unwillingness to
pursue the manifestations of power); with 31–4 he will indicate that
this way of life will confer fame on Maecenas too. Despite Maecenas'
aloofness from public office he will equal the likes of Camillus, be
spoken of by the public, share in Caesar's fame and have, in his
reputation for loyalty and trustworthiness, the equivalent of a victor's
trophies. Maecenas is made the climax of the catalogue of excellence:
the artists of 9–16 had a verse each, Maecenas receives a dozen. His
greatness and his fame consist in refusing the prominence and epic
glory that his closeness to Caesar would allow: despite being one of
the most powerful citizens (2 n.), he never held one of the formal
magistracies of the Roman state. In this sequence, however, verses
21–2 play no part. Where it stands in the manuscripts *at* (21) can
only contrast the *natural* inclinations of 20 with the *precepts* that
determine P.'s behaviour. The couplet apparently belongs in a lacuna*
apparent before verse 35.

23–4 tu looks ahead to the verbs in 29 (compare 1.6.31, 1.20.7 for the
holding over of a subject pronoun).   **Romano dominas in
honore secures:** 'axes that dominate among Roman magistracies'.
The axes were tied round with bundles of sticks (*fasces*) and carried
by lictors to symbolize executive power.   **cum . . . secures | et
liceat . . . ponere iura:** 'although you could place axes and lay down
laws [*or* dispense justice]': a syllepsis*: the meaning of *ponere* shifts
from physical to abstract.

25–6 arcus: the transmitted *hostes* is clearly wrong. Helvetius'
arcus is tempting because Medes, like other Easterners, were
regarded by the Romans as using bow and arrow as their pri-
mary weapon (cf. 3.12.11); but the alternative *hastas* would also

make sense. Cf. 3.4 for such a campaign; but the idea that
Maecenas could have had a successful military career is scarcely
serious. He was apparently present at the battles of Philippi (42)
and Actium (31), but he cultivated an image of softness (Sen. *Ep.*
114.4–7).   **fixa per arma**: 'with arms fastened up': spoils
of war could be fixed on the walls of a victorious general's house
as well as in temples (e.g. Gallus fr. 3 [F], *Aen.* 7.183–6).

27–8 ad effectum: i.e. 'to achieve this'; for *ad* marking purpose see 19;
3.14.9; 3.22.41; 3.24.26.   **uires det Caesar**: Maecenas' power
comes from Caesar, not from popular election.   **faciles**: the
adjective is used adverbially: 'easily'.   **insinuentur**: 'flow in
(to your purse)'. The line draws attention to the wealth accruing to
members of the regime: cf. 3.4.1–2 n.

29–30 parcis: 'you show restraint' (*OLD* 2d).   **in tenues humilem te colligis umbras**: 'you humbly gather yourself into the narrow
shadows': for the use of *umbra* to communicate withdrawal from the
hurly-burly of the public world, see *OLD* 5. *tenues* (3.1.5, 8 nn.) and
humilem (2.10.11) associate Maecenas with the 'unambitious' elegiac
style commended by Callimachus.   **uelorum plenos subtrahis
ipse sinus**: 'you yourself reef up the full belly of your sails'. *sinus* is poetic
plural; P. avoids the repetition of *uelorum plenum . . . sinum.* The sails
could be full if Maecenas wanted. This recalls the nautical imagery of
3–4; again a parallel is drawn between P. and Maecenas—the latter
shortens sail in order not to gain glory as consul or conqueror and
magistrate, the former sails too small a boat to accomplish Maecenas'
request (so Butrica, *ICS* 21 [1996], 143).

31–2 crede mihi: when Horace in *Odes* 1.1 moves on to himself at the
climax of his list of human roles, he defers to Maecenas' judgement
(1.1.35 *si me lyricis uatibus inseres* [if you will insert me among the
lyric poets]); P. offers his judgement when he places Maecenas at the
climax of his list.   **magnos aequabunt ista Camillos iudicia**:
'those decisions of yours will equal the great Camilli', i.e. heroes such
as Camillus, the conqueror of the Gauls, hailed as second founder of
the city (Livy 5.43–55; 3.11.67 n.). For such generalizing plurals
(often grouped) compare Plaut. *Bacch.* 649, Cat. 14.18, and *Camillos*
itself at Verg. *Geo.* 2.169 and Cic. *Cael.* 39. The comparison of the

Maecenas who shuns the limelight with the great military hero is a playful touch; but Camillus was a private citizen when summoned back to Rome from exile at Ardea after the Gauls had captured the city.   **uenies tu quoque in ora uirum**: *uirum* is the shortened form of the genitive plural. Once again Maecenas is aligned with the poet: there is an allusion* to the poet Ennius' epitaph on himself, *uolito uiuu' per ora uirum* [still living (*uiuus*), I flit on the lips of men], but also to Prop. 2.1.1–2: *Quaeritis...* | *unde meus ueniat mollis in ora liber* [You (i.e. readers) ask...how my book comes in elegiac form (*mollis*) onto people's lips].

33–4 Caesaris et famae uestigia iuncta tenebis: 'and you will keep your footsteps adjoined to Caesar's fame'.   **erunt**: the subject is the singular *fides* ('loyalty') but it has been attracted into the plural by the complement to the verb, *uera tropaea* ('the true trophies', pl. for s.).

21–2, 35–46 The catalogue of sources of *fama*, reinforced by the echoes of Horace, *Odes* 1.1, may lead a reader to expect a contrasting culmination in the poet himself. But this is delayed until after the picture of Maecenas, and introduced in a different way: Maecenas provides a model for the poet in his unwillingness to deal in warfare and sail on an epic sea. If the poet overcomes Maecenas, it is only through following his example, avoiding epic and writing in the tradition of Callimachus and Philitas, thus winning the admiration of the young of both sexes.

21–2 at provides the link between the paragraph on P. himself and the previous one on Maecenas: the poet contrasts the fame Maecenas wins for himself through his self-restraint with the example that he offers the poet.   **cogor**: paradoxical with *te superare*, but nicely implying the pressure a patron can bring to bear (cf. 52). For *cogi* used of poetic compulsion, see already 1.1.8, 1.12.14 *nunc primum longas solus cognoscere noctes* | *cogor et ipse meis auribus esse grauis* [Now for the first time I am compelled to get to know long nights spent alone, and to be a burden to my own ears]; and 3.21.18, 3.24.11.   **superare**: 'to prevail over', i.e. in argument; but the verb is a striking one when it has as its object one of the most important men in Rome.

35–6 uelifera tumidum mare … carina: the return to sailing imagery (3–4 n., 30) is compounded by the epic compound epithet and the anti-Callimachean *tumidus* (= παχύς, used of Antimachus' *Lyde* in Call. fr. 398 'a fat [*or* swollen] book and not lucid', and translated into *tumido… Antimacho* by Catullus at 95.10; Ovid has metapoetic* instances at *Am.* 1.9.13, *Met.* 1.460, 8.437). **findŏ:** the *o* scans short: after a long syllable this is unique in P., though Ovid takes the liberty at *Am.* 3.2.26 (*tollŏ*), *ex P.* 1.7.56 (*credŏ*). Some have therefore given weight to the omission of the verse in N and thought it a medieval invention to fill a gap; but Housman observed that 'every change must have a beginning' (*CP* 276), and in its epic imagery and diction the verse is perfect. **tuta … nostra mora (e)st:** 'our time is spent safely'. Between *nostra* and *mora* we can hear *mora*'s anagram, *amor*. *nostra* can include Cynthia as well as the poet himself. For *tuta*, cf. 3.3.24. **sub exiguo flumine:** 'down in (*OLD* 2; i. e. beneath the banks of) a tiny river': cf. 2.32.39 *sub antro* ('down in a dell'). Springs are more often the watery symbols of the small-scale and refined (3.1.3 n.), but cf. 2.10.26 *Permessi flumine lauit Amor* (**P**).

37–42: the poet rejects the material of the two archetypal military epics, the *Thebaid* and the *Iliad*. Each story features in a contemporary epic mentioned by P. (Ponticus' *Thebaid*: 1.7.1–2, 1.9.10) or Ovid (Macer's completion of the *Iliad*: *Am.* 2.18.1–2, *ex P.* 2.10.13–14). Besides the *Iliad* itself we also have fragments* of two archaic Greek epics on Argive-led campaigns against Thebes, (a) the *Thebaid* proper, telling of the unsuccessful Seven against Thebes, including the exiled Theban prince Polynices, who kills and is killed by his brother Eteocles; and (b) the *Epigoni* ('those born next'), who sack Thebes in revenge for their fathers; see e.g. West 2003: 3–11, 42–59. P. refers to the later episode first (cf. 49–51; 3.1.25–30, where the Trojan Horse is mentioned first before episodes from the *Iliad*; 3.12.24 n.).

37–8 non flebo in cineres arcem sedisse tepentes / Cadmi: 'I shall not lament that the citadel of Cadmus sank into warm ashes': *tepentes* or *parentis* ('father Cadmus') appear the most plausible substitutes for the transmitted *paternos* (which could not refer to the fathers of the Epigoni: see Morgan, *CQ* 36 (1986), 186–8). **nec septem**

proelia clade pari: 'nor the seven battles with equal disaster', i.e. 'the seven equally disastrous battles': each of the seven champions dies.

39–42 Scaeas: understand *portas*. In the *Iliad* Troy has a number of gates (2.809 = 8.58). Their significance is that they are the location that divides off the security of the town from the danger of the battlefield. They mark some key events: the meeting of Hector and Andromache (6.392–495), Hector's approaching death (22.6, 194) and the predicted killing of Achilles (22.359–60).   **Pergama, Apollinis arces**: *Pergama* (n. pl., and perhaps influencing the choice of the poetic plural *arces*) was the citadel of Troy built for king Laomedon by Apollo and Neptune (41): *Il.* 7.452.   **Danaum decimo uere redisse rates**: lit. 'that the ships of the Greeks returned in the tenth spring': P. freely mixes noun objects (*Scaeas et Pergama*) with clauses. The reference here can be to the end of the war after ten years, or to the epic *Nostoi* ('Returns'), of which the greatest is the *Odyssey* (which also tells of the journey in general [so the song of Phemius at 1.325–7], and of Menelaus in particular, at 4.351–592).   **moenia cum Graio Neptunia pressit aratro | uictor Palladiae ligneus artis equus**: the idea is compressed: turning the active *pressit* into a passive may be the best way to preserve the effect in a translation: 'the walls of Neptune were overwhelmed with a Greek plough by the victor, the horse built by Pallas' ingenuity'. The horse is represented as ploughing over the razed city, though of course it was the device that enabled this to happen later. Compare Hor. *Odes* 1.16.19–21 where anger was the cause *cur perirent | funditus imprimeretque muris | hostile aratrum exercitus insolens* [why they (i.e. lofty cities) were razed to the ground and an insolent army drove a hostile plough down upon their walls]. Pallas Athena was the goddess of carpentry (3.20.7–8 n.) and helped build the horse.

43–4 inter Callimachi … libellos: 3.1.1 n: the small scale of his writing is implicit in the diminutive *libellos* (3.2.17, 3.19 nn.).   **sat erit placuisse**: 'it will be enough to have pleased …': P., like his model, has a sense of what is enough.   **modis, Coe poeta, tuis**: 'in your metres [i.e. elegiac couplets], Coan poet'. Though *Coe* is a conjecture, we can be sure that Philitas is meant here: he is regularly paired with Callimachus (3.1.1 n.; 2.34.31–2, 4.6.3–4). The transmitted *dure* (which would imply 'epic') is due to a scribe's reminiscence of 2.34.44 *dure poeta.*

45–6 haec urant scripta: 'may these writings fire': with love, and with admiration for the poet. P.'s elegiacs have the power of Cupid himself to make young readers fall in love: cf. 1.7.23–4, 3.3.19–20, Ov. *Ars* 3.329–34, *Rem.* 757–66; this is a very different kind of didactic to that aimed by Horace at *uirginibus puerisque* (*Odes* 3.1.4).   **meque deum clament et mihi sacra ferant:** in the first line of the book, P. talks of *sacra* paid to Philitas (3.1.1 n.); he now envisages himself receiving such worship.

57–8, 47–56 Something seems to have been lost between 37–46, announcing that the poet will not write epic but continue with erotic elegy, and 47–56, which suddenly reveal an intention to compose not just epic, but the grandest epic, on the battle between gods and titans, or Roman historical themes. *te duce* (47) can operate as a conditional ('if you lead'), but the context needs immediately to mark it as such: more than this phrase is needed for so fundamental a change of tack. Rather than just marking a lacuna*, it seems that verses 57–8 should be transposed here: in *tu* they have a marker of the fresh appeal to Maecenas, and of a new sequence of thought as well. The couplet asks for guidance of the poetic career already begun (*coeptae... iuuentae,* 57; *immissis... rotis,* 58), and thus leads into verses 47–56, where the poet tells Maecenas that, if he leads the way (and assumes a great public office—which is inconceivable), he himself will write a grand epic, on national and Augustan themes.

57–8 mollia tu coeptae fautor cape lora iuuentae, | dexteraque immissis da mihi signa rotis: 'you should take the pliant reins as patron of my youthful life [*lit.* the youth I have begun] and give supportive signals to my rolling wheels'. As Camps observes, Maecenas is asked to be both a supportive onlooker (a *fautor* giving *dextera signa*) and to hold the reins himself. For equestrian (including chariot) imagery used of poetic composition, cf. 2.10.2 (P); 3.1.10–14; 3.3.18, 21; 4.1.70; Pindar, *Olymp.* 9.80–1, *Pyth.* 10.65; Verg. *Geo.* 2.542, Ov. *Ars* 1.39–40, *Rem.* 397–8, and especially Lucretius 6.92–5, the invocation to Calliope:

> **tu** mihi supremae praescripta ad candida callis
> *currenti* spatium praemonstra, callida Musa
> Calliope, requies hominum diuumque uoluptas,
> **te duce** ut insigni capiam cum laude coronam.

You should show the course in advance to me *as I run* to the white line of the furthest goal, inventive Muse, Calliope, relaxation for men and delight of gods, so that **under your guidance** I may gain a garland along with splendid praise.

47–8 te duce alludes to Lucretius 6.95 (just cited) and evokes those other places where it is used of statesmen who, unlike Maecenas, really do lead (Verg. *Ecl.* 4.13 Pollio; Hor. *Odes* 1.2.52 Caesar; 1.6.4 Agrippa). **Iouis arma**: the grandest of themes: cf. 2.1.19–20, 39–40, and Innes, *CQ* 29 (1979), 165–71.   **Coeum**: a titan (Verg. *Geo.* 1.279, Hesiod, *Theogony* 134).   **Phlegraeis... iugis**: 'on the Phlegraean mountains', which authors place either in southern Italy or in Thessaly in northern Greece. As well as symbolizing the grandest epic, gigantomachy* becomes a pointer to Roman civil war: 3.11.37; Statius, *Siluae* 5.3.196; cf. also Hor. *Odes* 2.12.6–7, 3.4.43–64.   **Oromedonta**: Oromedon appears as a mountain in a metapoetic* passage of Theocritus (7.46), and may well have had an existence as a giant in some lost passage; but it is tempting to amend the word to *Eurymedonta* since Eurymedon is king of the giants at *Odyssey* 7.58.

49–50 celsaque Romanis decerpta Palatia tauris: 'the lofty Palatine grazed by Roman bulls'. *Palatia* is poetic plural: 'the Palatine hill', as at 4.1.3, 4.9.3. As in both those passages, the poet looks back to the early history of the Roman nation when cattle grazed on what was to become the site of the city: cf. also Tib. 2.5.25, Virg. *Aen.* 8.360–1. **ordiar**: 'I would begin to recount' (*OLD* 2b).   **caeso...Remo**: Romulus killed Remus when he contemptuously jumped over the walls of Rome, which the former was in the process of founding: cf. Livy 1.7.2 (a different version is told by Ovid at *Fast.* 4.835–44; cf. also Dionysius Hal. 1.87). The text suggests that the death of Remus was in some way a human sacrifice which made the walls inviolable for the future (cf. 4.1.50 *Auentino rura pianda Remo* [fields to be purified with <the sacrifice of> Remus of the Aventine]).

51–2 eductosque pares siluestri ex ubere reges: 'and the royal partners brought up by a wild beast's [*lit.* woodland] dug'. For the story of

Romulus and Remus suckled by a she-wolf, see Livy 1.4.6; *Aen.* 8.630–4; Ov. *Fast.* 3.49–54; Dionysius Hal. 1.79.5–8. As in 37–8, P. reverses the chronological order of events. For *ex* = 'by' (*OLD* 19a), cf. 4.3.4 *e lacrimis facta litura* ('a blot made by tears').   **crescat**: 'would grow': Camps' conjecture for *crescet*. The other verbs in the sentence (*canam, ordiar, prosequar*) could be subjunctive or future indicative; but the change after 43–6 and the sense of *te duce* (47) show that the meaning is hypothetical and the verbs are thus subjunctive.   **et** is postponed* (as perhaps also in 53, though 'also' is a possible translation there).   **sub tua iussa**: 'up to the level of your orders'. Cf. Verg. *Geo.* 3.41 *haud mollia iussa* (L; also addressed to Maecenas).

53–4 currus utroque ab litore ouantes: 'chariots coming in triumph from either shore'. P. reworks Verg. *Geo.* 3.33 *bisque triumphatas utroque a litore gentes*; the poets seem to foresee a triumph to cap Caesar's triple triumph of 29 BC which celebrated victories in Illyricum, at Actium, and over Egypt; cf. *Aen.* 8.724–8.
Parthorum astutae tela remissa fugae: 'the loosing of the arrows of the Parthians' cunning flight'. *tela remissa* could mean 'arrows laid aside' or 'unstrung bows'; in either case the reference would be to an easing of hostilities with Parthia (3.4 intro.) around the time of the battle of Actium (31 BC): cf. Dio 51.18. However, the meaning could simply be 'arrows shot backward', referring (as *astutae fugae* does) to the famous tactics of the Parthian horse-archers (3.4.17 n.).

55–6 claustraque Pelusi Romano subruta ferro: 'and the bastions of Pelusium undermined by Roman steel'. Pelusium was a fortified town on the Canopic mouth of the Nile. According to Dio's account (51.9.5–6) it was not stormed but surrendered to Octavian. **graues in sua fata**: 'grievous for [i.e. to bring about] his own death'. Antony committed suicide at Alexandria in 30 BC.

59–60 nunc mihi, Maecenas, laudes concedis: 'as things stand, Maecenas, you grant me praise'. The manuscripts offer *hoc mihi...laudis concedis*: 'you grant me this (much) of praise': after a sequence of imperatives and subjunctives this offers a description of present circumstances that (given *hoc*) needs to pick up an idea from what precedes, and yet provides no adverb or conjunction to mark a contrast or a resumption of earlier thought. *nunc* provides the necessary contrast: Maecenas is not going to change his life style and so P. will not write on the themes referred to in 47–56. Thus the situation as it now stands is that P. will have the glory of being acknowledged as sharing Maecenas' approach to life (21–2). **et a te (e)st**: 'and it is thanks to you': cf. the conjectural restoration at 2.14.29 *nunc a te est, mea lux, ueniatne ad litora nauis* [now, light of my life, it is down to you whether my ship comes to the shore]. P. has four hexameters that end with three consecutive monosyllables: 2.27.11 (*et a qua*), 3.1.9 (*et a me*), 3.8.3, 4.5.17 (both *et in me*); this verse adds a fourth monosyllable, *est*, which prodelides after *te*. This effect is to slow the line down and lay emphasis on *te* (= Maecenas). **quod ferar in partes ipse fuisse tuas**: 'that I am said to be in [*or* have come into] your faction'. For *in* + accusative so without a verb of motion, see *OLD* 15d; it is particularly found with set phrases, as at Cicero, *Div. Caec.* 66 *nationibus quae in amicitiam populi Romani dicionemque essent* [nations that fell into the friendship and influence of the Roman people]; Sallust, *Jug.* 112 *cum talem uirum in potestatem habuisset* [since he had such a man in his power].

Additional bibliography: Wimmel 1960: 250–63; Gold 1982: 103–17.

3.10

1–4: I wondered why the Muses were standing smiling by my bed at dawn: they gave a signal to mark my girl's birthday. 5–10: Let it be a day of calm and free from sorrow. 11–18: You, my dear, should rise and pray to the gods. Wash, do your hair, and put on the dress in which you first caught my eye. Seek continuing beauty and rule over me. 19–26: Then, when the incense has burnt brightly, let there be eating, drinking, as night comes on, and perfume; music and dancing; unrestrained talk to keep sleep at bay, and noise to fill the neighbourhood. 27–32: Let us cast dice to see which loves the other more; and, the drinking over, let us perform the final birthday rite for Venus in our bedroom.

For other birthday poems, see Tib. 1.7 (to his patron Messalla, combined with celebration of a triumph), 2.2 (to Cornutus, including wedding elements); the Sulpicia poems, [Tib.] 3.11 & 12; Hor. *Odes* 4.11, Ov. *Tristia* 3.13 (his own), 5.5 (his wife's); Statius, *Siluae* 2.7 (the poet Lucan, decades after his death). In Greek we have epigrams by the first-century BC poet Crinagoras (*Anth. Pal.* 6.227, 261, 345); and Callimachus, *Iambus* 12 (fr. 202) is a poem that celebrates a birth, marking the ceremony that happened after seven days. The passage with the most in common is the opening of Tib. 2.2 (we have no clear evidence of priority):

> Dicamus bona uerba: uenit Natalis ad aras:
> quisquis ades, lingua, uir mulierque, faue.
> urantur pia tura focis, urantur odores
> quos tener e terra diuite mittit Arabs.
> ipse suos Genius adsit uisurus honores,
> cui decorent sanctas mollia serta comas.
> illius puro destillent tempora nardo,
> ille satur libo sit madeatque mero;
> adnuat et, Cornute, tibi, quodcumque rogabis.
> en age, quid cessas? adnuit ille: roga.
> auguror, uxoris fidos optabis amores.

Let us speak fair words: the birthday god is coming to the altar: any man or woman present, keep silent. Let pious incense be burnt in the hearth, and the perfumes that the soft-living Arab sends from his rich land. Let the Genius come himself, to see the honours paid him, with a soft garland decorating his sacred hair. Let his head drip with pure nard-oil; let him be full of honey-cake and soaked in wine; and let him nod to grant you whatever you ask, Cornutus. Hey, why do you hesitate? He nods: do ask. I prophesy, you will seek the loyal love of your wife.

P. does not include Cynthia's *Iuno* (*OLD* 4), the female equivalent of the 'Genius' who symbolizes a man's identity; instead he concentrates on Cynthia's dress and actions: she is the deity here. He writes the poem for her, but makes no mention of presents (which turn birthdays into days of ill omen for lovers at Ov. *Ars* 1.417–18: see James 2003: 98). Moreover, she is asked to wear an old, if special, dress and no make-up (13–15), in contrast to the extravagant Cynthia of 1.2, 1.15, 2.18.23–36. Any expenditure goes on the party (21–3).

1–2 Mirabar: wonder is a theme of the next section of the book: 3.14.1 n.   **quidnam:** *nam* adds a note of puzzlement. The line is as spondaic as a hexameter can be, reflecting the slow-moving operation of the poet's newly awakened consciousness, an effect furthered by the muzzy alliteration of *m*s and *n*s, and continued by *ante…stantes…rubente* in the pentameter.   **risissent:** 'had smiled'. Another conjecture for the transmitted *misissent* ('what the Camenae had sent') is *uisissent* ('why they had come to visit').   **Camenae:** the goddesses of a spring just outside the Porta Capena at Rome (Livy 1.21.3). The Muses are also associated with water (already in Hesiod's *Theogony*: **A**) and the two groups were identified (as here) at least from the time of Livius Andronicus (second half of the third century BC): cf. the first line of his translation of the *Odyssey* (the rest is almost entirely lost): *Virum mihi, Camena, insece uersutum* [Tell me, Camena, of the cunning man]. Water returns in verses 6, 8, 13 (but perfume and wine take over after that). It is perhaps a joke when Horace echoes the line-ending at *Epist.* 1.19.5 *uina fere dulces oluerunt mane Camenae* [the sweet Muses generally stank of wine in the morning].   **stantes:** cf. the Penates appearing to the sleeping Aeneas at *Aen.* 3.150 (*uisi ante oculos astare*). Deities more often appear to mortals in the country-side, as Apollo and the Muses in 3.3, and the Muses to Hesiod (*Theog.* 22–3 [**A**]) and Callimachus (*Aetia* fr. 2). But the bedroom is P.'s workplace (cf. also Cynthia's appearance at 4.7.3–12, and 3.3 intro. on epic dreams).   **sole rubente:** 'as the sun grew red': the backdrop is a Homeric rosy-fingered dawn, which together with the appearance of the Muses sets up epic expectations that are revisited but repeatedly disappointed in this, the poem their appearance does inspire.

3–4 natalis nostrae signum misere puellae: 'they gave the signal for my girl's birthday'. *signum mittere* is a technical term for giving the signal that starts a race: cf. Ennius, *Annales* fr. 79–80 Skutsch: *ueluti consul cum mittere signum | uult, omnes auidi spectant ad carceris oras* [as, when the consul is going to give the signal, everyone eagerly looks to the barriers of the starting stalls].   **manibus faustos ter crepuere sonos:** lit. 'they three times clapped propitious sounds with their hands'. The Muses inaugurate the birthday—and

the poem—favourably. Note the crisp alliteration of *ter crepuere.*
The first two couplets provide an appealing dawn scene for the
beginning of the poem and a vivid allegory of poetic inspiration.

5–10 P. sets up Cynthia's birthday celebrations in imitation of
Callimachus' instructions for the hymn to Apollo (*Hymn* 2.17–24):

> εὐφημεῖτ᾽ ἀίοντες ἐπ᾽ Ἀπόλλωνος ἀοιδῆι.
> εὐφημεῖ καὶ πόντος, ὅτε κλείουσιν ἀοιδοί
> ἢ κίθαριν ἢ τόξα, Λυκωρέος ἔντεα Φοίβου.
> οὐδὲ Θέτις Ἀχιλῆα κινύρεται αἴλινα μήτηρ,   20
> ὁππόθ᾽ ἱὴ παιῆον ἱὴ παιῆον ἀκούσηι.
> καὶ μὲν ὁ δακρυόεις ἀναβάλλεται ἄλγεα πέτρος,
> ὅστις ἐνὶ Φρυγίηι διερὸς λίθος ἐστήρικται,
> μάρμαρον ἀντὶ γυναικὸς ὀιζυρόν τι χανούσης.

Silence, listeners, for the hymn to Apollo. Silent is even the sea, when
singers tell of either the lyre or the bow, instruments of Lycorean Phoebus. Not even Thetis, his mother, sings a song of woe for Achilles when
she hears 'Hië Paieon, hië Paieon' [i.e. the ritual cry for Apollo]. Even the
tearful rock postpones its grief, the wet [*and* living] stone that is set in
Phrygia, a piece of marble in the shape of a woman gaping some
pitiful cry.

Thetis (goddess of the sea) and Niobe both appear in mourning in
Iliad 24 (84–6; 602–17). Like Callimachus, P. rejects these epic
symbols. The stillness of the sea is broadened to include fair weather
in general (*aëre*, 5, echoes Callimachus' ἠέρι, 2.5). Thetis, a mythological doublet of the sea in the model, is omitted; and replaced by a
general rejection of grieving. Niobe is retained, and in this briefer
version named; *et* reproduces the καί of the original. Cynthia is to
have her day marked with the fair weather and absence of grief
required for a divine epiphany.

5–6 No clouds, high winds or rough waves: hence no epic storm for
the elegiac beloved, a point brought out by the positive *molliter* ('in
elegiac fashion': cf. 3.1.19 n.).

7–8 aspiciam nullos...dolentes: for Cynthia's birthday, a striking
change from 3.8.23–4 *in amore dolere uolo* etc.   **Niobae...
ipse lapis:** 'the very stone that was [*lit.* of] Niobe'. Niobe boasted
that she was superior to Latona, not least in having umpteen children

rather than the goddess's two, Apollo and Diana; in punishment, all her children were killed and she was turned into a rock on Mount Sipylus which wept in eternal mourning: 2.20.7–8; Ov. *Met.* 6.146–312. She is thus a symbol of endlessly sorrowing bereavement: 'like Niobe all tears' (*Hamlet* I.ii.149). The grief which is to be absent from the birthday is distanced here and in 9–10 by the poet's use of mythology to point to an underlying permanence of sorrow which is juxtaposed with the prospective joy of this one day (n.b. *hodierna luce*, 7).

9 alcyonum positis requiescant ora querelis: 'let the mouths of the halcyons lay aside their complaints and rest'. Ovid recounts the myth at length at *Met.* 11.410–748: Ceÿx leaves behind his loving wife Alcyone when he sails off to consult an oracle; he is shipwrecked and killed; a dream tells her of his death, and when his body is eventually carried home by the waves, in her grief she becomes a bird and flies out to greet him; he too is transformed. The birds referred to are in fact kingfishers, but to translate the Latin word in that way is to lose the resonant associations of the name 'halcyon'. The halcyon's cry was said to sound like 'ceÿx', i.e. the husband's name. *querelae* are elsewhere a marker of elegy: 3.6.18 n.

10 increpat absumptum nec sua mater Ityn: 'and may his mother not moan over the dead Itys'. *increpat* has connotations of indignant complaint. Poets freely use parts of *suus* to refer not to the subject of the sentence, but to a significant noun, here the object, *Ityn* (the Greek accusative of *Itys*). Procne was married to Tereus, king of Daulis, and had a son called Itys by him. Tereus raped Philomela, Procne's sister, and tore out her tongue to stop her telling anybody, but she wove her message into a robe. The sisters killed Itys and served him up as food for Tereus. When he discovered this, Tereus pursued them, but all three were changed into birds, the sisters into a nightingale and a swallow, Tereus into a hoopoe (Ov. *Met.* 6.438–673). The nightingale's song is presented as a lament for her son already in a beautiful simile at *Od.* 19.518–23. Catullus adapts Homer's simile to express his grief over his brother's death (65.12–14):

> semper maesta tua carmina morte canam,
> qualia sub densis ramorum concinit umbris
> Daulias, absumpti fata gemens Ityli.

Always I shall sing songs made sad by your death, such as the Daulian bird sings beneath the dense shade of branches, moaning over the fate of lost Itylus (*alternative name for* Itys).

absumptum echoes this, and brings out the point that P.'s elegy, at least for this day, is not concerned with lamentation.

11–20 P. tells Cynthia to get up and make her birthday prayers to the gods (like wishing as one blows candles out on a birthday cake); 13–16 then give more instructions about her dressing, and 17–20 about the worship.

11–12 felicibus edita pennis: 'born under happy omens'. *penna* is lit. 'a wing' but the flight of birds was regularly used to tell the future. The sad bird stories of 8–10 have been suppressed and the avian imagery is now propitious.   **praesentes iusta precare deos:** 'pray to the present deities for what is just'. The Camenae are divinities currently present and willing to help (*OLD praesens* 3), but so implicitly are Cynthia's 'Juno' (see intro.; [Tib.] 3.12.1), Cupid and Venus (28–30). *praesentes* is an emendation for the transmitted *poscentes*: it is implausible that the gods should *demand* her prayer.

13–14 primum: referring to her first action, i.e. before she prays. Where an epic day might begin with a warrior arming (*Iliad* 11.1–46), the elegist has his mistress dressing (though this too has an Homeric model: Hera preparing to seduce Zeus at *Il.* 14.153–86).   **pura...lympha:** a pleasing combination of ritual and an everyday action: the pure water will wake her up, but also wash away any pollution.   **nitidas presso pollice finge comas:** 'arrange [*OLD* 4b] your shining hair with finger pressed against thumb' (lit. 'with pressed thumb'). *nitidas* may mean 'lustrous' (i.e. thick and healthy) or 'shining with hair-oil'.

15–16 qua primum oculos cepisti ueste Properti | indue: 'put on the dress in which you first captured the eyes of *Propertius*': there is a pointed echo of 1.1.1 *Cynthia prima suis miserum me cepit ocellis*; the poet's own name replaces Cynthia's. A similar sense of vivid reminiscence occurs in Thomas Hardy's poem *The Voice*, in which, looking back poignantly to his early relationship with his recently deceased first wife, he writes of 'the original air-blue gown'. On eyes in P. see K. O'Neill in Ancona and Greene (eds.) 2005: 243–68.   **nec uacuum flore relinque caput**: 'and do not leave your head free of flowers'. The garland suits the festal occasion, the party that will follow, and Cynthia as mistress of a poet. P. uses *flos* only in the singular*; it is collective also at 1.20.40, 4.3.57.

17–18 qua polles: 'in which your strength lies': the relative clause is dependent on the noun *forma*.   **inque meum semper stent tua regna caput**: 'and that your reign over me [*lit.* my head] may be established for ever'. Even on this happy occasion P. asserts the power Cynthia has over him. For erotic *regna*, cf. 2.16.28, 2.34.57, 4.7.50, and the imitation, addressed to Cerinthus by Sulpicia, at [Tib.] 3.11.3–4:

> te nascente nouum Parcae cecinere puellis
> seruitium et dederunt regna superba tibi.

At your birth the Fates predicted a new slavery for girls and they gave you proud rule.

19–20 inde ... ubi: 'Next, when ...'   **ture piaueris**: 'you have consecrated with incense' (cf. Tib. 2.2.3 [intro.]).   **luxerit**: 'has shone': the word is placed with effective suddenness at the start of the line (*et* being postponed*). The flame blazes up when the incense is thrown on it.

21 sit mensae ratio: 'let there be thought of the table [i.e. food]'. **noxque inter pocula surgat**: i.e. 'let night arise amid our cups [i.e. drinking]'. The leap from morning (1–18) reflects the hectically sensual nature of the relationship as the poet's thoughts rush forward to the night. As often, *nox* is treated as a heavenly body. *currat* is transmitted, but there is no reason for P. to want the night to pass quickly (lovers traditionally want night to linger: cf. Ov. *Am.* 1.13; Donne's *The Sunne Rising*; and the dismissal of sleep in verse 25).

22 crocino nares murreus ungat onyx: 'let an onyx jar full of myrrh anoint our nostrils with saffron'. *crocino* is an adjective agreeing with *unguento* ('ointment'), which is omitted but understood. *onyx* (a valuable kind of marble) refers to an ointment jar made out of the stone. The line luxuriates in the richness and colour of saffron (yellow), myrrh (reddish brown) and onyx; it also appeals to the senses of smell and touch in the vivid phrase *nares ungat*.

23–4 Now the poet appeals to the ear. **tibia continuis succumbat rauca choreis:** 'let the pipe grow hoarse and give way to the constant dancing': the idea is that pipe player stops in exhaustion. **adsint nequitiae libera uerba tuae:** 'let unrestrained talk back up your lasciviousness': *OLD adsum* 11a. For *libera uerba* as a key part of erotic drunkenness, cf. 2.34.22, Tib. 1.9.26.

25–6 dulcia . . . conuicia: 'sweet arguments': cf. the similar oxymoron* at 3.8.1 *Dulcis ad hesternas fuerat mihi rixa lucernas.* Broukhusius' conjecture *conuicia* (for *conuiuia*, 'parties') fits verse 25 into sequence between the *libera uerba* of 24 and the reference to noise in the pentameter. **publica uicinae perstrepat aura uiae:** lit. 'let the public air of the neighbouring street ring' (i.e. with our partying). *publica* implies 'open to all'. Public access is something conventionally disdained by the Callimachean* (3.16.25–6 n.); but the public on this occasion only gets to hear Cynthia, not to see her (contrast 1.2; 2.32.8–10, 1–2). Note the explosive alliteration of *ps*.

27–8 sint sortes nobis talorum interprete iactu: 'let us cast lots, with the throw of the dice deciding . . .'. The highest throw was known as *Venus* and would of course be particularly fortunate in this context: cf. 4.8.45–6 (P. partying in Cynthia's absence) 'when I aimed at the lucky Venus-throw with the dice, it was always the damnable dogs [the worst throw] that came up'. **quem grauius pennis uerberet ille puer:** 'which (of us) that boy [i.e. Cupid] beats more heavily with his wings'. For the lovers' playful argument, cf. Cat. 45, Hor. *Odes* 3.9. *quis* is used fairly widely for 'which of two' (normally *uter*): see Kenney 1996 on Ov. *Her.* 19.174.

29–30 fuerit . . . exacta: 'shall have passed'. P. uses parts of the perfect system of *esse* with past participles also at e.g. 1.4.9 *si . . . fuerit collata,* 2.31.2 *porticus . . . aperta fuit,* 3.23.11. **multis . . . trientibus:** 'with many cups': a *triens* is a third of a *sextarius*, i.e. about half a pint. **hora:** simply 'time' in this context. **noctis et instituet sacra ministra Venus:** 'and Venus as attendant will set up the ceremonies of night'. The goddess of love becomes the acolyte of the lovers (cf. 3.16.20).

31–2 annua soluamus sollemnia: 'let us perform our annual rites':
the ritualistic language looks back to the religious observances of 12,
17–20, as well as to the poetic *sacra* of 3.9.46.   **peragamus
iter**: 'let us complete the course': closural language, as in 29. The
journey is not an epic one, but the programme of events for the
birthday, and perhaps also the intercourse that is to conclude it: cf.
2.33.22, 3.15.4. The purity of the poem's opening has led to this
joyously sexual conclusion.

Additional bibliography: R. O. A. M. Lyne and J. H. W. Morwood,
G&R 20 (1973), 38–48; Heyworth, *MD* 33 (1994), 52–4.

3.11

*1–8: Why are you surprised that a woman controls my life? Why do you
criticize me for not breaking the yoke? I used to utter your views; mine is
an example to fear. 9–26: Examples of dominant women are Medea,
Penthesilea, Omphale, Semiramis. 27–32: Why use heroes, or gods, to
provide examples (Jupiter is a disgrace)? What of Antony and Cleopatra? She sought Rome's subservience as her dowry. 33–8: Egypt, you
robbed Pompey of his triumphs: a permanent stain on you, Rome. Better
if he had died elsewhere. 39–46: Whore queen, you dared to threaten
our gods and to impose Egyptian culture on Rome. 47–56: What use is
the driving out of the Tarquins if a woman had to be endured? Cry
triumph and pray for Augustus. You fled to the Nile, were captured, and
saw the snakes bite your arm. 57–70: The gods founded and protect this
capital city: if Caesar is safe, Rome would scarcely fear Jupiter. Where do
the victories of Scipio, Camillus, Pompey rank now? The defeats of
Hannibal, Syphax, Pyrrhus? There are memorials to the achievements
of Curtius, Decius, Cocles, Corvinus. Apollo's temple on Leucas will
record the great victory at Actium. 71–2: Sailor, you should remember
Caesar wherever you are in the Ionian Sea.*

Elegy 1.12 begins and ends thus (1–4, 20):

> Quid mihi desidiae non cessas fingere crimen
> quod faciat nobis Cynthia, Roma, moram?

> tam multa illa meo diuisa est milia lecto
>   quantum Hypanis Veneto dissidet Eridano. . . .
> Cynthia prima fuit; Cynthia finis erit.   20

Why don't you cease inventing a charge of sloth against me, on the
grounds that Cynthia is causing us a distraction, Rome? She is as many
miles separated from my bed as Hypanis [*a river in the Ukraine*] is
distant from the Venetian Po... Cynthia was the start; Cynthia will be
the end.

With its critical response to the charges of others the opening serves
as a model for 3.11: in particular the words *Quid... fingere crimen
quod* recur, and so does the charge of sloth (*desidia, mora*; cf. *ignaui*,
3.11.3). But the development of the two poems is very different: after
femina in the first line of 3.11 Cynthia is not only not named, she is
not mentioned. She has, with Propertius, become an *exemplum** (6),
the fitting start of a list of dominant women from myth and history.
Such a list recalls the *Catalogue of Women*, a now fragmentary* poem
by the Alexandrians' favourite model, Hesiod (on which see the Loeb
edition, vol. 2, and Hunter (ed.) 2005). As he will again in 3.19, P.
extends his catalogue for its own sake and does not return to Cynthia;
but here he moves on to contemporary politics, to Antony and
Cleopatra, and to the Roman who defeated them and did not succumb to Cleopatra's charms.

The opening lines present P. as enslaved, and the notion of *seruitium* surfaces repeatedly in the poem, as the women overcome and
control men and the world around them (9, 16, 19–20, 26, 30, 32,
49): for discussion of *seruitium amoris*, see 3.6 intro.

1–2 The poet at play: after a poem that begins *Mirabar, quidnam* we
find one that begins **Quid mirare** (= *miraris*). For address of an
unspecified second person (reprised in *tu*, 8, but thereafter forgot-
ten), cf. 4.2, 4.8.1, and a number of fragments from Book 2 (e.g.
2.4.1–4, 2.17.5–10). The plural is used in openings at 2.1.1, 3.13.1,
4.6.5–7; generic addressees in verse 71 (*nauita*) and at, e.g., 2.8.2
amice, 3.5.14 *stulte*, 4.1.1 *hospes*.   **uersat:** 'governs' (*OLD*
6b): cf. 3.17.12, 4.5.63 *animum nostrae dum uersat Acanthis
amicae* [while Acanthis controlled the mind of my mistress].
addictum sub sua iura uirum: 'a man indentured into her power':

addico can mean 'assign the custody of a debtor to his creditor' (*OLD* 1b); more generally it can simply mean 'enslave' (*OLD* 6b).

3–4 crimina ... ignaui capitis: 'charges of (being) a slothful creature [*lit.* head]': the genitive is used to convey the nature of the charges (G&L §361.2).   **quod:** 'on the grounds that': i.e. these are the charges: hence the subjunctive *nequeam*.   **fracto rumpere uincla iugo:** for the yoke of love, see 3.24.28 n.; heroines impose them on men at Ov. *Her.* 6.97, 9.6. 'Bonds' of love appear also at 3.20.23 (n.) and 3.15.10 (an embrace).

7–8 ista uerba: 'those words of yours', i.e. 'charges like that'. **praeterita ... iuuenta:** 'in my bygone youth', i.e. 'in the past when I was young': P. describes such a change of attitude at 1.1.3, 2.3.47–50. **exemplo disce ... meo:** P. presents himself as a source of understanding to others repeatedly in Books 1 (especially Gallus in 1.5, 10; Ponticus in 1.7, 9), and 2 (e.g. Lynceus in 2.34). At 1.15.24 he offers Cynthia the chance to become a *nobilis historia* like a Calypso or Hypsipyle grieving over the lover's departure; at 2.3.42 she is a possible *exemplum** for artists; here he casts himself as the first in a sequence of *exempla*.

9–12 Colchis: 'the Colchian woman', i.e. Medea, a princess with magical powers from Colchis, east of the Black Sea. She enabled the Greek hero Jason to yoke fire-breathing bulls (*flagrantes tauros*), and to sow the ground with dragon's teeth from which sprang up armed warriors, and by lulling the dragon guarding it to sleep she helped him take the Golden Fleece (*aurea lana*, 12): Apollonius, *Arg.* 3.1026–4.211; Ov. *Met.* 7.7–158. Jason later abandoned her, as is told in various *Medea* plays (3.19.17 n.). The poet focuses not on her erotic power but on her ability to control her world through intelligence and magic. All the actions are here attributed to her, not Jason. **adamantina ... iuga:** 'adamantine yokes': cf. 4. Adamant was the hardest of all substances ('unconquerable' in Greek), used for the yokes so they withstand the fire of the bulls.   **proelia seuit:** 'sowed (the seeds of) battle'.   **feros hiatus:** lit. 'the savage gapings', i.e. 'the savagely gaping jaws'.   **Aesonias ... domos:** 'to the house of Aeson [Jason's father]': accusative of motion towards, without a preposition, as is normal with *domum* and frequent in poetry after *ire* (cf. 2.8.24 *Thebanam ire... domum*; Verg. *Ecl.* 1.64 *ibimus Afros*; Austin on *Aen.* 1.2).

13–16 ausa: supply *est*. **Maeotis...Penthesilea:** 'Penthesilea from lake Maeotis', that is the sea of Azov, north of the Black Sea. Penthesilea was queen of the Amazons, who fought with arrows on horseback. The *Aethiopis*, a lost epic in the Trojan cycle (West 2003: 108–17), is said to have been joined to the end of the *Iliad* (after the burial of Hector) with the words ἦλθε δ' Ἀμαζών [There came an Amazon (i.e. Penthesilea)]. She fought beside the Trojans and was killed by Achilles. When he removed her helmet, he fell in love with her beauty. A famous vase by Exekias in the British Museum (GR 1836.2–24.127 Vase B210) shows Achilles and Penthesilea locking eyes at the moment of her death.   **Danaum...rates:** 'the ships of the Greeks'.   **aurea cui postquam nudauit cassida frontem:** 'after her golden helmet laid bare her face', i.e. by being removed. *cui* is possessive dative.   **uicit uictorem candida forma uirum:** a classic application in the erotic sphere of the turning of tables: the dominant figure himself becomes subservient; cf. Ov. *Her.* 9.2 *uictorem uictae succubuisse queror* (Deïanira complains that Hercules has succumbed to Iole; cf. 17–20 n.).

17–20 Hercules' period as Omphale's slave is a powerful example of the thesis being propounded here. Where the cause of the enslavement is given, it is usually a punishment (for the murder of Iphitus); but here it is a consequence of the beauty of the 'Lydian girl'. For accounts in which Omphale dresses Hercules in women's clothing and makes him spin wool while she wears his lion-skin and brandishes his club, see 4.9.47–50; Ov. *Her.* 9.53–118, *Fast.* 2.303–58. As Antony had idenitifed himself with Hercules (Plutarch, *Ant.* 4, 60.5; cf. Griffin 1985: 32–47 = *JRS* 67 (1977), 87–105), these lines can be seen to look ahead to 29ff.   **quin etiam:** 'nay, too', 'on top of that': this is Heinsius' reading for the transmitted *Omphalē*, which is tautological* (with *Lydia puella* following) and involves a metrical oddity: in order to scan, the long *ē* would have to be shortened before the vowel of *in*; such correption* is common in Homer, rare in Latin poetry, and in elegy is only securely attested at Ov. *Am.* 2.13.21 *făuĕ Īlīthÿĭă* (which also involves a Greek name).   **in tantum formae...honoris:** 'to such distinction of beauty', looking ahead to

ut (19).   **Gygaeo tincta...lacu**: 'bathed in Gyges' lake': a
lake in Lydia near Sardis (*Il.* 2.865, 20.390; Plin. *Nat.* 5.110), associated with the gold-bearing river Pactolus, whence king Gyges and his
successors drew their wealth (3.18.28 n.). The implication is that
Omphale's beauty has come from the golden waters of the lake (cf.
4.7.85 *aurea Cynthia*); for water as a source of pigmentation, see
3.13.16 n.   **statuisset**: the verb is in the subjunctive because it
stands in a relative clause which is part of the result clause (*ut...
traheret*): G&L §629.   **columnas**: the 'Pillars of Hercules', set
up by the hero at the straits of Gibraltar to celebrate his removal of
monsters from the (Mediterranean) world (*pacato orbe*). Note how
the hero's self-assertion is placed in the epic hexameter, his adopting
of a female role in the pentameter.   **traheret** is used of drawing the wool from the distaff in the spinning process.   **mollia
pensa**: 'soft quantities [i.e. of wool]'. The epithet sets the feminine
activity of spinning against the hard hands of the hero (cf. 3.1.19 n.);
the effect is compounded by the predominance of nasal consonants in
the second half in contrast to the dentals of *tam dura traheret*.

21–6 Semiramis was queen of Nineveh in the 9th century, and a
founder of Babylon (Strabo 2.1.31). As with Medea in 9–12 there is
no reference to her sexual power here; her mighty public achievements are stressed instead. However, (as is clearly the case with
Medea) informed readers are invited to pick up the implication:
when she appears at Ov. *Am.* 1.5.11 it is because of her beauty and
sexual availability; and at a number of places Diodorus' historical
account links Semiramis' power to her sexuality—Onnes, her first
husband, is absolutely enslaved by her (Diod. 2.5.2). She has a similar
effect on Ninus (2.6.9ff.), and after his death, as sole sovereign, she
takes her pleasure with handsome soldiers, and then has them killed
(2.13.4). All four of the catalogued women have qualities that will be
displayed by Cleopatra, as queen, and in her relations with Roman
leaders. Domination by a woman is a fate the poet shares with the
whole world, it seems—except Augustus.   **statuit**: cf. *statuisset* (19). Fedeli (on 16) notes how the separate items in the list are
bound together by repeated vocabulary: *feros* (11), *ferox* (13); *aurea*
(12, 15; and cf. 18); *forma* (16), *formae* (17); this example is especially
effective in that it shows Semiramis performing the action of a hero.

cocto...aggere: 'with a baked mass' i.e. a wall of baked brick. The balanced structure of the line is appropriate to the description of a well-built wall.   **ut duo in aduersum mitti per moenia currus | nec possent tacto stringere ab axe latus**: 'so that two chariots could be sent in opposite directions along the walls and be able not to scrape the side with the touching of an axle-hub'. *possent* is understood in both lines, and *nec* in the pentameter negates *stringere* rather than *possent*. The detail about the chariots is recorded also by Diodorus (2.7.4) and Curtius (5.1.25).   **Euphraten**: though Semiramis' tale belongs in prose genres, history, and romance (Ctesias' lost *Persica* and the fragmentary* Ninus romance: see S. A. Stephens and J. J. Winkler, *Ancient Greek Novels: the Fragments* (Princeton, 1995), 23–71), she shows epic prowess in founding and conquering cities; and the river she controls is the one familiar from Callimachus' rejection of epic scale (*Hymn* 2.108 [C]). **medium quam condidit arcis**: 'through the middle of the city which she established': for *medius* with the genitive, see *OLD* 1. **subdere caput**: 'bow its head'. Semiramis' involvement with the capture of Bactra is described in Diodorus 2.6.

27–8 There is a slight problem here: all the males charged so far have been heroes; the male to be arraigned climactically in 28 is a god. How illogical then to say 'For why should I force heroes to face the charge, why gods?'. Rothstein was probably right to take 27 as a signing off device ('<Enough,> for why should I talk of heroes, why of gods? What of Antony and Cleopatra?'), with 28 as a parenthesis, economically making good the lack of gods on the charge-sheet, and comically belittling Jupiter, the obvious climax to such a list.   **nam**: the conjunction can be used to signify that a matter is to be passed over: G&L §498.4 cites Cic. *de Oratore* 1.18 *nam quid ego de actione ipsa plura dicam?* ('for why should I say more about delivery itself?', after discussion of other aspects of the orator's craft).   **crimina**: cf. 3. P. has taken on the rejected stance of the prosecuting addressee.   **Iuppiter infamat seque suamque domum**: Jupiter's notorious and varied love life is referred to here. He brings disgrace on his house with his sexual susceptibility, just as a Roman might. This mimics the social comedy present in the Homeric epics (*Iliad* 1.493–611, *Od.* 8.266–366), continued by

Apollonius (*Arg.* 3.7–155), Ovid (*Fast.* 5.17–34, 6.21–90; *Met.* 3.318–38) and even Vergil (*Aen.* 4.90–128).

29–30 quid modo qui nostris opprobria nexerit armis: 'what of the man who recently bound insults to our arms', i.e. involved Roman arms in a disgraceful conflict. For the historical background, see pp. 16–17. Baehrens' *qui* for the transmitted *quae* causes this line to refer to Antony (cf. 2.16.37 *cerne ducem, modo qui,* 'look at the leader who recently'), not Cleopatra, who is added in the pentameter (*et...femina*: Augustan poets never use the name Cleopatra). There has been no condemnation of Jason, Achilles, Hercules, or of Propertius himself; and it is not clear what condemnation there is of Antony; his involvement with *armis* brings *opprobria*, but his subservience to Cleopatra is part of the natural order. Indeed 'Propertius' poetry shows some affinity for the defeated man whose public reputation of devotion to a woman at the expense of the state made him an attractive model for the elegiac lover' (Welch 2005: 125). One can, however, observe that the poem will move from an initial endorsement of the proposition that it is understandable for a man to be enslaved by a woman to the final celebration of one man (Caesar) who was not enslaved.   **famulos inter...trita suos:** 'ground at by her slaves': for the word order, see p. 40. The verb *tero* is used, with some coarseness, of sexual intercourse (3.20.6 n.; *OLD* 1b; Adams 1987: 183). For Cleopatra as uncontolled and insatiable in her passion, see Hor. *Odes*, 1.37.9–12, Dio 51.15.4.

31–2 coniugii obsceni pretium: '(as) the price of her obscene marriage': for the sentiment and construction compare Flor. 2.21.2 (*mulier Aegyptia ab ebrio imperatore pretium libidinum Romanum imperium petit* [the Egyptian woman sought the Roman empire from the drunken general as the price of his pleasures]), *eleg. in Maec.* 53.   **addictos in sua regna patres:** 'senators indentured into her sovereignty': cf. 2—Cleopatra 'has done to Rome just what Cynthia does to Propertius' (Stahl 1985: 239). The two consuls and possibly as many as 300 senators had left Rome to join Antony in 32 BC (see p. 16).

33–8 A digression, inveighing against the damage done to Rome by Egyptian immorality. Here begins a passage that in its transmitted

form contains an extraordinary sequence of second-person verbs
(some without vocatives) and vocatives (some without second-person
verbs); emendation is required but is especially uncertain when there
is such a concatenation of problems.

33–5 Alexandria and Memphis were the two chief cities of Egypt and
stand for the whole country. The verb 'to be' should be supplied in
33: 'guilty Alexandria is...'.   **totiens:** i.e. in the Alexandrian
Wars fought by Julius Caesar and by Octavian against Antony
and Cleopatra.   **nostro...malo:** predicative dative, 'to our
misfortune'.   **Memphi:** Greek   vocative   of   *Memphis*.
tres tua Pompeio detraxit harena triumphos: 'your sand stole away
three triumphs from Pompey'. After his defeat by Julius Caesar at the
battle of Pharsalus (48 BC), Pompey the Great fled to Egypt and was
treacherously killed there on a boat near the coast. His head was cut
off and the rest of his body was thrown naked out of the boat. It
was soon cremated on the shore (Lucan 8.712–872; Plutarch, *Pomp.*
79–80). Hence *harena*. Vergil's picture of Priam's headless corpse on
the shore was designed to evoke Pompey's death (*Aen.* 2.557–8,
reworked by Lucan at 1.685–6). He had celebrated triumphs for
his victories in Africa over the enemies of Sulla, in Spain over
Sertorius, and over Mithradates, king of Pontus. *Pompeio* is dative
of disadvantage (3.1.21 n.), like *tibi* in 36.

36–8 Roma: the vocative sets Rome against *Memphi* (= Egypt).
notam: 'mark of disgrace' (*OLD* 4c).   **issent Phlegraeo
melius quam ibi funera campo:** 'death would have come better on
the Phlegraean fields than there', i.e. than in Egypt. If the conjecture
quam ibi is correct, the *Phlegraeus campus* will refer to Thessaly, where
the battle of Pharsalus, in which Pompey was defeated, was fought. If
Pompey had died there, he would not have fled to Egypt and involved
Rome with Cleopatra: though P. does not refer to Julius Caesar's affair
with her (she bore him a son and was residing in Rome when he was
assassinated), the Medea and Semiramis *exempla** have trained the
reader to look for unmentioned affairs. The 'Phlegraean plain' is
where the battle between the gods and the giants took place (2.1.39,
3.9.48; Ov. *Met.* 10.151). This is placed in Thessaly by the ancient
commentator Servius (on *Aen.* 3.578), but the phrase could have two
other possible meanings in this context: (a) on a battlefield of the Civil

War: the association of gigantomachy* with civil war is regularly implicit (3.9.48 n.), but explicit at Statius, *Siluae* 5.3.196; (b) the volcanic area of Campania where Pompey was dangerously ill in 50 BC, leading Cicero to make the point that it would have been fortunate if he had died then rather than later by the hands of slaves (*Tusc. Disp.* 1.86). P. is likely to be aware of both possibilities: (a) works here; and the reader is teased into thinking (b) might. The transmitted *melius tibi* would lead to the meaning: 'better if death had come to you on the Phlegraean plain', with *tibi* addressed to Pompey; but a vocative is lacking and *tibi* has been directed at Rome in the previous line. **uel sua si socero colla daturus erat:** 'even if he was going to bow his neck to his father-in-law'. To seal their power-sharing agreement in 59 BC, Pompey married Caesar's daughter Julia; though she died in 54, well before the war between them started, the marriage is often characterized as between *socer* and *gener* (father-in-law and son-in-law): e.g. *Aen.* 6.830–1, Lucan 1.289–90. The phrase *colla dare* seems designed to recall the cutting off of Pompey's head and *socero* the presentation of the head to a disgusted Julius Caesar by the agents of Ptolemy (Lucan 9.1010–1108, Plutarch, *Pomp.* 80.1–5).

39–40 incesti meretrix regina Canopi: Canopus was a town on the western mouth of the Nile. Though it stands for Egypt as a whole (cf. 33–4), it is relevant to the rest of the line: like other ports it was known for its brothels (NB *meretrix*) and loose living (Sen. *Ep.* 51.3; Statius, *Siluae* 3.2.111; Juvenal 15.46).   **una Philippei sanguinis usta nota:** 'woman uniquely branded with the mark of Philip's blood'. Cleopatra was of Macedonian descent; hence the association with Philip, the father of Alexander the Great. The text and meaning of this line remain very uncertain (see *Cynthia*).

41–2 ausa: the same word is used of Penthesilea's entry into the Trojan War in 13; but also of Cleopatra in Hor. *Odes* 1.37.25, at a very different moment in her story, her boldness in committing suicide (cf. 53–4):

> **ausa** et iacentem uisere regiam
> uultu sereno, fortis et asperas
>   tractare serpentes, ut atrum
>   corpore conbiberet uenenum,
> deliberata morte ferocior

Having dared with a calm expression to see her palace lying in ruins, bold to handle fierce snakes, so she might drink the fatal poison in with her body, the fiercer for having decided on death.

es: a conjectural addition to the transmitted text: Cleopatra appears in the second person in 51, and it looks as though *meretrix regina* (39) must be vocative to lead up to this. *es*, which would be easily lost (3.7.1), clarifies the grammar quickly. **latrantem ... Anubin:** the Egyptian god Anubis was portrayed with a dog's head. In his description of the battle of Actium on Aeneas' shield Vergil makes similar play with the contrast between the Roman and Egyptian gods (*Aen.* 8.698–9): *latrator Anubis | contra Neptunum.* **Tiberim Nili cogere ferre minas:** 'to force Tiber to endure the threats of Nile': note the juxtaposition of the opposed rivers.

43–4 pellere: 'to drive out' or 'defeat', but playing on the usage with percussion instruments (*OLD* 1b). **tubam ... sistro:** the Roman war-trumpet is set against the rattle used in the worship of the Egyptian goddess Isis: cf. *Aen.* 8.696 *regina ... patrio uocat agmina sistro* [the queen summons her forces with her native sistrum]. **baridos et contis rostra Liburna sequi:** 'and to pursue the beaks of Liburnian ships with the poles of her barge': *baridos* is the genitive, Greek in form, of *baris* (= a Nile barge). Liburnian ships were light galleys modelled on those used by the piratical Liburni, an Illyrian tribe. Octavian had used them successfully at Actium: cf. Hor. *Epod.* 1.1–2 *Ibis Liburnis inter alta nauium, | amice, propugnacula* [You will go, my friend [Maecenas], in Liburnian vessels amid the lofty ramparts of ships (i.e. the enormous boats of Antony)], *Odes* 1.37.30. *rostra* evokes the Forum, where the 'beaks' of enemy ships adorned the speakers' platform (thus called the *rostra*: Livy 8.14.12).

45–6 conopia: 'mosquito nets', evoking Hor. *Epod.* 9.16. **Tarpeio ... saxo:** Traitors were thrown down to their deaths from the Tarpeian crag on the Capitoline Hill (probably where the north-eastern summit, the Arx, overlooks the Forum). Elegy 4.4 will tell the aetiology* of the name, derived from the Vestal Virgin Tarpeia who betrays her city out of love for the Sabine leader Tatius; he has her killed for her treachery (cf. also Livy 1.11.6–9). The contrast between rugged Rome and decadent Egypt has become scornful, perhaps funny.   **iura dare**: the act of a Roman magistrate (cf. 3.9.24). Dio 50.5.4 describes this as Cleopatra's intention. The short *e* scans long before the two consonants at the start of the next word: see p. 34. Many editors supply *et* before *statuas*, but P. freely uses asyndeton* in lists, and postpones* *et* to third place only in the second half of a pentameter or after set phrases (*quo magis et*, 1.4.15).   **statuas inter et arma Mari**: the trophies of Gaius Marius' victories over Jugurtha, the Cimbri and the Teutones, were set up on the Capitol, removed by Sulla, and brought back there by Julius Caesar (Velleius 2.43.4; Suetonius, *Diu. Jul.* 11; Plutarch, *Caes.* 6). *inter* regularly stands between two nouns that it governs (e.g. Hor. *Odes* 3.23.10 *quercus inter et ilices* [between oaks and ilexes]; *Aen.* 2.632 *flammam inter et hostes* [between fire and the enemy]).

47–50 quid nunc iuuat: 'what help is it now (that...)': the subject of *iuuat* is the accusative and infinitive noun-clause *Tarquinii fractas... esse secures*. Tarquinius Superbus (Tarquin the Proud) was the last king of Rome, driven out by anger at the tyrannical behaviour of himself and his son (Livy 1.56.7–60.3; Ov. *Fast.* 2.685–852). The kings were attended by twelve 'lictors' (Liv. 1.8.2), men carrying axes surrounded by bundles of wooden rods; the practice was then taken over by the magistrates of the Republic (3.9.23 n.; Livy 2.5.8, where the rods and axes are used for punishment by the first consuls).   **nomine...simili**: the 'similar name' is of course Superbus.   **si mulier patienda fuit**: getting rid of the kings will have been pointless if Rome must endure a *meretrix regina*: it is as if the war is still going on (*nunc*, 46), the poet's horrified excitement carrying the thought over from one couplet into the next. *fuit* directs our attention to the moment of danger in the past (cf. *fui*, 55): with the gerundive there is no need for a subjunctive verb (Kennedy §441b).   **cane, Roma, triumphum**: Roman triumphs were greeted by the cry 'io triumphe' from the crowd: Tib. 2.5.118 [= Ov. *Trist.* 4.2.52] *miles 'io' magna uoce 'triumphe' canet* [the soldier will sing 'io triumphe' loudly]; Ov. *Am.* 1.2.34; Hor. *Odes* 4.2.49–50. Here the city is invited to celebrate the conquest of Cleopatra, as if it were just being announced; but the triumph has already taken place, on the second and third days of the triple triumph in Sextile (later known as August) 29 BC. **longum Augusto salua precare diem**: along with the celebration of victory comes a prayer for 'long life' for Augustus, now that Rome is 'safe'. For once, P. has moved away from his stance as an elegist, who approves of male subservience to women (or at least regards it as inevitable), and has adopted the view of a writer of Augustan panegyric: celebration must continue. But the sincerity of the enthusiasm must be judged against the background of passages such as 1.21–2, 2.15.41–8, 3.4–5.

51–2 The poet returns to addressing Cleopatra. **fugisti tamen**: i.e. despite your audacity (as described in 41–6), you fled: verses 47–50 are a digression. For the flight cf. Hor. *Odes* 1.37.16–20. **timidi…Nili**: compare and contrast the personification* of the Nile at *Aen.* 8.711–13:

> contra autem magno maerentem corpore Nilum
> pandentemque sinus et tota ueste uocantem
> caeruleum in gremium latebrosaque flumina uictos.

But opposite <Vulcan had depicted> the enormous Nile grieving [i.e. at Egypt's defeat], and opening up his chest, and with all his clothing summoning the conquered into his dark lap and his streams that offer a chance to hide.

uaga flumina: 'wandering': the reference is to the many streams of the Nile delta or the distance the river travels (Lucan 9.752 *Nilum…per rura uagantem*). **accepere tuae Romula uincla manus**: an inversion of what has earlier been presented as the natural order (n.b. *uincla*, 4; *manu*, 20): a male force imposes bonds on a woman. *Romula* is a shortened form of *Romulea* (4.4.26), = 'of Romulus', the first king of Rome, hence 'Roman'.

53–4 bracchia spectasti sacris admorsa colubris: 'you watched your arms bitten by the sacred snakes': Cleopatra committed suicide by applying asps to herself. *colubris* could be understood as instrumental ablative or dative of the agent (G&L §215, 354). For the short *a* of *bracchia* before the opening two consonants of *spectasti*, see 67, and p. 34. Horace also pictures Cleopatra observing her own downfall (*Odes* 1.37.25–9, cited on 41): both poets may have been influenced by the image of the queen carried in the triumph, with snakes attached (Plutarch, *Ant.* 86, Dio 51.21.8). *spectaui* is transmitted, but reference to the triumph and P. himself is intrusive here. Cf. also *Aen.* 8.697 *necdum etiam geminos a tergo respicit angues* [not yet does she see the twin snakes behind her].   **et trahere occultum membra soporis iter**: 'and your limbs drinking in the hidden advance of sleep [i.e. death]': for the use of *trahere* cf. 3.7.52, and *OLD* 7.

55–6 The speaker is Cleopatra: in P.'s imagination even her wine-sodden tongue had (before her death) acknowledged the power of Octavian.   **non hoc, Roma, fui tanto tibi ciue uerenda**: 'I was not to be feared when you had this great citizen [i.e. Octavian]'. *hoc tanto ciue* is an ablative absolute ('there being such a citizen'); and *tibi* functions both as possessive dative with this and dative of the agent with *uerenda*.

57–8 septem urbs alta iugis: Rome is often characterized by reference to the seven hills enclosed by the Servian wall (Capitoline, Palatine, Aventine, Caelian, Esquiline, Viminal, Quirinal).   **Verse 58** is omitted in the oldest manuscript N; in its transmitted form (*femineas timuit territa Marte minas* [terrified by war <the city> feared the threats of a woman] it is both repetitive (*timuit territa*) and imprecise (*Marte* lacks an epithet). Moreover, it does not fit with the flow of thought here. The threat of Cleopatra has built up to a climax in 49, only to be broken by the entry of Augustus; there is a recapitulation in the description of her defeat (51–4), and in the assertion of Augustus' supremacy in the list of heroes who have made and protected Rome's greatness (55 ff.). With 49 the moment of danger is past, and, bar 58, all that follows serves to heighten and celebrate Caesar's triumph. The obvious conclusion is that the original has been lost and the transmitted verse is a medieval attempt to repair the couplet. The sense of the lost line could have been something on the lines of: '(the city) stands, not to be cast down by human hand' (F. H. Sandbach, *CQ* 2 (1962), 264). (If the lost line ended with *manu* as 68 does, the homoeoteleuton* would explain the omission and transposition of 65–8; alternatively the five lines might have been lost together, and only the two complete couplets restored to the text, though in the wrong place.)

65–8 The transposition of 67–8 before 59–60 has been widely accepted: 59–60 lacks the construction that 67–8 provides. In addition 65–6 interrupts the link between the memorials of 61–4 and 69; it makes a good hinge between the Rome of 57 and the review of past memorialized achievements, which are belittled in comparison with the victory at Actium (67–8, 59–64).

65–6 haec di condiderant, haec di quoque moenia seruant: as often in such balanced phrasing there is a word (*moenia*) that should be taken with both clauses: cf. *hiemis* and *natasse* in 3.12.32 *totque hiemis noctes totque natasse dies.*   **uix timeat saluo Caesare Roma Iouem.** If Caesar can master Cleopatra, he's certainly the equal of Jupiter, famously subordinate to the power of love. According to the poem's argument, he alone is capable of avoiding female domination, a point hinted at by *saluo* (cf. 2.9.3–4 *Penelope poterat bis denos salua per annos | uiuere* [Penelope managed to live unharmed (i.e. faithful) for twenty years]; Dio 51.12 presents Cleopatra as attempting to sway Caesar emotionally, but he is quite unmoved 'and said nothing affectionate'). In his lack of susceptibility to Cleopatra, he is contrasted with the submissive heroes, most directly with Antony, implicitly with his adoptive father Julius; but in his virtual superiority to the infamous Jupiter he is raised to the level of—Propertius himself: cf. 2.13.16 *possum inimicitias tunc ego ferre Iouis* [then (if Cynthia returns my love) I can bear the enmity of Jove himself] echoed at 2.34.18.

67 nunc ubi Scipiadae classes, ubi signa Camilli. The poet looks back on Rome's tradition of military greatness, but in asking where they are, he implies that in comparison with Actium they count for nothing.   **Scipiadae classes:** 'the fleets of Scipio': *Scipiadae* is genitive. As *Scīpiō* does not fit in hexameters, *Scīpĭădēs* is the standard form in poetry; found first in the second-century satirist Lucilius (394, 1139 Marx), it recurs in passages of Lucretius (3.1034) and the *Aeneid* (6.843) that tell of the family's greatness in war. The elder Scipio Africanus sailed to Africa with an army that brought about the end of the Second Punic War with Hannibal (59; Liv. 28.45, 29.24–7); his adoptive grandson Scipio Aemilianus was the commander who defeated Carthage in the Third Punic War and destroyed the city (146).   **signa Camilli:** for the military hero Camillus, see 3.9.31 n. He recovered Rome from the Gauls and regained the standards (*signa*) captured at the river Allia (*Aen.* 6.825 *referentem signa Camillum*). Camillus and the Scipios were

paired already by Vergil at *Geo.* 2.169–70 *magnosque Camillos,* |
Scipiadas duros bello et te, maxime Caesar [<Italy produced> great
Camilli, the Scipios tough in war, and you, Caesar, the greatest].

68 aut modo Pompeia, Bospore, capta manu: the word *signa* (67)
must be understood with *capta*: 'or those recently captured, Bosporus, by Pompey's hand [*or* band]'. In 65 BC, in the Third Mithri-
datic War, Pompey had finally defeated Mithradates, King of Pontus
(on the south coast of the Black Sea), and he retreated to another
power-base, Cimmerian Bosporus (on the northern coast); there in
63 BC during a revolt led by Pharnaces, one of his sons, he was
assassinated (Livy, *Periochae* 102). Pharnaces then accepted Rome's
sway. It is not clear what part of this story P. evokes.

59–60 After Roman victories the text turns to those defeated; *nunc ubi*
<*sunt*> continues to govern the list of nouns.   <**fera tela**>
Syphacis: Syphax, king of Numidia, sided with Carthage in the Second
Punic War and was defeated by Scipio in 203 BC. The *exempli gratia*
suggestion *fera tela* avoids the clunking reiteration of *monumenta* in
successive hexameters.   **Pyrrhi:** Pyrrhus, king of Epirus
(north-western Greece), after success in battles in southern Italy in
280–79, was eventually defeated by the Romans at Malventum in 275
BC. After this event, the town was renamed Beneventum.

61–4 P. now lists other heroic actions commemorated in Rome; the first
two involve horses and self-sacrifice.   **Curtius expletis statuit
monumenta lacunis:** 'Curtius set up a memorial by filling in the chasm'.
Marcus Curtius rode fully armed into a chasm (*lacunis*, poetic plural, like
monumenta) that had opened up in the forum: soothsayers had said that
sacrifice of the thing 'in which the Roman people were most powerful'
(*quo plurimum populus Romanus posset*) would ensure that the Roman
state lasted for ever (Livy 7.6; other aetiologies* are given by Varro, *Ling.
Lat.* 5.148–50). Stones were later laid on the spot, and Ovid mentions
altars (of which traces may have been found by archaeologists): *Fast.*
6.403 *Curtius ille lacus siccas qui sustinet aras* | *nunc solida est tellus, sed
lacus ante fuit* [the *Lacus Curtius* which supports dry altars is now solid
ground but was previously a lake]. In using *statuit* of Curtius' descent P.'s
language is pointedly paradoxical.   **admisso…equo:** 'on a
galloping horse'. The Decius Mus of three successive generations

vowed himself and the enemy to death (*deuotio*), rode alone into the thick of the foe and was killed, thus securing a Roman victory (Cicero, *Tusc. Disp.* 1.89, *Fin.* 2.61 *equo admisso in mediam aciem Latinorum irruebat*): at Vesuvius in 340 (Livy 8.9), at Sentinum in 295 (Livy 10.28–9), at Ausculum, against Pyrrhus, in 279 (but there are problems with this third case, not least that the battle was not won: see T. J. Cornell, *CQ* 37 [1987], 514–16).   **rupit proelia:** 'broke (the enemy's) battle(-line)s'.   **Coclitis:** just after the expulsion of the Tarquins, Horatius Cocles saved Rome from the Etruscans by holding the bridge to the city until it was broken down; he then plunged into the Tiber (Livy 2.10; n.b. the first of Macaulay's *Lays of Ancient Rome*). We know nothing about 'the path of Cocles'.   **est cui cognomen coruus habere dedit:** 'there is a man to whom a crow has given its name to keep'. *habere* is an epexegetic* (i.e. explanatory) infinitive. When Marcus Valerius was serving against the Gauls in 348 BC, a crow perched on his helmet and harried the Gaul he was fighting (Livy 7.26.2–5). As a memorial *Coruus*, or its adjectival form *Coruinus*, became his *cognomen* (often a name derived from an achievement), and thus that of his family.

69–70 Leucadius … Apollo: the temple of Apollo above the white cliffs of Leucas, from which the flight of Cleopatra and Antony's forces after the battle of Actium was visible; but P. perhaps conflates this with another temple at Actium itself: cf. Suetonius' account of the memorialization (*Augustus* 18.2): 'So that the memory of the victory at Actium might be more celebrated even in the future, he founded the city of Nicopolis near Actium and set up games there to happen at four-yearly intervals, and having increased the size of the old temple of Apollo he adorned the place he had used for his camp with naval spoils and dedicated it to Neptune and Apollo.' Nicopolis ('Victory-city') was on the north side of the inlet to the Ambracian Gulf; Actium itself and the temple to Apollo on the south side; the island of Leucas a little to the south-west. Vergil apparently mentions all three places in his account of Aeneas's visit at *Aen.* 3.274–89.   **tantum operis belli sustulit una dies:** 'a single day of war took away so much labour': cf. Ennius, *Annales* fr. 258 Sk. *multa dies in bello conficit unus* [many things does one day bring about in war]. For *tantum operis,* cf. 3.3.4, where the phrase refers to the mammoth enterprise undertaken by the poet. The echo implies that a single day has not only brought warfare to an end; it has destroyed the potential for military epic. All that is possible now is the composition of Augustan panegyric. It is less attractive to take *belli* with *tantum operis* ('a single day took away so much labour of war'), as that creates a phrase with a double genitive.

71–2 The poem does not revert directly to the dominance of women, but ends with Caesar. The poet addresses a sailor about to make for, or set out from, harbour on the Ionian sea, from which Caesar has swept Rome's enemies: cf. p. 14, Hor. *Odes* 4.5.19 *pacatum uolitant per mare nauitae* [sailors fly over a peaceful sea], Suetonius, *Aug.* 98.2. The nautical language recalls that of the metapoetic* couplets 3.3.23–4, 3.9.35–6. P. alludes to one of the epigrams in the new Posidippus papyrus* (39.1–2, 7–8 A.-B.):

> Καὶ μέλλων ἅλα νηὶ περᾶν καὶ πεῖσμα καθάπτειν
> χερσόθεν, Εὐπλοίαι 'χαῖρε' δὸς Ἀρσινόηι, ...   2
> εἵνεκα καὶ χερσαῖα καὶ εἰς ἅλα δῖαν ἀφιεὶς
> εὐχὰς εὑρήσεις τὴν ἐπακουσομένην.   8

Both when you are about to cross the sea in a ship, or to fasten the cable from the shore, give 'greetings' to Arsinoe who brings a fair voyage, ... For this reason, heading both for dry land and for the divine sea, you will find that she will listen to your prayers.

Arsinoe has been replaced by the conqueror of her descendant: Rome is learning to treat its rulers as Alexandria treated the Ptolemies; and significant within this poem is that a male leader has replaced a female, the elegist's world turned upside-down.

[**5–6 uenturam melius praesagit nauita mortem**: 'A sailor better foresees coming death'. This is very vague (better than when, or than who?) and not integrated within the context. It is similar to a line in an inscribed poem, *CLE* 1552A.63 *uenturae citius dicant praesagia mortis*, a fact that helps protect the transmitted *uenturam...mortem* and confirms the commonplace nature of the couplet. As the pentameter is no better attuned to the context Georg's deletion is very likely to be right. The couplet will have originated in the margin, as a pair of *sententiae* designed to illustrate verse 8.   **uulneribus**: 'from his wounds'.]

Additional bibliography: W. R. Nethercut, *TAPhA* 102 (1971), 411–43; R. J. Baker, *Antichthon* 10 (1976), 56–62; G. Mader, 'Heroism and hallucination: Cleopatra in Horace *c.* 1.37 and Propertius 3.11', *GB* 16 (1989), 183–201; Stahl 1985: 234–47; J. L. Butrica, 'Propertius 3.11.33–8 and the death of Pompey', *CQ* 43 (1993), 342–6; Gurval 1995: 189–208; A. Tronson, *AClass* 42 (1999), 171–86; E. Fantham, in Günther (ed.) 2006: 196–8.

3.12

1–6: Could you bring yourself, Postumus, to abandon Galla and go to fight for Augustus in Parthia despite her pleas? A curse on all who greedily put war before love! 7–14: You shall suffer military hardships in the east; meanwhile she will waste away over rumours, fearing that your courage lead you to death at the hands of Persian archers or cavalry and your remains come back in an urn. 15–22: You are very fortunate in her chastity, and deserve a different wife. What will a girl do amid Rome's luxury when she is protected by no husband? Don't worry: she will not be seduced by gifts despite your hardness of heart. 23–38: Whenever you return she will embrace you: in his wife Postumus will be another Ulysses. He was not harmed by undergoing ten years of war and a fearful series of adventures. When he put an end to these by killing the suitors with his bow, it was not in vain, for his wife Penelope had sat faithfully at home. Aelia Galla outdoes Penelope.

In 1.6 Propertius refuses to leave Cynthia in Rome by taking a place in the cohort of Volcacius Tullus, who was governor of the province of Asia in 30–29 BC; the potential or actual separation of the two of them by travel is explored further in 1.8, 1.11–12, 1.17, 2.19. In 3.4–5 he takes as a given fact that he will remain in Rome when others go out to fight; but he continues to explore the fear of separation through service in the army with this poem and 4.3. In each he writes about a contemporary married couple, his sympathies emphatically with the wife, who remains at home, faithful and anxious. Poem 4.3 will have a distinctive feature: it takes the form of a letter written by Arethusa to her husband Lycotas. This became a major model for Ovid's *Heroides*, letters written by mythical heroines to husbands and

222 A Commentary on Propertius, Book 3

lovers from who they are separated. *Heroides* 1 has Penelope writing
to Ulysses in the twentieth year of his absence and thus displays a
debt to this poem too. P. was himself perhaps influenced by Horace,
Odes 3.7, where Gyges has been detained by stormy weather the other
side of the Adriatic, and his wife Asterie is first reassured of his
fidelity, then warned about her own behaviour.

The opening poem has given a summary of the *Iliad* and other
poems from the Trojan cycle; here we get a long if tendentious
paraphrase of the *Odyssey* to give emphatic point to the assertion
of the closing couplet.

1–2 Postume...Gallam: both were common names, and both were
later used by Martial (repeatedly) and Juvenal (6.21, 28, 377;
1.125–6) to give apparent identity to generic individuals. See
also on 38. *Postumus* conventionally refers to someone born
after his father's death; this resonance is used expressively by
Horace in *Odes* 2.14.1–2 *Eheu fugaces, Postume, Postume | labuntur
anni* [Alas, Postumus, Postumus, the fleeting years slip away].
This is one of six poems in Book 3 to have a named human
individual as addressee: the others are 3.6 (Lygdamus), 3.7
(Paetus), 3.9 (Maecenas), 3.22 (Tullus), 3.24 (Cynthia).
plorantem: the tearful Galla is marked from the first as an elegiac
figure (cf. 2.14.14, 4.3.26).   **miles et...sequi:** 'and as a
soldier to follow'.

3–4 tanti: 'of so great importance': genitive of value (G&L §380).
ulla...spoliati gloria Parthi: 'any glory gained from despoiling the
Parthian': lit. 'any glory of the despoiled Parthian': *Parthi* is defining
genitive, and a collective singular*, implying the whole group who
are so named. On the hostile relationship between Rome and the
Parthians see p. 9, 15, 3.4 intro.   **tantine...fuit | ne faceres
Galla multa rogante tua:** the structure is difficult to determine here,
and the text possibly corrupt. In *tantine ut lacrimes Africa tota fuit*
(3.20.4) *tantine* in a very similar context (commenting on a man's
departure from Rome for a province) leads on to a consecutive
clause. Normally the negative of consecutive *ut* is *ut non*; but *ne* is
also found (e.g. at Columella 5.6.12, Tacitus, *Ann.* 2.29.2, and especially in clauses that might be read as final, such as Hor. *Ars Poetica*
152), so we might translate 'worth so much that you not do many

things when your Galla asks you' (this would be easier with *cuncta*, 'everything', for *multa*). On the other hand, *ne* could straightforwardly introduce a negative indirect command after *rogante*: 'when your Galla is asking you much not to do it'. But what then is the force of *faceres*? For this construction we should surely read Heinsius' *fugeres* ('not to depart'); and *multa* will display an adverbial use of the neuter plural: 'much', i.e. 'repeatedly'.

5–6 si fas est: the poet softens the aggressiveness of his wish by acknowledging that it may not be 'right' (in accordance with divine law) to wish for the death of Postumus and his like. The alliteration on *s* beginning here is reinforced by an emphatic sequence of *ps* later in the couplet.   **auari:** 'greedy', i.e. for Parthian booty. The assumption about Postumus' motive allies this poem closely with 3.4, where much stress is put on the wealth of the eastern countries that Augustus is attacking.   **arma** enhances the link by recalling the first word of 3.4 (important too at 3.5.47): it also of course opens the *Aeneid*, a poem in which the hero forsakes the faithful bed of Dido in favour of Italy and the warfare he encounters there.

7–8 tamen: there are two possible ways to take this, not mutually exclusive. It could refer back, i.e. in spite of Galla's pleas in 4, or the curses on such behaviour in 5–6. Alternatively it could look ahead to 9: *tamen* and *quidem* can mark the different clauses in an antithetical or concessive sentence: 'While you…, yet she…'. Cf. 2.8.28 *mors inhonesta quidem, tu moriere tamen* [though the death be dishonourable, yet you shall die]; Ov. *Her.* 7.27–30; and for *tamen* = 'though' 3.15.35 n.   **immunda…lacerna:** 'in a grubby cloak'. P. evokes the discomfort of a military campaign with vivid detail: the implication is that a *lacerna* is no more his usual clothing than a *galea* is his drinking vessel. *immunda* is a conjecture for the transmitted *intecta* ('uncovered'), which has clearly arisen from a scribe's anticipating the following word *tectus*. *iniecta* ('thrown on') has been the correction generally favoured, but the participle contributes nothing to the sentence, and the conjecture ignores the cause of the error.   **uesane** = *insane* (the prefix *ue-* has a negative force, as in *uegrandis*, 'unbig' i.e. 'small'). P. uses such epithets elsewhere of love and lovers (cf. 1.1.26, 2.14.18, 2.15.29, 3.17.3), and this is a pointed inversion of the conventional judgement, as when he calls the Forum 'insane' at 4.1.134.   **galeā**: i.e. 'from your helmet'.   **Araxis**: the river Araxes on the Armenian-Median border flows into the Caspian. It appears as a symbol of Roman territorial ambition in the East at 4.3.35 and *Aeneid* 8.728 (the final item on Aeneas' shield).

9–14 quidem: 'on the other hand' (see on *tamen*, 7).   **ne**: 'for fear lest'. Like *neu* in 12 this has been postponed* to third position in its clause.   **uirtus**: Postumus' activity is focalized through Galla's eyes—but from the poet of 7–8 this reads like sarcasm. **amara tibi**: the *uirtus* may turn from a matter of pride to a cause of pain to Postumus: the vague expression here leads on to explicitness in 11–13. P. may have written not *tibi*, but *sibi*: it is Galla who will feel the real bitterness of her husband's death.   **laetentur caede**: to be understood also with *cataphractus* in the pentameter. *caedes* can mean 'blood' (*OLD* 4) as well as 'slaughter'. The Median arrows are personified* and imagined as rejoicing in the blood they have shed. Alternatively, *Medae sagittae* could mean 'Median archers' (by metonomy*; cf. *surdo remige*, 34).   **cataphractus**: an armoured soldier on an armoured horse, as *ferreus* and *armato... equo* make clear. For the armour of the Parthian cavalry, cf. 4.3.8; Sall. *Hist.* 4, fr. 64–6; Curtius 4.9.3. *armato* replaces the transmitted *aurato*: it would be strange for the horse's armour to be gilded, thus far outdoing its rider in splendour.   **aliquid de te flendum**: 'something of you to be mourned [*lit.* wept]'. The sense of *de* might initially be 'about', but *in urna* confirms the physical nature of *referatur* ('be brought back', rather than 'be reported'), and thus that *de* is partitive (*OLD* 10).   **sic redeunt illis qui cecidere locis**: 'so return the men who have fallen in those places': the matter-of-fact explanation implies Postumus' unwillingness to believe this simple truth.

15–16 in casta felix ... Galla: *es* is implied: 'you are fortunate in the chastity of Galla'.   **moribus his**: apparently ablative absolute (the non-existent present participle of *esse* being assumed) 'this being her behaviour [*or* character]'; but possibly equivalent to *coniuge alia <quam> moribus his <coniuge>* [a wife different from a wife of this character]. In view of Postumus' hardness of heart, Galla is too good for him.   **coniuge** reveals that Galla is married to Postumus, a point confirmed in 22.

17–18 quid faciet: 'what will a [*or* the] girl do?' The text interweaves the threat of infidelity with moments of reassurance.   **nullo munita ... marito:** 'protected by no husband'. The transmitted *timore*, here emended to *marito*, represents Galla as *un*fearful, which is clearly not the case.   **cum sit luxuriae Roma magistra suae:** 'when Rome is a teacher of its own lascivious ways'. *luxuriae* looks back to 3.5.3–6, 3.7, and ahead to 3.13. *suae* is a conjecture for *tuae*; an equally plausible change would be *sis* instead of *sit* (with *Roma* taken as a vocative).

19–20 securus eas: 'you may go without anxiety' (jussive subjunctive). P. uses *ire* with adjectives as a more dynamic alternative to *esse* (e.g. 2.1.8, 2.7.16, 2.34.45); but here there is an additional implication: 'to Parthia'.   **duritiae:** his hardness of heart in stubbornly rejecting her requests; but also his anti-elegiac preference for *arma* over love (see pp. 31–2; 3.1.20, 3.5.2 nn.).   **non erit illa memor:** she will forget not him, but his failure to be swayed by her words. Again the phrasing is suggestively threatening.

21–2 Here we find an evocation of the close of Tib. 1.3, a poem in which the elegist describes how, having followed Messalla as part of his cohort, he is stranded, ill, in Phaeacia, the mythical island visited by Odysseus (whose adventures he also recalls with a description of the eroticized underworld that will receive him if he dies: 57–82). He regrets the invention of travel, and looks forward to the day on which he returns to Delia's busy, sober household (like Cynthia's in 3.6):

> at tu casta precor maneas, sanctique pudoris
>   adsideat custos sedula semper anus. ...   82
> tum ueniam subito, nec quisquam nuntiet ante,
>   sed uidear caelo missus adesse tibi.   90
> tunc mihi, qualis eris, longos turbata capillos,
>   obuia nudato, Delia, curre pede.
> hoc precor, hunc illum nobis Aurora nitentem
>   luciferum roseis candida portet equis.

But you, I pray, are to remain chaste, and an old woman should sit constantly at your side, a careful guardian of your sacred chastity. ... Then

I shall suddenly come, and no one is to announce me in advance, but let me seem to you to be there sent down from heaven. Then whatever state you are in, your long hair in disorder, run to meet me, Delia, barefoot. This I pray for, let a fair dawn bring for us this shining day on her rose-red horses.

23–4 alter... Vlixes: 'another [*or* a second] Ulysses [*the Roman version of* Odysseus]'.   **miranda coniuge:** 'thanks to his wonderful wife': ablative of respect (G&L §397).   **non illi longae tot nocuere morae:** 'he was not harmed by so many long delays', the point being that his wife remained faithful, so all was well in the end. In apposition*, to *morae*, the following lines offer a resumé of the *Odyssey*, Odysseus' adventures as he seeks to return home and be reunited with Penelope. For similar summaries of Ulysses' adventures, see Eur. *Tro.* 433–43, [Tib.] 3.7.54–78. P. deviates from the *Odyssey* in the ordering of events: Homer places the Lotus-eaters between the Cicones and Polyphemus, the visit to the dead and the Sirens before Scylla and Charybdis. Such re-ordering happens in the Euripides passage and in P.'s synopses of other poems (e.g. Ennius, *Annales* at 3.3.7–12); moreover, the *Odyssey* itself had already broken away from chronological order, the hero narrating many of the stories in the reminiscences of Books 9–12.

25 castra decem annorum: 'the expedition of ten years', i.e. the Trojan War. Though it lasted ten years, it is given a strikingly small part in the list of delays.   **Ciconum mors, Ismara capta:** 'the death of the Cicones on the capture of Ismara': hendiadys*, lit. 'the death of the Cicones, captured Ismara'. The reference is to the first of Ulysses' adventures after leaving Troy (*Od.* 9.39–40: 'a wind carrying me from Ilium brought me to the Cicones, to Ismarus; here I sacked the city and killed them'). *capta* is an emendation of the transmitted *Calpe* (Gibraltar): the word would be abnormally isolated in the final foot, and the place does not feature in the *Odyssey*.

26 exustaeque tuae nox, Polypheme, genae: 'and the darkness of your burnt-out eye, Polyphemus': cf. *Od.* 9.318–466, where the hero effects an escape from Polyphemus' cave for himself and most of his crew by getting the man-eating monster drunk, and burning out his eye with his staff, sharpened and heated in the fire; Polyphemus cannot see them to take vengeance, but is still able to roll back the boulder at the mouth of the cave to let out his flock of enormous sheep, under whom they escape. The text given here (with *nox* rather than the transmitted *mox*) gives the Cyclops just one eye. While the *Odyssey* (unlike later versions) nowhere states that he had a single eye, the story of his blinding would not work were that not the case. *gena* usually means 'cheek' but for instances referring to the eyes see *OLD* 2; it is rare in the singular in any sense, but so used where the meaning requires it, as it does for a Cyclops.

27 Circae fraudes: Circe's deceit was in seeming to offer hospitality, while in fact perpetrating magic that turned her visitors into animals, in the case of Odysseus' crew into pigs. He himself survives with the help of a magic plant ('moly') and advice from Hermes; when he threatens her with his sword, Circe returns his men to human form, and becomes truly helpful and hospitable (to the extent that she invites Odysseus into her bed): *Od.* 10.210–405. But the stay with Circe lasts a full year (9.467–70), and the delay might well have harmed the hero.   **lotosque herbaeque tenaces**: 'and the retentive vegetation of the lotus' (hendiadys*). The vegetation is called *tenax* because the lotus deprived travellers of any desire to return home (including three of Odysseus' men: 9.83–104). *lotos* uses the nominative ending of the Greek second declension. *herbae tenaces* could also refer to the drugs used by Circe to make men forget their homeland (10.235–6), as Odysseus himself is in danger of doing (10.472–4).

28 Circe warns Odysseus about the monster Scylla and the whirlpool Charybdis at 12.85–126; the ship passes between them at 12.234–59, and, as they avoid the pull of Charybdis, a man is seized by each of Scylla's six mouths.   **alterna saeua Charybdis aqua**: 'Charybdis, savage in the ebb and flow of water'. *saeua* is a conjecture for the transmitted *scissa* ('split'), which does not aptly describe the action of the whirlpool.

29–30 Lampeties Ithacis ueribus mugisse iuuencos: 'the fact that the cattle of Lampetie bellowed on Ithacan spits': the list of nouns functioning as subjects of *non nocuere* in apposition to *morae* is superseded now by noun clauses using the accusative and infinitive construction. Odysseus' men (like him from Ithaca) were driven by adverse winds and hunger to the disastrous killing and eating of the cattle of the Sun god (12.260–419). The flesh of the cattle produced lowing noises as it was roasted on spits (12.394–6). *Lampeties* is the Greek genitive of *Lampetie*, one of the daughters of the Sun god: as the pentameter explains, she had tended the cattle before they were slaughtered (*Od.* 12.127–36); she does this with her sister Phaëthusa, but it is Lampetie who reports the crime to their father, at 12.374–5. **Phoebo:** 'for Phoebus', dative of advantage. *Odyssey* 12 uses the names Helios and Hyperion for the Sun; but the equation with Phoebus Apollo is a common one.

31–2 fugisse: Ulysses must be understood as the subject of this and the subsequent infinitives (lit. 'it did not harm him to have fled'). **Aeaeae flentis … puellae:** the 'weeping girl from Aeaea' is most easily taken as Calypso, since for P. she is the *puella* who weeps on Ulysses' departure (1.15.9–14 *Ithaci digressu mota Calypso … fleuerat*), and it was after leaving her that Ulysses sailed for seventeen days and nights, and swam for three more (*Od.* 5.278, 388–90). The oddity is that in Homer, Aeaea is the island of Circe; but she has been referred to already in 27, and the name is applied to Calypso's island also at Hyginus, *Fab.* 125.16, Mela 2.120. One reason for P. to follow this variant tradition may be the etymological play in *Aeaeae flentis*: it is Calypso who is known for weeping, and so she appropiately becomes the inhabitant of the island of 'Alas' (αἴ or αἰαῖ in Greek). In using the genitive form *Aeaeae* P. reduplicates the sound of woe. **totque hiemis noctes totque natasse dies:** 'and to have swum so many nights and so many days of storm'. Cf. *Od.* 5.388 δύω νύκτας δύο τ᾽ ἤματα ('two nights and two days'), and on the shared phrasing in balanced clauses see 3.11.65 n.

33–4 The shades of the dead, dumb until given the power to speak through drinking the blood of the sheep Odysseus sacrifices (*Od.* 11.23–50, 140–54), are set against the alluring music of the Sirens, and the deafness of the crew.   **nigrantes domos:** though Odysseus' encounter with the dead is not set beneath the earth, but in the far west, the darkness of the place is emphasized by Homer (11.15–19).   **surdo remige:** lit. 'with deaf oar', i.e. 'with deafened oarsmen': while Odysseus is bound to the mast, the crew have their ears stopped with wax so they can not fall under the spell of the

Sirens, whose songs lure mariners to their doom (12.166–200). **lyras:** Though Homer gives the Sirens no instrument, they often have a lyre in art. The transmitted *lacus* has not been satisfactorily explained and illustrated, and a reference to the Sirens' music is desirable.

35–6 ueteres arcus leto renouasse procorum: 'to have brought back into use [*lit.* renewed] the old bow [*poetic plural*] through the death of the suitors'. In *Odyssey* 21 Penelope, inspired by Athena, responds to the demands of the suitors that she choose another husband by setting a challenge—to string Odysseus' bow and shoot an arrow through the holes in a series of axes. None achieves the feat; but in the closing lines of the book (404–34) the old tramp who has just arrived does, for it is Odysseus himself; and in Book 22 he turns the bow and its arrows against the men who have been consuming his wealth and threatening his family. **statuisse modum:** 'to have set a limit' i.e. 'to have reached the end'.

37 nec frustra: 'and not in vain'. This does not refer to the sentence as a whole, but to the noun clauses in 31–6, especially the final couplet. Putting an end to his wandering by routing the suitors was worth while because Penelope had remained faithful to him.

38 uincit Penelopes … fidem: does the hyperbole* simply flatter Galla, or are we to imagine that her *fides* is tried in even more severe ways than Penelope's? Is her husband away longer? Is he less worth waiting for? Are those who try her chastity able to offer more than the nobles of Ithaca could (cf. 3.13.4–8)? **Aelia Galla:** a surprise: we find at the last that Galla has a specific identity. It is implied that she, and thus her husband too, is a real individual. We still cannot identify them with confidence, but some have speculated that he might be C. Propertius Postumus, a senator and proconsul mentioned in *CIL* 4.1501, and perhaps a relative of the poet (see e.g. Cairns 2006: 16–20). The sense of specificity makes even more striking the tone of rebuke with which P. points out the damage that continuing warfare does to the marriages so forcefully encouraged by Augustan policy (see p. 21). (Note that *Aelia* is a conjecture, though a very plausible one: the *l* of *laelia galla* in the manuscripts is likely to have arisen through misreading of the long final *s* in the Greek genitive *Penelopes*, which is itself corrupted to *Penelope* by the tradition.)

Additional bibliography: Nethercut, *CPh* 65 (1970), 99–102; Jacobson, *ICS* 1 (1976), 161–4.

3.13

1–8: You ask how girls have come to be greedy and nights of love so expensive that fortunes are used up. The cause is clear: the road to luxury is too open: gold comes from India, pearls from the Red Sea, purple dye from Tyre, spices from Arabia. 9–14: These weapons capture even girls who are locked up or chaste. A matron parades wearing the spoils of adultery. There is no respect in asking or giving; delay is removed for a price. 15–24: Happy is the practice of suttee for eastern husbands: a crowd of wives stands round the funeral pyre and they compete to see who accompanies her husband. The victors rejoice as they embrace their men and burn. But here today wives are unfaithful. 25–32: Happy the youth of the past, whose riches were harvest and tree: gifts for them were peaches and berries, plucked violets, lilies in baskets, grapes in vine-leaves, or a multicoloured bird. 35–46: In the countryside such seductions bought kisses; a fawn's skin covered a pair of lovers; deep grass provided a bed, a pine shade. <...> The ram led the pastured sheep back to the fold. <...> There was no punishment for seeing goddesses naked. All the gods and goddesses of the fields offered kindly words: 'Friend, you shall hunt hare or bird on my land; summon me, Pan, as your comrade, whether you hunt with hound or rod.' 47–50: But today sacred groves are deserted; everyone worships gold. Gold destroys fidelity, buys the law and chastity too. 51–8: Brennus attacked and burnt the temple of Apollo at Delphi, but Parnassus covered his army in snow. Having received gold Polymestor was a wicked host to Polydorus. Eriphyla destroyed her husband Amphiaraus for gold bracelets. 59–66: May I be a false prophet in proclaiming that Rome is being broken by its own wealth. My words are certain, but there is no belief—just as Cassandra should have been held true. She alone said Paris was causing Troy's downfall, that the horse was a trick. That inspiration could have been useful; her tongue achieved nothing and found that the gods are true.

In earlier books Propertius sometimes attacks interest in material possessions: love counts for more than clothes or cosmetics (1.2, 2.18.23–30), a grand house on the banks of the Tiber (1.14), or travel in search of wealth (1.6, 8). He contrasts himself with those who can provide expensive presents (2.16A and B). When Cynthia goes to the countryside (2.19), he accepts the innocence of such surroundings, and promises to join her. He even makes moral judgements, attributing modern immorality and lack of religion to obscene wall-paintings (2.6). But all of this is related to his own affair with Cynthia; and it is not until Book 3 that we find general attacks on luxury and the pursuit of wealth. In poems 4, 5, and 12 he presents Roman warfare as a misguided attempt to gain riches, and 7 imagines the painful death of Paetus, who has headed to Egypt as a trader in search of *pecunia*. Now the focus switches to women, in a striking contrast with poem 12: there Postumus is presented as *auarus*, whereas his wife Galla is a faithful Penelope, indifferent to the luxuries of modern life; here *puellae* ask for the costly presents that come to Rome from all over the empire and beyond, and lovers are ruined by their demands. (Poem 14 will praise the simplicity of sexual life in Sparta.)

The poem separates passages on the disgraceful behaviour of contemporary Rome (1–14, 23–4, 47–50) with contrasting scenes, distant in place or time: conjugal fidelity is represented by the Indian practice of suttee (15–22), primitive innocence by a pastoral idyll (25–46), in which all the gifts a lover might offer are available in the local countryside, while nature and the gods offer their assistance too. The wickedness of acting on a desire for gold is illustrated by one historical and two mythological examples (Brennus; Polymestor, Eriphyla); the punishment of the perpetrator is mentioned only in the first case, but implied in the other two, as P. moves on to predict ruin for Rome too, taking on the role of Cassandra.

Such a poem is as close as P. gets to 'diatribe'*, the name modern scholars apply to moral sermonizing in a lively style: see e.g. Kenney 1971: 17–20; K. Freudenburg, *The Walking Muse* (Princeton, 1993), 7 n. 14; Moles in *OCD*³ 'diatribe'. The form is traced back to the work of the fourth-/third-century travelling popularizer of philosophy, Bion (see J. F. Kindstrand, *Bion of Borysthenes* (Uppsala, 1976)), which survives only in fragments*: F17, 34–46 give some of his statements about avarice and wealth. It seems to have influenced a variety of Latin authors, such as Lucretius (e.g. 3.870–1093), Horace (*Satires* 1.1–3, 2.3; *Odes* 1.3, 2.14–15, 3.24), Seneca (*Ep.* 78) and Juvenal (*Sat.* 1, 6): they at any rate inveigh against human folly, including avarice, luxury, and female infidelity, P.'s targets here (female lust again in 3.19). The theme and a number of details are also shared with Tib. 2.3.35–58 and 2.4.27–34, which (unless they were published before Tibullus' death) are more likely to have been influenced by than an influence on this poem; note in particular 2.4.29–30, which encapsulates themes and diction from verses 1–6:

> addit auaritiae causas et Coa puellis
> uestis et e Rubro lucida concha mari.

Additional reasons for greed are given to girls by Coan cloth and the shining pearl from the Red Sea.

Despite the vividness of the writing, the tone of 3.13 is very hard to assess. Though the poet's preference for love over wealth is persistent, he nowhere else presents himself as inspired by social conditions more generally—it is Cynthia who provides him with *ingenium* (2.1.4; contrast the generality of Juvenal's *facit indignatio uersum*, 1.79). He has cast himself as a *haruspex* at 3.8.17, moved by the torments of love, and as a *uates* twice in Book 2: in a similar couplet at 2.17.3–4, where he is filled with the bitterness of being a locked-out lover, and at 2.10.19 *uates tua castra canendo | magnus ero* [I shall become a great and inspired poet in singing of your campaigns]— but he never fulfils, and apparently never intended to fulfil, this promise to Augustus. Some hint of the expansion of role has come when he calls himself *sacerdos* at 3.1.3; that alludes to Hor. *Odes* 3.1.3, and we probably should see here an imitation of the use of the concept of *uates* (priest-poet-prophet) by Vergil and Horace to provide divinely inspired and thus authoritative comment on matters social and political, as Horace notably does in *Odes* 3.1–6 (see J. K. Newman, *The Concept of* Vates *in Augustan Poetry* (Bruxelles, 1967), and, for instances of *uates* of the poet, *Ecl.* 7.28; *Aen.* 7.41; *Epod.* 16.66; *Odes* 1.1.35, 1.31.2, 2.20.3). But is P.'s adoption of the poses of moralist and *uates* emulation or parody?

Where a poet introduces a new stance or different material, it seems appropriate to wonder whether he is reflecting on his future genre, all the more so in a sequence like this, where instead of the conventional love elegies familiar from Books 1 and 2, we find synopses of the *Odyssey* (3.12) and the tragedy *Antiope* (3.15), a hymn (3.17) and an epicedion* (3.18). This poem offers a generic miscellany of which diatribe* and vatic utterance form but part: verses 5–8 and 15–22 smack of paradoxography*; 15–22 could be more precisely described as ethnographical, a style that will be pursued in 3.14's account of Spartan life; 43–6 translates an epigram of Leonidas, and the interest of 5–6 in the origin of minerals recalls the *Lithica* of the Posidippus papyrus* (*Epigrams* 1–20 A.-B.). Pastoral is the subject of the most prolonged passage, however, 25–46, which reads not as an aspiration for the future, but as a celebration of the poetry of his lost youth (25 n.)

1–2 Quaeritis: 'you ask': when the same word opens Book 2 (and Ov. *Fast.* 5), the poet addresses his readers in general: cf. 3.11.1 n., and the specific addressees of *quaeris* in 1.22.2, 2.31.1. Here the device creates a sensation of orality that leads well into a sermonizing poem. **unde auidis nox sit pretiosa puellis:** 'why girls are greedy and nights are costly'. *auidis puellis* is an ablative absolute: 'girls (being) greedy'. The satire on the avaricious Roman girl looks back to Lucretius 4.1123–32, and ahead to Juvenal 6 (6.7 actually evokes P. by naming Cynthia). For the realities behind such passages, see Griffin 1985: 1–31 = *JRS* 66 (1976), 87–105; James 2003: esp. 93–4. **Venere exhaustae damna querantur opes:** 'wealth used up by love complains of losses'. The word order and the striking personification* of wealth invite the reader to think at first of *puellae* exhausted by Venus, and of their complaints as they seek *opes*. In this untypical poem *queri* is a gesture towards elegiac norms: 3.6.18 n.

3–4 certa quidem ... et manifesta: *quidem* stresses the answer to the (indirect) question posed in the first couplet: 'quite certain and clear'. **tantis ... causa ruinis:** 'the cause of such great ruin': for *causa* with the dative, cf. 2.19.10 *peccatis plurima causa tuis*, 2.33.21. For the plural of *ruina* cf. Cic. *Cat.* 1.14 *ruinas fortunarum tuarum*. **luxuriae ... uia:** 'the road to *or* for luxury': for the genitive ('road to') see *OLD uia* 8; for the dative 3.16.18, Ov. *Trist.* 4.3.76 *publica uirtuti per mala facta uia est* ('through public misfortunes a path was made for courage': other manuscripts read *uirtutis*), Hor. *Odes*

3.16.7–8 (cited on 9). The first sense keeps the pentameter as a variant on the hexameter, with *causa* replaced by *uia*, and *ruinis* by *luxuriae*: the ruin is the loss of the man's fortune lamented in 2, the luxury now easily available to greedy *puellae* (1). The second sense, in giving a less abstract force to *uia*, looks ahead to the following lines, which present places where the Roman may travel and whence luxuries may freely come to the city (*mittit*, 5; *uenit*, 6). An empire such as Rome's collects riches from all over the world.

5–8 Similar lists of exotic Roman luxuries desired by the beloved are found at Tib. 2.3.53–8 (dresses of Coan silk, Indian slaves, dyes from Carthage and Tyre) and 2.4.27–30 (emeralds, Tyrian dye, Coan silk, *conchae* from the Red Sea: see intro.); cf. within P.'s text 1.2.1–4 (Coan silk, myrrh from the Orontes), 1.8.39 (gold, Indian *conchae*), 1.14.11–12 (gold from the Pactolus, gems from the Red Sea), 4.5.21–6 (eastern chrysoliths, Tyrian shellfish [i.e. dye], Coan silk, cloth-of-gold from Asia Minor, Egyptian goods, and fluorspar goblets from Parthia); and Verg. *Geo.* 1.56–7 (Tmolus supplies [*mittit*] saffron, India ivory, the Sabaeans incense).   **cauis ... metallis**: 'from hollowed out mines'. Herodotus 3.102–5 (paraphrased by Pliny at *Nat.* 11.111) describes how in India ants bigger than a fox brought up gold from underground as they burrowed the sand in the desert, and the locals harnessed camels to go and collect bags of the gold-rich sand. (There is presumably some confusion between ants and a burrowing mammal.) P.'s interest may have been provoked by the briefer reference at Callimachus, *Iambus* 12 (fr. 202.58–9). **e Rubro ... salo**: 'from the Red Sea', which implies not only the modern 'Red Sea', between Egypt and Saudi Arabia, but also the Persian Gulf and the north-western portion of the Indian Ocean. **concha Erycina**: 'the shell of Venus'. Venus is *Erycina* because of her cult centre at Eryx in Sicily. She was born from the foam of the sea and carried to land on a shell. As in the other passages listed above, *concha* could mean either pearl or mother-of-pearl here. **Tyros ... Cadmea**: 'Tyre, (city) of Cadmus': Cadmus, who was to be the founder of Thebes, was sent by his father from Tyre to find his sister Europa, kidnapped by Jupiter in the form of a beautiful bull (Ov. *Met.* 2.836–3.25); he is relevant here as a traveller to Europe. **ostrinos ... colores**: 'purple dyes': the Tyrians were famous for their manufacture of purple cloth. Their dye, which produced a glowing purple colour, was made from an extract from a vein of the whelk (a shellfish) and was enormously expensive. A German scholar called L. Friedländer used 12,000 molluscs to produce 1.5 grams of dye (R. J. Forbes, *Studies in Ancient Technology*, 2nd edn (Leiden, 1964), vol. 4, 118). Pliny expatiates on the species, the process and the luxuriousness of the product at *Nat.* 9.124–37 (after a discussion of the costliness of pearls worn by Lollia Paulina and consumed by Cleopatra: 9.117–23).   **cinnamon et culti messor odoris Arabs**: 'and the Arabian harvester of cultivated spice (provides) cinnamon'. After three lines that refer to colour, we move on to scent. *culti messor* is a conjecture for the transmitted *multi pastor*. *pastor* ('herdsman') is irrelevant to the context, and makes any interpretation of *multi... odoris* very awkward: if taken with *pastor*, the phrase suggests the stink of goats rather than perfume; both word order and the redundancy of the expression discourage one from taking it with *cinnamon*. For Arabia as the source of perfumes and spices, see 2.29.17, Tib. 2.2.2–3 *odores / quos tener e terra diuite mittit Arabs* [scents that the soft-living Arab sends from his rich land], [Tib.] 3.8.17–18 *possideatque metit quicquid bene olentibus aruis | cultor odoratae diues Arabs segetis* [let her possess whatever the wealthy Arab, cultivator of a scented crop, harvests in his sweet-smelling fields].

9–10 etiam clausas ... puellas: 'even locked up girls'. That wealth can storm any castle is a truism attributed to Philip of Macedon (Cic. *Att.* 1.16.12). We should also think of Danaë, locked up by her father so that she could not conceive the son who was destined to kill him; Jupiter entered the tower as a shower of golden rain, interpreted by Horace, among others, as bribery (*Odes* 3.16.7–8): *fore enim tutum iter et patens | conuerso in pretium deo* [the route would be safe and open for the god turned into money]. *puellas* is an emendation for the transmitted *pudicas* ('locked up chaste girls'): the use of two adjectives without a noun or a conjunction suggests textual corruption.   **quaeque gerunt fastus, Icarioti, tuos**: 'and those who display disdain like yours, daughter of Icarius [i.e. Penelope]'. *Icarioti* is a Greek vocative form of the patronymic. For the use of *gero* to convey the possession of a quality of mind displayed in behaviour, cf. Tac. *Hist.* 4.85 *quos spiritus* *gessisset uultu ferebat* [he displayed in his expression the spirit he had], Val. Max. 8.3.1 (of Maesia, who successfully defends herself in court) *sub specie feminae uirilem animum gerebat* [she bore a man's spirit under the form of a woman]. *fastus* is used by P. to describe arrogant indifference to sex or rejection of the affections of others at 1.1.3 *tum mihi constantis deiecit lumina fastus* [she forced me to drop my look of resolute pride], 1.13.27 *nec tibi praeteritos passa est succedere fastus* [nor has she allowed your past disdain to come over you], 1.18.5 *unde tuos primum repetam . . . fastus?* [Where am I to seek the first cause of your disdain?], 2.14.13, 3.19.11, 3.24.35. This presentation of Penelope is in decided contrast to the previous poem, where she is the model of faithfulness whom Galla can surpass though assailed by *luxuria* (18–19), and to line 24 of this one. The inconsistency may suggest a lack of seriousness in the moral stance.

11–12 matrona: a very honourable position in the Roman world, here degraded. **incedit . . . spolia opprobrii nostra per ora trahit**: the matron compounds her adultery by public display ('in front of our eyes [*lit.* faces]') of the gifts for which she has sold herself (*spolia opprobrii* is literally 'the spoils of her shame'): cf. the use of *incedere* ('parade') at 2.1.5, 2.2.6, Plaut. *Epidicus* 226 *quasi non fundis exornatae multae incedant per uias* [as if many women weren't parading through the streets adorned in estates]; *trahit* implies the length of her dress, but with *spolia* also plays on the sense 'carry off as plunder' (*OLD* 5). If she is wearing eastern gold or pearls (5–6), she is like the Indian wives of 15–22 in dress, but not behaviour. **census induta nepotum**: 'dressed in the fortunes of wastrels'. Like other verbs that describe what a person does to their own body, *induere* can be used in the passive, especially in the participle, with an accusative equivalent to that accompanying the active voice ('I put *x* on': for examples see *OLD* 2b; G&L §338 n.2). Ovid repeats the use of *census* in such a context at *Ars* 3.172 *quis furor est census corpore ferre suos*. *nepos*, lit. a 'grandson', came to mean 'playboy, spendthrift' (*OLD* 4; 4.8.23), presumably because of the indulgence of grandfathers (see Watson on Hor. *Epod.* 1.34); Horace has vivid accounts of *nepotes* at *Sat.* 1.4.49–52 and 2.3.224–38. The word strongly contrasts with *matrona* at the start of the verse.

13–14 nulla est poscendi, nulla est reuerentia dandi: 'there is no proper respect in asking, there is none in yielding'. Both gerunds apply to the man and the woman: thus *dandi* refers to the giving of the gift the woman requests, or her giving of herself.   **tollitur ipsa mora:** 'the very delay is removed': *reuerentia*, the sense that a love affair is a serious undertaking, not to be entered into lightly, or that turning it into a financial transaction might be improper and require restraint, here becomes a momentary hesitation, itself to be dismissed for money.

15–16 felix: introduces a beatitude*, as in 25; cf. 1.12.15 *felix qui potuit praesenti flere puellae*, Verg. *Geo.* 2.490 *felix qui potuit rerum cognoscere causas* ('happy the man who has been able understand the causes of things': he thinks of Lucretius); *fortunatus* is used similarly (3.20.9 n.).   **lex illa funeris:** 'that funeral law', i.e. suttee, a Sanskrit word referring to the self-immolation of a Hindu widow on her husband's pyre, a practice that fascinated the Romans (see W. Heckel and J. C. Yardley, 'Roman writers and the Indian practice of suttee', *Philologus* 125 (1981), 305–11), and modern Europeans too, as is illustrated by the prominence of the ceremony in M. M. Kaye's novel *The Far Pavilions*: suttee persisted into the nineteenth century. **Eois…maritis, quos Aurora suis rubra colorat aquis:** as elsewhere the dark skin of Indians is attributed to the waters they bathe in (3.11.18, 4.3.10; Martial 7.30.4 *a rubris et niger Indus aquis*). *Eous*, the adjective from 'Ἠώς, the Greek for dawn, is glossed by *Aurora*; and *suis* in stressing the association of the waters in the east with *Aurora rubra* suggests that they too are 'red' (cf. 6 *Rubro salo*) because the goddess rose from them.

17–22 mortifero: 'corpse-bearing': this meaning is unique, the word elsewhere having the sense of 'bringing death'; but P. uses *mors* for 'corpse' at 2.13.22, 3.6.24. The compound epithet, together with those in 32, 34, 39, 51, 53, adds a note of epic grandeur to the style. **uxorum…certamen:** the Eastern husband had a number of wives but not all of them are granted the supposed privilege of burning with him on his pyre. P. may have been influenced by the account at *Tusc. Disp.* 5.78 *quae est uictrix, ea laeta, prosequentibus suis, una cum uiro in* *rogum imponitur. illa uicta maesta discedit* [The winner rejoices and having been led out by her relatives she is placed on the pyre together with her husband. The loser departs disappointed]. Cicero goes on to complain that Romans in contrast have been corrupted by luxury and sloth.   **quae uiua sequatur | coniugium:** an indirect question in apposition* to *certamen* (the verb therefore being in the subjunctive): the contest of death is to *decide* who is to follow the husband. For *coniugium* used of a partner in marriage, see *OLD* 3a. **gaudent:** for the joy of the victorious wife see *Tusc. Disp.* 5.78 (above), Diod. 19.34.3, Val. Max. 2.6.14. Stephanus' emendation replaces the transmitted *ardent* ('they burn'); this comes too soon if taken literally, and is inappropriately limited to the winners if read as indicating burning desire.   **imponunt ... ora perusta:** 'they place their burnt lips': P. replaces Cicero's passive *imponitur* with an active form to bring out the eagerness of the wives, and gives it an object that ends the account with an erotic moment (cf. the picture of Cynthia at 4.7.7–10).

23–4 hoc genus ... nuptarum: 'the group of brides here', i.e. here in present-day Rome (so too *hic*).   **nulla ... nec ... nec:** the accumulated negatives do not cancel each other out: cf. 2.19.5 *nulla neque ante tuas orietur rixa fenestras* [nor will any row arise outside your window], Livy 2.49.3. It lends emphasis to the fact that no girl these days is an Evadne or Penelope.   **Euadne** flung herself onto the funeral pyre of her husband Capaneus (one of the 'Seven against Thebes'), and thus provides a Greek example of suttee. Her surpassing devotion to her husband became a frequent *exemplum** in Latin poetry from 1.15.21–2 on. She accompanies Penelope (and others) at Ov. *Ars* 3.21–2, *Trist.* 5.14.36–8, *ex P.* 3.1.111–13, Sen. *Contr.* 2.5.8. We first find the episode in Euripides' *Suppliant Women* (980–1071), where, in an extraordinary *coup de théâtre*, we actually see Evadne's leap. The witnesses, the chorus and her father Iphis, respond to her suicide with horror and despair respectively (1072–9). Euripides presents her as a woman running wild, abandoning herself to utterly un-Greek behaviour: there may well a note of irony in P.'s choice of her as a model of wifely fidelity.   **pia Penelope:** the adjective echoes the *uxorum pia turba* in 18, and Penelope takes us back to 10, and once again to 3.12, where Galla is presented as a clear counter-example to the claim made here about the lack of modern Penelopes.

25–46 A surprising passage from an urban poet: when he accepted Cynthia's visit to the countryside in 2.19, it was only because it seemed less of a threat than the city, or a seaside resort (cf. 1.11). But here he shows real gusto for the pastoral idyll he describes, admittedly as something from a past age. Most similar is 2.34.67–76, where he gives more verses to evoking Vergil's *Eclogues* than to the *Aeneid* or *Georgics*, in particular emphasizing the innocence of the rustic gifts given by the herdsmen to the beloved. One might read this as a cry of regret for the poetry that was published during his youth (*iuuentus*, 25).

25–6 agrestum: the regular genitive plural in dactylic* verse (Verg. *Geo.* 1.10, and later), where *agrestium* will not scan; cf. the participle forms *silentum* (3.12.33), *amantum* (3.16.27), *luctantum* (3.22.9). **quondam**: 'once', implying 'in ancient times', but allowing a reference to the 30s, the period of the *Eclogues* and P.'s own youth. The adverb looks ahead to the contrasting *nunc* in 47.   **diuitiae quorum messis et arbor erant**: 'whose riches were harvest and tree'.

27–32 Cydonia (i.e. *māla*): 'Cydonian fruits', i.e. 'quinces'. For the giving of fruit, cf. 2.34.69–71; Theoc. *Id.* 3.10; Cat. 65.19; Verg. *Ecl.* 2.51–3, 3.70–1; *Daphnis & Chloe* 3.33–4. According to Plutarch, *Solon* 20.3 (and *Coniug. praec.* 1) the Athenian statesman and elegist said that a new bride should eat a quince before going to the bridal bed.   **et dare**: 'and giving': the infinitive looks back to the word *munus* ('gift') in the previous line and forward to *tondere* ('plucking'), *referre* ('bringing back') and *portare* ('carrying') in 29–31.   **nunc mixta referre | lilia uimineos lucida per calathos**: 'now bringing back shining lilies intermixed in [*lit.* by means of] wickerwork baskets'. *mixta* implies that the brilliant white lilies are set off against the violets picked in the first half of the line. The line echoes *Ecl.* 2.45–6 *tibi lilia plenis | ecce ferunt Nymphae calathis* [for you the Nymphs bring lilies, look, in full baskets]; Vergil goes on to mention *uiolas* in 47, and then other flowers. P. transfers the adjective *plenus* to the blackberry baskets in 28. The picking of flowers often heralds a scene of abduction or rape (so e.g. Hylas at 1.20.35–40, Proserpina at Ov. *Fast.* 4.425–46), but here lovers join without the need for force.   **uariam plumae uersicoloris auem**: 'a pied bird of colour-changing plumage': its plumage is iridiscent: cf. Lucr. 2.801–7.

33–4 his tum blanditiis furtiua per antra puellae | oscula siluicolis empta dedere uiris: 'Then girls in secret caves gave to the men dwelling in the woods kisses bought by these acts of courtship.' Both word order and the distribution of epithets between separate nouns suggest that *furtiua* is to be taken with *antra* rather than *oscula*. But the secrecy still gives an edge of excitement to the affair. *empta* recalls *mercaris* at 2.34.71, and *siluicolis* continues the evocation of the *Eclogues*: *siluae* is (with *umbrae*, 'shadows') Vergil's most important marker of the pastoral genre (1.1–5 [H], 2.60–2, 4.3 *si canimus siluas, siluae sint consule dignae* [if we sing of woods, let them be woods worthy of a consul], 6.2, 10.63).

35–6 hinnulei pellis: 'the skin of a fawn'.   **operibat**: an alternative form of the imperfect for this fourth-conjugation verb; $\breve{o}p\breve{e}r\bar{\imath}\bar{e}bat$ will not scan in dactylic verse*.   **iunctos... amantes**: 'conjoined lovers'. *iunctos* is an emendation for the transmitted *totos*: rather than the togetherness of the lovers the latter oddly stresses the size of the fawn skin (which is unlikely to cover them completely). As emended the text makes play with the one blanket/two lovers contrast that we find at *Anth. Pal.* 5.169.3–4 (Asclepiades): ἥδιον δ' ὁπόταν κρύψηι μία τοὺς φιλέοντας | χλαῖνα [but sweeter is when one cloak covers lovers], and *Daphnis & Chloe* 3.24.2.   **natiuo... toro**: dative: '(to form) a natural bed': the grass was suitable *for* a bed where it grew.   **creuerat**: 'had grown', i.e. was *now* deep. Simple shepherds enjoyed the delights provided for gods at *Iliad* 14.347–50, where the earth produces a bed of grass and flowers for Zeus and Hera to make love on.

37 lentis circumdabat umbras: 'put shade around the relaxing lovers'. *lentis* is an emendation of the transmitted *lentas* which is not easy to apply to the shadows cast by the pine tree (unlike the 'pliant' plants such as vines to which it is regularly attached); if it is correct, it will probably be a transferred epithet meaning e.g. 'lazy'. The adjective is another key term in the *Eclogues*: in the iconic opening (H) Meliboeus describes Tityrus as lying *lentus in umbra* (picked up again by P. at 4.10.29 *pastoris lenti*).

39–40 Where transmitted, this interrupts the sequence on deities, and is separated by 38 from the scene where the herdsman is with the beloved and not concentrating on his duties: it seems clear that one or more couplets has been omitted and the restoration done inaccurately in a subsequent copy.   **corniger...dux aries:** 'the horn-bearing guide, the ram'.   **Arcadii** is a conjecture; the impossible *atque dei* is transmitted. Vergil identifies singers in two *Eclogues* as 'Arcadian', which became a marker of the idyllic world of pastoral (7.4, 26; 10.31–3; also the contemporary epigram *Anth. Pal.* 6.96). Another possibility is *Idaei*, which would establish a clear focus on Paris (38 n.; and cf. 2.32.35–40).   **uacuam:** 'empty', i.e. 'unguarded', in the herdsman's absence with his girl. The ability of livestock to herd themselves is a marker of the Golden Age at *Ecl.* 4.21–2 (*ipsae* lacte domum _referent_ distenta capellae | ubera [the goats on their own will bring back home udders swollen with milk]), Hor. *Epod.* 16.49–50, Tib. 1.3.45–6; but as relevant here may be Theoc. 11.12–13 'Often the ewes came back on their own from the green pasture to the fold, while he [Polyphemus] was singing of Galatea'.

38 nec fuerat...poena: 'and it was not a (cause of) punishment'. For the pluperfect *fuerat* see 3.7.31, 3.8.1. In the background to this line are (a) Actaeon, who accidentally saw Diana bathing while he was hunting; Diana transformed him into a stag and he was torn to pieces by his hounds; and (b) Tiresias, who, also on a hunt, saw Athena bathing and was blinded. Both stories appear in Callimachus' fifth hymn, Actaeon in Ov. *Met.* 3.138–252 (a different account of Tiresias' blinding follows at 3.316–38). Callimachus, *Hymn* 5 also refers to the judgement of Paris (17–26), which some have thought significant here. He was working as a humble shepherd when he preferred Venus to Juno and Minerva (explicitly judged naked at 2.2.13–14); the punishment he suffered takes us to Troy and the world of epic, but it was caused by the anger of the defeated goddesses, not by the fact that he saw them naked.

41–2 dique deaeque omnes quibus est tutela per agros: 'all gods and goddesses whose protection extends across the fields'. There is a reminiscence of the opening invocation in Vergil's *Georgics*: *dique deaeque omnes* studium quibus arua *tueri* (1.21: 'and all you gods and goddesses whose interest is protecting the fields'). **dextris...focis**: 'at [*or* along with, *ablative absolute*] their favouring altars'. The transmitted *uestris* turns *dique deaeque* into a vocative and leaves *praebebant* without an effective subject. *dextris* sums up the gods' kindly disposition.

43–6 As an illustration of the integration of the divine with the pastoral world of the past, P. offers a careful translation of an epigram by Leonidas of Tarentum (*Anth. Pal.* 9.337), in which Pan addresses a prospective huntsman:

> Εὐάγρει, λαγόθηρα, καὶ εἰ πετεεινὰ διώκων
> ἰξευτὴς ἥκεις τοῦθ' ὑπὸ δισσὸν ὄρος,
> κἀμὲ τὸν ὑληωρὸν ἀπὸ κρημνοῖο βόασον
> Πᾶνα. συναγρεύω καὶ κυσὶ καὶ καλαμοῖς.

Have a good hunt, pursuer of hares, and if you have come beneath this two-peaked mountain as a bird-catcher in pursuit of flying creatures; and call upon me, Pan, the watcher in the woods, from a crag. I join you in the hunt, with both dogs and [bird catchers'] rods'.

et is awkward in itself, and does not correspond to anything in the original, so corruption has been suspected. **quicumque uenis** looks ahead to the vocative *hospes*. **Pana**: the Greek accusative of *Pan*. **meo tramite**: 'in my glen': the commentator Servius on Verg. *Geo.* 1.108 defines *tramites* as valleys hemmed in by mountains. **uocato**: the 'second' imperative is chiefly used in legal documents and maxims; but it has an application to the future, which is appropriate with *petes* here; it also mimics the sound and rhythm of Leonidas' βόασον. **calamo**: a jointed rod, the top of which was smeared with bird lime (*OLD* 5).

47–50 at nunc marks the contrast of the wickedness of the current world with the simplicity and ease, the erotic delights and the integration of human and divine in the pastoral past (25–46). **cessant sacraria**: 'shrines are neglected': for this meaning of *cesso* see *OLD* 4b. **uicta...pietate**: compare *nondum spreta pietate* at Cat. 64.386. These lines resemble the end of Cat. 64 more

generally: there the distant past, in which deities visited homes and
mingled with mortals at sacrifices and in war, is contrasted with the
criminality of the current age, when gods keep themselves hidden
from human sight (384–5, 407–8); however, the modern world
appears to include the heroic age, famous for crimes listed in
397–404 (399 recalls Ariadne's involvement in the death of her
half-brother, the Minotaur, at 150, 181). An earlier response had
come in *Ecl.* 4 (cf. 39–40 n.), where Vergil foresees the return of a
Golden Age in which gods will be seen among men (15–16). P.
reasserts that such days are gone: no Augustan optimism for him,
and when he talks about the neglect of shrines he does not even allow
the possibility of rebuilding, as Horace does in *Odes* 3.6.1–4: *Delicta
maiorum immeritus lues,* | *Romane, donec templa refeceris* | *aedesque
labentes deorum et* | *foeda nigro simulacra fumo* [Roman, though you
do not deserve to, you will pay for the crimes of your ancestors until
you restore the falling shrines and temples of the gods and the images
fouled by black smoke].   **auro uenalia iura**: 'justice can be
bought by gold'. The word *aurum* is given tremendous emphasis by
its fourfold repetition and its use in anaphora* and asyndeton*. Ovid
will imitate this with a new twist when he discusses girls' preference
for gifts over poetry at *Ars* 2.277–8: *aurea sunt uere nunc saecula:
plurimus auro* | *uenit honos: auro conciliatur amor* [The age is truly
golden now; the greatest respect has come to gold; love is won
through gold].   **mox**: 'afterwards': when gold has subdued
the law, all sense of shame is abandoned.

51–4 torrida sacrilegum testantur limina Brennum: 'the burnt doorway
testifies that Brennus was sacrilegious'. The reference is to the attack on
the temple of Apollo at Delphi by Gauls under Brennus in 278 BC
(Callimachus, *Hymn* 4.171–85; Lucan 5.134–5); Cicero (*Diu.* 1.81) described how a snow-storm then miraculously overwhelmed the Gauls;
Pausanias 10.23.1–4 adds mention of thunderstorms and landslips,
perhaps drawing on Herodotus' similar account (8.34–9) of the Persians'
attack on Delphi in 480 BC.   **Pythia regna**: 'the Pythian kingdom': *Pythius* was the cult title of Apollo ('the unshorn god'), who had
killed the monstrous Python which occupied Delphi until the god's
arrival there (Call. *Hymn* 2.97–104, Ov. *Met.* 1.438–9).   **mons**

laurigero concussus uertice: 'the mountain, shaken on its laurel-bearing summit'. The mountain is Parnassus, on whose slopes Delphi is situated; it is represented here as like the god himself, with a laurel-wreath on its head. An earthquake or landslide helps the snow-storm frustrate Brennus' attack: cf. 2.31.13 *deiectos Parnasi uertice Gallos*.

55–8 Having started with an example from history, P. moves back to the world of epic (the Trojan and Theban cycles) and tragedy: like Catullus (48 n.) he presents human criminality as no recent thing. The punishment of sacrilegious greed is shown in 53–4; here it is implied through the familiarity of the myths.   **scelus...
Polymestoris**: i.e. *scelestus Polymestor*. At the start of Euripides' *Hecuba*, the ghost of Polydorus explains how his father Priam, fearing that Troy would fall, had sent him, the Trojan king's youngest son, for safety to Polymestor, king of Thrace. Priam also smuggled out a vast quantity of gold with him. In an impious abuse of the obligations of guest friendship, Polymestor eventually killed Polydorus and seized the money (so too *Aen.* 3.49–57: the poem of *pius Aeneas* is evoked by *pio* in 56). Euripides' play shows him suffering a terrible revenge from Priam's widow Hecuba, who blinds him and murders his sons.   **Eriphyla ... Amphiaraus**: The pious seer Amphiaraus was persuaded by his wife Eriphyla, who had been bribed by golden bracelets (elsewhere a necklace), to join the expedition of the Seven against Thebes: this was against his better judgement, for he knew it would fail; during the attack on Thebes a chasm opened up and swallowed him and his four-horse chariot: cf. *Od.* 15.244–7, Eur. *Suppl.* 500–1, Stat. *Theb.* 7.794–8.20. Eriphyla's son, Alcmaeon (3.5.41 n.), subsequently killed her to avenge his father; cf. 2.16.29 *aspice quid donis Eriphyla inuenit amari* [see what bitterness E. found in gifts].   **nusquam est**: 'is nowhere', i.e. 'has disappeared', as at Hor. *Sat.* 2.5.102.

59–60 proloquar: future.   **patriae**: 'for my fatherland'.
falsus: an emendation, probably by Petrarch, of the transmitted *uerus*. Though the conjecture may seem bold, scribes often write the opposite of what they should (some manuscripts have *liberae* for *captae* at 3.19.4, e.g.); and it is hard to believe that P. is praying that he be a true prophet, i.e. that his announcement of Rome's doom should be fulfilled.   **frangitur ipsa suis Roma superba**

bonis: the warning is an imitation of Hor. *Epod.* 16.2 *suis et ipsa Roma uiribus ruit* [Rome rushes to ruin through its own strength]. Where Horace sees the threat as the military might (ῥώμη) on which Rome is founded (with etymological aptness), for P. it comes from 'goods' (i.e. the luxuries of 5–8).

61–2 certa loquor, sed nulla fides. The poet now decides that his pronouncement in 60 is certain, but no one believes him, like Cassandra in Troy (given prophetic powers by Apollo, but then cursed with universal disbelief when she finally rejected his love: see e.g. Aesch. *Ag.* 1202–12). **nempe Ilia quondam | uerax Pergamei Maenas habenda mali:** 'to be sure the Trojan Maenad [Cassandra] once ought to have been held truthful over the disaster of Pergamum [the citadel of Troy]': *Pergamei mali* is an objective genitive after *uerax*. The text here and up to the end of the poem is seriously problematic and uncertain: see *Cynthia*.

63–4 sola..., sola | ... dixit: the anaphora* indicates the continuity of structure, with *dixit* understood in both clauses introducing the accusative and infinitive construction. **Parim Phrygiae fatum componere:** 'that Paris was building destruction [*OLD fatum*, 6] for Phrygia [i.e. Troy]'. Cassandra made such a prophecy at Paris' departure for Greece in the lost *Cypria* (West 2003: 68–9; cf. Paris's comments to Helen at Ov. *Her.* 16.121–6). **fallacem Troiae:** 'treacherous to Troy'. **serpere:** 'was gliding'. The snake-like connotations suggest the insidious nature of the entry of the Trojan horse into the city, as at *Aen.* 2.240 (*inlabitur*); cf. *Aen.* 2.246–7 for Cassandra's unheeded warning.

65–6 utilis: this must mean 'which could have been useful'. The notion of a useful *furor* is a striking one: in the *Aeneid* it is the polar opposite of the ideal of *pietas* (n.b. *Furor impius*, 1.294). **parenti:** i.e. Priam. **experta est ueros irrita lingua deos:** 'her tongue in being ineffectual found that the gods are true to their word'. The gods were found to be true to their word in that Troy fell; in addition Apollo's curse that Cassandra would not be believed proved only too true.

Additional bibliography: Nethercut, *CPh* 65 (1970), 99–102; Jacobson, *ICS* 1 (1976), 161–4.

3.14

1–14: We admire the way in which you organize athletics, Sparta, espe-
cially the involvement of girls. A woman can exercise naked in the
company of men without shame, whether playing ball, rolling hoops,
running, fighting in the pancration, boxing, throwing the discus, riding,
arming as if for war, like the Amazons. 15–20: Now she goes hunting,
<and now...>, like the young Pollux and Castor, with Helen between
them, bearing arms, bare-breasted, without embarrassment. 21–8: In
Sparta lovers are together in public; there is nothing to fear from guards
or stern husbands. You may speak for yourself: any rejection comes quickly.
No expensive cloth deceives the eye; there are no elaborate hairstyles. 29–
34: Girls in Rome are surrounded by attendants and unapproachable. You
cannot discover their character; the lover stumbles in the dark. Rome, if
you had followed Spartan practice, I would like you better.

This poem takes further the rhetorical mode of 3.13, presenting the
reader with what can be seen as a declamatory *thesis* or *quaestio*: 'Should
a state encourage women to engage in athletic pursuits, as the Spartans
do?' S. F. Bonner, *Roman Declamation in the Late Republic and Early*
Empire (Liverpool, 1949), 1–11 discusses the history of declamation
and gives many examples (3–4), e.g. 'Should a man marry?' 'Should one
prefer fame to riches?', 'How should captives be treated?', 'How is virtue
to be attained—by nature or training?' For discussion of *theses*, and
related aspects of declamatory practice, see Cicero, *Topica* 79–90; Quintilian 2.4.24–32, 3.5.5–18; the references to *iura* (1, 33) and *lex* (21)
make a link also with the *laus legis* discussed by Quintilian at 2.4.33–42,
though the poem is scarcely structured as a reflection on a law.

In his *Tusculan Disputations* (2.36) Cicero introduces a passage
from an anonymous lost Roman tragedy. The Spartans, he says,
wanted 'nothing of this sort' (i.e. a soft, sequestered life) for their girls,

> apud Lacaenas uirgines,
> quibus magis palaestra Eurota sol puluis labor
> militia studio est quam fertilitas[5] barbara.

[5] As Lycurgus is said by Xenophon and Plutarch to have wanted to prepare the
girls for motherhood, the word is almost certainly corrupt; the context suggests that a
noun meaning softness or luxury has been displaced.

among the maidens of Sparta, for whom the wrestling ground, the Eurotas [*the river of Sparta, i.e. swimming*], the sun, dust, the work-out, military service are more a concern than the child-bearing[1] of barbarian women.

Xenophon (*Constitution of the Lacedaemonians* 1.4) says that physical training for girls was introduced by Lycurgus, the semi-mythical founder of the Spartan system; and Plutarch gives a list like P.'s here: 'running, wrestling, throwing the discus and the javelin' (*Lyc.* 14.2). Other Greeks were horrified: at Euripides, *Andromache* 595– 600 Peleus makes a scathing denunciation of the practice to the Spartan Menelaus: 'A daughter of the Spartans could not be chaste [*or* modest] even if she wanted: in the company of young men they abandon their homes, with tunics tucked up to bare their thighs, and they share running tracks and *palaestrae* with them in a way I can't bear.' P. clearly responds to a strong tradition; but as with 3.13 one wonders how far the poem is parodic ('another spoof', Newman 2006: 345).

Suetonius tells in his life of Augustus (43–5) how the *princeps* encouraged athletic activities with the institution of formal games and in other ways (cf. Dio 52.26.1); but women take no part, and even as spectators they are separated from the men (*feminis ne gladiatores quidem, quos promiscue spectari sollemne olim erat, nisi ex superiore loco spectare concessit* [44.2: he did not allow women to watch even gladiatorial shows except from the higher rows, though it was previously the custom for them to be watched by mixed crowds]). From athletic games they are excluded altogether (*athletarum uero spectaculo muliebre secus omne... summouit* [44.3: but he kept women away from athletic games entirely]). We have no indication when these restrictions were introduced, but the difference between *princeps* and poet could hardly be more stark.

In view of this it is surprising that Cairns 2006: 369–403, suggests the piece was commissioned by someone close to Augustus, perhaps in connexion with a visit to Sparta in the late 20s. However, his prime concern is to demonstrate how P.'s account tallies with contemporary belief about Sparta and 'even with the facts' (370); this perhaps understates the use of literary models (illustrated in the notes below), but he reasonably concludes that the poem's humour lies more particularly in the elegiac application of the material. Sparta is normally a byword for austerity, but here becomes the home of nakedness and free love (cf. Nethercut, *CPh* 65 (1970), 100–1).

1–2 Multa points to the wealth of detail that the poem will offer on Sparta.   **Spartē**: this form (as opposed to the commoner *Spartă*) is first found here; each has a Greek equivalent. This opening vocative is matched by the address of *Roma* in the final couplet. **miramur**: wonder is present in the opening also of 3.10 and 3.11; Galla is *miranda* at 3.12.23; and, though the term is not used, 3.13 describes *mirabilia* of other lands (esp. 15–22) in a way that links up with the handling of Sparta here.   **palaestrae … gymnasii**: Sparta's alien customs are denoted with imported Greek words, prominent at the end of the lines: so too *trochi* (6), *pancratio* (8: like *gymnasii* this is given added weight as a rare non-disyllabic word at the end of the pentameter); *disci* (10) is less emphasized; *gyrum* begins 11.   **mage** = *magis*, 'especially'. For the form cf. 1.11.9, 4.8.16; for the sense 3.9.13.   **tot bona**: i.e. 'the many benefits'. The noun closely follows the instance at 3.13.60, where it means 'luxury items'; now it is used for what are more properly called 'goods'.

3–4 non infames exercet corpore ludos: 'plays physical sports without ill repute'.   **luctantes nuda puella uiros**: the word order vividly places the girl, naked, among men, whose nakedness is implicit in the fact that they are wrestling: this, like most ancient sport, was performed *nudus*. *luctari* is not only a word that stresses physical contact, but it is actually a common metaphor for sexual intercourse: Adams 1987: 157–8; cf. 2.1.13, 2.15.5 *nudatis mecum est luctata papillis* [she wrestled with me bare-breasted]. There is no reason to think male and female regularly wrestled with each other in Sparta, and the word *nudus* can allow for scanty clothing (*OLD* 2), as can its Greek equivalent γυμνός, used by Plutarch when he recounts how Lycurgus laid it down that girls would be 'naked' in processions and as they danced and sang at certain festivals with the boys looking on (*Lyc.* 14.2). But even if P. is playing with ambiguities here, the main point is surely to titillate the reader. On nudity in Latin poetry, see Griffin 1985: 88–111.

5–6 cum pila ueloces flectit per inania iactus: 'when the ball curves its swift flights through the void [i.e. the air]'. The transmitted text has *fallit per bracchia* in place of *flectit per inania*. Shackleton Bailey's strained translation shows the difficulty of staying faithful to that text: 'when the ball hides the swift casts <as it passes> through the arms <of the players>'. The literary tradition of girls playing catch goes back to Nausicaa and her maids at *Od.* 6.99–117: though they are not naked (unlike Odysseus, who will awake and surprise them), they do throw off their veils, symbols of modesty (100). **increpat et uersi clauis adunca trochi:** 'and the rolling hoop's hooked stick clatters'. The hooked stick makes a noise as it drives and steers the hoop: similarly Martial 11.21.2 *arguto qui sonat aere trochus* [a hoop that resounds with its shrill bronze]. The initial *increpat* draws attention to the onomatopoeia* of the line. For the use of the hoop in exercise, cf. Hor. *Odes* 3.24.57 (and Nisbet & Rudd *ad loc.*), Ov. *Trist.* 3.12.20; at *Ars* 3.383 Ovid includes it in a list of physical pastimes open only to men in Rome:

> sunt illis celeresque pilae iaculumque trochique
> armaque et in gyros ire coactus equus.

They have swift ball games and javelin and hoops, and military training and forcing a horse to tread prescribed circles.

7–8 ad extremas stat ... metas: 'stops at the final mark': for *sto* with the meaning 'stop', see *OLD* 10. Naturally the woman will be dusty by the end of the race.   **patitur:** *patientia* was a perceived purpose of Spartan training: Cic. *Tusc. Disp.* 5.77.   **duro ... pancratio:** 'in the tough pancration', a combination of boxing and wrestling in which anything was permitted apart from biting and gouging. The picture of female athletic activity is becoming somewhat surreal.

9–10 nunc ligat ad caestum gaudentia bracchia loris: 'now she ties to the glove fore-arms that take delight in the thongs'. *gaudentia* implies the pleasure of the girl: cf. Valerius, *Arg.* 1.109–10 *umeris gaudentibus arcus | gestat Hylas* [Hylas carries the bow on rejoicing shoulders]. Greek boxing gloves consisted 'of two parts, a glove and a hard leather ring encircling the knuckles ... This ring is formed of three to five strips of hard, stiff leather, bound together by small straps, and held in its place by thongs bound round the wrist' (E. N. Gardiner, *Greek Athletic Sports and Festivals* (London, 1910), 409). At *Aen.* 5.401–8 Vergil gives a vivid description of the gloves worn by the

Sicilian boxer Entellus; and the fight that follows shows the damage
even less fearsome gloves could do. Boxing returns with Pollux in 17–18.
in orbe: 'in a circle', before the discus leaves her hand.

11–14 gyrum pulsat: 'she pounds the training ring'. For *gyrum*,
see 6 n., 3.3.21 n.   **niueum latus:** again the girl's attractive
physicality is put on show.   **cauo...aere:** i.e. with a helmet.
Though Spartan women certainly did not go to war, it is possible
P. has training exercises in mind.   **qualis Amazonidum...**
bellica...turma: 'just as the warlike squadron of the Amazons...'
Women in armour will always call to mind the Amazons; here the
tradition that they fought bare-breasted makes their presence especially appropriate, as does their part in various erotic myths, notably
Penthesilea and Achilles (3.11.13–16).   **Thermodontiacis...**
uagatur agris: 'roam in the fields by the Thermodon', a river in
Cappadocia, the Amazons' original home. The transmitted *lauatur*
aquis has the Amazons washing in the Thermodon, which lessens
their similarity to the Spartans and removes the point of the reference: any woman bathing might have bare breasts.

15–16 et modo: *modo* in the sense 'at one time' requires a second
modo or an alternative adverb; if the transmitted order is correct, the
simile in 13–14 separates this too strongly from *nunc...*, *nunc* in 9–10,
and something has been lost. The missing couplet, probably beginning
et modo (which would explain the omission), will have led more neatly
than this does on to the introduction of Castor, Pollux, and Helen as
exemplars of Spartan athleticism.   **Taygeti:** Taygetus is the
mountain above Sparta; in the Nausicaa scene at *Odyssey* 6.103 it is
mentioned as a place where Artemis hunts (cf. 5 n.). Another model is
Aen. 1.315–16 where Venus appears to her son Aeneas in the guise of a
Spartan huntress: *uirginis os habitumque gerens et uirginis arma* |
Spartanae [with the features and dress of a maiden and the weapons
of a Spartan maiden].   **crines aspersa pruina:** 'her hair
speckled with hoar-frost'. *crines* is accusative of the part affected
(compare the related phenomena discussed at 3.13.11, 3.24.14).
The cold of the mountain brings out the hardiness of the girl.
patrios...canes: 'the local dogs': Sparta was celebrated for its

'Laconian' hounds: Pindar, fr. 106 Maehler (associated with Taygetus); Sophocles, *Ajax* 8; Hor. *Epod.* 6.5; Verg. *Geo.* 3.405.

17–20 Eurotae … harenis: 'on the sand of the Eurotas', the river of Sparta. Theocritus in the epithalamium for Helen at *Idyll* 18.22–3 has his chorus of Spartan maidens describe themselves as those 'who, oiled up like men, take part in the same race [i.e. as Helen] by the bathing places in the Eurotas'. Callimachus evokes Helen by alluding to this at *Hymn* 5.24–5: in preparation for the Judgement of Paris, Pallas Athena runs 'just like the Lacedaemonian stars by the Eurotas', i.e. Castor and Pollux, who became the constellation Gemini. P. brings the two connected passages together; Pallas' dislike of mixed (i.e. perfumed) oils, which is at the heart of the Callimachus passage (25–30), is relevant to verse 28 here. **hic … ille**: 'the one … the other', Pollux and Castor respectively. They were the sons of Jupiter and the Spartan Leda; their sister Helen looks in vain from the walls of Troy for Κάστορά θ' ἱππόδαμον καὶ πὺξ ἀγαθὸν Πολυδεύκεα (*Il.* 3.237: 'Castor the horse-tamer and Polydeuces [= Pollux] good with his fists'); similarly balanced patterns are found of the pair also at Hor. *Odes* 1.12.26–7 *hunc equis, illum superare pugnis* | *nobilem*; Ov. *Met.* 8.301–2 *spectandus caestibus alter,* | *alter equo*, *Fast.* 5.700 *hic eques, ille pugil*. Pollux's famous boxing victory over Amycus during the voyage of the Argo to Colchis is described by Apollonius at *Arg.* 2.1–97, and also by Theocritus at *Idyll* 22.26–134, followed by an account of Castor's fight with Lynceus at 137–211. **pugnis**: strictly ambiguous: either from *pugnus* ('with his fists)' or from *pugna* ('in fights': *OLD* 1b); but the cited parallels favour the former. **uictor … futurus**: distributed between the two clauses, as often happens in balanced verses (cf. 4.10.19): take each with both *hic* and *ille*. We are shown the heroes as young men in training for the triumphs they will achieve. **Helene … capere arma … fertur**: one might have expected a perfect infinitive here ('Helen is said *to have taken up* arms') but for the present infinitive referring to a past action in indirect statement, cf. Cat. 64.124–8. **erubuisse**: 'to have blushed/felt shame in the presence of' (*OLD* 1g). **deos**: Castor and Pollux eventually achieved divine status, and received a temple in the Roman forum.

21–4 igitur: 'therefore', in the sense of 'consistently with that'.
secedere: 'to go apart'.   **licet in triuiis ad latus esse suae:** 'it
is possible [for a man, *implied*] to be at the side of his girl at the
crossroads'. This could simply mean they walk through the town
together (contrast 29–30), but at 4.7.19 Cynthia reminisces about
sex at the crossroads (*Venus triuio commissa*).   **nec timor est
ulli clausae tutela puellae:** 'neither is a guard on a girl who is kept
indoors a [source of] fear for anyone': contrast 3.13.9, where girls are
shut away indoors, but still vulnerable to the insidious attack of
luxuriae.   **austeri...uiri** echoes *austeros...uiros* at 3.3.50,
where Calliope says P.'s poetry is designed to help the lover outwit
such men: in Sparta there would be no need for elegy.

25–8 nullo praemisso: 'without sending anyone on ahead [i.e. as go-
between]'.   **tute:** emphatic *tu*. The form occurs only here in
elegy, just once in Catullus (30.7) and once in Vergil (*Ecl.* 3.35), but it
is frequent in earlier Latin as far down as Lucretius.   **longae
nulla repulsa morae:** 'no rejection involves [*lit.* is of] long delay':
longae morae is a genitive of quality (G&L §365). The immediacy and
directness of the Spartan life-style make a woman's feelings clear at
once, whereas in Rome access is almost impossible, and expenditure
of money, time, and effort may produce no result: besides 29–32, cf.
2.23.3–9 (written as if during an estrangement from Cynthia):

> ingenuus quisquam alterius dat munera seruo
>   ut promissa suae uerba ferat dominae? ...
> deinde ubi pertulerit quos dicit fama labores
>   Herculis, haec scribet 'muneris ecquid habes?' —
> cernere uti possis uultum custodis amari?

Does any well-born individual give gifts to the slave of another so that he'll
take the words as promised to his mistress? ... Then when he has endured
what gossip terms the labours of Hercules, will she write 'do you have any
gift?'—just so that you can gaze at the face of an unpleasant guard?

The street-walker is there preferred, and her behaviour is strikingly
akin to the Spartan girl's (2.23.11–16), unencumbered by clothes and
guards, and causing no delay:

> contra reiecto quae libera uadit amictu
>   custodum nullo saepta timore placet.

> cui saepe immundo Sacra conteritur Via socco   15
> nec sinit esse moram si quis adire uelit.

On the other hand, the woman who walks free, with her wrap thrown back, protected by no fear caused by guards—she pleases. The Sacred Way is often worn away by her soiled slipper, and she lets there be no delay if anyone should wish to approach.

Tyriae uestes: here P. makes explicit the underlying contrast between Spartan simplicity and the Roman decadence expounded in its predecessor: cf. 3.13.7.   **errantia lumina fallunt:** 'mislead eyes into error': *errantia* is proleptic*.   **odoratae cura molesta comae:** the attention given to hair is 'troublesome', because time-consuming, deceptive and unnecessary. *odoratae* points to the use of perfumed hair-oils: Ovid echoes the phrasing at *Ars* 2.734 and in his work (mainly lost) on female cosmetics *Medicamina faciei femineae: uultis odoratos positu uariare capillos* [19: you wish to vary the arrangement of your perfumed hair]. P. complains about Cynthia spending effort on her hair at 1.2.1–3, 1.15.5, 2.18.23–30. More generally on female coiffure in Rome, see Ov. *Ars* 3.133–68, and Gibson's commentary (with many further references to texts ancient and modern). Horace implies that the Spartan girl tied up her hair in a simple knot: *Odes* 2.11.23–4.

29–30 at nostra: 'but our woman', i.e. 'a Roman woman': the poem turns to the closing contrast.   **nec digitum angusta est inseruisse uia:** 'nor is it possible (*OLD sum* 9) to insert a finger in the packed street': the woman is so hemmed in by attendants that the lover cannot find an opening to slip a finger through and make bodily contact with her. What P. has in mind is clarified by Ov. *Ars* 1.605–6 *insere te turbae, leuiterque admotus eunti* | *uelle latus digitis, et pede tange pedem* [insert yourself in the crowd, and subtly moving up to her as she goes along feel her side with your fingers and touch foot against foot]. The perfect infinitive is freely used by the elegists as an alternative to the present when it is metrically convenient (e.g. 1.1.15 *potuit domuisse*, 3.5.19–20 n.; and see Platnauer 109–11).

31–2 nec quae sint faciles nec quae dent uerba roganti | **inuenias:** 'and you would not find which girls are easy and which deceive the man who asks'. For *facilis* so ('accommodating', 'susceptible to love'):

OLD 9), cf. 2.24.5, 2.29.33, 2.34.76. If the transmitted *facies*, not *faciles*, is correct, the meaning would be that it is impossible for the Roman man to discover what a girl looks like, so closely is she guarded, but this sits ill with the second half of the line: if he cannot even see her, how can he proposition her? For *uerba dare* + dative = 'I deceive, hoodwink', see *OLD uerbum* 6.   **caecum uersat amator iter**: 'the lover treads a path of darkness'.

33–4 iura...pugnasque: 'the regulations and bouts' or 'the fighting regulations' (hendiadys*).   **fores...imitata**: either = *imitata esses* ('you had imitated') or (with *fores* offering a future element) = 'you would be going to have imitated' (equivalent to *imitareris*, 'you were imitating': P. never has the second person singular imperfect subjunctive either passive or deponent). **hoc...bono**: 'thanks to this benefit'. The poem's final word looks back to *bona* in 2, just as *iura* (33) echoes *iura* in 1: an extremely common technique, known as 'enclosure'*.

Additional bibliography: B. Weiden Boyd, *CQ* 37 (1987), 527–8; Keith 2008: 36–7.

3.15

3–8: After I gained the liberty of adulthood Lycinna initiated me in love, without the need for gifts. Two years have now passed: I have scarcely spoken to her. 9–10, 45–6, 1–2, 43–4: My love for you is total; no other has embraced me. Do not listen to stories about me; even in death I shall love only you: on this basis may our love run smoothly. But you should not persecute Lycinna with the anger that women are prone to. 11–18: Dirce will support the point, so savage because Antiope had slept with Lycus. Often the queen pulled out her hair and scratched her face; often she overworked her and forced her to sleep on the ground and to live in a dark hovel; she denied her water. 19–22: Jupiter, are you not helping Antiope in her distress? It is a disgrace that your girl is a chained slave. 23–34: Using her own strength she broke the bonds, and ran away up Cithaeron in the cold of the night. Often she feared that her mistress was after her. She found Zethus harsh and Amphion softened by her tears,

*but was driven away. Like the sea growing calmer after a storm, she fell
to her knees. 35–42: Eventually the sons realized their mistake: old man,
protector of Jupiter's sons, you restored the mother to her boys. They tied
Dirce to a bull. Antiope, Jupiter has given you victory, and Dirce's limbs
are scattered in death. Zethus' fields are drenched in blood, and Amphion
celebrated with a paean.*

Antiope was a play of Euripides, now mainly lost, though over thirty
fragments* survive, including one of 116 verses from the final act
(223): see the Loeb volume *Euripides VII: Fragments* (ed. C. Collard
and M. Cropp), 170–227. It was famous in antiquity, being cited by
Plato, for example (*Gorg.* 485e–6d), and Dio Chrysostom, *Orat.* 73.10.
The second-century tragedian Pacuvius wrote a version in Latin, a
translation according to Cicero, *Fin.* 1.4; of his play we have nineteen
fragments*, none more than seven lines in length; for full commentary
(in German), see P. Schierl, *Die Tragödien des Pacuvius* (Berlin, 2006),
91–130; for an English translation see the Loeb volume *Remains of
Old Latin II* (ed. E. H. Warmington). Specific echoes are treated in
individual notes.

The myth is summarized in Hyginus, *Fab.* 7 and 8, the latter
purporting to be a summary of Euripides' play: 'Nycteus, king in
Boeotia, had a daughter called Antiope; attracted by her great beauty,
Jupiter made her pregnant. When her father wanted to punish her for
her depravity and was making dangerous threats, Antiope ran away.
It so happened that Epaphus of Sicyon was staying in the very place
to which she came; he took the woman home and married her.
Nycteus was angry at this and when he was dying, in an earnest
appeal he charged his brother Lycus, to whom he was leaving his
kingdom, not to leave Antiope unpunished. After Nycteus' death
Lycus came to Sicyon; he killed Epaphus, put Antiope in chains
and took her to Mount Cithaeron. Antiope gave birth to twins and
left them there; a shepherd brought them up and called them Zethus
and Amphion. Antiope was given to Dirce, the wife of Lycus, for her
to torture; she seized an opportunity and took to flight; she came to
her sons, of whom Zethus, thinking her a fugitive, did not take her in.
Dirce was brought to the same place through the ecstasy inspired by
Bacchus; she found Antiope there and started to drag her out to her
death. But the young men were informed by the shepherd who had

brought them up that she was their mother; they quickly caught up, seized their mother back, tied Dirce to a bull by her hair and killed her. When they were about to kill Lycus, Mercury forbade them, and at the same time ordered Lycus to yield the kingdom to Amphion.'

The retelling of a tragic narrative at such length adds to the generic complexity of the sequence of poems: see the final paragraph of the intro. to 3.13. However, *Antiope* does not take us as far from elegy as other tragedies might. In the first place, the story is brought in as an *exemplum** designed to affect Cynthia's behaviour: though it is different in extent, it is similar in function to the many *exempla* that were a distinctive feature of Book 1 (e.g. 1.2.15–20, 1.15.9–22); in fact 1.20 is similarly structured, with a long narrative backing up an initial warning. Secondly, Dirce's behaviour is very like Cynthia's, the physicality of her anger recalling the start of 3.8, for example, and her vindictiveness towards slaves will be echoed in 4.7 and 4.8, whereas Antiope's fearful night-time journey matches what P. himself will face in 3.16; he too has an aggressive *domina* (3.15.28, 3.16.1). Exclamations (6, 13, 15) and apostrophes* (19, 36, 39, 42) make the style emotional. But perhaps most significant is the character given to Antiope's two sons, brought out by Euripides' often cited *agon** in which Zethus attacked his brother for the time he wastes singing rather than working the farm (Eur. fr. 183–8) and Amphion responded strongly, arguing for the morality of the quiet life that concerns itself with things of the mind (fr. 193–202). The antithesis is like those central to Propertian poetry: action versus pleasure; wealth versus ease; male versus female; *arma* versus *amor*: see 29, 41–2 nn.

When a group of lines is omitted in the copying of a text, a subsequent reader may notice the omission (perhaps when formally checking against the exemplar) and try to put it right. Unless the error has occurred at the top or bottom of a page it will be difficult to find room for the missing lines in the margin adjacent to the point where they are to be inserted, and sometimes they get broken up, with the result that when they are restored, further dislocation or loss results (cf. 3.4.17–18, 3.6.3–4, 3.13.39–40, 3.22.15–16). One place where omitted couplets end up is at the beginning or end of a poem, where an interstice* may provide space and where they may seem less to interrupt the sequence of thought. This poem has an obvious lacuna* between 10 and 11, for Dirce cannot be a witness (11) to P.'s fidelity (10); the mad excess of a woman's jealous anger is what Dirce illustrates (and the punishment that can result), and that has been rightly found in verse 44. But there are compelling reasons to think that verses 1–2, 45–6 are also misplaced, and they seem to belong in the same lacuna (see *Cynthia* and nn. below). Some MSS indicate the start of a new poem at verse 11, perhaps because a mark of omission has been misunderstood.

3–4 Vt mihi praetexti pudor est releuatŭs amictūs: 'when the restraint of boyhood clothing was removed from me'. 'The change from the status of [upper class] child to man was marked by the change in dress from a *toga praetexta* with a purple stripe [the *praetextus amictus* referred to here] that all [upper-class] adult males wore. The age at which this change took place varied, but tended to occur by a male's seventeenth birthday...' (M. Harlow and R. Laurence, *Growing Up and Growing Old in Ancient Rome* (London, 2002), 67). It was the public sign that he had reached puberty and that the time was ripe to engage in adult activities; for the elegist this means not politics or warfare, but sex.   **libertas noscere Amoris** [*or* amoris] **iter:** all four words occur in 1.1, *libertas* in 28, *Amor* in 4 and 34, and 1.1.30 reads *qua non ulla meum femina norit iter* [where no woman may know my route]. The echoes strengthen the sense of a return to the beginning developed in 5–6. For the connotations of *iter*, cf. 3.10.32 n. On *Amoris*, see 3.21.2 n.: here too the text uses the capital to bring out the personification*, which may otherwise be missed: 'the path to [*or* travelled by] Amor'.

5–6 illa: looking forward to *Lycinna* in the next line: 'it was she, Lycinna, who...'   **conscia:** 'sharing in secret' or possibly 'expert' (cf. Valerius, *Arg.* 3.301 *mens conscia uatum* [the informed minds of prophets]).   **primas:** this overturns the implication of the opening words of 1.1 *Cynthia prima*, reprised at 1.12.20; the juxtaposition <u>*conscia primas*</u> seems designed to produce an echo. **imbuit:** 'initiated', often found, as here, in combination with words like *rudis* and *primus*.   **heu:** the poet expresses regret that the generous spontaneity of Lycinna is in strong contrast with his subsequent experience of women. P. thus touches on the elegiac *puella*'s desire for expensive presents, a major theme of the previous two

258   *A Commentary on Propertius, Book 3*

poems.   **Lycinna:** a rare name, possibly a corruption of
Lycaena: it may be no coincidence that a woman named *Lycaenion*
performs a similar role for Daphnis in *Daphnis & Chloe* 3.15–19. In
either form it plays on the Greek for 'she-wolf' and thus hints at
the Latin *lupa* ('she-wolf', and 'prostitute'). Only the analogy with
Antiope supports the commentators' notion that Lycinna is Cynthia's
slave. She appears nowhere else in the corpus*.

7–8 tertius (haud multo minus est) iam ducitur annus: 'The third
year is now passing (it is not much less)'. This is not to be taken as
biographical truth: to judge from the indicated dates, seven years
separate the publications of Book 1 (*c.*29 BC), which introduces
Cynthia, and 3 (*c.*22 BC). There seems to be a similar contraction of
the real time-scale in Book 2 (a month's gap after 1: 2.3.3–4; six
months: 2.20.21–2).   **nobis uerba coisse decem:** 'that we had
shared ten words', lit. 'that ten words had come together for us'.
Butrica (*Phoenix* 48 (1994), 136) suggests that there is a play on the
verb *coisse*: any recent intercourse with Lycinna was strictly verbal.

9–10 cuncta tuus sepeliuit amor: a striking image, which perhaps
plays on the repeated address of Cynthia as *uita* ('life'): love of her
has hidden everything else and made it as if dead. But the phrasing
also equates his love for Cynthia with death, which overcomes everything in the end (3.5.13–18, 3.18.20–8).   **nec femina post te:**
the poet forgets the earlier claim to have two mistresses (2.22B) and
to prefer street-walkers (2.23–4)—or implies that they were fiction.
dulcia uincla: 'sweet bonds' i.e. embraces; the metaphorical *uincla*
contrast with the real ones borne by Antiope (20–4).

45–6 is isolated where it is transmitted, at the end of the poem, and
provides a neat restatement of 9–10.   **fabula:** each of the
lovers is troubled by being the subject of gossip, once the publication
of Book 1 has made them famous (2.24.1–2): *cum sis iam noto fabula
libro / et tua sit toto Cynthia lecta foro* [though you are a byword since
your book became known, and your Cynthia is read all over the
forum]; P. repeatedly questions or affirms the credibility and power
of rumour (2.5.29; 2.18.37; 2.32.21–30).   **concitet aures:** 'let
it rouse your ears', i.e. pass through your ears and rouse your anger. P.
gives ears qualities or emotions that might more often be attributed

to the mind or the whole individual (in 1.1 for example they are
'easy', 31, and 'slow', 37).   **et lignis funeris ustus:** 'even if
burnt by funeral logs', i.e. even in the ashes of my pyre. The image of
burial appears in 9; he now envisages himself cremated.   **te
solam ... amem** is a variant on the classic elegiac assertion of love, *tu
mihi sola places* (2.7.19; [Tib.] 3.19.3; quoted humorously by Ovid
at *Ars* 1.42).

1–2 Richardson comments *ad loc.*: '*Sic ... iam norim ... nec ueniat*:
this is a wish or prayer formula regularly followed by *ut* with the
indicative, ... Here the *ut* clause of line 3, no matter how we emend
it, can be nothing of the sort; it is the beginning of the narrative of
explanation that then follows.' He saw that the couplet must affirm
some statement of committed love: hence the repositioning of the
couplet here.   **sic ego non ullos iam norim** (= *nouerim*) **in
amore tumultus:** 'so may I know no storms [*or* violent disorder] in my
love in future'. See 3.6.2 n., and, for the negative in a wish used to mark
an asseveration*, Verg. *Ecl.* 10.4–5.   **nec ueniat sine te nox
uigilanda mihi:** 'and may no night come for me to spend awake without
you'. *sine te* is crucial: wakeful nights come in two kinds for lovers, those
spent in bed with the *puella*, and those in discomfort, locked out on the
doorstep (3.20.22; Tib. 1.2.78 *cum fletu nox uigilanda uenit*).

43–4 non meritam ... Lycinnam: 'Lycinna, who does not deserve it
[i.e. such treatment]'.   **parcas:** for *parco* + infinitive meaning
'refrain from', see *OLD* 2c.   **nescit uestra ruens ira referre
pedem:** 'the anger of your sex does not know how to retreat once it
begins to charge'. For the reference to women generally, cf. 3.19.2–4.

11–12 testis erit: for the future ('will serve as a witness'), cf. 2.32.28.
tam uero crimine saeua | Nyctĕŏs Antiopen accubuisse Lyco: 'so
savage at the true accusation that Antiope, (daughter) of Nycteus,
had slept with Lycus'. *Nycteos* (Eur. fr. 223.42) and *Antiopen* are Greek
genitive and accusative respectively. Some have changed *uero* to *sero*
('late') or *uano* ('empty'), but according to Hyg. *Fab.* 7 (a somewhat
different version from 8, translated in the intro.) Antiope had married Lycus ('wolf' in Greek), just as P. has had a relationship with
Lycinna (6 n.). The mythological parallel warns Cynthia of the
consequences of unrestrained anger, not of false accusation.

13–14 a quotiens begins a sequence that continues with *a quotiens* (15), *saepe* (17), *saepe* (18): similarly Tib. 2.3.17–23, Ov. *Her.* 17.81–5. **pulchros ... capillos**: a striking and apparently unique combination; Dirce's hair plays a part at the end of story, unspoken here, but cf. Hyginus 8.   **molliaque immites fixit in ora manus**: the orderly expression of this golden* line heightens by contrast the violence which it describes. The diction marks Dirce as grand (*regina*) and harsh (*immites; iniquis*, 15), Antiope as elegiac in nature (*pulchros capillos; mollia* contrasted with *dura*, 16, 20—and n.b. 29).

15–18 famulam: Antiope's subject status is conveyed; cf. *dominae*, 28. **pensis ... iniquis**: 'with unfair tasks': she has quantities (lit. 'weights') of wool to work on, like Cynthia's slaves at 3.6.15, and they are so big as to weigh her down (*onerauit*).   **caput in dura ponere ... humo**: i.e. in order to sleep. Here and in 17 it is the text of Pacuvius that is brought to mind (though presumably Euripidean phrasing lies behind it): *Antiope* fr. 8–10, esp. 9 Schierl (= 24 Warmington) *perdita illuuie atque insomnia* [desperate through dirt and lack of sleep]. **tenebris**: the noun is used of dark and squalid buildings (*OLD* 1b), and the detail is shared with Hyginus, *Fab.* 7 *imperauit* [i.e. *Dirce*] *famulis ut eam in tenebris uinctam clauderent*.   **uilem ieiunae saepe negauit aquam**: 'often she refused a mean drink of water to the thirsty girl'. *ieiunae* normally means 'hungry', which is also possible here, adding another detail to her inhumane treatment.

19–20 Iuppiter: Jupiter is addressed as the ravisher of Antiope and the father of her twins. She talks of the neglect of the 'gods' in Eur. fr. 208.   **nusquam**: 'at no juncture', 'under no circumstances': *OLD* 4.   **tot mala** echoes Eur. fr. 204 'Mankind has many troubles', perhaps spoken by Antiope herself (cf. also fr. 211).   **corrumpit**: 'spoils'.   **dura catena manus**: *molles* is implied with *manus* (14 n., 29 n.)

21–2 si deus es: such conditional clauses do not necessarily express real doubt, but strengthen what follows; cf. T. C. W. Stinton, '*Si credere dignum est*: some expressions of disbelief in Euripides and others', *PCPhS* 22 (1976), 60–89 = *Collected Papers* (Oxford, 1990), 236–64.   **tibi turpe tuam seruire puellam**: 'it is shameful for you that your girl is a slave', a sentiment enhanced by the alliteration. Eur. fr. 217–18 are exclamations over the misfortunes

of slavery.   **inuocet Antiope quem nisi uincta Iouem?**:
'whom except Jupiter is Antiope to call on in her chains?' *inuocet*
can be read as deliberative subjunctive. *uincta* looks back to *catena*
(20) and on to *manicas* (24).

23–4 tamen: despite Jupiter's lack of assistance.   **quaecumque aderant in corpore uires**: lit. 'whatever strength there was in her
body'; the grammar is separated from the main clause, but one may
understand 'with' or 'using' before 'whatever'. Shackleton Bailey
helpfully adduced Livy 45.1.1 *uictoriae nuntii...quanta potuit ad-
hiberi festinatio celeriter Romam cum uenissent* [when those reporting
the victory had come to Rome, <with> as much haste as could be
produced].   **regales manicas**: 'the manacles which the queen
had put on her'.   **utrāque manu**: i.e. 'with her two hands'.

25–8 The influence of a dramatic telling might explain the surprising
sequence in which she heads to Cithaeron (25; Map 2), lies down to
sleep (26), and then goes along the valley of the Asopus, which lies
between Thebes and Cithaeron (27–8). Such events are sometimes
revealed in tragedy through a mixture of iambic narrative and lyric
exchange with the chorus (*timido pede* could serve as a commentary
on the latter, in its secondary sense 'in fearful rhythm': 3.1.6 n.).
Cithaeronis...in arces: 'to the heights of Cithaeron', the mountain
where her sons had been exposed, and now live.   **sparso triste
cubile gelu**: 'her bed was grim with scattered frost', *erat* being understood.   **uago Asopi sonitu permota fluentis**: 'alarmed by the
wandering sound of the river Asopus [*lit.* of the flowing Asopus]': *uago*
may be a transferred epithet, implying the meandering of the river;
more straightforwardly, it conveys that the sound is 'shifting' or
'uncertain' (*OLD* 3), and thus easily misinterpreted as Dirce in pursuit.

29–30 et durum Zethum et lacrimis Amphiona mollem | experta est:
'she found Zethus harsh and Amphion softening at her tears'.
Amphiona is a Greek accusative. The antithetical phrasing
(3.1.19 n.) evokes the *agon** between the two brothers (see intro.),
in which each identifies Amphion with the weak and feminine (cf.
mollis), at fr. 185.3, 199.1. The presence of *lacrimis* makes him seem
especially elegiac (cf. 1.6.24 *lacrimis omnia nota meis*, and *Cynthia* on
4.1.120).   **stabulis...abacta suis**: 'driven from the homestead

that was properly hers'. Her sons should have welcomed their mother to their humble country dwelling and made it her home; but according to Hyginus (see intro.), Zethus treated her as a runaway slave and refused to take her in. *stabulis* occurs, presumably of the 'pens' or 'stalls' of Zethus and Amphion, at Pacuvius, *Antiope* fr. 16 Schierl (= 15 Warmington) *nonne hinc uos propere stabulis amolimini* [are you not moving yourselves swiftly away from our farmstead]; the plural makes it unlikely that this was addressed to Antiope.

31–4 The changing motion of the sea is one of the most persistent of similes, especially in epic (e.g. *Il.*2.144–9, 4.422–7; *Aen.* 7.528–30, 10.97–9; most similar to this is Silius 7.253–9). Here, in elegy, the image is transferred from great armies to a single woman. The point seems to be the move from passionate excitement to quiet despair: a diminuendo before the dramatic entrance of the old man, and the revelation to the twins of their unconscious impiety.   **ac ueluti:** *ac* is rare in P., apparently restricted to this set phrase (2.3.47, 2.15.51) and *ac primum* (3.10.13).   **magnos cum ponunt aequora motūs:** 'when the sea gives up its mighty motions'.   **aduersus ire Noto:** 'to go in opposition to Notus'. The opposition of the winds (mythologically brothers) has been seen as providing an image of the *agon** between Zethus and Amphion.   **litore subtractae sonitus rarescit harenae:** 'the sound of sand dragged down on the shore lessens'.   **cadit inflexo lapsa puella genu:** the pleonasm* perhaps marks the stages of a gradual collapse; cf. also *Aen.* 6.310 *lapsa cadunt folia* [the leaves slip and fall].

35–8 sera tamen, pietas: 'though late, piety (comes)': for *tamen* marking a concessive clause, cf. 2.34.50 *trux tamen, a nobis ante domandus eris* [fierce though you are, you will need taming first by us], 3.24.30 (= 25.10).   **digne Iouis natos qui tueare senex:** *digne* and *senex* are vocatives, the former leading into a generic relative clause: 'old man worthy to protect the sons of Jupiter'. The poet addresses the old man who found and brought up the boys and has now revealed their identity to them and their mother. **pueris...pueri:** after the repetition *natis...natos*, which stresses their relationship with Jupiter and Antiope, this verse stresses their youth.   **Dircen:** Greek accusative. Her fate is illustrated in the famous sculpture in the National Archaeological Museum at

Naples known as the Farnese Bull. According to Pliny, *Nat.* 36.33–4, such a sculpture (possibly this one) was put on display at Rome by Asinius Pollio (76 BC–AD 4): the poet will have seen it. **sub trucis ora bouis**: 'under the eyes of a fierce bull': this is literally true of Dirce in the case of the Farnese Bull.

39–40 Antiope…; Dirce: the unusual strong break before the final foot of the line increases the emphatic antithesis between the two names. **cognosce Iouem**: 'acknowledge Jupiter', i.e. recognize that he had an unseen part in the working out of events: she now has fame (as Jupiter's mistress, for her heroism in the escape, and as the mother of the (re-)founders of Thebes), whereas her tormentor undergoes a horrific death. **in multis…locis**: Dirce will meet her death 'in many places' because her body is scattered as the bull drags her all over the area. The lacunose* fr. 221 of the Euripides play apparently has her becoming part of the countryside, dragged by the bull along with rock and oaktree (cf. also 223.62, 81). There is no hint here of her traditional transformation into the spring called Dirce with which Thebes was identified (3.17.33 n.). At Eur. *Bacch.* 1219–21 Pentheus' body is scattered over Cithaeron by the Maenads.

41–2 prata cruentantur Zethi: for fields fertilized by human blood, cf. 1.22.10 (implicit), Verg. *Geo.* 1.491–2 *sanguine nostro | Emathiam et latos Haemi pinguescere campos* [that Thessaly and the broad plains of Haemus grow rich with our (i.e. Roman) blood]; Hor. *Odes* 2.1.29–30. **uictor**: though applied to Amphion (and perhaps carrying the implication that he was victor in their war of words), this is valid for both brothers in terms of the action of the *Antiope* and thus appropriately stands next to the name of Zethus. **paeana**: Greek accusative of the word *paean*, a victory song. **Aracynthe**: a peak, like Cithaeron, on the border between Boeotia and Attica: cf. Verg. *Ecl.* 2.23–4 (and Clausen *ad loc.*):

> canto quae solitus, si quando armenta uocabat,
> Amphion Dircaeus in Actaeo Aracyntho.

[I sing what, if ever he was summoning the herds, Amphion of Thebes (*Dircaeus* is ironic, as he killed her) was accustomed to sing on Attic Aracynthus.]

The couplet presents another striking antithesis between the brothers, marked by the initial words of hexameter (*prata*, summing up Zethus' concern with the farm) and pentameter (*paeana*, the song of Amphion, who later used his music to charm the rocks into building the walls of Thebes: 3.2.5–6); the former is associated with blood and death, the latter is marked by emotive engagement with the landscape (note the apostrophe* *Aracynthe*) and reminiscence of pastoral.

Additional bibliography: Macleod 1983: 169–70 = *CQ* 24 (1974), 92–3; E. W. Leach, 'The punishment of Dirce in a newly discovered painting in the Casa di Giulio Polibio and its significance within the visual tradition', *MDAI(R)* 93 (1986), 157–82; J. L. Butrica, *Phoenix* 48 (1994), 135–51.

3.16

1–4: I have received a midnight summons from my mistress to come to Tibur at once. 7–10: There is a danger of assault in travel by night but postponing the journey will provoke my mistress to tears and violence against me: she has attacked me in the past. 11–18: However, lovers are under a special protection from man and beast, and nobody assaults them. 19–24: Indeed, if I were to be killed, my death would be a benefit because my mistress would bury me and tend my grave. 25–30: I hope that my grave will be in an out-of-the-way place.

1–2 Nox media: a dramatic opening, itself cut short by the elision before *et*. Two previous poems, 1.3 and 2.29A, have *narrated* events from night-time. In each P. remembers being out on the street drunk before finding his way to Cynthia. In 1.16 a house door repeats the nocturnal complaints of a locked-out lover (similar to but not actually identified as the poet). Only in 2.33B has night been specified as the time of the poem: Cynthia drinks deep into the night, her compelling beauty unaffected by her partying. The rest of the couplet shows quickly and clearly that we have a very different situation here: P. is not straying from Cynthia, but commanded by her (compare the lover at Ov. *Ars* 2.227–30); and travel, which is in Book 1 repeatedly

presented as a symbol of estrangement (e.g. 1.6, 8A, 11, 17), is here
(as in 2.26B) a danger undertaken to maintain the relationship.
dominae mihi uenit epistula nostrae: P., like other authors, freely
uses the first person plural of himself, even in the same clause as the
singular (so at 3.5.3–4, 3.9.35–6). *mihi* itself is dative of advantage,
and here with the verb of motion (*uenit*) differs little in effect from *ad
me.*   **Tībŭrĕ:** 'at Tibur'. The locative of the third declension
can be in -ĕ or -ī; *Tībŭrī* is the usual form in prose, but cannot fit
into a dactylic verse*, so poets use this form (e.g. Hor. *Epist.* 1.8.12,
Ov. *Fast.* 6.670). Tibur (modern Tivoli) was a resort town at the edge
of the Sabine Hills to the east of Rome (Map 1), with spectacular
views over the Tiber valley and many grand villas. It is one of a
number of local towns mentioned as destinations for Cynthia's
outings in 2.32.3–6, and at 4.7.81–6 her ghost indicates *Tiburna
terra* as the place of her burial.   **missa ... mora:** 'without
delay', but literally 'delay having been abandoned', so that Cynthia's
instruction comes with the implication that P. should already have
come—and the poem itself shows that he does hesitate and think the
matter through despite her instruction.   **iussit:** 'she has
ordered', in her letter written in the past but still active in the present.

3–4 After the concise summary of the situation, we are given an
evocative description of Tibur. The falls of the river Anio were (and
are) a famous feature of the town, a drop of over 100 metres, often
celebrated in poetry (Hor. *Carm.* 1.7.13, Statius, *Siluae* 1.5.25), and
in paintings of the eighteenth and nineteenth centuries. The hexameter on the other hand is obscure and difficult: **candida qua geminas
ostendunt culmina turres** ('the place where white roofs make visible
the twin towers') does not bring out features for which Tibur was
known. Some have seen a reference to buildings perched on the
heights on either side of the falls; that would certainly give point to
geminas: compare Statius' description of the villa of Vopiscus, which
actually spanned the river (*Siluae* 1.3.1–2): 'the chill Tiburtine estate
of eloquent Vopiscus and the twin (*geminos*) homes threaded by
Anio' (Shackleton Bailey's translation). But in such close combination with *turres*, it is hard not to take *culmina* as 'roofs', and
ostendunt hardly fits this reading. An alternative would be to see
the *turres* as those of Rome (3.21.15), and to take *ostendunt* as 'afford

a view of' (*OLD* 2e). However, we would need to suppose that the text had been corrupted in transmission, with *qua geminas* replacing (e.g.) *ubi urbanas*.   **nympha Aniena**: The ancients associated all watercourses with nymphs (or, for grander rivers such as the Tiber, deities), and frequently the two are identified.

5–6 quid faciam? obductis committam mene tenebris, | ut timeam audaces in mea membra manus? Deliberative subjunctives: 'What am I to do? Am I to entrust myself to the covering darkness so that I fear the hands of reckless men on my person?' This translates *ut* as indicating result, but it may be concessive ('although': *OLD* 35). P. postpones* the question enclitic* -*ne* for metrical benefit also at 3.6.12.

7–10 A classic account of the relationship between P. and Cynthia: the tears that will follow any delay in carrying out her wishes (7–8), and the possibility of rejection (9) and violence (10) are far more of a threat to his well-being than any fear of highwaymen. The phrasing of 10 **in me** *mansuetas non habet illa* **manus** carefully picks up that of 6: *audaces* **in mea** *membra* **manus**, as *timore* (7) does *timeam* (6). The couplet 9–10 has interesting sound effects: eight *m*s (three of them in final -*um* in 9, three of them initial sounds in 10), seven *s*s, and the two verbs in 9 linked by initial *p*; on the clash of ictus and accent in the hexameter see p. 43.   **fletus saeuior**: supply *erit*. **peccaram**: the syncopated* form, for *peccaueram* ('I had made a mistake'). Though *semel* minimizes the wrong-doing, we are left to speculate on how serious the peccadillo might have been: arrival a few minutes late on one occasion, or real infidelity? The punishment is then emphasized by the contrasting *totum... in annum.*

11–12 Lovers are so strongly associated with the gods Venus (20) and Cupid (16) that they can be regarded as 'sacred' and thus protected from harm; they could travel confidently (*media uia*) even past the home of Sciron, a bandit who, according to mythology, lived near Megara on the coast between the Peloponnese and Attica. He forced travellers to bend down and wash his feet and then kicked them over the edge of a cliff; he was one of several such figures dealt with by Theseus as he travelled the dangerous road from Troezen to Athens (see 3.22.37–8). The hero pushed Sciron over the cliff himself, as he apparently narrated in the one-book epic *Hecale* by P.'s Greek model Callimachus. **tamen** contrasts the dangers of offending Cynthia with those threatened by the *nocturnus hostis.* **laedat:** the subjunctive shows that the relative clause is generic 'such as would harm sacred lovers'. **quis** = *quibus,* referring back to *amantes,* and dative with the impersonal verb *licet.* Relative pronouns, like other conjunctions, are regularly postponed* to the second half of the pentameter by the elegists. The manuscript tradition has *si licet* or *scilicet,* neither of which makes sense here.

13–14 Scythicis . . . oris: Scythia was for the Romans the distant area stretching north of the Black Sea (which is evoked by *oris,* 'shores'), a place of danger and alien attitudes, where one could expect the barbarian inhabitants not to respect strangers: Cicero uses Scythia as typical of *barbaria* at *Verr.* 2.5.150, *de Natura Deorum* 2.88; and Ovid increases the horror of his exile to Tomi on the Black Sea by placing it in Scythia; cf. also Curtius Rufus 4.6.3 *Scytharum bellicosissima gente et rapto uiuere adsueta* [the race of Scythians being the most warlike and accustomed to live on what they have stolen]. **erit . . . uolet:** gnomic* futures for the generalization: see G&L §242 n.1, and e.g. Publilius Syrus 40 *animo imperabit sapiens, stultus seruiet* [the wise man will command his feelings, the fool will be a slave to them]. **licet:** as well as 'it is possible' (as in 12), this word is used as a concessive conjunction with the subjunctive: 'let him walk, it is allowed' being equivalent to 'though he walk'. **adeo ut feriat barbarus:** 'barbarous to such an extent as to strike'.

 This couplet is one of many quotations found among the graffiti in Pompeii. In three respects this provides a better text than the oldest manuscript N: *ambulet > ambulat; adeo > deo; feriat > noceat. noceat* may well have arisen in an attempt to provide a verb to govern *deo;* 'no one will wish to be barbarian to harm a god' makes a kind of sense, but lacks an adverb to lead into *ut,* and hardly suits the context. A fourth reading of the inscription (*Scythiae*) is also possible, but it is the kind of substitution easily made by someone writing from memory.

19–20 The couplet moves from belittling the threat faced by the travelling lover to a description of the journey he may expect with Venus as his companion. In the transmitted text the same change of

268   *A Commentary on Propertius, Book 3*

topic has occurred, rather abruptly, between verses 14 and 15, and scholars have therefore seen that 19–20 has been displaced in the manuscripts, as happens quite regularly.   **spargatur:** *sanguine tam paruo* suggests that the lover would be so insignificant a prize that no ruffian would wish to attack him and be stained by his blood. But interpretation of the subjunctive *spargatur* is tricky. There seems little point in taking it as implying a hypothetical situation: 'the lover has so little blood, no one would be stained with it—if he were to attack him'. Perhaps then it indicates propriety or obligation: 'for what rogue is to be stained with the small amount of blood a lover has?' For the conventional feebleness of the lover compare e.g. 1.5.21–2, 2.22.21; Ov. *Am.* 1.6.5 *longus amor... corpus tenuauit;* lack of blood is regularly imputed to the elderly, e.g. Ov. *Met.* 13.409, Valerius Maximus 3.8.5, Sen. *Ag.* 657–8, Juvenal 10.217.   **ecce** marks the change of direction dramatically. *ecce suis it* is a conjecture for *exclusis fit:* it has been widely felt that the notion of the *exclusus amator* is alien to the poem. P. is generalizing from his own situation and he is not currently excluded from Cynthia's favour. For the verb, *it* is much more vivid than *fit,* and a common idiom when accompanied by *comes.*

16 ipse Amor concutit ante faces: well-to-do Romans were normally accompanied by slaves (so P. notes their absence at 2.29.1–2 *cum potus nocte uagarer | nec me seruorum duceret ulla manus* [when I was wandering drunk at night and no band of slaves was accompanying me]), and at night they would have carried torches (cf. 1.3.9–10 *cum... quaterent sera nocte facem pueri* [when the slave-boys were shaking the torch late at night]). Here Cupid does the job, for which he is admirably equipped since he carries a torch, which symbolizes his fanning of the fires of love.

17–18 saeua canum rabies = *saeui et rabiosi canes.* Cf. e.g. 1.20.15–16 *miser error Herculis* = *miser et errans Hercules.* P. has been influenced by phrases such as *Aeneid* 4.132 *odora canum uis* [the keenly scented power of hounds]. Guard-dogs, farm-dogs, feral dogs all have fearsome reputations in ancient literature as attacking strangers: cf. Cicero, *de Natura Deorum* 2.158 *canum... odium in externos;* Hor. *Epod.* 6.1; Apuleius, *Met.* 8.17 'the workers on an estate which we happened to pass...set dogs on us. These were mad, enormous creatures, fiercer (*saeuiores*) than any wolf or bear,... a mass of hotly excited dogs,... making the rounds of our entire convoy with snapping jaws (*morsibus*).' The pentameter ends the section with an appropriate generalization: 'the road is safe for this class [i.e. lovers] at any time at all.'

21–2 quod si certa meos sequerentur funera casus, | talis mors pretio uel sit emenda mihi: 'But if a particular <kind of> funeral would accompany my fall, it would be right for me actually (*uel*) to buy such a death for cash.' P. suddenly realizes that there is another reason why he should obey his mistress's call: the lover's safety does not matter, for death would be worth while if only it meant that Cynthia would bury him and tend his grave in a suitably elegiac manner.   **meos...casus:** Latin poets use plural for singular freely, even when (as here) there is no metrical benefit; **funera** is another example, though that word has to be in the plural to scan here.

23–30 Death, burial, and memorials are a characteristic theme for P. from Book 1 on, starting with 1.6.27–8 (**N**) and 1.7.23–4 (*nec poterunt iuuenes nostro reticere sepulchro: | 'ardoris nostri magne poeta, iaces?'* [nor will the young men be able to keep quiet at my tomb: 'Great poet of our passion, do you lie dead?']). It is Cynthia's reaction to his death that is most explored, however, as at 1.17.16–24, 1.19, and especially 2.13.17–58. In that poem death results from Cynthia's rejection of him, but he gives her instructions for his funeral, rejecting anything expensive or pompous (19–23) in favour of a plebeian event (23–4). But what matters most is the presence of his poetry (25–6) and Cynthia herself, passionately displaying her grief (27–8), and kissing him for the final time (29). His ashes will be collected in a little jar (32), his tomb will be small and shaded by a poetic laurel (33–4), and even his epitaph will be shorter than the two lines assigned to it (35–6). The emphasis in 3.16 on the small scale and the avoidance of the grand links with the opening of 2.13 (**Q**), which shows the poet favouring the 'slender Muses' of love poetry (3) rather than military matter of epic (1): see p. 7. Discussions of the poet's death and burial are also found at 2.1.71–8, 2.8.17–28, 2.27, 3.1.21–4.

23–4 haec at first might refer to *mors*, but in the pentameter it becomes clear that the reference is to Cynthia.   **unguenta... sertisque:** wreaths are a major feature of modern funerals too, and perfumes were expected in the ancient world: cf. e.g. 4.7.32–4; even in 2.13, where P. says *desit odoriferis ordo mihi lancibus* (23: 'there should be no column of scent-bearing dishes for me'), he still expects 'an onyx jar full of Syrian unguent' (30: *Syrio munere plenus onyx*). **custos:** The lack of a *custos* is one of the complaints made by Cynthia's ghost, at 4.7.25: guards were placed on tombs to ward off those who might steal the offerings buried with the dead (cf. Chariton, *Callirhoe* 1.7–10), witches, whose interest would be in the fresh cadaver itself, which might contribute to powerful spells (cf. Apuleius, *Met.* 2.21–6, 30; Hor. *Epod.* 5), and perhaps wild animals. Here, in P.'s imagination, Cynthia's commitment is such that she takes on the role herself: cf. the behaviour of the 'Widow of Ephesus' in Petronius, *Satyrica* 111 (but not in 112, when her attitude goes through something of a revolution!).

25–6 di faciant mea ne terra locet ossa frequenti | qua facit assiduo tramite uulgus iter: 'May the gods make sure she does not place my bones in a crowded place where the populace travels on a busy road.' Grammatically *mea* belongs after *ne*. Rejection of the common people, or at least their aesthetic judgement, is a repeated theme in Callimachus; see esp. Epigram 28.1–4 Pfeiffer (= 30 Loeb): 'I detest the cyclic poem, nor do I take pleasure in the road that carries many to and fro. I hate the promiscuous lover, and I do not drink from the public well: I abhor all common things.' Cf. Cat. 95.9–10 *parua mei mihi sunt cordi monumenta <sodalis>; | at populus tumido gaudeat Antimacho* [The writings of my <friend> are my delight; let the common people delight in swollen Antimachus (an early Greek poet, whose work was disliked by Callimachus)], and Hor. *Odes* 3.1.1 *Odi profanum uulgus et arceo* [I hate the irreligious crowd and keep them out].

27–8 post mortem tumuli sic infamantur amantum: given the run of thought, apparently to be understood as follows: 'Thus [i.e. if placed by a busy road] are the tombs of lovers maligned after death.' **arborea... coma:** This combines two features of earlier burial poems: the planting of a tree over the tomb (2.13.33–4) and (through the choice of *coma* to refer to foliage) the offering of hair by the leading mourner (1.17.21; cf. Achilles by Patroclus' pyre at *Iliad* 23.141–53, and Richardson 1993, *ad loc.*).

29–30 Here the correction of views expressed in 2.13 reaches its height (contrast also 3.1.37). Whereas in 2.13 he sees his tomb as gaining greater fame than the tomb of Achilles on which Polyxena was sacrificed (37–8), here P. follows his Callimachean* instincts further in his concern to avoid contact with crowds. So determined is he to stay away from the highway (30: cf. 3.1.14–18) that he now prefers the idea of burial in sand that is 'obscure' and 'unmarked' (*ignotae*). The poor were buried in mass graves, but the marble tombs of the better off normally stood by the main roads running out of a town and carried the name of the occupant (as Cynthia's appears in her epitaph at 4.7.75, on the road between Rome and Tibur). *harenae* might also suggest the seashore (3.7.26, 11.35), though that takes us away from the road to Tibur. **media ... uia:** cf. 12; here 'on the public road' (*OLD medius* 4b) rather than 'in the middle of the highway'. **nomen habere** is a pun. He neither wants his name to appear on a grand roadside tomb, nor wishes to have a reputation for following the well-travelled route.

3.17

1–6: Bacchus, I offer worship to you: please favour me. You are not inexperienced in love (7–8) and have the power to ameliorate its effects: wash away my folly. 9–12: Only death or wine can cure me; sobriety tortures lovers. 13–20: If you help me sleep, I shall plant vineyards; if my wine-making is successful, I shall become your poet. 21–8: I shall sing of your birth and your deeds. 29–38: I shall describe your appearance and how you are worshipped with dancing, music, and wine. 39–42: This will be in the grand style of tragedy or Pindar—provided you free me from my love and let me sleep.

Hymns and prayers are a major category in ancient poetry, featuring as parts of longer works (e.g. in epic *Iliad* 1.37–42 [to Apollo], *Aeneid* 8.287–302 [Hercules] and Ov. *Met.* 4.11–31; in drama Sen. *Oed.* 403–508 [Bacchus]) and as complete poems, both those that concentrate on single narratives (so, e.g., *Homeric Hymns* 1–7, of which 7 tells the story of the transformation into dolphins of the Etruscan pirates who capture Bacchus, and 1, now fragmentary, the reception of Dionysus on Olympus; Callimachus, *Hymns* 3 [Artemis], 4 [Delos]; Catullus 63 [Cybele]) and those that take a varied approach to the deity in asking for attention or favour (called 'cletic'* hymns when they specifically summon the god). This falls into this last group, alongside lyric hymns such as Sappho fr. 1 (Aphrodite); Cat. 34 (Diana); Hor. *Odes* 1.10 and 3.11 (Mercury), 1.19 and 30 (Venus), 1.35 (Fortuna), 3.21 (a parody, to a wine-jar); and, in elegy, Callimachus, *Hymn* 5 (Athena) and Tib. 2.5 (Apollo). Typical of such hymns are an opening vocative (1), often (though not here) with an appositional phrase (*o Latonia, maximi magna progenies Iouis* [daughter of Latona, great offspring of greatest Jove], Cat. 34.5–6) or a relative clause attached ('Our father, which art in heaven'), followed by the 'aretalogy'*, a list of the powers displayed by the god in general (3–5) and in specific myths (21–8), often starting with the birth myth (21): such lists are regularly bound together by anaphora* or polyptoton*, usually of *tu* (3–8). If a prayer is formulated specifically, it may come at beginning (2, 6) or end (41–2), perhaps with a vow (13–40), and general (3–5, 7–8) or individual (9–10) reasoning for the appropriateness of support. Evocation of the cult and its geographical spread (27–38, 22), alternative names for the deity and etymological play (5–6) are frequent features. The classic treatment of hymnic style is E. Norden, *Agnostos Theos* (Berlin, 1913), 143 ff. (in German). Also addressed to Bacchus are two Horatian odes that have hymnic elements (2.19, 3.25), and Ovid imitates this poem in his account of the Liberalia, a Bacchic festival, at *Fasti* 3.713–90. Catullus 76.17–26 is a prayer to the gods in general (*o di*) for relief from love treated as a sickness (cf. 4 n.).

The inversion of themes from earlier books (noted in 3.16) is even more marked in 3.17: as in 1.1 P. looks for a cure for his love; but here the poem does not end by denying the possibility of a cure. He thinks of moving from a life in which wine is part of partying and love-making (1.3, 2.15.41–2, 3.10; in 2.33B it is Cynthia who drinks—and is none the worse for it) to one where wine is a way of escaping from the pain of love. The basic sentiment and some of the language draw on the start of Tib. 1.2, where the elegist reacts to having to spend a night outside Delia's door:

Adde merum uinoque nouos compesce dolores
   occupet ut fessi lumina uicta sopor;
neu quisquam multo percussum tempora Baccho
   excitet infelix dum requiescit amor.

Give me more unmixed wine and with it restrain my new emotions so that
sleep may conquer and seize my tired eyes; and let no one rouse one
whose head has been struck by much Bacchus [i.e. wine: *see 6 n.*] until my
unfortunate love is asleep.

Besides the words for wine, note *compescere* (3), *uince sopore caput*
(42), *tempora* (13). In his birthday poem for Messalla (1.7) Tibullus
also celebrates the power of wine (33–48), within a hymn that
equates the Egyptian god Osiris with the Nile and with Bacchus.

As a poet P. conceives that he might really start writing in a grand
and hymnic style, that he might abandon the mode of the 'water-
drinking' Callimachean* poet concerned with sober artistry and instead seek inspiration from wine. There was a long-standing contro-
versy between scholarly 'water-drinkers', who depend on *ars* or τέχνη,
and the inspired, who seek *ingenium* in wine (see e.g. *Anth. Pal.* 11.20;
13.29.1–2 'Wine is a swift horse to a poet who charms; but if you were
to drink water you would produce nothing poetic', the second verse a
quotation from the fifth-century comic poet Cratinus; Hor. *Epist.*
1.19.1–11; N. B. Crowther, 'Water and wine as symbols of inspiration', *Mnemosyne* 32 (1979), 1–11). Callimachus associates his
poetry with water at *Hymn* 2.105–12, fr. 1.33 (cf. Prop. 3.1.1–6,
4.6.4), and sets himself against heavy drinkers at fr. 178, 544.

1–2 Nunc immediately brings out the change in circumstances.
tuis humiles aduoluimur aris: Worshippers abase themselves like
suppliants before their gods in ancient as in modern religions: similarly Statius, *Siluae* 5.1.73 *cunctis supplex aduolueris aris*. Derivation
from *humus* gives *humiles* the connotation 'on the ground'.
da mihi pacato uela secunda: 'what Propertius now seeks from
Bacchus is...tranquillity; therefore when he says *da mihi uela
secunda* he specifies the favour asked by adding *pacato*' (Housman,
CP 372). At Hor. *Odes* 2.16.1–2 (*Otium diuos rogat in patenti* |
prensus Aegaeo), and Lucr. 5.1229–30, it is the sea, not the worship-
per, that will be pacified if the prayer is granted; here P. himself is the
site of the storm, and the juxtaposition with *uela secunda* eases the

extension of the metaphor from sea to man wracked by passion. The
phrasing also implies a request for poetic support, the imagery of
sailing being used to convey the progress of a poem: cf. 3.3.22–4,
3.9.35–6, 3.24.15–16 nn. The motif is especially common in didactic
works, as at e.g. Vergil, *Geo.* 2.39–41 (J); Ovid, *Ars* 1.772, 3.99–100;
Fast. 1.466, 2.863–4, 3.789–90 *mite caput, pater, huc placataque
cornua uertas, et des ingenio uela secunda meo* ('Turn a kind face in
this direction, father, and placated horns, and grant to my poetic
genius sails with a following wind', addressed to Bacchus: the imitation gives some support to *placatus* here, as conjectured by Postgate).
pater: regularly used as an honorific title for deities, often with some
point: cf. *Sileni patris*, 3.3.29, *Mars pater*, 3.4.11. In Roman (and
Greek) iconography* Bacchus appears as a mature bearded god as
well as a carefree dissolute youth: *pater* brings the former to mind
here (contrast 29–31).

7–8 remind the god that he too (**quoque**) is experienced in matters of
love. Having found Ariadne abandoned on a beach by Theseus, with
whom she has eloped from Crete (Cat. 64.53–265, Ov. *Met.* 8.176–82),
he falls in love, marries, and elevates her to the heavens (cf. 3.20.18 n.).
This gives him reason to be sympathetic to other lovers and thus to help
P. in his affair; cf. Ov. *Ars* 1.525–6 *ecce, suum uatem Liber uocat: hic
quoque amantes / adiuuat et flammae qua calet ipse fauet* ('Look, Bacchus
summons his poet: he too [*quoque* echoes P.] aids lovers and he favours
the flame by which he himself is warmed', followed by a 38-verse account
of the rescue of Ariadne). In the transmitted order, however, the implication of *enim* is that because he is himself a lover the god should remove
love from the poet's mind. Moreover, if we leave 7–8 after 6, Bacchus's
affair with Ariadne interrupts the account of loving Cynthia as a misfortune (*uitium*, 6; *malum*, 10).   **testatur... Ariadna**: Poets call
on characters (and even places) from myth to bear witness to the truth of
their generalizations: e.g. 2.13.53, 3.15.11, 3.19.11–13; Ov. *Her.* 17.193,
20.101–3. Close to this instance is 2.26.47, where Amymone, raped by
Neptune, is called on as a witness that the god is susceptible to love.
non rudem ... amoris: 'inexperienced in, not innocent of love'. *in astris*
is transmitted for *amoris* (Burman's conjecture); the corruption is
demonstrated by a combination of flaws, the tautology* with *ad caelum*
and the lack of a genitive for *rudem*, which is not adequately defined by

the context. The change may have come about through either the intrusion of a gloss* or a psychological error, with a scribe, prompted by the pentameter, identifying the figure of Ariadne as the constellation Corona: cf. the ambivalences at Ov. *Ars* 1.557–8 *caelo spectabere sidus;* | *saepe reget* (*reges* other MSS) *dubiam Cressa Corona ratem* [you will be seen as a star in heaven; often the Cretan Crown will guide an uncertain boat]; *Met.* 8.177–82, *Fast.* 3.507–16.   **lyncibus**: these cats are regularly associated with Bacchus in Latin poetry (e.g. Verg. *Geo.* 3.264; Ov. *Met.* 4.25, 15.413 *uicta racemifero lyncas dedit India Baccho*: 'conquered India gave *lynxes* to cluster-bearing Bacchus'); spotted cats (anatomically cheetahs) are yoked to Bacchus's chariot in Titian's picture of the meeting of the pair, though that places not Ariadne but her crown, a circle of stars, in the sky.

3 insanae Veneris compescere flatus: 'restrain the blasts of mad Venus'. For love as a wind or a storm, see 2.12.5–8, Hor. *Odes* 1.5.6–12, Ov. *Am.* 2.9.31–3, Eur. *Iph. Aul.* 69, *Anth. Pal.* 5.190, 12.157, 12.167 (all Meleager); P. Murgatroyd, 'The sea of love', *CQ* 45 (1995), 9–25. *flatus* is a conjecture for the transmitted *fastus* ('disdain'), which does not fit a verb that expects as its object something violent or unrestrained. More distant palaeographically, but no less attractive in sense is another conjecture, *fluctus* ('waves'). Either would resume the metaphor of verse 2. *compescere* is used of calming winds and water by later writers, and of controlling passion with wine at Tib. 1.2.1 (intro.), Ov. *Her.* 16.231 *saepe mero uolui flammam compescere.*

4 medicina: for wine as a cure for love, see *Anth. Pal.* 12.49 (Meleager) 'Drink strong wine, you who are unlucky in love, and Bacchus the giver of forgetfulness will send to sleep the flame that makes you love boys. Drink…and drive out the hateful pain from your heart', Ov. *Rem.* 803–10; as a remedy for unspecified troubles, Alcaeus 335, *Anacreontea* 38, Hor. *Epod.* 13.17–18, *Odes* 1.18.3–4, 2.11.16–17, Sen. *Dial.* 9.17.8 *Liber…liberat seruitio curarum animum* [Liber…liberates the mind from the servitude of cares]. Verse 10 conceives of death as the only alternative open to P. But wine can also drive away love by sending the *willing* lover to sleep: so Ovid at *Ars* 1.565–8 instructs his pupil to pray to Bacchus that wine not cause him harm, and *Anth. Pal.* 11.49.5–6 sees the danger

of excess in leading to 'sleep, neighbour to death'.   **tuo...**
mero: 'by means of your wine'. The ancients regularly mixed their
wine with larger quantities of water (Athenaeus 38cd; H. Wilson,
Wine and Words in Classical Antiquity and the Middle Ages [London, 2003], Chapter 4); *merum* (i.e. 'unmixed <wine>') was thus a
convenient alternative to *uinum*, especially in contexts where heavy
drinking is implied.

5–6 soluuntur amantes... dilue, Bacche: both verbs play on the
etymology of the god's alternative name *Lyaeus* ('Loosener': see on
3.5.21 *uincire Lyaeo*). The presence of the balancing **iunguntur** may
remind us that Juno, the goddess of marriage, is the divinity who is
etymologically marked as joining lovers: cf. her words *conubio iungam* at Verg. *Aen.* 1.73 and 4.126.   **dilue** ('wash away') is
appropriately used of Bacchus, the deity's name being used as a
metonym* for wine (as e.g. at Tib. 1.2.3, cited in the intro.). Cf.
Hor. *Odes* 3.12.1–2 *dulci | mala uino lauere.*

9–10 hoc...quod ueteres custodit...ignes |...malum: fires in
Roman literature are often guarded by Vestal Virgins; it is neat irony
to have uncontrollable lust taking on the role for once. *hoc malum* is
the antecedent of *quod*. On fire as an image for love, see 3.6.39 n.; for
fire in the bones, cf. Cat. 45.16, Verg. *Geo.* 3.258, *Aen.* 1.660, 4.66.

11–14 play on literary scenes of sleeplessness: cf. Medea kept awake
by love and uncertainty at Ap. *Arg.* 3.744–54, Dido by a mixture of
love and anger at *Aen.* 4.522–32, the phrase *animum... uersat* of
Aeneas at *Aen.* 8.20–1, and the concentration on physical discomfort
at *Il.* 24.10–11 (Achilles grieving for Patroclus) or, in a lighter vein,
Cat. 50.11–15 (*uersarer, membra*): P. has similar passion, anxieties as
disturbing, but he proposes to get drunk so that he can sleep through
the night.   **uacuos**: 'alone': a key word. The lover who is not
alone will be pleased to lack sleep: cf. 2.15.1–10; and Statius in his
poem on insomnia, *Siluae* 5.4.14–15 *si aliquis longa sub nocte puellae |
bracchia nexa tenens ultro te, Somne, repellit* [if someone beneath the
long night holding entwined the arms of a girl willingly drives you
off, Sleep].   **spesque timorque... uersat**: Latin freely uses a
singular verb where a singular subject is expressed, even if there is
more than one.   **feruida**: 'glowing, flushed': wine was

thought to warm the body (Lucr. 3.476–7, Ov. *Fast.* 3.531), as seems reasonable given the redness of face that alcohol can induce.

15 ipse seram colles pangamque ex ordine uites: 'I shall myself sow hillsides and plant vines in rows.' Good drainage and favourable exposure to the sun make hillsides the best sites for vineyards (cf. Hor. *Odes* 1.20.12, Stat. *Theb.* 4.123–4). The line imitates Verg. *Ecl.* 1.73 *pone ordine uites,* and Tib. 1.1.7 *ipse seram teneras maturo tempore uites*: P.'s *ipse* has particular point when one remembers that in another poem Tibullus envisages Delia as the *frugum custos* (1.5.21), and her foot as treading the grapes (1.5.24 *pressaque ueloci candida musta pede* [white must pressed by a swift foot]: P. responds in 17–18—his must is a more vivid, and realistic, purple).

16 quas carpant nullae me uigilante ferae: 'and may no wild animals strip them <of fruit> on my watch'. The future *carpent* (Camps) would be simpler, and may be right. P. presents himself as a more committed guard of ripening grapes than the boy at Theocritus, *Idyll* 1.45–54, who weaves a cricket-cage while two foxes thieve at will (cf. also *Id.* 5.112–13, Varro, *Agr.* 1.8.5); wild boar are a notorious threat to modern vineyards.

17–18 Foaming vats of fermenting purple grape-juice ('must') and the stained feet of those treading the grapes are frequent in old representations of the vintage and may still be seen at traditional port-producers in the Douro valley. The staining of the feet here may evoke Bacchus' effect on P.'s poetry: cf. 'the dyer's hand' in Shakespeare's Sonnet 111.   **dum modo:** 'provided that' + subjunctive.

19–20 quod superest uitae: *uitae* is partitive genitive; and we supply a notional *id* (accusative of time throughout which): 'for that part of life which remains', i.e. for my future life.   **per te et tua cornua uiuam:** difficult and possibly corrupt. *per* can hardly be *per* adjurative* ('I swear by you and your horns I shall live'), for even if we take *uiuam* in the sense 'live to the full', we lose the identification with Bacchus that creates a sense parallel to the pentameter. And yet the addition of *tua cornua* introduces the god in his physical aspect and thus makes interpretations such as 'live in accordance with your lifestyle' or 'live by means of your gifts' seem awkward. In themselves

Bacchus' horns are an identifying feature that characterizes him as a bull, vigorous and fertile: cf. Tib. 2.1.3, Ov. *Fast.* 3.789 (see 2 n.). **uirtutisque tuae, Bacche, poeta:** P. will become a writer of the ἀρεταί (excellent qualities) of Bacchus, *uirtutis* translating the technical term into Latin.   **ferar:** 'I shall be called' (*OLD* 34).

21–38 dicam ego introduces an account of the poetry P. will compose (a self-fulfilling prophecy in the Pindaric mode: Cairns 1972: 97). Typically in sequences dependent on a single verb P. has a mix of nouns (21, 23, 24), often with participles attached (22, 27), and noun clauses (25–6): so e.g. 3.3.7–12, 3.12.25–36.

21–2 maternos Aetnaeo fulmine partus: Bacchus was born prematurely when his mother Semele made her lover Jupiter appear to her in full armour, flashing lightning, but was saved by being sown into his father's thigh till he reached the maturity for birth: Eur. *Bacch.* 2–3, 88–100, Ov. *Met.* 3.287–312. Normally a causal ablative such as *Aetnaeo fulmine* would be attached to a verb, but here the placing of the phrase between adjective and noun shows that it goes closely with *partus*: 'the birth from your mother due to the thunderbolt made under Etna'. From Hesiod, *Theog.* 139–41 on, Jove's thunderbolts are regularly presented as the main production of the furnaces worked by the Cyclopes; for the location, under Etna and the other volcanoes nearby, see e.g. Call. *Hymn* 3.46–61, Verg. *Geo.* 4.170–5, *Aen.* 8.416–32.   **Indica Nysaeis arma fugata choris:** The god was reared by nymphs on the mythical Mount Nysa (*Hom. Hymn* 1.9 ff.), and they formed his first group of singing and dancing companions. He then travelled in the east, his band of Maenads routing all opposition, before returning to spread his cult in Greece. *choris* is dative of the agent.

23–4 uesanumque noua nequiquam in uite Lycurgum: 'Lycurgus pointlessly mad at the newly discovered vine'; cf. the use of *in* + abl. at 1.13.7, 3.8.28, 3.19.28. Lycurgus, King of Thrace, opposed Bacchus, and was induced by a mad vision of the hated vine to attack, according to various versions, either his son or himself. **Penthĕŏs:** Greek genitive of *Pentheus*, Bacchus' cousin and king of Thebes after the retirement of its founder Cadmus. Euripides'

Bacchae depicts his persistent refusal to acknowledge the divine power of Dionysus and his eventual dismemberment at the hands of three troops of maddened Theban Maenads, led by his mother Agave and her two sisters. For *grata* cf. 2.34.40 *Capanei magno grata ruina Ioui* [the fall of Capaneus that delighted mighty Jove]; but the use here is bitterly ironic: the final act of the *Bacchae* shows Cadmus revealing to Agave the horror of what she has done in her blinded state.   **gregi:** In context the choice of collective noun perhaps casts the Maenads as animals: so at Ov. *Met.* 3.536–7 Pentheus criticizes the Thebans as defeated by *femineae uoces et mota insania uino | obscenique greges et inania tympana* [female voices, madness provoked by wine, foul flocks and hollow drums]; for other instances of the word applied to human beings in demeaning ways, cf. Hor. *Odes* 1.37.9, *Epist.* 1.4.16 (jocularly on himself) *Epicuri de grege porcum* [a pig from Epicurus' herd].

25–6 curuaque Tyrrhenos delphinum corpora nautas | in uada pampinea desiluisse rate: 'and that as the curved bodies of dolphins the Etruscan sailors leapt into the waves from the vine-covered ship': the entwined word-order confuses the grammar and thus evokes the confusion of the moment of metamorphosis: the tale of how the god takes vengeance on the Etruscan pirates who abduct him originates in the seventh Homeric Hymn, and Ovid gives us a version from the point of view of the (innocent) helmsman at *Met.* 3.582–691. On the change of construction (still after *dicam*), see 3.4.13–18 n.

27–8: Naxos (or Dia), the largest of the Cyclades, is where Bacchus was said to have found the abandoned Ariadne: his cult was important on the island, and it is a suitably Bacchic notion to picture it flowing with streams of wine.   **tibi:** possessive dative ('your streams [i.e. of wine]' or 'for you').   **Diam . . . Naxia:** the rare name is glossed by the more familiar adjective. In the tradition *Naxon* (Greek acc.) stands instead of *Diam*: presumably a reader's explanation has replaced the original text; but others have suggested alternatives for *Naxia* (*Bacchica* Shackleton Bailey, *ebria* Watt) or tried to find rhetorical point in the repetition.   **turba** evokes the confusion of Bacchic ritual; as in English the collective noun can take a plural verb.

29–30 'I shall burden your fair-skinned neck with spreading ivy-clusters'. In familiar fashion (cf. e.g. 3.3.41–2) the poet is presented as performing what he describes. The implication 'in my poetry' carries over to all the succeeding futures.   **candida**: though very much a god of the outdoors, Bacchus is regularly presented as fair-skinned (e.g. Eur. *Bacch.* 457), and thus, in ancient terms, as attractively youthful (cf. also *lēuis* ['smooth'], 31). As a fast-growing and luxuriant plant, ivy is associated with him nearly as often as the vine (cf. 4.1.62; *Hom. Hymn* 7.38–41).   **Bassaricas**: adjective from the Greek *Bassaris*, used for a Thracian Maenad; cf. *Bassareu* addressed to Bacchus at Hor. *Odes* 1.18.11.   **Lydia mitra**: the 'Lydian bonnet' characterizes Bacchus as typically Eastern and effeminate.

31–2 odorato ... oliuo: olive oil was used as a basis for perfumes and unguents in the ancient world.   **feries nudos ueste fluente pedes**: *ferire* with an ablative normally implies more purpose or force than the brushing of feet with a long robe. However, there is similar phrasing in a passage of Valerius Flaccus (1.385) *palla imos ferit alba pedes*.

33 mollia ... tympana: it is not so much the drums that are 'soft' as the worshippers who pound them: cf. *seruitio superbo* ('servitude to an arrogant woman') in 41.   **Dircaeae ... Thebae**: the story of the wicked queen Dirce and her vicious punishment has been told in 3.15; but her name is also attached to one of the two rivers of Thebes, and thus becomes a marker of the city: see D. W. Berman, 'Dirce at Thebes', *G&R* 54 (2007), 18–39.

34 Panes and Fauns (the Roman equivalent) are regularly associated with Satyrs, Silvani, and Nymphs (Lucr. 4.580–9; Verg. *Geo.* 2.494; Ov. *Met.* 1.192–3, 14.637–9, *Fast.* 1.397–8), and so fit in Bacchus' wild train, though they are not regular attendants: cf., however, Hor. *Epist.* 1.19.4 *male sanos* | *adscripsit Liber Satyris Faunisque poetas* [Bacchus enlisted intoxicated poets among the Satyrs and Fauns].   **capripedes** ('goat-footed') is otherwise found only of Satyrs (Lucr. 4.580; Hor. *Odes* 2.19.4, in a Bacchic context).   **calamo ...hiante**: 'on the open-ended (*lit.* gaping) pipe', another phrase drawn from Lucretius' passage on echoes: *Pan...* | *unco saepe labro calamos percurrit hiantes*

(Pan often with hooked lip ran along the gaping pipes: 4.586–8). Ovid narrates the invention of the Pan-pipes at *Met.* 1.705–12; cf. also Verg. *Ecl.* 2.31–4.

35–6 'nearby Cybebe, great goddess with tower-crowned head, will clash noisy cymbals for Idaean dances'. **Cybēbē** (or *Cybĕlē*) was worshipped in Rome from 205 BC as the 'Mother of the Gods'. Her worship came from Phrygia (hence **Idaeos**, from Mount Ida, the setting for the Attis and Cybele narrative in Cat. 63) and so suited a Rome which traced its origins to Aeneas' escape from Troy. It involved inspired dancing and music-making, and the similarities with Bacchic cult were explained by the story that the god spent time with his grandmother before heading east. They are associated already at Pindar, fr. 70b.6–14, Eur. *Bacch.* 78–9, 120–34; and adjacent shrines made them neighbours on the Palatine (Martial 1.70.9–10). Ovid gives a detailed account of Cybele's cult and myths at *Fast.* 4.179–372, including the reason for her 'tower-bearing' crown: that she first provided towers for cities (220).

37–38: 'before the doors of the temple a priest will offer libations from a mixing bowl of gold'. Sacrifices took place in front of temples. **cratere ... et auro**: a hendiadys*: cf. Verg. *Geo.* 2.192 *pateris libamus et auro* ('we make libations from dishes of gold'): P.'s god gains an even more impressive golden utensil. **ante fores templi** perhaps helps evoke another programmatic* description of ritual by a temple, that with which Vergil announces his future epic at *Geo.* 3.13–39 (L): cf. esp. 13 *templum de marmore ponam*, 16 *Caesar ... templum ... tenebit*, 26 *in foribus*.

39–40 sums up the proposed composition, a move away from the 'low' style of a Callimachus to the lofty thundering of tragedy (associated with Bacchus through the Athenian festivals) or Pindar (Hor. *Odes* 4.2.1–24; Quintilian 10.1.61). **coturno:** the buskin, a frequent symbol of tragedy, cf. 2.34.41 *Aeschyleo coturno*; Verg. *Ecl.* 8.10 *Sophocleo coturno*; Hor. *Sat.* 1.5.64 *tragicis coturnis*; *Odes.* 2.1.12 *Cecropio* [i.e. Athenian] *coturno*; *Ars Poetica* 80 *hunc socci cepere pedem grandesque coturni* [This foot (i.e. iambic* metre) was taken up by <comic> slippers and grand buskins]. **qualis ... spiritus** = *tali spiritu, qualis Pindarico ore tonat*: cf. e.g. 1.2.21–2 *facies aderat*

nullis obnoxia gemmis, | qualis Apelleis est color in tabulis [they had a
beauty reliant on no gems, and of such colouring as there is in the
paintings of Apelles].   **tonat:** P. takes over this image of
grand style from Callimachus, *Aet.* fr. 1.20 (**B**) ('It is not my place to
thunder, but Jove's'): so too 2.1.39–40 *neque . . . intonat angusto pectore
Callimachus,* 4.1.134.

41–2 'Just set me free from my servitude to an arrogant woman
[33 n.]'. The caution expressed by **modo** may seem likely to be
justified: using wine as a remedy is often shown as exacerbating the
symptoms (Hor. *Epod.* 11.8–14, Tib. 1.5. 37–8 *saepe ego temptaui
curas depellere uino;* | *at dolor in lacrimas uerterat omne merum*
[Often I tried to drive away my cares with wine; but pain had turned
all the alcohol to tears]). But, after trying other cures for an unsuccessful affair: a new lover in 20, travel in 21, the poet will end the
book separating from Cynthia.   **uacuum:** contrast the usage
in 11, which means 'free of the beloved', not 'free of love'.
hoc . . . caput: 'this head' i.e. mine.   **sopore:** Sleep has ended
an earlier poem (1.3.45–6 *me iucundis lapsam Sopor impulit alis:* | *illa
fuit lacrimis ultima cura meis* [Sleep with his pleasant wings pushed
me to fall: that was the final cure for my tears.].

Additional bibliography: R. J. Littlewood, *Latomus* 34 (1975), 662–9;
J. F. Miller, *AJPh* 112 (1991), 77–86; G. Mader, in C. Deroux (ed.),
Studies in Latin Literature & Roman History 7 (Bruxelles, 1994),
369–85; Hunter 2006: 55–6, 68–72; Keith 2008: 63–5.

3.18

*1–8: Baiae was once visited by Bacchus; but what hostile god has settled
there now? 9–10: <Marcellus> was overwhelmed by misfortune there
and sank into the waters of the Styx. 11–16: What use to him was his
virtue or his family connexions? his celebrated games or his early
maturity? He is dead, in his 20th year. 17–20: Go on, imagine triumphs
and public applause; collect luxuries: you will give these things to the
pyre. 21–4: Everyone treads the unpleasant road to the Underworld,
and encounters Cerberus and Charon. 25–8: There is no protection in*

*iron or bronze; nor in beauty, might or wealth. 31–4: But let the
ferryman carry you on the route your ancestor Claudius took, or Caesar,
transported to the stars.*

Marcellus, the son of Augustus' sister Octavia, fell ill and died in 23
BC, aged 19 (Dio 53.30–1). He was already seen as a possible succes-
sor for Augustus, and his death was given a prominent place in
Vergil's *Aeneid*, close to the end of Aeneas' meeting with his father
Anchises in the underworld, at 6.860–83:

> una namque ire uidebat   860
> egregium forma iuuenem et fulgentibus armis,
> sed frons laeta parum et deiecto lumina uultu....
> 'o gnate, ingentem luctum ne quaere tuorum;
> ostendent terris hunc tantum fata nec ultra
> esse sinent. nimium uobis Romana propago   870
> uisa potens, superi, propria haec si dona fuissent.
> quantos ille uirum magnam Mauortis ad urbem
> campus aget gemitus! uel quae, Tiberine, uidebis
> funera, cum tumulum praeterlabere recentem!
> nec puer Iliaca quisquam de gente Latinos   875
> in tantum spe tollet auos, nec Romula quondam
> ullo se tantum tellus iactabit alumno.
> heu pietas, heu prisca fides inuictaque bello
> dextera! non illi se quisquam impune tulisset
> obuius armato, seu cum pedes iret in hostem   880
> seu spumantis equi foderet calcaribus armos.
> heu, miserande puer, si qua fata aspera rumpas!
> tu Marcellus eris....'

For he could see there too a youth outstanding in beauty and gleaming arms,
but his face was not happy and his eyes had a downcast expression.... 'My
son, do not ask about the great grief of your people; the fates will only show
him to the earth and not allow him to exist for long. The Roman race
seemed to you, gods, too powerful, if these gifts had been granted as their
own. What lamentations will that plain raise by the great city of Mars! Or
what a funeral you will see, father Tiber, as you flow past the new tomb!
Neither will any boy from the Trojan race exalt his Latin grandfathers to so
great an extent in hope, nor will the land of Romulus pride itself so much in
any child. Alas, the piety, alas, the antique honesty and the hand unconquerable in war! Not with impunity would anyone have come face to face
with him in arms, whether he was going against the enemy on foot or

digging with spurs at the flanks of a foaming horse. Alas, poor boy, if only you might in some way break the harsh fates! You will be Marcellus.'

Seneca also included panegyric of Marcellus in his account of the unending grief of his mother, *Cons. Marc.* 2.3–5:

Octauia Marcellum <i.e. amisit>, cui et auunculus et socer incumbere coeperat, in quem onus imperii reclinare, adulescentem animo alacrem, ingenio potentem, sed frugalitatis continentiaeque in illis aut annis aut opibus non mediocriter admirandae, patientem laborum, uoluptatibus alienum, quantumcumque inponere illi auunculus ... uoluisset laturum

Octavia lost Marcellus, on whom his uncle and father-in-law [i.e. Augustus] had begun to rely and to place the burdens of ruling the empire, a youth of keen intelligence and powerful ability, but with a frugality and restraint in behaviour that was highly admirable for his age and wealth, able to endure hard work, antagonistic to pleasure, and ready to bear whatever his uncle might have wished to place on him.

Propertius responds to the outpouring of public grief; but the tone in which he does so is open to interpretation. He approaches Marcellus not through the underworld but via Baiae (Map 4a), the infamous resort near to which he died, a place used by Cicero in the *pro Caelio* to condemn by association the depravity of Clodia (see e.g. 28, 35, 38, 49), and by P. himself in 1.11 to suggest Cynthia's search for new lovers (1–2, 27–30):

> Ecquid te tepidis cessantem, Cynthia, Baiis,
>   qua iacet Herculeis semita litoribus, ...
> tu modo quam primum corruptas desere Baias:
>   multis ista dabunt litora discidium,
> litora quae fuerunt castis inimica puellis:
>   a pereant Baiae, crimen Amoris, aquae!

Is it the case that while you, Cynthia, are on holiday in warm Baiae, where a path lies on the Herculean shore, ... <any care for us creeps up on you >? ... Only leave corrupt Baiae as quickly as you can: that coast will cause a break-up to many, the coast which has been an enemy to chastity in girls. Ah, damnation take the waters of Baiae, a charge against Amor.

For Ovid too, at *Ars* 1.255–8, it is a town that makes the visitor fall in love; for Seneca (*Ep. Mor.* 51) it is a byword for *luxuria*. Here, to the conventional features of the place (1–4) is added a historical perspective:

once visited by a celebrating Bacchus (5–6), it is now (7–8) cursed by the presence of a less propitious god, but not, as we might expect, *Amor*. We have apparently lost the couplet in which Marcellus was introduced, but in 9–10 his death is connected to the presence in the area of portals to the Underworld (mention of Stygian waters also takes us back to Avernus in line 1). Verses 11–16 sum up the excellence of Marcellus' short life, but the rhetoric is less generous than Vergil's: instead of *nec quisquam in tantum* (875–6, e.g.) we read *quid profuit?* And the sense that public achievement is pointless is confirmed by 17–28 (triumphs and riches do not last beyond the funeral pyre; all men take the road to the Underworld). The difficult last two couplets do seem to offer alternative routes, however, including ascent to the heavens (34).

1 **Clausus ab umbroso qua ludit pontus Auerno**: 'Where the sea plays, enclosed by shady Avernus': cf. Tib. 2.3.45–6 *claudit et indomitum moles mare, lentus ut intra | neglegat hibernas piscis adesse minas* [A breakwater corrals the untamable sea so that within it the fish may peacefully ignore the imminence of winter's threats], where the leisure of the fish is analogous to that of the sea in our line (*ludit*): in this resort even the sea finds a secluded spot for play. The sea had recently, and notoriously, been linked to Lake Avernus by the works of Agrippa in creating the *portus Iulius* for the navy; a key intertext* is Verg. *Geo.* 2.161–4 (**K**: *claustra, ponto, sonat, Auernis* are all echoed here). There were woods on the shores of Lake Avernus (*Aen.* 3.442), but the significant point in *umbroso* is the link with the 'shades' of the Underworld, to which it provided access (*Aen.* 5.732).

2 **fumida . . . stagna tepentis aquae**: Baiae was famous for its volcanic springs, used as hot baths (Plin. *Nat.* 31.4–5; Statius, *Siluae* 3.2.17; Martial 1.62.4). The line as transmitted (*fumida Baiarum stagna*) is without construction. Since it refers to bodies of water different from those of the hexameter, it can hardly be in apposition*. The whole of the opening four lines says 'at Baiae'; the poet leads up to the name in 7 with an elegant and allusive description. The bald *Baiarum* in the second verse spoils the effect by coming so soon, and the genitive is not elegant in a line that contains another genitive phrase. Deficiency and superfluity in combination mark corruption. Either a reader's gloss mentioning *Baiae* has replaced the original phrasing or perhaps

the text of these lines was partially obliterated (cf. 3, 5): hence the illustrative conjecture *fumida* <*que exundant*> *stagna* ('<and> steaming pools <overflow>').

3–4 The trumpeter Misenus accompanied Aeneas to Italy, but fell from the cliffs at Cumae when he challenged the sea-god Triton; his death and burial are prominent in *Aeneid* 6 (151–235). Again the text printed (Heinsius' conjecture **Euboica tubicen Troianus harena**) assumes that the transmitted version (*et Troiae tubicen Misenus harena*) has been affected by an intrusive gloss or physical damage. *et* is superfluous, and *harena* lacks an epithet: *Euboica* is appropriate because Cumae was founded by settlers from Cyme on the Greek island of Euboea: *Aen.* 6.2, 42; 9.710.   **sonat** echoes *Geo.* 2.163 (**K**), and is thus to be taken of the noise of the sea. Note the contrast with the silenced trumpeter in the hexameter. **Herculeo structa labore uia**: the causeway that separated the Lucrine lagoon from the sea was supposed to have been built by Hercules (cf. 1.11.2, cited in the intro.). Hercules, like Misenus, and Marcellus, died young—but he became a god.

5–6 hic picks up *qua* (1, 3): 'here, in the area of Baiae'. **Thebano...deo** could in itself refer to Hercules, but *cymbala* shows that we have here an otherwise unattested visit by Bacchus, which contrasts with the familiar pictures of the opening four lines. The couplet describes a propitious visit by a god who brings joy; this past event (*olim*) provides a foil for the reflections of 7–8 on the identity of the evil deity who can be assumed now (*nunc*, 7) to have taken up residence in Baiae's waters.   **olim, <Hesperias> dexter cum quaereret urbes**: 'once, when he was propitiously making for the cities <of Italy>'. The MSS read *ubi mortales dexter etc.*, but the unfamiliarity of this episode makes it an awkward continuation of the opening couplets, and *mortales* is pointlessly redundant with *urbes* when we could be given a more precise epithet to indicate the cities of Italy or the West. Given the corruption in 2 and 3, there is good reason to accept a radical change here too. *Hesperia* and its adjective are regularly applied to Italy as the Trojans' destination in the *Aeneid* (e.g. on their arrival at Cumae in 6.6). *dexter* shows the god's good-will (in contrast to his conquest of the East or his return to Thebes, e.g.: see 3.17.22–6). *quaerere* is found with a geographical object in the sense 'head for' at *Aen.* 1.380 *Italiam quaero patriam.* Bacchus presumably came to Baiae on a proselytizing tour of the west; cf. Silius 7.171–2, a passage which, like ours, has the god visiting a particular place in Italy (Falernus) whilst on a general tour: *attulit hospitio pergentem ad litora Calpes | extremumque diem pes dexter et hora Lyaeum* [a lucky foot and hour brought Lyaeus as a guest when he was on his way to the shores of Gibraltar and the furthest west].

7–8 inuisae magno cum crimine Baiae: 'Baiae, hated along with your great crime', *inuiso* being understood with *crimine* (*OLD cum* 3). The resort has been cursed at the end of 1.11 (see intro.) and described as a *crimen Amoris*, because of the way that it is leading Cynthia astray (as P. believes). But it proves to be an illusion that we are reading an erotic elegy (so T. M. Falkner, *CJ* 73 [1977], 11–18).   **uestra:** second-person plural because the vocative *Baiae* is plural.   **constitit:** 'has stopped' = 'is settled'.   **hostis** is set against *dexter* (5).

9–10 his pressus ('overwhelmed by these') has nothing to which it can reasonably be referred (*stagna* being too distant), and Marcellus has still not been mentioned. Either we must replace the phrase, or mark a lacuna* between 8 and 9, as in the text here. Marcellus' sinking into the underworld (a short trip from Baiae, as Aeneas had found) will have been introduced by an account of his sickness in this place, with reference to the forces that overwhelmed the young man. The imagery has returned in 8 to the water of the opening couplet, and here exploits the link between Avernus and the Underworld; it is as if Marcellus has been drowned and found himself immediately in the river Styx (9) or some other infernal water (10), now transformed into a spirit, wandering as the shades of the dead do (4.7.89–90; *Aen.* 6.329).

11–14 After three nouns as subjects of *quid profuit illi*, an accusative and infinitive noun clause follows and then two participial phrases in 13–14: 'What has been the use to him [i.e. none at all] of his birth or excellence or his noble mother, and the fact that he embraced the hearth of Caesar, or the awnings fluttering recently in so crowded a theatre and all the things done by hands so young?' For such a catalogue of ultimately useless qualities in an *epicedion**, see Ov. *Am.* 2.6.17–20 (and McKeown *ad loc.*).   **amplexum Caesaris esse focos:** Both *amplecti* ('to become emotionally attached to', *OLD*

6) and *focus* ('house' or 'family' as symbolized by the household hearth, *OLD* 2) are used metaphorically. We might compare the phrasing at *Aen.* 3.133–4 *gentem | hortor amare focos.* But the combination 'embrace the fire' is bizarre and perhaps comic, like Priapus trying to rape Vesta, the normally formless goddess of the hearth in Ov. *Fast.* 6.319–48 (contrast 6.295–302). Marcellus was both nephew of Augustus and husband of his daughter Julia, so *focos* could imply two households, but it can also be taken as a conventional plural for singular.   **modo tam pleno fluitantia uela theatro**: with Augustus' help he had put on spectacular games as aedile in 23 not long before his death (v. 18; Dio 53.31.2–3); coloured awnings above the theatre were familiar by the time of Lucretius (4.75–83; cf. also 4.1.15), but in association with his games Marcellus had hung cloths to provide shade in the Forum (Plin. *Nat.* 19.24), and P. apparently combines the two. The theatre named after Marcellus was ready for the *Ludi Saeculares* in 17 BC and formally opened later (Dio 54.26.1; Plin. *Nat.* 8.65); presumably the games referred to here were in the Theatre of Pompey, the first such permanent structure in Rome, but possibly at a temporary site.   **per maturas omnia gesta manus**: Marcellus had already taken part in the Spanish campaigns in the years leading up to 23, but the reference is rather to his promised progress up the *cursus honorum* (the sequence of magistracies), accelerated by ten years (Dio 53.28.3). The presence of *mater* in 12 has led to the corruption of *maturas* to *maternas* in the manuscripts. For comments on such precociousness see Ov. *Ars* 1.181–90.

15–16 misero: possessive dative, with *illi* understood.   **steterat**: 'had come to a halt' (*OLD* 10): his twentieth year was not completed. **tot bona tam paruo clausit in orbe dies**: 'time (*OLD dies* 10) has closed so much good in so small a circle (*OLD orbis* 16b)'.

17 i (both with and without **nunc**) frequently adds a sarcastic tone: so *ite* in 3.7.29; *Aen.* 7.425–6; and Ovid in two lines that recall this one, *Am.* 1.7.35 *i nunc, magnificos uictor molire triumphos* [go now, as a victor put on magnificent triumphs]—he is pretending to celebrate his beating of Corinna; and just after Deianira has described Hercules' submission to Omphale, *Heroides* 9.105 *i nunc, tolle animos et fortia gesta recense* [go now, exalt your spirit and rehearse your brave deeds]. It is left unclear whether P. addresses the reader in

general or Marcellus in particular (as he seems to in 31).   **in**
plausum: 'for [i.e. to offer] applause' (*OLD in* 21; 3.9.56). For
applause in the theatre giving pleasure, cf. Lucan 1.133 (*plausuque
sui gaudere theatri*) in a description of Pompey's delight in popularity.

19–20 Attalicas supera uestes: 'outdo clothes made with cloth of gold'.
This form of expensive ostentation was thought to have been invented
by Attalus III, last king of Pergamum (138–133). The structure is
paratactic*, the *supera* (and *sint*) having the force of verbs in a
concessive clause ('though...') leading up to *ignibus ista dabis*.
omnia conchis | gemmea sint Indis: 'let everything be jewelled with
Indian pearls'. *conchis... Indis* is Housman's conjecture for *magnis...
ludis*, which awkwardly maintains reference to the games in a couplet
where wealth, not public glory, is the issue. India was known for its
jewels (Plin. *Nat.* 37.200) and *Indis* looks secure, but there are other
nouns that might have been replaced by *magnis* (Housman himself
suggested *bacis* and *granis*, either of which would mean 'pearls').

21–4 There are, not surprisingly, many ancient observations on the
inevitability of death for all: see e.g. Hor. *Odes* 1.28.15–16 *sed omnes
una manet nox | et calcanda semel uia leti* [but one night awaits all
and the path of death to be trodden only once] and 2.14.9–21 *unda...
omnibus... enauiganda, siue reges siue inopes erimus coloni....
uisendus... Cocytus.... linquenda tellus* [the water to be crossed by all,
whether we be kings or poor peasants.... Cocytus (a river of the Underworld) must be seen... The earth must be left...]. Catullus also uses a
gerundive in expressing the same notion less explicitly at 5.5–6 *nobis... |
nox est perpetua una dormienda* [we must sleep one perpetual night]; he
too has the image of death as a path to hell—for a pet sparrow (3.11–12).

23–4 'The three barking throats of the dog have to be won over; the
public ferry-boat of the grim old man has to be embarked on.' For
Cerberus' triple head and aggressive nature, see e.g. 3.5.43–4, 4.7.52,
Aen. 6.417–23. Vergil's passage has striking phrases to describe both
the barking (*latratu trifauci*, 'three-throated', 417) and the *colla*
(*horrere uidens iam colla colubris*, 419 [seeing his necks were already
bristling with snakes]).   **publica:** 'open to all, universal'.
cumba: 'virtually a technical term for Charon's boat' (Austin on
Aen. 6.303: the following line describes him as *senior*).

25–6 Though some have thought of Acrisius, who in vain locked his daughter Danaë in a bronze tower so she would not produce the grandson fated to kill him, this does not fit the phrasing **se condat.** We may think of a man in a suit of armour or a room lined with metal.   **ille ... cautus:** 'the cautious man' or (as if pointing) 'that man ... cautiously'.   **licet** (lit. 'it is possible', 'he may') is used with the subjunctive as a concessive conjunction, 'although', reinforced here by *tamen* in the main clause.   **mors:** though printed here without a capital, the personified* figure of death might be imagined hauling out the corpse.   **caput** can be taken either as 'head' or as 'individual'.

27–8 After Achilles, himself the greatest warrior, Nireus was the most handsome man in the Achaean army at Troy (*Il.* 2.673–4). **Pactoli quas parit umor opes:** 'the wealth which the water of Pactolus produces'. Croesus was the fabulously rich king of Lydia in the mid sixth century (3.5.17 n.): the kingdom's wealth was thought to have derived from the gold carried by the river Pactolus (1.14.11; Soph. *Phil.* 394; *Aen.* 10.142), in the waters of which Midas was said to have washed off his golden touch (Ov. *Met.* 11.85–145).

31–4 A difficult pair of couplets, perhaps not fully corrected by the four conjectures accepted here. As printed, the text turns to address Marcellus, who has been the centre of attention from before verse 9, with a prayer that the ferryman who conveys 'pious souls' may carry his lifeless body on the route which was followed by a major ancestor, that of the hero Claudius Marcellus, who captured Syracuse for the Romans in the Hannibalic war (211 BC), and that of the deified Julius Caesar, who left the path normally taken by mankind and ascended into the stars (pp. 9–10). The concept of separate routes for the dead is found at 4.7.55–62; we need not be troubled then to find a Charon who is defined as transporting *pias umbras*. But why is he introduced at all if the soul is headed for heaven? It seems that P. is conflating two possibilities. For the notion that heaven and the Elysian Fields are alternative destinations for the virtuous, see 4.11.101–2; Sen. *Hercules* 743–4; Statius, *Siluae* 2.7.107–12, 5.3.19–27.   **hac:** supply the ablative *uia*, as again with *qua* in 33.   **animae ... corpus inane suae:** 'your body empty of its soul [*or* life]': cf. Ov. *Met.* 13.488

corpus ... animae tam fortis inane.   **Claudius:** the name helps
activate the implied puns in *Clausus* (1), *clausit* (16), *inclusum* (26):
the door is closed on one of the Claudii.

[**29–30** The presence of this couplet must be due to a feeble attempt
to find a home for a stray piece of text (which may have been a
marginal addition taken from another elegist). Without a context,
any prolonged attempt at interpreting the couplet will be labour in
vain. The reference is to the disasters that befell the Achaeans as
a result of Apollo's plague (*Iliad* 1.51–3) or (conceivably) Zeus'
withdrawal of support after Book 7.   **magno ... stetit:**
magno is ablative of cost (as at 4.9.57); for *sto* in this sense see *OLD*
23.   **alter amor:** Agamemnon's love for Chryseis (*Il.* 1.111–
15), or perhaps, in a looser expression, for Briseis, subsequently
snatched from Achilles as recompense for the loss of Chryseis.]

Additional bibliography: T. M. Falkner, 'Myth, setting and immorality
in Propertius 3.18', *CJ* 73 (1977), 11–18.

3.19

*1–4: You criticize me for male lust but women's sexual appetite knows
no bounds. 5–10: The impossible will happen before anyone could keep
it in check. 11–22: Examples of uncontrolled women from mythology
who prove my point are Pasiphaë, Tyro, Medea, Clytemestra, Myrrha,
and Scylla. 23–8: Scylla offered her father's city to an enemy out of love.
Maidens, enjoy a happier wedding: Minos was just and she was dragged
behind his departing boat.*

Mythical *exempla* are a major feature of Book 1 (and to a lesser extent
Book 2); very often these occur in lists (e.g. 1.2.15–20 cosmetics were
not used by the attractive heroines Phoebe and Helaira, Marpessa,
Hippodamia; 1.3.1–8 the sleeping Cynthia is like Ariadne, Androm-
eda, a Maenad; 1.15.9–22 Cynthia did not behave like Calypso,
Hypsipyle, or Evadne facing up to the loss of lovers; 2.14.1–10
P. rejoiced like Agamemnon at the fall of Troy, Ulysses returning to
Ithaca, Electra finding Orestes is alive, Ariadne seeing Theseus
unharmed). A poem that offers a sequence of such heroines as examples

of female lust thus looks like a return to a previous mode, a point that is reinforced when we notice that Cynthia has complained about P.'s wandering lust in 1.3.35–46. However, there is little sense of occasion here, and 3.19 is unlike the earlier poems (though like 3.11) in the number of *exempla* and their cumulative length, and in not engaging with Cynthia at the end of the sequence: the final, extended case, that of Scylla, features the departure of the stern-minded Minos (cf. 3.21). The poem is untypical as a Cynthia poem and, if read so, perhaps rather lifeless; but that seems pointed: as we head towards the rupture that will end the book, the myths now interest the poet more than Cynthia herself does (cf. the movement from the particular *te* to the general *uobis* in the opening couplet). There is also real vigour in its opening onslaught on women's sexual voracity, and from verse 11 a fascinating engagement with the literary tradition.

Listing exempla is rhetorical (Quintilian 5.11) and at home in diatribe* (3.13 intro.), but it is also poetic. Disgust at women's allegedly unbridled sexual appetite is expressed already by Hesiod in the story of Pandora at *Works and Days* 70–105, and in the archaic iambists Archilochus, Hipponax, and Semonides (fr. 7). There is a hysterical outpouring of detestation of women put into Hippolytus' mouth by Euripides (*Hipp.* 616–68: Seneca gives a Latin equivalent to his Hippolytus at *Phaedra* 483–564). Ovid imitates P.'s poem in his argument supposedly intended to encourage the nervous man that women are likely to be interested in sex: *Ars Amatoria* 1.269–344 lists Byblis, **Myrrha**, **Pasiphaë** (at length), **Aërope**, **Scylla**, **Clytemestra**, **Medea** (and some men who were victims of female lust: those in bold can be found in 3.19). Given the prominence of incest, bestiality, and disaster, it seems Ovid is not entirely serious. Another notable list of female faults occurs in Juvenal's sixth satire. And we find such disgust in Shakespeare's plays, most strikingly in Lear's outburst on the cliffs near Dover (IV.v.116–24).

The theme seems at home then in didactic, iambic, and tragedy, so P. may wish to imply that his disgust at Cynthia's lusts is pushing him towards generic infidelity. But we should not ignore the elegiac affiliations, with his own earlier poetry, as we have seen, but also the catalogues of love affairs presented in the fragments* of Hermesianax and of Phanocles' homosexual *Erotes* (each of which acknowledges a debt to Hesiod's *Catalogue of Women*, another influence both here and in Book 1: see Hunter (ed.) 2005: 259–98).

1–2 Obicitur... mihi: 'is brought as a charge against me'. T. Rein-
hardt, 'Propertius and Rhetoric' in Günther (ed.) 2006: 214 notes
that *Obicitur* opens the declamation at [Quint.] *Decl. min.* 328.2.
Legal diction continues, e.g. in *testis* (11, 13) and *crimen* (15).
totiens: 3.24.7 n.   **nostra... uobis:** referring to 'us men'
and 'you women' respectively: cf. 2.29.32 *me similem uestris moribus
esse putas?* [do you think I'm like the behaviour of you men], which
illustrates the use of the plural possessive and the charge on Cynthia's
lips.   **ista** = *uestra*: the second-person element in *iste* is
strongly apparent (3.6.8 n.). A famous mythological story may lie
behind the idea that women are more subject to lust than men.
Tiresias, who had experience of being both a man and a woman,
was called in by Juno and Jupiter to settle an argument as to which
sex experienced the greater sexual enjoyment. He replied that women
derived ten-ninths as much pleasure from it as men (magnified to ten
times, in some sources). Juno was so furious that she blinded him.
See e.g. Ov. *Met.* 3.316–38.

3–4 contempti rupistis frena pudoris: two stages are imagined: initial
contempt for *pudor* (i.e. a sense of proper behaviour), then breaking
of the bridle, with the implication that women career away like a
horse that has broken the bit. The imagery continues in 9–10.
nescitis + infinitive = 'you do not know how (to)': *OLD* 3.
captae mentis habere modum: 'to keep control [*lit.* a limit] of
the mind that has been possessed'. Cf. Livy 39.13.12 *uelut mente
capta... uaticinari* [prophesy as if with mind possessed]; 39.15.3
*non illos qui prauis et externis religionibus **captas mentes** uelut furia-
libus **stimulis** ad omne scelus et ad omnem **libidinem** agerent* (note the
shared diction; 'not the sort [i.e. of gods] who would drive minds
captured by degrading foreign religions as if with maddening goads
towards every kind of wickedness and lust').

5–6: the first of two couplets of *adynata** ('impossibles'), cited here
in order to emphasize the unlikelihood of female restraint. Rivers
returning to their fountainhead is a classic example: cf. 1.15.29,
2.15.33; Eur. *Medea* 410, Hor. *Odes* 1.29.10–12.   **flamma
per incensas citius sedetur aristas:** 'more swiftly would a flame be
calmed down amid burning corn'. Ovid picks up this less common

image and transmutes *flamma* into the fire of love in his encapsulation of verses 1–6 at *Ars Amatoria* 1.281–2:

> parcior in nobis nec tam furiosa libido;
> legitimum finem flamma uirilis habet.

In us [i.e. men] desire is more sparing and not so maddened; the flame in a man has an end that is permitted.

7–8 Syrtes: dangerous sandbanks off the coast of North Africa, where (e.g.) three of Aeneas' vessels are trapped (*Aen.* 1.110–12). They are the subject of *praebeant*, understood from *praebeat* in the next line. **hospitio saeua Malea suo:** 'Malea, savage in its typical reception'. Malea, the southernmost promontory of the Peloponnese, was notorious for its dangerous seas: cf. *Odyssey* 3.287. *suo* has its emphatic sense 'properly belonging to it'.

9–10 uestros ... reprehendere cursus: 'restrain your career'. There may be a play on the meanings of *reprehendo* here. The most common meaning of the verb is 'find fault with'—as this is precisely what P. is doing here, it is thus anything but an impossibility. Clearly the primary meaning here must be 'restrain', but is there a hint of 'woe betide the man who criticizes'?   **rabidae stimulos frangere nequitiae:** 'break the goads of your maddened lasciviousness'. *stimulos frangere* might call to mind the goad used by the driver of an ox-cart as much as anything equestrian (cf. Tib. 1.1.30 *stimulo tardos increpuisse boues* [to urge on the slow oxen with a goad]), and thus perhaps look to the *exemplum** in the next couplet. But charioteers and horsemen have *stimuli* (whips or spurs) at Ov. *Met.* 2.399, Lucan 7.143, Statius, *Thebaid* 3.429, and *rabidae* is less appropriate of oxen than horses. Moreover, riding is a repeated image for sexual intercourse, especially when the woman is astride the man: Hor. *Sat.* 2.7.50 *clunibus aut agitauit equum lasciua supinum* [or she lustily urged on with her buttocks her supine horse]; Ov. *Ars* 2.732 *admisso subdere calcar equo* [apply the spur and get the horse galloping] and 3.777–8 *parua uehatur equo; quod erat longissima, numquam | Thebais Hectoreo nupta resedit equo* [let a small girl ride on a horse; because she was very tall, the wife from Thebes (Andromache) never sat on Hector's horse (i.e. Hector himself)]; Adams 165–6. Two Hellenistic* epigrams (*Anth. Pal.* 5.202–3) suggest that this imagery could be realized physically in the accoutrements of prostitutes: Plango and Lysidice dedicate to Aphrodite a whip and a spur respectively. Evocation of such activity gives a physical urgency to the whole passage.

11–12 testis Cretaei fastūs quae passa iuuenci: 'a witness is the woman who, having endured the indifference of the Cretan bull, . . .'. Pasiphaë, the wife of Minos, king of Crete, fell in love with a bull that her husband had refused to sacrifice. Daedalus constructed a life-like hollow cow of wood (12) and the bull mounted this with Pasiphaë inside. The monstrous coupling resulted in the birth of the Minotaur. As well as Ov. *Ars* 1.289–326, the story was told in Euripides, *Cretans,* of which only fragments* survive, and Verg. *Ecl.* 6.45–60.

13–14 testis Thessalico flagrans Salmonis Enipēo | quae uoluit liquido tota subire deo: 'a witness is the daughter of Salmoneus who, burning for Thessalian Enipeus, was willing to submerge herself entirely in the liquid deity'. Tyro, daughter of Salmoneus, fell in love with the river-god Enipeus. P. here asserts that she was willing to drown to fulfil her burning passion for the god (the mixture of fire and water imagery recalls 5–8). Neptune disguised himself as Enipeus and she gave birth to the twins Pelias and Neleus. She is one of the famous women met by Odysseus in the underworld (*Od.* 11.235–59), and thus she appears among the dead beauties at 2.28.51, as well as at 1.13.21–2 (stressing the utter involvement of Gallus and his girl):

> non sic Haemonio Salmonida mixtus Enipeo
> Taenarius facili pressit amore deus.

Not to such an extent did the Taenarian god (Neptune), mingled with Thessalian Enipeus, overpower the daughter of Salmoneus in a willingly given act of love.

17–20 nam: cf. 3.11.27.   **quid Medeae referam . . . quidue <tuum facinus>:** The paired structure shows how we are to read these lines: *referam* must be read with *quid* in 19, and to 19 we must look for the object in each case, to which *Medeae* is attached as a genitive. Unfortunately, that noun has been lost when the gloss* *Clytaemestrae* was interpolated, and we cannot be at all sure what was lost, hence the placing of Housman's *tuum facinus* in pointed brackets: 'why should I mention <the crime> of Medea, . . . or why

<yours, Clytemestra>'.   **quo tempore matris | iram natorum caede piauit amor:** 'at the time at which a mother's love appeased her anger through the slaughter of her sons'. Medea killed her children in order to take revenge on their father Jason, who had abandoned her. The story was told in extant plays by Euripides and Seneca, in lost ones by Ennius and Ovid. The meaning of 18 is that she sacrificed her maternal love to appease her anger, but the use of the verb *piare* with its religious significance and its evocation, through *pietas*, of duty to the family adds a savage force to this summary of a horrific perversion of a mother's love.

19–20 tuum: i.e. Clytemestra's, or possibly Aërope's; for the structure cf. e.g. Ov. *Rem.* 764 *uel tua* <i.e. *carmina*>, *cuius opus Cynthia sola fuit* [or the poems of you whose only work was Cynthia]. **propter quam tota Mycenis | infamis stupro stat Pelopea domus:** 'on whose account the whole house of Pelops stands infamous for adultery in Mycenae'. Clytemestra, wife of Agamemnon, king of Mycenae and descendant of Pelops, had an affair with his cousin Aegisthus and killed her husband on his return from Troy. Agamemnon too had committed adultery, bringing his mistress Cassandra back home with him and, in Aeschylus' *Agamemnon*, asking his wife to look after her (950–1). Again there is a later version by Seneca, still extant. However, *tota Mycenis* is awkward because the ill-repute of Clytemestra and the house of Pelops spread far beyond Mycenae, and *tota* rules out a contrast between the house of Pelops at Mycenae and Menelaus' line at Sparta. This difficulty is removed if we see a reference to the less familiar Aërope, mother of Agamemon and Menelaus, wife of Atreus, but seduced by his brother Thyestes and thus a contributor to the infamous quarrel between the two.

15–16 has been moved because otherwise 21–2 lacks a construction. The transposition also improves the structure of the poem, the *exempla* falling into three pairs, linked by *testis* (11–14), *quid* (17–20), and here **crimen,** 'a reproach [to the female sex]'.   **patria succensa senecta:** 'inflamed by her father's old age [i.e. her (comparatively) old father]'. Myrrha fell in love with her father Cinyras, king of Cyprus, and tricked him into incest. When he found out what had happened, he tried to kill her. Having fled into the desert, she was metamorphosed into the first (*nouae*) myrrh-tree, which then

gave birth to the beautiful Adonis, beloved of Venus. The myth was
the theme of the lost *Smyrna* of the neoteric* poet Cinna (d. 44 BC),
and is told by Ovid at *Met.* 10.298–518.   **condita:** 'formed',
but with a suggestion of the 'hiding' of her human identity.

21–4 tuque: 'and you too', parallel to *illa* in 15, with *crimen fuisti*
understood.   **Minoa uenumdata Scylla figura:** 'Scylla, sold
for [*or* bought by] the beauty of Minos'. For the short *a* of *uenumdata*
before the double consonant in *Scylla*, see p. 34. *uenumdata* is the full
form from which *uendita* is contracted. *Minoa figura* is ablative of
price. Scylla was the daughter of Nisus, king of Megara, whose
kingdom depended on a purple lock of hair on his head. Minos
was besieging Megara and Scylla fell in love with him. She tried to
buy his love by cutting off her father's purple lock. Minos captured
the city and punished her for her treachery by dragging her at the
stern of his ship till she drowned. The version told by Ovid at *Met.*
8.6–151 ends with the metamorphosis of Scylla and Nisus into sea-
birds, as does the *Ciris*, a 541-line poem once attributed to Vergil (it
ends with lines on the birds, copied from *Geo.* 1.406–9) ; there is
evidence for earlier Greek versions too (26 n.). She is different from
Scylla, the sea-monster, who terrorizes Odysseus and his crew
(2.26.53, 3.12.28), but Latin poets like to confuse them at times (so
4.4.39–40).   **tondens** ('shearing') is a play on the name of
the bird she becomes, the *ciris*, derived from the Greek verb κείρειν,
'to cut'.   **purpuream, regna paterna, comam:** 'the purple
lock, your father's kingdom'. The enclosed apposition* (3.3.31 n.)
neatly marks the lock as identified with the kingdom (Ov. *Met.* 8.8–
10): when Nisus died, his kingdom would inevitably fall. *regna
paterna* is poetic plural.   **igitur:** apparently implying that it
was because of the identification of lock and kingdom that she had
offered this as her dowry (**dotem**).

25–6 felicius urite taedas: 'burn your torches with happier outcome':
the reference is to the torches in the wedding procession escorting
the bride to her husband's house. The day when Scylla expects
her wedding turns out rather different: desertion and death.
pendet . . . tracta . . . rate: the story of the dragging of the girl behind
the boat in punishment is attributed by two late commentators to the
first-century BC Greek poet Parthenius (fr. 24 Lightfoot). There is a

suggestion of flying in *pendet* (*OLD* 8), so we may see a hint of the version of the myth in which Scylla is transformed into the *ciris* (*Met.* 8.148–51).

27–8 tamen: i.e. despite his apparently cruel punishment of Scylla. Minos was rightly (*non . . . immerito*) made judge of the dead (*arbiter Orci*; cf. 4.11.21; *Od.* 11.568–9; Plato, *Gorg.* 523e–524a; *Aen.* 6.431–3): he was just in punishing Scylla's act of treachery towards her father, even though through it he gained absolute power as conqueror. The abstinent Minos is a fitting figure with which to end this contrast of male and female libido. But the less innocent reader will be reminded of his wife Pasiphaë, with whom the list began (11–12).   **in hoste:** 'in the case of his enemy', i.e. Scylla, or Nisus, in taking vengeance for him.

Additional bibliography: C. W. Wootten, 'Rhetoric in Propertius 3.19', *CW* 69 (1975–6), 118–19.

3.20

1–6: The man who left you has no memory of your beauty: the riches of Africa wouldn't justify making you cry. You are being foolishly hopeful when he is probably making love to another. 7–10: You are beautiful, artistic, and have a distinguished family: your house is blessed, if your lover is faithful. I'll be faithful: come to bed with me. 11–14: Phoebus, shorten the long summer day: provide room for my first night. Moon, linger over the night. 19–20, 15–18: How many hours of talking before we go to bed! A new affair needs a contract to be signed, with Love putting his seal on it and Ariadne as the witness. 21–4: When a union is bound by no agreement, the gods don't exact punishment, and the bonds are loosened. 25–30: So let whoever breaks our sacred agreement feel the pains of love and become a victim of gossip; may he always love without fruition.

The scene enacted in this poem makes a strong contrast with the upright Minos of the preceding verses. Propertius addresses a girl abandoned by her *uir*, who has gone to Africa without her. This recalls the situations of 1.8A–B, where Cynthia ends up not accompanying P.'s rival to Illyria (2) or Greece (35–6), and 2.21, where

Panthus has married another and is compared to Jason and Ulysses (11–14); cf. also 2.9, where Cynthia has returned to the man who previously left her behind to go abroad (23–4, 29–30), and 2.16B, where the praetor returns from Illyria. But perhaps most significant is the relationship with 3.12, where Postumus has left his wife Galla to go war, as Ulysses did Penelope; in 17–20 Galla's chastity is seen as threatened by her husband's hard-hearted absence and gifts, but P. is sure she will outdo Penelope's steadfastness. Yet here he is himself playing the part of one of the suitors: in 3 he calls the man *durus* (cf. *duritiae*, 3.12.20); he does not woo with gifts, but points to the way money has been preferred to the girl—he will be faithful (10).

All of this would be relatively unproblematic if the poem were addressed to Cynthia, to whom he has been faithful, in spirit, if not at every moment (1.17, 2.22A, 22B, 23). After all it uses expressions reminiscent of those addressed to her earlier in the corpus* (see notes on 4, 5, 7). Some have concluded that these lines also must be addressed to Cynthia (e.g. R. J. Baker, *AJPh* 90 [1969], 333–7). The 'learned grandfather' of 8 is, however, a new and distinctive touch (at 2.13.10–11 P. rejects grand ancestry as irrelevant in comparison with Cynthia's own learning), and so is Africa as the lover's destination: these help us to read the address as to a different girl. Moreover, the tone is that of a seduction—the poet makes no mention of previous involvement. And when we find *primus* three times in 13–14 and *nouus* in 16, it is clear that the coming assignation is with a *new* mistress; the compact discussed in the closing lines confirms this. If this is a 'Cynthia' poem, why is she not named to allow the reader to comprehend the dislocation (the natural home would be early in Book 1)? A new mistress does not need to be addressed by name, for the poem gradually makes the new development clear.[6] At this point P. begins his run of closing poems: what could better express his alienation from Cynthia than an attempt to seduce another? He illustrates male insincerity by using again compliments and promises previously marked as unique. The stress on oaths and fidelity is wonderfully ironic in this poem that exposes the poet as philandering. This

---

[6] There is thus no need to consider breaking the sequence in two after line 10 as Scaliger did (followed by some modern editors).

is the Propertius that stimulated Ovid to write (e.g.) the two Cypassis poems (*Am.* 2.7, 2.8), in the first of which he expresses horror at Corinna's charge that he has been having sex with her maid, and in the second asks Cypassis how Corinna found out, and tells her to come round that afternoon—or he'll admit the whole truth.

As background to the second half of the poem, there is a useful exploration of legal terminology in Latin poetry in E. J. Kenney, 'Ovid and the law', *YCS* 21 (1969), 241–63 (with a table of usage on 253).

1–2 Credis will usually make the best sense as a question (you do not normally tell someone what they believe), and so it proves here. **eum**: most parts of *is* are rare in Augustan poetry, but *eum* is used comparatively freely (also at 2.29.8).   **meminisse**: with genitive, as often (e.g. 2.20.28).   **quem**: grammatically belongs before *uidisti*.   **a lecto...dare uela tuo**: both the setting sail and the departure from the bed are literal actions, but the combination is typically daring: it is as though the husband or lover has stepped directly from bed to boat. Cf. 2.21.14 *uidit amatorem pandere uela suum* [she (Calypso) saw her lover (Ulysses) spread his sails], and Cat. 64.122–3 where Theseus leaves Ariadne sleeping on the seashore (as in 1.3, P. here figures himself as a Bacchus, come to save her).

3 durus: supply *est. durus* could mean 'tough' (in being able to overcome the heartache), but the sense 'hard-hearted' is uppermost. Cf. Tib. 2.3.2 *ferreus est, eheu, quisquis in urbe manet* [made of iron, alas, is anyone who remains in the city], i.e. when love is in the countryside; [Tib.] 3.2.3–4 *durus et ille fuit qui tantum ferre dolorem,* | *uiuere et erepta coniuge qui potuit* [Hard too is he who could bear such pain, who could live even when his wife is snatched away]. This is like a negative equivalent of the beatitude* (9 n.).   **mutare** is followed by accusative of the noun given up in exchange for a noun in the ablative: the girl has been traded for money.

4 tantine ut lacrimes Africa tota fuit? 'Was all Africa so valuable that you should weep?' *tanti* is genitive of value. Africa is implied as the destination of the departed lover; making money is the implied goal whether he has gone as a representative of Roman government or to trade. Tears are put in the balance with the whole province, and found to weigh more. The first three words are Heinsius' conjecture for *tantisne in lacrimis*, which is confirmed by the closeness of the phrasing to passages in three related poems: 1.6.13–18 (**N**); 1.8.3–4 *et tibi iam tanti ... iste uidetur,* | *ut sine me... ire uelis?* [does he seems to you worth so much that you are willing to go without me?]; and 3.12.3–4 (cf. intro.). Cf. also Tib. 2.6.42 *non ego sum tanti ploret ut illa semel* [I am not worth so much that she cry once].

5 stulta: cf. 2.21.18 *experta in primo, stulta, cauere potes* [Having gained experience in the first case (Panthus: cf. intro.), you can be careful, you foolish girl].   **tu ... deos, tu fingis inania uerba**: the theme, the unreliability of lovers' words, is a common one, but the line is very difficult, perhaps corrupt. Traditionally lovers swear by the gods to be faithful—and then break their oaths with impunity (e.g. Callimachus, *Ep.* 25 Pf. translated as Catullus 70; Tib. 1.4.21–6; Ov. *Ars* 1.631–6; *Rem.* 678; cf. too Cat. 64.139–48). We find the pairing of words and gods in such a context also at Eur. *Medea* 21–2; Ov. *Am.* 3.11.21–2

> turpia quid referam uanae mendacia linguae
> et periuratos in mea damna deos?

Why should I recall the shameful lies of a deceitful tongue and the gods by whom, to my harm, false oaths have been made?

and *Rem.* 687–8

> at tu nec uoces (quid enim fallacius illis?)
> crede nec aeternos pondus habere deos.

You should not believe that either voices (for what is more deceiving than they?) or the eternal gods have weight.

Interpretations of the Propertian line include the following: (a) 'you invent <oaths by the> gods, you invent empty promises' (i.e. the girl claims that her man said things he did not), but this would be very different from the usual motif, and without attention drawn to the difference (nothing to say 'he didn't even swear an oath', e.g.). (b) 'You deceive yourself with talk of the gods and empty promises.' For *fingo* with this sense of self-deceiving, however, no parallels have been offered. (c) 'You falsely imagine the gods <by whom he swore will take vengeance>; you put together empty words'. This leaves too much to be provided by the reader, and the syllepsis*, the change in the sense of *fingis*, adds to the awkwardness. A further complication is the uncertainty over *inania*: is this P.'s claim or the girl's?

6 forsitan: elsewhere in P. used with the indicative, but the subjunctive is normal Latin too.   **alio pectus amore terat**: as we read, the phrasing may look abstract ('with another love his heart . . .'), but *terat* makes it persuasively physical ('he perhaps is rubbing his chest on another love'): cf. the extraordinary image of a skeletal embrace with which Cynthia's ghost ends her speech at 4.7.94 *mixtis ossibus ossa teram* [I shall grind bone with intermingled bone], and 3.11.30 n. *alio*, as often, = *altero* ('a second').

7–8 est tibi: possessive dative, 'you have' or 'your <beauty> is'; similarly *sit tibi* (9).   **forma potens**: cf. 2.5.28 *Cynthia forma potens*, and 3.10.17.   **castae Pallados artes**: cf. 1.2.30 *omnia quaeque Venus, quaeque Minerua probat* [<you are not lacking> all that Venus, and all that Minerva approves]. The omission of Venus and the presence of *castae* makes the poet's interest here seem less physical. *castae* can be taken with either *Pallados* (Greek genitive) or *artes*. The many arts associated with the virgin goddess Minerva are listed by Ovid at *Fast.* 3.815–34: learning, spinning, weaving, dyeing, shoemaking, carpentry, medicine, teaching, sculpture and painting. Spinning and weaving are the conventional crafts of the respectable (i.e. *casta*) Roman lady (3.6.15–16 n.). For Cynthia's combination of beauty and artistry (not associated with Pallas), see also 2.3.9–22.   **docto** perhaps implies that the grandfather was a poet: cf. 2.34.89 *docti Calui*, Tib. 1.4.61 *doctos poetas*, Ov. *Am.* 3.9.62 *docte Catulle*, Hor. *Epist.* 2.1.56; but it is also used of philosophers (3.21.26, Hor. *Satires* 2.4.3), orators (Ov. *ex P.* 1.2.117), lawyers (Hor. *Sat.* 2.1.78), and generally learned men (Hor. *Epist.* 1.19.1).

9–10 fortunata domus: for *fortunatus* introducing a beatitude*, see 3.2.17, Verg. *Geo.* 2.493 and 458–9 (qualified, as this is) *o fortunatos nimium, sua si bona norint,* | *agricolas* [o too lucky farmers, if only they knew their advantages]; cf. *felix* (3.13.15 n.).   **modo**: 'provided that', 'if only'.   **in nostros curre, puella, toros**: another very physical expression of a sentiment that might have been treated more abstractly ('be mine'), and a very swift move from the *castae Pallados artes* of 7.

11–12 Having in verse 10 encouraged the girl to run into his bed, P. instructs Phoebus, the sun-god, also (**quoque**) to hurry. **aestiuos spatiosius exigis ignes**: it is summer, and Phoebus is presented as driving his chariot (which carries the fire of the sun) out on a wider course. He is therefore asked to shorten the route on which he is taking the light of the day, which will otherwise linger (**moraturae contrahe lucis iter**).

13–14 nox mihi prima uenit: this explains why the sun should hurry: a night of love, the first, has been promised. The pentameter will make a corresponding request of the moon, that she linger, to lengthen the first night.　　　**primae da tempora nocti**: 'give up time for the first night', completing the address to Phoebus. This is Palmer's emendation of the transmitted *primae date tempora noctis* (where the incomprehensible second-person plural has arisen from dittography*, and *primae* has been read as genitive). *dare tempora* functions as an alternative to the common phrase *dare locum*; it suits the sun, the marker of the hours.

19–20 As transmitted, these verses intervene disastrously between the emphatic assertion of the inevitability of an agreement and the explanation (introduced by *namque*, 21) of why a compact is needed. When the couplet is set next to 15–16, *prius* and *ante* stand properly in parallel, as do the conversations (*sermonibus*) and the treaties settled within them.　　　**quam multae**: P. has the combination *quam multi* rather than *quot* also at 2.15.3, 2.34.91.　　　**cedent**: see p. 30.　　　**ante…quam**: *antĕquam* is often separated into its constituent parts, with the adverb (*ante*) in the main clause separate from the conjunction (*quam*); in dactylic* verse the separation is necessary.　　　**dulcia quam nobis concitet arma Venus**: 'before Venus may rouse our sweet warfare'. *arma* is used with a direct reference to sex also at 1.3.16 and 4.8.88 *toto soluimus arma toro*. The subjunctive *concitet* marks this as a hope, not a necessary consequence of 19: see 1.15.29–31, G&L §577 for the potential subjunctive after *ante quam*.

15–16 We move away from the erotic notes of 10, 14, 20, and enter the world of lawyers, with a profusion of gerundives of obligation (**ponenda, signanda, scribenda**) and legal terminology (**foedera, iura, lex**), which will continue in subsequent couplets. The notion may be to reassure the girl with the formality of a quasi-marriage. At the same time, the repetition of *foedus* will recall the epigrams of Catullus, e.g. 87.3 *nulla fides ullo fuit umquam in foedere tanta* [in no alliance has there ever been loyalty so great], though the imagery there is rather of political association.   **mihi**: dative of the agent, as is usual with gerundives.   **in amore nouo**: the newness of the affair is stressed once again (as also in *omina prima*, 24).

17–18 ipse suo ... signo: 'with his own signet ring': Love identifies himself as a party to the contract and confirms its binding nature. As often *ipse* is used to strengthen the force of *suus*: cf. especially 4.8.41 *Magnus et ipse suos breuiter contractus in artus* [Bigboy, briefly compressed into his own limbs], where *Magnus ipse* on its own would have no point.   **constringet pignora**: see p. 30. **testis sidereae torta corona deae**: Ariadne's crown (or, rather, garland, which would have stems twisted together: cf. 4.2.25 *torto faeno*) was elevated to the heavens as a constellation and often identified with her: see 3.17.7–8, Ov. *Ars* 1.527–64, *Met.* 8.176–82, *Fast.* 3.505–16. It is called on as a witness because of its association with love, the everlasting love of the goddess and her Bacchus—and, perhaps, because of Ariadne's experience of broken oaths: 'Are you departing like this,' she asks Theseus, sailing away, at Cat. 64.134–5, 'neglecting the power of the gods, ... and carrying home your accursed perjuries?' Moreover, at Apollonius, *Arg.* 3.997–1005 Jason cites the tale of Theseus and Ariadne in his seduction of Medea, and mentions the constellation as a sign that the gods approved the princess's actions: 'and as a sign in the middle of the sky her *starry crown* [ἀστερόεις στέφανος], which men call "Ariadne's", turns [ἐνελίσσεται] all night long among the heavenly constellations'. The verbal echoes confirm the allusion*; particularly neat is the transference of the notion of 'turning' from the celestial movement to the earthly creation of the garland. Into his seduction P. introduces the *corona* not as an *exemplum**, but as a witness, one ever available in the night sky as a symbol of pledged love. Like Jason he leaves unmentioned the inauspicious elements of Ariadne's story.

In casting himself as Bacchus, the male who brings consolation to the abandoned girl, he once more recalls material from early in the Cynthia cycle (1.3).

21–2 nox uigilata: P. implies that the gods should be taking vengeance on the departed *amicus* (as they did on the forgetful Theseus); but rather than the girl's abandonment he focuses on a tribulation the man is more likely to face, the night spent awake outside the beloved's door.

23–4 quibus imposuit soluit mox uincla libido: supply *illis* (dative of disadvantage): 'lust subsequently loosens the bonds *from those* on whom it has placed them'. The imagery of binding continues from *constringet* (17), *uincītur* (21); see 3.11.4 n.   **omina prima:** cf. Janus's words at *Fasti* 1.178–80: 'Omens are regularly present in beginnings. Men apply fearful ears to the first thing said, and the augur consults the bird he sees first.'

25–7 tacta sic ... ara: 'having touched the altar so [i.e. in the way I do now]'. *sic* is a vivid marker of the formal act (cf. what the late antique commentator Servius suggests are Dido's demonstrative words as she stabs herself at Verg. *Aen.* 4.660 *sic, sic iuuat ire sub umbras*). Cf. *Aen.* 12.201–2 *tango aras...:* | *nulla dies...foedera rumpet* [I touch the altar;...no day will break the agreement]: the language of religion is added to that of law (so too in *polluerit* and *sacra*).   **qui foedera ruperit...pollueritque..., illi sint:** we cannot be certain whether the verbs are future perfect or perfect subjunctive, and it may not have been clear to contemporary readers. The usage is like that in laws such as Cicero cites (in archaic form) at *de Legibus* 2.22.5 *sacrum...qui clepsit rapsitue, parricida esto* [let the man who has stolen or seized a sacred object be treated as a parricide].   **sacra marita:** the affair is treated as a marriage; Ovid repeats the phrase when Medea quotes Jason's oath to her at *Her.* 12.87.

28 caput argutae praebeat historiae: 'let him make himself the object of shrill story-telling'. *caput* is frequently used for one's person, identity or character. External disgrace is here added to internal pain; for anxiety about public notoriety, cf. 2.5.1–2, 2.24.1–8, 2.32.21–6; 3.15.45, 3.24.4 nn.

29–30 nec... dominae patefiant nocte fenestrae: instead of the usual door, a more dramatic route is evoked for illicit assignations: cf. 4.7.16, where Cynthia speaks of her *nocturnis trita fenestra dolis* [window worn by night-time deceits]; Ov. *Ars* 2.246, 3.605. Despite the formality of their agreement (n.b. 26), P. envisages the stolen pleasures he has had with Cynthia.   **fructu:** ablative after **egens.**

Additional bibliography: R. E. White, 'The unity of Propertius 2.34 and 3.20', in M. F. Gyles and E. W. Davis (eds), *Laudatores Temporis Acti: Studies in memory of W. E. Calder* (Chapel Hill, 1964), 63–72; Courtney, *Phoenix* 24 (1970), 48–51.

3.21

1–8: I'm going to Athens to free myself from love, which grows through looking. I've tried everything else in vain. She seldom lets me in, or, if she visits, sleeps on the edge of the bed. 9–16: The only solution is to move out of sight. Comrades, let's launch ship and set sail. Farewell, Rome, and friends, and my girl. 17–24: Now for the first time I shall be carried over the Adriatic, praying to the sea-gods, and through the Ionian Sea to the Isthmus of Corinth. Hurry across, feet. Having arrived in Piraeus, I shall head into Athens. 25–30: There I shall improve my mind with Plato or Epicurus, study the oratory of Demosthenes and sample Menander's wit, or at least enjoy looking at pictures or sculpture. 31–4: Time or distance will soothe the wounds in my heart. And if I die, it won't be of love, and that will be an honourable death.

This poem is, like 3.20, a strong pointer to the end of the Cynthia collection. In the first half of Book 1, Propertius has made it clear that neither he nor Cynthia can leave the other and sail abroad: especially relevant is 1.6 (**N**), where he rejects the idea of going with Tullus as part of his uncle's cohort (cf. 3.22), but see also 1.8A, where Cynthia is about to depart to Illyria with a magistrate, and 1.8B, where she has decided to remain with Propertius. Having set up the norm, he plays with it, by having her go off to Baiae in 1.11 (she is still absent in 1.12). And in 1.17 he describes himself as stranded by a storm at sea (*Et merito, quoniam potui fugisse puellam*, 1 [deservedly, since I could abandon my girl]). However, that journey never leads anywhere, and in verse 17 of this poem he denies that he has been on such a voyage before, at least across the Adriatic.

Travel is a familiar suggestion for those trying to escape love. Ovid will dedicate a section of the *Remedia amoris* to it (213–48), and P. has already considered it in 1.1.25–32, esp. 29–30:

> et uos, qui sero lapsum reuocatis, amici,   25
> quaerite non sani pectoris auxilia, ...
> ferte per extremas gentes et ferte per undas
> qua non ulla meum femina norit iter.   30

And you, friends, who are attempting too late to revive one who has perished, look for some aid for my love-sick heart. ... Take me through the peoples at the world's end, take me across the sea, where no woman may know of my route.

Horace will produce a sardonic rejection of travel as a cure for anxiety at *Epist.* 1.11.27, *caelum, non animum, mutant qui trans mare currunt* [those who hurry across the sea change their surroundings, not their character]. P. himself has already denied the efficacy of the supposed cure for love at 2.30.1–2:

> quo fugis a demens? nulla est fuga: tu licet usque
> ad Tanain fugias, usque sequetur Amor.

Where are you running to, you mad fool? There is no escape: though you run all the way to the river Don, Love will follow all the way.

Here he commits himself, with apparent confidence (31–4), to trying the remedy; and he does so in terms that present him initially as like an epic hero, pursued by a deity, and setting out on a great quest: *magnum* as the first word overturns the Callimachean* interest in the small scale and rejection of the large, and the account of the journey to come has a number of evocations of epic, especially Apollonius' *Argonautica* (11–13 nn.). But he is heading for Athens, and that proves not to be an epic destination.

1–2 Magnum iter... proficisci: 'to set out on a great journey' (internal accusative: G&L §332–3). On *magnum* see intro.; previously the adjective has been associated with the manifestly grand (1.14.17 *heroum uires*; 1.16.1 *triumphi*; 2.1.26, 2.7.5, 2.31.2 *Caesar*; 2.8.9

tyranni; 2.28.44, 2.34.40 *Iuppiter*; 3.8.12 *Venus*; 3.9.31 *Camilli*; 3.17.35 *Cybebe*), with aspirations P. never means to fulfil (2.10.6, 12, 20, 21; 3.3.5), and with himself, his poetry or love only by way of paradox (1.7.24, 2.7.16, 2.13.25; and see C. Weber, *AJPh* 103 (2008), 184–8 on 1.19.12). The phrase *magnum iter* will be reprised at 4.10.3 in an entirely metapoetic* sense, describing the journey to create a poem on the *spolia opima*.   **ad doctas … Athenas:** *ad* is not normally used with the name of a town to convey 'motion to', but here the sense is 'set out *for*'. Athens was the major centre for tertiary education in the Roman period, especially for the study of philosophy and oratory: see 25–7; but *doctas* also evokes its poetic traditions (3.20.8 n.). P. recalls 1.6.13 where he uses the phrase *doctas cognoscere Athenas* (**N**): he is no longer bothered by any pain he may cause her (cf. 1.6.15–18).   **cogor:** explained by the following lines, especially 5–6: everything else has been tried. As Fedeli notes, the form occurs six times in Book 1, so it contributes to the sense of reminiscence here; cf. 18 n.   **graui soluat Amore:** 'release me from the heavy weight of Love'. With *deus* in verse 6 P. compels us to think of the god rather than simply the emotion. *premit* there involves the same image as *graui* here: cf. 2.30.7–8 *semper Amor … instat amanti* | *et grauis ipse super libera colla sedet* [Love always looms over the lover, and himself sits heavy on the neck of the freeborn]. It makes sense therefore to print *Amore* with a capital, though P. will not have made any such differentiation between proper names and other words: modern readers are not so used to turning their emotions into deities. We may contrast 33, where the lack of *ab* to mark an agent and the force of *turpi* together remove the possibility of personifying *amore*.

3–4 crescit … assidue spectando: 'grows through looking constantly': cf. Lucr. 6.457 (clouds) *coniungendo crescunt*; Publilius Syrus 43 *Audendo uirtus crescit, tardando timor* [courage grows through daring, fear through delaying], *Aen.* 4.175.   **ipse** serves to heighten the paradox of the god providing food for himself.

5–6 omnia sunt temptata mihi quacumque fugari | **possit:** 'Everything has been tried by me by which [*lit.* by whatever path] he could be put to flight.' Lucretius has similar phrasing at 5.187–91 (repeated at 422–6) 'primordia rerum | ex infinito iam tempore … | … consuerunt … | … *omnia*pertemptare, / *quaecumque* inter se *possint* congressa creare' [the first beginnings of things have for an infinite amount of time now become accustomed to trying out everything, whatever they could come together and create].   **usque:** Heinsius' *usque* is far more forceful than the transmitted *ipse*: cf. *usque* and *semper* in 2.30.1–2 (intro.). It reinforces the sense of **exsomnis** (Barber) as do the accusatives of time at *Aen.* 6.555–6 *Tisiphone...| uestibulum exsomnis seruat noctesque diesque* [Tisiphone watches the entrance unsleeping night and day]. After *omnia* in 5, corruption of *exsomnis* to *ex omni* was very easy.   **premit:** cf. 1.1.4 *pressit Amor pedibus* (p. 1).

7–8 bis tamen aut semel admittit, cum saepe negarit: 'She admits me <only> once or twice, although she has often said no.' Amor has been the subject of the previous clause, but the association of god and Cynthia confuses the identity of the grammatical subject as early in the corpus* as 1.1.3 *deiecit* (cited p. 1). *tamen* marks the *cum*-clause as concessive; but (given the need to supply 'only') it has possibly been corrupted from *tantum*. *negarit* is the syncopated* form of the perfect subjunctive *negauerit*. For *bis* before *semel* cf. Ov. *Tr.* 4.10.58, *Nux* 74.   **seu uenit:** 'or, if she comes': 33 has another instance of this use of *seu*.   **extremo dormit amicta toro:** the first three words all contribute to the disappointment: she keeps as far away from the poet as the bed allows, she keeps her clothes on, and she sleeps (rather than having intercourse of any kind with P.). Both clothes and sleep are (playfully) criticized in a passage about a night P. and Cynthia spent together, 2.15.1–24; and when Corinna arrives (*uenit*) in Ovid's bedroom at *Am.* 1.5.9, she proves willing to have her clothes torn off.

9–10 auxilium occurs only twice in the corpus*, and is one of a number of details that recall P.'s opening poem (1.1.26 *auxilia*, cited in the intro.). Another is the use of the name **Cynthia** for the first time in Book 3; the reference to eyes also looks back to 1.1.1–3 (p. 1). Other lovers are advised in 1.1 not to change place when they grow used to a love (36: *neque assueto mutet amore locum*: cf. **mutatis terris**). This is combined with reminiscence of 1.12.3–4 (where it is Cynthia who has left Rome): *tam multa illa meo diuisa est milia lecto | quantum Hypanis Veneto dissidet Eridano* [She is as many miles separated from my bed as Hypanis (in the Ukraine) is distant from Venetian Eridanus (the Po)].

11–12 nunc agite: the combination both points to a new section in the poem (similarly *nunc age* fourteen times in Lucretius), and gives an urgency to what follows (cf. Plaut. *Persa* 469; and, for continuing urgency here, *properate* in 21). The line's four dactyls* add to the sense of pace (cf. also 17–18, 21); we might compare the rowing of Menelaus' men at *Od.* 4.580.   **socii:** an epic address for those who travel (*Aen.* 1.198; cf. ἑταῖροι at *Od.* 1.5 etc.). Both those who go with him as comrades, and the friends to whom he says farewell in 15 recall the *amici* of 1.1.25.   **propellite** evokes προπροβιαζόμενοι ('forcing onward') in the description of the launch of the Argo at Apollonius 1.386.   **remorumque pares ducite sorte uices:** apparently 'in pairs take your places at the oars in accordance with the lot': cf. *Arg.* 1.395–6 κληῖδας μὲν πρῶτα πάλωι διεμοιρήσαντο, | ἄνδρ' ἐντυναμένω δοιὼ μίαν [first they assigned rowing benches by lot, two men taking one bench].

13–14 felicia lintea: 'fair-weather canvas'. *felicia* brings a good omen for the voyage: as the wind is set fair, the sail can be hauled to the top of the mast (**extremo mālo**). The couplet works as a précis of *Arg.* 1.563–79, where the Argonauts raise the mast and sail with the breeze astern. **liquidum ... aura secundat iter:** 'the breeze renders the journey favourable and smooth'. *secundus* (derived from *sequi*) means 'following', hence 'favourable' of a wind; *secundare*, the verbal equivalent, is rare enough to cause the lexicographer Nonius Marcellus (third/fourth century) to cite this line (the only time he cites elegy).

15–16 qualiscumque mihi: 'of whatever kind to me', i.e. 'however you have treated me'. The pronoun has been used of Cynthia, with a similar connotation, but in a more affirmative context, already at 1.18.31 *sed qualiscumque es, resonent mihi 'Cynthia' siluae.* **tuque:** deferred to the second half of the pentameter, where *que* provides a helpful short syllable (cf. 2.32.14).

17–18 ergo ego nunc: another new beginning, as if the poet is finding it hard actually to leave.   **rudis Hadriaci ... aequoris hospes:** unlike *rudis*, *hospes* is not regularly used with a genitive, but the phrase perhaps functions as a whole: 'an inexperienced visitor to the Adriatic Sea'.   **cogar et undisonos nunc prece adire deos:** this echoes 1.1.8 *aduersos cogor habere deos*; but the gods there are erotic and here, as the gods of the sea, described with a compound epithet, they are epic. Other occurrences of *undisonus* come in later epic, but earlier poetry has a number of compounds in -*sonus*, including Cat. 64.52 *fluentisono*, at the start of an epic ecphrasis, in which Theseus abandons Ariadne and sails to Athens. Abandoning Cynthia and going to sea means a change of genre for the poet.

19–20 'Then when my yacht, having been carried across the Ionian Sea, rests its weary sails in the calm waters of Lechaeum...' The word-order is complicated, *cum* being postponed*, and the three adjective-noun phrases are entwined: VECTUS ... *fessa* Lechaei...placida *uela* PHASELUS aqua. Any sense of epic sweep is quickly removed: the sails are tired not after a great storm (e.g. *Aeneid* 1.81–123), but simply when they have passed through the Ionian Sea (between Sicily and Greece at the foot of the Adriatic). The water is described as calm. Like many Romans P. will arrive at Lechaeum, the port of Corinth on the western side of the Isthmus, and a name not previously found in poetry. And as a *phaselus* his boat recalls the yacht of Cat. 4: a lyric vessel (only later in epic, at Lucan 5.518).

21–2 quod superest: 'for the future'. There are good parallels at *Aen.* 9.157, 11.15, in each of which some action is described as finished and then contrasted with an imperative relating to the future. Here the phrase is odd, because the pentameter, in continuing the thought, limits that future to a restricted locality (contrast 3.17.19); and in the next couplet we find the clear implication that P.'s feet are indeed to carry him only over the Isthmus: he will sail on again, from Cenchreae on the eastern coast of the Isthmus, to Piraeus, the port of Athens. The oddity appears to be tactical, however: this voyage is only implied and we have no further account of sailing. The poet's feet and verse (**pedes**) remain landbound in what follows.   **Isthmos qua terris arcet utrumque mare:** descriptions of the Isthmus of Corinth occur frequently in later poetry (e.g. Ov. *Her.* 4.105–6, 12.104; *Fast.* 6.495–6; Sen. *Ag.* 564–5, *Thy.* 111–13; Lucan 1.100–3; Stat. *Theb.* 1.120, 4.61–2). It has an obvious function as an image of transition (Jacobson, *ICS* 1 (1976), 167 n. 19), but here it seems mainly to give P. firm ground from which he can ward off the sea, that epic element; he certainly does not meet the monsters encountered by Theseus on his journey from Troezen to Athens (as narrated in lost portions of Callimachus' *Hecale*); cf. 24, [3.22.37–8]).

23–4 Piraei ... litora portus: 'the shores of the port of Piraeus'. There are similar, if shorter, periphrases* at Cat. 64.74 *curuis a litoribus Piraei*, Ov. *Met.* 6.446 *Piraea litora.*   **scandam ego Theseae bracchia longa uiae**: the twelve-kilometre road from the port to Athens was protected by 'long arms' (*bracchium, OLD* 7): cf. Livy 31.26.8 *muri qui bracchiis duobus Piraeum Athenis iungit* [of the wall which joins Piraeus to Athens with two arms]. The route is one that was taken (in the other direction) by Theseus when heading to Crete—and Ariadne (17–18 n.).

25–6 in spatiis animum emendare Platonis: *spatiis* ('porticos') is the conjecture of the early eighteenth-century editor Broukhusius (for *studiis*, which comes from *studium* in the same position in the next hexameter); it evokes the Academy (the school founded by Plato), offering a feature to match the gardens of Epicurus, and one that is mentioned by Cicero (*Fin.* 5.1.1 *Academiae ... nobilitata spatia*; *Orator* 12 *ex Academiae spatiis*). For young Romans studying philosophy in Athens, see the report of Cicero's son in *Fam.* 16.21, and Hor. *Epist.* 2.2.43–5: after a literary schooling at Rome Athens gave him a little more education and he sought 'the truth in the woods of the Academy'. At *Trist.* 1.2.77 Ovid contrasts his current journey into exile with that to Athens as a student.   **docte** (28 n.) **Epicure**: Lucretius, conveying Epicurus's philosophy in Latin, attacks the follies of love (4.1037–1287), so his teachings might well be useful to P.

27–8 After considering philosophy as his Athenian pastime, he moves on to rhetoric and the reading of comedy: he will devote himself to anything except elegy.   **studium linguae, Demosthenis arma**: we have sixty-one speeches attributed to the Athenian orator Demosthenes (384–322 BC), a significant proportion dealing with foreign policy, and in particular his *Olynthiacs* and *Philippics*, through which he attempted to persuade the Athenian assembly to resist the aggression of Philip of Macedon. Hence the relevance of *arma* (which involves the added joke that Demosthenes' father made swords: Juv. 10.129–32). However, it is the tongue itself that constitutes the arms of Demosthenes, not the *study* of eloquence: as an accusative, not a genitive, *arma* breaks the standard rule of apposition*, and the text is possibly corrupt. **libabo**: 'I shall taste'. Suringar's brilliant conjecture replaces the awkwardly feeble *librorum* ('your wit of books'?) and provides an appropriate verb for *sales* ('witticisms', lit. 'samples of salt'; *OLD* 6b). **munde Menandre**: 'refined Menander'. Menander (*c.*343–291 BC) was the greatest writer of New Comedy, the form that gradually developed in the fourth century BC, concentrating on stories of social interaction and love temporarily thwarted, in realistic manner and unextravagant style. His plays were lost, but much has been recovered from papyri*. Many Roman comedies are versions of his plays, and he is mentioned by P. also at 2.6.3, 4.5.43. At *Ars* 3.332 Ovid encourages the erotically inclined girl to read his work (along with Sappho and the elegists). *munde* (also applied to Menander at 4.5.43) is Kuinoel's conjecture for *docte*, which a scribe has apparently repeated from 26: the descent from mind (25) to tongue (27–8) to eyes and hands (29–30) suggests that the intellectual epithet is more appropriate with *Epicure* than *Menandre*. However, it is not inconceivable that the repetition of *docte* in 26, 28 is the author's, intending to emphasize the shared nature of these different citizens of 'learned Athens'.

29–30 Relevant for the whole passage, but this couplet in particular is Livy 45.27.11 *Athenas inde, plenas quidem et ipsas uetustae famae, multa tamen uisenda habentes, arcem, portus, muros Piraeum urbi iungentes, naualia, <monumenta> magnorum imperatorum, simulacra deorum hominumque, omni genere et materiae et artium insignia* [thence to Athens, itself full of ancient fame, but containing much worth seeing, the acropolis, the ports, the walls linking Piraeus to the city, dockyards, <memorials> of great generals, images of gods and men, objects distinguished in every kind of material and craft]. **aut certe tabulae**: 'or at any rate pictures', marking the decrease in ambition. **capient mea lumina**: 'will captivate my eyes'; an inversion of 1.1.1 *me cepit*, where it is Cynthia's eyes that captivate the poet (perhaps also to be set against *capient me*, 23 and *spectando*, 3). **siue ebore exactae seu magis aere manus**: 'or [3.8.24 n.] works of art finished off in ivory or preferably in bronze': cf. Petronius 83.1 *Zeuxidos manus* ('masterpieces by Zeuxis': in a passage where Encolpius seeks

314 A Commentary on Propertius, Book 3

consolation for lost love in an art gallery). Why does P. prefer bronze statues? In the first place bronze sculpture commanded immense admiration. But there may be an implied preference between two enormous cult statues of Athena on the Acropolis, both by the great sculptor Phidias: the gold and ivory (chryselephantine) statue in the Parthenon and the even taller Athena Promachos outside. The latter, which would have commanded the view when P. entered the sanctuary, was made of bronze.

31–2 profundi: 'the deep', i.e. the sea.   **lenibunt:** an alternative form of the future for this fourth-conjugation verb; *lēnĭēnt* will not scan in dactylic* verse.   **tacito...sinu:** 'secretly in my breast', with the double implication that P. will write no more while time and distance imperceptibly heal his wounds (cf. 3.2.24 *annorum tacito pondere*).

33–4 seu moriar, fato, non turpi fractus amore: 'or, if I die, <I shall die> thanks to fate, not broken by a shameful love affair.' For the ellipse, cf. 4.11.79 *et si quid doliturus eris, sine testibus illis* [and if you grieve at all, <grieve> without their seeing]. For the sequence *aut...seu* (= 'either...or, if'), cf. perhaps 2.22.43. P. has exploited the notion of death from love at 1.6.25–8, 2.1.77–8, 2.13.17–58 (cf. the wounds of 32).   **illa mihi mortis honesta dies:** *honesta* ('respectable') is the antonym* of *turpi* in the hexameter. There is a fundamental contrast with two passages from Book 2. In 2.8 he thinks in his despair of killing the two of them with the same sword, and concedes *ista mihi mors est inhonesta futura* (27: 'that death of yours will be dishonourable for me'). In 2.26B, Cynthia plans a sea-voyage, and he envisages their journey together, culminating in shipwreck and death (57–8):

> quod mihi si ponenda tuo pro corpore vita,
>   exitus hic nobis non inhonestus erit.

But if my life has to be laid down for your body, this will not be a dishonourable end for us.

Additional bibliography: R. Daut, in P. T. Brannan (ed.), *Classica et Iberica* (Festschrift J.M.F. Marique; Worcester, MA, 1975), 293–302; Jacobson, *ICS* 1 (1976), 164–73.

3.22

1–4: Have you lived in Cyzicus, Tullus, for so many years now? 5–6 (incl. 15–16): Whether you delight in the cities of the Hellespont, or the rivers Cayster or Maeander, <....................> and be moved by my longing for you. 7–14: You may see the marvellous sights visited by Perseus and Hercules in the West and follow the voyage of the Argo to the East. 17–25: But they all yield to the wonders of Italy. Our strength lies in piety and the sword. Here are the rivers Anio and Clitumnus, the Marcian aqueduct, lakes and springs. 27–36: There are no dangerous snakes or monsters here. Italy is not the setting for tragic mythology. 39–42: This is your origin and home, the country in which you should pursue ambitions in the spheres of politics and your future family.

Propertius continues to move towards the close of his Cynthia cycle. In addressing Tullus, he recalls his first book, which has four poems (including the first and last) addressed to him. 1.14 contrasted Tullus as a rich man with Propertius (note the opening *Tu licet*, recalled at 7 of this poem, and the sense in 1.14.3–6 that Tullus is an idle spectator). But more powerful are the links between the poem and (once again) 1.6 (**N**). That poem sent Tullus off east as a Roman dignitary as a way of stressing Propertius' commitment to Cynthia in Rome. In 3.21 P. marks the end of this commitment by announcing his departure from Rome. Now he turns to Tullus, who has lost any care he may have had for his *armata patria* (1.6.22), and whose continued absence announces his rejection of the *cursus honorum*. Like 3.21 this poem draws on Apollonius' *Argonautica* (2–3, 10–14 nn.): again a move of genre might be implied, but Tullus is presented as a sightseer who no more fits into the role of an epic hero than P. did. To tempt him to return, P. recalls the delights of Italy as expressed by Vergil in his famous[7] *laudes Italiae* (*Geo.* 2.136–76 [**K**]). Points of contact are:

7–17 < *Geo.* 2.136–9
19–21 < *Geo.* 2.145–8, 167–72

---

[7] Famous, but not at all straightforward, and for some modern readers disturbing: see e.g. D. O. Ross, *Virgil's Elements* (Princeton, 1987), 116–28, and Thomas 1988, *ad loc.*

23 *Anio* (voc.), *Clitumnus* < *Geo.* 2.146 *Clitumne*
23–6 (without the stress on oceanic scale) < *Geo.* 2.158–64
39 *parens* < *Geo.* 2.173
17 *Romanae*, 20 *Roma* < *Geo.* 2.148, 172, 176
28 *Itala* < *Geo.* 2.138

Especially noteworthy is that P. also emphasizes the absence of the monsters and crimes found in Greek myth (27–36; cf. *Geo.* 2.140–2, 151–4). As a response to Vergil this looks ahead to a major aspect of Book 4 (esp. poems 1A, 6, 9); 21–2 even bring in the *Aeneid* which will be the main focus there. Establishing the tone of the imitation itself is more difficult. Critics such as Williams have been disappointed by the piece as emulation; an alternative is to read it as parody.

1 Frigida: like *Magnum* (3.21.1) an initial word with metapoetic* significance. Of a town in a Mediterranean climate the adjective is positive ('cool': Cyzicus has a well-ventilated position on the strait); but it is also used of literary style: *OLD* 8 (Catullus 44 is based on the conceit that the poet read a speech so bad he caught a cold from it). **Cyzicus:** a town on an island off the south coast of the Propontis connected to the mainland by a causeway or isthmus (2): cf. Strabo 12.575, Plin. *Nat.* 5.142; and see Map 4b. Roman citizens were killed in disturbances there in 20 BC (almost certainly after the publication of Book 3). It is a feminine noun like many other Greek cities, such as *Miletus*.

2 Tulle: see intro.   **Propontiaca qua fluit isthmos aqua:** 'where the isthmus flows with the water of Propontis'. Appropriately for a Greek settlement, *Propontiaca* has a Greek ending, and *isthmos* a Greek spelling. Propontis is the stretch of water through which boats pass coming from the Aegean before (*pro*) they reach the Black Sea (*Pontos*). At *Argonautica* 1.936–52 Apollonius describes the setting of Cyzicus in Propontis, including 'the isthmus flooded by the waves' (ἐπιμύρεται ἰσθμός: 1.938). The watery start of the poem looks forward to the celebration of Italian waters in 23–6. As at 3.21.22 the isthmus could be seen as contributing to the sense of transition, a point reinforced by the appearance of the *uia Ditis* in 4, the route between earth and underworld.

3 Dindymis…Cybebe: 'and <there is> Cybebe, goddess of
Dindymon, made from wood of the sacred vine'. Cybebe (or
Cybele), the great mother-goddess of Anatolia, was a goddess of
fertility and wild nature: see Cat. 63, Ov. *Fast.* 4.179–372. Her
ecstatic cult was associated with a number of mountains called
Dindymon (Map 3), one near Pessinus in Galatia (to the west of
the centre of modern Turkey: Herodotus 1.80 seems to think of
another, further west), the other on the peninsula above Cyzicus.
Valerius Flaccus (3.19) and Claudian (20.262) are the only other
Latin authors who in naming the mountain specify the locality
more precisely than 'Phrygian'. Silius 17.20 refers to *gemino…
Dindyma monte*, which has been taken as an etymological gloss*
(cf. δίδυμος 'twin'), but might well refer to the uncertain geography. Apollonius gives an account of the dedication of a vine-
wood statue to the Dindymian Mother at Cyzicus (*Arg.* 1.1117–21;
Herodotus 4.76 already places her cult at Cyzicus). It was carved
by Argus, the builder of the Argo.

4 raptorisque tulit quae uia Ditis equos: 'and the road which carried
the horses of the rapist Dis'. The rape of Persephone by the god of the
Underworld is usually placed at Enna in Sicily (Ov. *Fast.* 4.419–66),
but she was associated with many other sites including Cyzicus
(Appian 12.75; Plutarch, *Lucullus* 10.1–3).

5 Helles Athamantidos: 'of Helle, daughter of Athamas', whose
drowning in its waters gave the strait the name Hellespont ('the sea
of Helle'). The two words are Greek genitives, the nominative of the
second being *Athamantis*. The cities of the Hellespont include Lamp-
sacus, and Sestus and Abydus, the homes of Hero and Leander (cf.
Ov. *Her.* 18–19).

15 siue et olorigeri uisenda est ora Caystri: 'if the bank of Cayster,
home of swans, is also (*et*) to be visited by you'. From *Iliad* 2.460–1
on, swans are associated with the Cayster, so *olorigeri* (lit. 'swan-
carrying'; cf. *olorifer* at Stat. *Theb.* 4.227, Claud. *Carm. min.* 31.12) is
a plausible replacement for the transmitted *orige*, which is nonsensical. Another conjecture is *Ortygie*, an ancient name of Ephesus, the
city at the mouth of the Cayster (Plin. *Nat.* 5.115); but it would stand
in awkward apposition* with *ora Caystri*.

16 et quae serpentes temperat unda uias: 'and the water that governs a serpentine route': the famously meandering Maeander, which flows into the Aegean south of Priene, described by Seneca at *Epist.* 104.15 as *poetarum omnium exercitatio et ludus* ('school exercise of every poet': see e.g. 2.34.35–6, Ov. *Met.* 8.162–6, Seneca's own version at *Her. f.* 683–5). The transmitted *septenas uias* looks like a reference to the seven streams of the Nile delta, which would take us away from Asia Minor abruptly in the middle of a couplet.

6 The lacuna* may have had the sense 'even so, return to your native land'.   **desiderio...meo:** i.e. 'my longing for you'. **mouere:** passive imperative.

7 tu licet aspicias: 'you may see...', lit. 'it is permitted (that) you may see': for *licet* + subjunctive with this meaning see *OLD* 1c. **Atlanta:** Greek accusative of *Atlas*, the giant who supported the sky on his shoulders and encountered both Perseus and Hercules: he is identified with the Atlas mountains in Morocco. The legendary sights referred to in 7–10 are all in the far west.

8 sectaque Persea Phorcidos ora manu : 'and the face of the daughter of Phorcys cut by the hand of Perseus'. The daughter of Phorcys was the Gorgon Medusa, whose appearance was so terrible that anyone who looked on her face was turned to stone: her face is not in fact a sight to behold! Perseus killed her by using his shield as a mirror: see Ov. *Met.* 4.772–86, where she is placed in the same general region as Atlas. *Persēā* is an adjective: 'of Perseus'.

9–10 Geryonae: genitive of *Geryones*, alternatively known as Geryon. Geryon was a three-bodied monster who lived in the far west beyond the pillars of Hercules on the island of Erythea. Hercules' tenth labour was to kill him and drive off the herd from his cattlesheds: cf. 4.9.1–2. We might think of another labour of Hercules which works against the logic of this poem, that in which the hero killed Cacus, a fire-breathing monster who dominated the future site of Rome itself and stole some of these cattle from him there (4.9.1–20, *Aen.* 8.185–269, Livy 1.7).   **luctantum in puluere signa |** **Herculis Antaeique:** 'the traces where Hercules and Antaeus wrestled in the dust'. Antaeus, a Libyan giant famous for his wrestling, was beaten at this activity by Hercules (Pind. *Isthm.* 4.52–60,

Apollodorus 2.5.11). He too lived in the west near the garden of
the Hesperides (Plin. *Nat.* 5.3). For the elision at the caesura of the
pentameter, cf. 1.5.32. **Hesperidumque choros**: possibly 'the
dancing places of the Hesperides' (a Greek rather than Latin meaning
of *choros*) as well as their performances. The Hesperides ('goddesses of
evening') guarded the golden apples in their western garden. According
to Apollonius, *Arg.* 4.1399, they sang charmingly until the arrival of
Hercules, whose eleventh labour was the theft of the apples.

11 Colchum... Phasin: 'to Phasis, (the) Colchian (river)'. We now
move from the far west to the extreme east: Colchis is on the
eastern side of the Black Sea; the chief river is the Phasis which
flows into the sea from the Caspian mountains. Jason and the
Argonauts went there to get the golden fleece, passing through the
Bosporus (13–14). *Phasin* is Greek accusative. **propellas**:
either 'you may drive <your ship>' or 'you may drive ahead'
(intransitive). **tuo... remige**: 'with your oarsmen': collective singular* : see *OLD remex* b.

12 Peliacae... trabis: 'of the ship built with wood from Mount Pelion',
i.e. the Argo. The cutting of the trees on Mount Pelion in north-east
Greece is referred to at the start of Euripides' and Ennius' *Medea* plays
as well as Catullus 64. In all three works there follow accounts of a love
affair that has gone disastrously wrong (Medea and Ariadne; cf. also
Cicero's citation of Ennius' passage when he characterizes Clodia
Metelli as a 'Palatine Medea', *Cael.* 18): there is no sign that Tullus
has yet found his Medea to abandon. **legas**: 'you may trace |
follow', but punning, in this allusive context, on the sense 'read' (as
Catullus does at 64.4, where he describes the Argonauts as *lecti iuuenes*
[youths who have been chosen (*or* read about)]).

13–14 rudis... in faciem prorae pinus adacta nouae: 'the inexperienced pine shaped into the new form of a ship'. *nouae* is
transferred from *faciem* (as often happens where a genitive is
attached to a noun). The Argo is often treated as the world's
first ship (Cat. 64.11–18). **immissa... columba**: 'after a
dove was sent on ahead', ablative absolute. This is how Jason
confused the timing of the Clashing Rocks, which tried to crush
ships sailing between them (Ap. *Arg.* 2.549–618). Heyworth's

emendation of the transmitted *Argoa* to *immissa* avoids a very abnormal ablative of attendant circumstances: 'with the Argo's dove'; *Argo* has presumably come from an explanatory gloss* written above the line.   **natat**: historic present.

17–18 The pay-off after 7–14: though you go to the west or to the east, 'everything wonderful will yield to the Roman land'.   **quicquid ubique fuit**: 'whatever has been anywhere': cf. Ov. *Ars* 1.55–6:

> tot tibi tamque dabit formosas Roma puellas
> 'haec habet' ut dicas 'quidquid in orbe fuit.'

[Rome will give you so many and such beautiful girls that you will say 'This city has anything that has existed in the world.']

19–20 armis apta magis tellus quam commoda noxae: 'a land more fit for arms than suited to wrong-doing': vocative with *Roma* in 20. The background here shifts to the *Aeneid*: one thinks for example of the words of Anchises at *Aen.* 3.539, *bellum, o terra hospita, portas* [you bring war, hospitable land]; and **Famam...pudet** may recall Fama at *Aen.* 4.173–95 disapproving of the love affair between Aeneas and Dido.   **Roma, tuae...historiae**: a reminiscence of Cornelius Gallus (3.2: F).

21–2 nam quantum ferro tantum pietate potentes | stamus: 'for we stand powerful as much through piety as the sword'. **uictrices temperat ira manus**: 'anger tempers [i.e. directs] our hands when they are victorious'. The first part of the couplet has used an Ennian structure (*moribus antiquis res stat Romana uirisque*, 156 Skutsch) to articulate the simple message of Vergil's poem: armed strength and piety are the twin pillars on which Rome stands. And it may well be to the *Aeneid* that we should look for an explanation of those paradoxical words *uictrices temperat ira manus*: anger does not restrain; it provokes to violence. The epic's closing scene in which Aeneas kills Turnus gives a remarkable picture of the man who symbolizes Rome rejecting restraint out of anger: *temperat* here hints at restraint while recalling the way that anger 'controls' the hero's action at the moment of final victory (see Putnam, *ICS* 2 (1977), 244). The confusion of the *Aeneid*'s moral message is thus encapsulated in the Propertian phrase.

23–4 The waterfalls of the Anio at Tibur (3.16.3–4 n.); the source of Clitumnus, a spring near Spoleto in Umbria famous for its clear, abundant water and for its white cattle (cf. *Geo.* 2.146 [**K**] and Plin. *Ep.* 8.8); the aqueduct called *Aqua Marcia* (3.2.14 n.) with its supremely clear, cold and healthy water (Plin. *Nat.* 31.41), which was repaired by Agrippa around this time (see pp. 15–16): all were famous wonders of Italy.   **ab Umbro tramite**: 'from the Umbrian upland': for the meaning of *trames*, see 3.13.44 n. **aeternum ... opus**: the structure of the *aqua Marcia* will last for ever.

25–6 Lakes Albanus and Nemorensis (now known as Nemi) are in volcanic craters some 20 kilometres south and east of Rome: they are beauty spots, and the Pope has his summer residence above the former at Castel Gandolfo.   **foliis ... abundans**: Housman's emendation of the improbable *socii ... ab unda* ('from the water of an ally') is both etymologically and descriptively apt: Ovid describes the lake as surrounded by a shady forest (*Fast.* 3.263–4 *silua praecinctus opaca | est lacus*), as it still is. *abundans* ('overflowing') is nicely joky, when used of a lake's leaves.   **potaque Pollucis nympha salubris equo**: 'The health-giving water-nymph drunk by the horses of Pollux' refers to the *fons Iuturnae* (the spring of Juturna) in the Roman forum between the temples of Vesta and Castor at the foot of the Palatine hill. It was here that Castor and Pollux watered their horses after the Roman victory at Lake Regillus: Dion. Hal. 6.13; cf. Ov. *Fast.* 1.706–8. A square basin fed by two springs, it is still visible. Its waters were considered especially wholesome: Frontinus, *Aq.* 1.4, Varro, *Ling. Lat.* 5.71.

27 cerastae: nominative plural of the Greek form *cerastes*, the horned Egyptian snake or asp. According to Herodotus 2.74 it does not harm human beings, but it is highly poisonous in Nicander, *Theriaca* 258–81. Vergil celebrates the absence of large snakes from Italy at *Geo.* 2.153–4.   **squamoso ... uentre**: 'with [*or* on] scaly bellies', i.e. ablative of description or means.

28 Itala portentis nec furit unda nouis: 'nor does Italian water boil [*lit.* rage] with strange monsters': Italy has no hydra or *cetus*, the sea-serpent to which Andromeda was exposed (29). It is appropriate too that there be no frenzy (*furor*) in Italian waters, for *furor* is the antitype of Roman *pietas* (21–2 n.). But *portentis* suggests prodigies and there could be a reference, subversive in the context of Augustanism, to the fact that the opening of the Portus Iulius (see p. 14) was marked by a storm so great that it was reckoned a *prodigium* (Servius Danielis *ad Geo.* 2.162). Vergil writes of 'the sea howling in indignation where the Julian wave echoes from afar' (*Geo.* 2.162–3: K). P. does not describe this great feat of Augustan engineering itself, but simply evokes this intertext*.

29 pro matre: 'in place of her mother'. Andromeda's mother Cassiope had boasted of being fairer than the Nereids. As a result Neptune sent a sea-monster to ravage her country, Ethiopia (we are back in Africa), and an oracle declared that Andromeda must be bound to a cliff to be consumed by it. She was saved by Perseus, who turned the monster to stone by showing it the Gorgon's head. Cf. 8 n., 1.3.3–4, 4.7.65–6, Ov. *Am.* 3.3.17–18, *Met.* 4.670–764, Manilius 5.538–618; and Euripides' play *Andromeda*, now mainly lost.

30 nec tremis Ausonias, Phoebe fugate, dapes: 'nor, Phoebus [*vocative*] put to flight, are you fearful of Ausonian [i.e. Italian] feasts'. The reference is to the banquet at which Atreus, king of Argos (or Mycenae) led his brother Atreus to consume the flesh of his own children. The sun god (Phoebus Apollo) turned back his chariot in horror at the sight: the story appeared in a number of tragedies both Greek and Roman, all now lost bar fragments* except for the later *Thyestes* of Seneca; see also Ov. *Am.* 3.12.39, *Ars* 1.329–30, *Tr.* 2.392, Hyginus, *Fab.* 258.

31–2 nec cuiquam absentes arserunt in caput ignes: 'nor have fires burnt at a distance against [i.e. to destroy] the life of anyone'. The Fates told Meleager's mother Althaea that his life would be coextensive with that of a log burning on the hearth. She hid the log away, but when Meleager killed her brothers, she burnt it and thus destroyed him. The story, the subject of fragmentary* plays by Euripides and Accius, and of Ovid, *Met.* 8.445–525, is set in Calydon in western Greece. *cuiquam* is a possessive dative.   **exitium nato matre mouente suo**: 'a mother creating destruction for her son', an ablative absolute making the main clause more specific (but still without a name).

33 Penthea: Greek accusative of *Pentheus* (3.17.24 n.), who spied from a pine tree on the Theban women who have become bacchants, his mother included; they hunt him down and tear him to pieces, his mother taking the lead: Eur. *Bacch.* 1063–152.

34 nec soluit Danaas subdita cerua rates: 'nor does a substituted hind release the Greek boats'. Diana was offended by Agamemnon and becalmed the Greek fleet which had assembled at Aulis to go to Troy. He had to sacrifice his daughter Iphigenia to appease the goddess. According to one version of the myth, she was miraculously rescued at the last moment from being sacrificed and a hind was put in her place. The story is told in Euripides' posthumous tragedy, *Iphigenia at Aulis*, and the version of the work that we have includes the miraculous substitution in a passage of doubtful authorship (1540–1612). The myths referred to in 29–34 all deal with terrible crimes within families, grim violations of *pietas* (as had been emphasized for the Iphigenia story at Lucr. 1.82–101).

35–6 nec ualuit . . . Iuno: 'nor has Juno had the power'.   **paelice:** the 'mistress' of Jupiter referred to here is Io. We see another family at war: Jupiter's wife Juno jealously put curving horns on Io's head, transforming her into a cow: 2.33.9, Aeschylus, *Supplices* 299. (Elsewhere it is Jupiter who transforms Io to hide her: Ov. *Met.* 1.610–12; we do not know which version Calvus, Catullus's friend, followed in his *Io.*).   **aut faciem turpi dedecorare boue:** 'or to spoil her appearance with the disgraceful (features of a) cow'.

40 hic tibi pro digna gente petendus honos: 'here is office to be sought by you as suits your distinguished family'. *honos* ('magistracy') is collective singular*; *tibi* dative of the agent, as is usual with a gerundive.

41–2 hic tibi ad eloquium ciues: 'here you have citizens for [i.e. to inspire] eloquence'.   **ampla nepotum spes:** an ironic echo of *Aen.* 2.503 *spes tanta nepotum* referring to the fifty bedrooms of Priam's sons in his palace. The poem concludes by looking forward to fulfilment within the family in strong contrast to the myths of 29–36. But there is no sign that the long-absent Tullus (nor indeed P. himself) is seriously expected to fulfil these hopes of grandchildren or even a wife: as in Vergil, the *laudes Italiae* are inspiring, but also disturbing.

[37–8 This couplet is impossible to construe since there is no verb in it. The references are to at least one of the labours of Theseus. Sinis destroyed travellers by a hideous punishment involving pine trees, and he met the same fate at the hands of Theseus. The rocks, however, are appropriate to Sciron, another monstrous figure killed by Theseus. After forcing travellers to wash his feet, he would push them into the sea at a place called the Scironian Rocks where a huge tortoise tore their bodies to pieces. This reference would lead to the couplet being structured as a Sinis–Sciron–Sinis schema, which seems highly unlikely. Later readers often embellish lists with their own examples: cf. e.g. 1.15.15–16, 2.28.21–2, 3.7.23–4; Ov. *Her.* 8.67–72, 9.85–100.]

Additional Bibliography: Williams 1968: 417–25; Stahl 1985: 205–12; Cairns 2006: 352–4; Heyworth, *BICS* 50 (2007), 95–7.

3.23

1–6: Our writing tablets have disappeared. They were well used, worn, familiar, and eloquent. 7–10: They had no gold on them, just boxwood and wax. But they were always reliable and effective. 11–18: Perhaps they had a message on them: 'I'm cross you were late. Do you prefer someone else? Are you inventing accusations against me?' or 'Come today: we'll spend the night together', and the witty things a willing girl says. 19–24: A miser is keeping his accounts on them. There is a reward if they are returned. Put this up on a column, boy, saying your master lives on the Esquiline.

The poet plays in verses 1 and 11–16 with the idea of an occasional poem, but 3.23 is not in fact tied to specific circumstances. The lost writing tablets drift between being a physical object (7–8) and the symbol for Propertius' whole poetic output (2, 6). They might offer responses from his readers too (12–18). Their loss means the loss of *tot bona scripta* (2)—even if we do not take this as a reference to the elegies, it does at least suggest P. knows what was on the tablets; whereas he later speculates on what message they might have contained from a girl—perhaps an angry complaint about his failure to turn up the previous day, with conjectures about his reasons for absence (12–14), or else an invitation for the coming night, with appropriate witticisms (13–16): though each case reveals a girl in love, the hypothetical background differs, and he apparently does not know to which girl he has written. In losing the means of such communication, P. seems to face the end of his love life as well as his elegy. But there is realism here as well as symbolism: the imagined messages are informal in phrasing (Tränkle 1960: 168–71 comments on the imperative future in 15, *quoniam, nescioquae*; add *heri, hodie*, used in Ovid's *Fasti* only in direct speech for example), and the poem finishes with arrangements for a notice and a reward.

To the reader who has already seen the closural elements in the preceding poems the symbolism is not hard to read: the tablets have been an intermediary in his passing love affair with Cynthia, the vehicle for his writing, and now even they are lost. This theme is taken further by the move within the poem from his own *scripta* (2), to the writing of hypothetical *puellae* (12–16; cf. 2.23.8, cited at 3.14.25–6 n.), then some *miser* (19), and finally his slave-boy (24).

Writing tablets play an important role in Latin literature, e.g. in plays of Plautus, such as *Bacchides* 714–1052, *Curculio* 420–37, *Persa* 195–250, 459–548, *Pseudolus* 1–102. In poem 50 Catullus describes how he and Calvus had an enjoyable day composing verses on tablets (which is important in showing that poetry is not conceptually incompatible with writing on wax); in 42 he sends his hendecasyllables to claim back his *pugillaria* (small *tabellae*); and elsewhere he addresses other writing materials (35.2 *papyre*; 36.1 *cacata charta*). Later Ovid will imitate this poem with a pair, *Am.* 1.11–12, in the first of which he sends off Nape, Corinna's maid, with a message. He speculates on possible positive responses, and promises to garland the tablets with laurel and dedicate them to Venus if they return with the simple instruction *ueni* ('come'). In 1.12, the tablets have returned with a negative response, and he curses them as *inutile lignum* ('useless wood') and deserving to lie amid a miser's *ephemerides* (1.12.25–6: cf. 20 n.). In *Ars.* 3.469–98 he gives instructions to (primarily female) lovers in the use of wax tablets in carrying on an erotic conversation; but the letters in the *Heroides* do not seem to be conceived of as written on tablets. There is a famous collection of tablets that survive at Vindolanda, near Hadrian's Wall (but many of these are written not on wax with a stylus, but directly onto the wood in ink).

1–2 Ergo: 'And so...' (3.7.1 n.); P. reflects on some recently delivered news.   **doctae:** 'learned', but with the particular implication 'poetic' (cf. 3.20.8, 3.21.1 nn.).   **nobis:** dative of disadvantage. Like *nostris* (3) this could stand for the first person singular, but it allows the sense 'mine and Cynthia's', at least as far as verse 5.   **scripta quibus pariter tot periere bona:** 'along with which so much fine writing has gone': it is as if the *tabellae* still contained all that had been written on them, including the elegies. (Strangely enough, some of the wax tablets from Vindolanda preserve traces of multiple messages where the stylus has pierced the wax and scratched the wood.) *tot* contributes to this evocation of the poet's work in echoing *totiens* at 2.1.1, *non tot* at 2.13.1 (perhaps the first line of the original third book: see pp. 22–3). *OLD* (*pariter* 4b) takes the relative *quibus* as a dative after the adverb; alternatively one may think of it as an ablative with *pereuntibus* understood: cf. 2.8.37 *sera captiua est reddita poena* <*reddita*> [the captive was given up, a late recompense <being given>]; *Aetna* 590 *exstinctosque suo Phrygas Hectore* <*exstincto*> [the Phrygians destroyed, their Hector <having been destroyed>].

3–4 has quondam nostris manibus detriuerat usus: 'frequent usage in our hands had worn these away long ago'; but *usus* has legal connotations too (*OLD* 5: rights won through continuous usage), and these are perhaps brought out by *signatas* and *fidem* in the pentameter.   **non signatas:** To confirm that a letter was authentic and had not been tampered with, the boards were fastened together, melted wax applied and an impression made with a 'signet' ring, to identify the author. It is ironic that in a poem which has something of the nature of a *sphragis* (i.e. 'seal': 24 n.) the only reference to the sealing of the tablets is negative.   **habere fidem:** 'to carry credence'. The tablets are worn and so recognizable by those to whom they are familiar, so no signature is needed; but in *non signatas* there is a hint that they were trusted, perhaps even when they did not deserve to be.

5–6 plācāre: 'placate' (as at 1.14.23 *dum plācata aderit*, 'while she comes in a good mood', he will despise power and wealth), but perhaps also recalls 1.7.11 *me... doctae solitum plăcuisse puellae* [me who regularly pleased a learned girl].   **puellas:** from this point on, the tablets' correspondence is shown to be with a plurality of girls. Generalization of the poet's erotic prowess has begun already at 2.34.57, and is a marked feature of the second poem of this book (3.2.10, 17). **sine me**: the repeated phrase brings out the peculiar power of written text to work in the writer's absence. **norant placare** = *nouerant* 'they had come to know', i.e. 'they knew how to please'. **atque eaedem**: 'and they also'. This is Heinsius' conjecture for *et quaedam*, which is both vague in sense and apparently unPropertian. For *eaedem* as a disyllable, see 3.6.36 n. **loqui**: in Euripides' *Hippolytus* Phaedra's tablet, with its false evidence against Hippolytus, is repeatedly personified* in this way; e.g. it wishes to speak (865), it shouts (877), it accuses (1058).

7–8 caras: that they were 'dear' to the poet is shown by his offer of a reward (21–2), but it is nothing to do with their value as an object. Others presumably did have ostentatious tablets with gold fittings. **uulgari buxo sordida cera fuit**: 'the common box-wood had poor-quality wax'. *buxo* is possessive dative. Cf. Ov. *Am.* 1.11.28 *uile fuistis acer* [you were cheap maple].

9–10 qualescumque: in a poem that discusses the quality of the writing material, the evocation of Cat. 1.9 *qualecumque* is especially strong. That poem, which ends by hoping that his book may last more than one generation 'whatever the quality', has begun by describing the *lepidum nouum libellum,* | *arido modo pumice expolitum* [charming new little book, freshly polished off with dry pumice]. Catullus starts one collection by dedicating his exquisite new *libellus* to Cornelius Nepos; P. ends (or very nearly) by losing his cheap and old *tabellae*. **fideles**: P. had also applied *qualiscumque* to Cynthia (3.21.16 n.). Unlike her, the tablets remained faithful; now even they have gone wandering off. **semper et effectus promeruere bonos**: 'they always earned good results' is not what he says when he complains about Cynthia (cf. e.g. 2.25.2 *excludi...sors mea saepe fuit*; 2.29B.42 *ex illo felix nox mihi nulla fuit*; 3.21.7 *cum saepe negarit*). Note the echo of 1.10.28 *effectu saepe fruare bono* ('you would often enjoy a good result', addressed to Gallus).

11 forsitan...fuerunt mandata: 'were perhaps entrusted' (for the pleonasm* see 3.10.29 n.). P. has *forsitan* with the indicative twice

(2.9.22, 2.15.54), once with the subjunctive (3.20.6); but Housman saw that as the perfect indicative follows in verse 15 (*dixit*), it should stand in 11 too. For the scansion, see p. 38.

12 irascor quoniam es, lente, moratus: the reader has seen Cynthia's anger over lateness implied at 2.29.8–20, 2.31.1, and expressed at 1.3.35–46; similarly P. in 1.15, calling her *lenta* in verse 4. *es* prodelides, so the placing of *quoniam (e)s* is no more unusual than that of *numquam (e)st* before the caesura at 3.13.58.

13–14 Compare P.'s own words at 1.18.9–10

> quid tantum merui? quae te mihi crimina mutant?
> an noua tristitiae causa puella tuae?

Why have I come to deserve so great a punishment? What charges are changing your attitude towards me? Is a new girl the cause of your bad temper?

Accusations against Cynthia are made or mentioned in 1.15, 2.4.1–2, 2.5, 2.6, 2.32.1–30. At 2.20.13 on the other hand, he says he will refuse to hear anything said about her behaviour. She responds with her own countercharges at 1.3.35–44, 2.29.31–8, 3.6.21–34, 3.19.1. He admits an interest in other women in 2.22A and B.   **non bene:** 'unpleasantly' (cf. Cat. 11.16, cited in 3.24 intro.). The independent manuscripts have *bona*, but the epithet is both stylistically and semantically* superfluous with *crimina ficta*.

15–16 uenies hodie: in invitations the future is used with imperative effect: cf. Hor. *Epist.* 1.7.71 *post nonam uenies* [come after the ninth hour], Plautus, *Curc.* 728 *tu, miles, apud me cenabis*. For the substance, cf. the invitation Catullus requests from Ipsimilla at 32.3: *iube ad te ueniam meridiatum* [bid me come to you to spend the afternoon (i.e. in bed)].   **cessabimus una:** 'we will relax together'. **tota nocte:** ablative (as opposed to the commoner accusative) of time throughout which; cf. 2.14.28 *tota nocte receptus amans*; Apuleius, *Met.* 2.10.6 *tota...nocte tecum...proeliabor* (the lascivious maidservant Photis to Lucius: 2.11, 15 describe the preparations).

17–18 et quaecumque uolens reperit non stulta puella | garrula cum blandis ducitur hora iocis: 'and all the clever things a willing girl thinks up when a gossipy hour is spent on pleasant conceits' or 'all the things a willing, intelligent girl . . .' As *uolens* must function as an adjective with *puella*, and poets prefer to distribute adjectives around their nouns, *non stulta* perhaps belongs with *quaecumque*, even though elsewhere in P. adjective and noun in *-a* at line end are always in agreement: the decision is not crucial to the effect of the words. In the pentameter it is clear that *garrula* belongs with *hora*: *puella* certainly does not need another epithet. *garrula* is used of wordy writing in Ovid's response, at *Am.* 1.12.23. *cum* is postponed* after a dactylic* adjective in *-a* at 3.7.40, e.g. For *duco* + ablative of spending time on an activity, see 1.14.10 *facili totum ducit amore diem*; 4.6.85: the reference is to the contents of the letter, not some promised meeting. The conjecture *iocis* ('witticisms') fits more easily than the transmitted *dolis* ('tricks'), both in combination with *blandis* and in a sequence that imagines a charming and positive response, and has no word at all of deception. The final word of the couplet is especially liable to alteration.

19–20 me miserum: accusative of exclamation. In this closural sequence we should hear the inversion of the phrase in 1.1.1 *Cynthia prima suis miserum me cepit ocellis*: cf. Hinds 1998: 29–34.   **auarus:** an alien figure, like the *senes seueriores* in Cat. 5 (cf. the *senes duri* at 2.30.13). Ovid's curse on his tablets imitates the picture (*Am.* 1.12.25–6): *inter ephemeridas melius tabulasque iacerent* | *in quibus absumptas fleret auarus opes* [they would better lie among the day-books and tablets in which a miser bewails (i.e. writes sorrowfully) the wealth he's lost]. **duras . . . ephemeridas:** 'heartless account-books'. *ephemerides* (Greek ἐφημερίς) are literally the place where the day's income and expenditure are registered. The better part of the manuscript tradition has *diras*, which, if right, would have a humorously exaggerated tone: 'awful', 'frightening'. But *duras* makes an appropriate contrast with the elegiac content of the *tabellae* while they remained in P.'s hands, a point Ovid picks up in his phrase *mollia uerba* at *Am.* 1.12.22.

21–2 Save for the imprecision over amount, a realistic announcement: cf. the Pompeian inscription (*CIL* IV.64) *urna aenia perit* [cf. 2] *de taberna. si quis rettulerit, dabuntur HS LXV* [A bronze urn has disappeared from the tavern. If anyone returns it, 65 sesterces will be given (i.e. as a reward)].   **donabitur auro:** 'he will be rewarded with gold'.   **ligna . . . uelit:** other than neuter pronouns, the direct object after *uelle* is not common (*OLD* 2), but

cf. 2.23.22 *nolim furta pudica tori* [I would not want an affair in a
marital bed], 4.4.88.

23–4 i, puer, et citus haec aliqua propone columna | et … scribe:
the climax of the closural elements in the poem is this reworking of
Hor. *Sat.* 1.10.92 (the final line of the book): *i, puer, atque meo
citus haec subscribe libello* [go, boy, and quickly write these lines at
the end of my book]. Horace's *haec* refers to the poem itself; the
echo invites us to take P.'s *haec* similarly (though in context it more
obviously means the notice about the reward). Like P. Horace has
described his poems as *qualiacumque* (9 n.), but he cares only for
a few distinguished readers, such as Maecenas and Vergil (72–90).
P. replaces *libello* with *columna*: his poem is to be issued informally
and to the public who chance upon it. Cynthia's ghost at 4.7.83–6
asks that an inscription marking her grave be put on a column, out
on the road near Tibur.   **dominum:** only here applied to P.
himself: so far has he changed from the lover who is characterized
as a captive and slave from the very beginning (Cynthia is *domina*
already at 1.1.21; P. *seruus* in his epitaph at 2.13.36 e.g.).
Esquiliis: his home also at 4.8.1. As in the *sphragis** poem 1.22,
we are given not a name but geographical pointers. If he was much
involved with Maecenas (something we doubt), it may have been
convenient to live near to his grand house, also on the Equiline
(Keith 2008: 9); the Subura, a centre of Roman night-life, where
Cynthia remembers meeting (4.7.15), is on the other side of the
hill.

Additional bibliography: R. J. Baker, *CPh* 68 (1973), 109–13; E. A.
Meyer, 'Wooden wit: *tabellae* in Latin poetry', in E. Tylawsky and
C. Weiss (eds.), *Essays in Honor of Gordon Williams* (New Haven, CT;
2001), 201–12; C. B. R. Pelling, *SIFC* 20 (2002), 171–81.

3.24

*1–8: You put too much trust in your appearance, Cynthia, thanks to the
tributes paid by my love elegies. I'm ashamed that I made you famous,*

praising the version of you invented by Love. Your complexion was owed to cosmetics. 11–14, 9–10: When saying these things I was under compulsion, shipwrecked, tortured, captive and bound. Neither friends nor witchcraft could save me. 15–20: Port is safely reached after a dangerous voyage; now at last I am recovering, my wounds healing. I dedicate myself to the goddess Good Sense, as Jupiter has been deaf to me. 21–4: I was a laughing stock when I served you for five years. You will miss my fidelity. 25–30: I am unaffected by your tears, as I have found they are a trick. I shall weep as I leave, but the hurt is stronger than tears: you stop us being a couple. Farewell to the doorway. 31–2, 35–8: May old age come upon you; may you be excluded in turn, and mourn what you did. My page has uttered these threats: be afraid of the outcome.

Cynthia has been named in the book only at 3.21.9, and not addressed at all since that poem. The closing sequence would have made grim reading for any Cynthia: besides that assertion of the intention now at last to depart for Athens, explicitly as a way of putting distance between them, she has seen an attempt to seduce another woman in 3.20, an announcement that marriage and a family are the duty of a Roman (3.22.41–2), and the revelation in the poem about the lost writing tablets that the poet has been carrying on correspondence with a number of *puellae*. To her, as to the public reader, it can be little surprise that the end of the relationship is now formally announced. Catullus 11 is a model for this, the poem in which Furius and Aurelius are asked not to accompany the poet to the ends of the earth (cf. 3.21 and 22), but to pass on a simple message (15–17): *pauca nuntiate meae puellae | non bona dicta: | cum suis uiuat ualeatque moechis* [Take a few unpleasant words to my girl: let her live with her adulterers and fare well].

P. marks the end of the book with continuing reminiscence of phrasing, imagery, and themes from earlier in the corpus*: e.g. love as torture (11, 13), as slavery (11, 14, 23), as sailing (12, 15–16); cosmetics (7–8), medical treatment (11, 17–18), gossip (21–2), tears (25–9), the *exclusus amator* (29–30, 35–6). He discusses the causes and effects of his poetry (1–14, 29). Having stressed the past, he makes threats for the future (31–8).

Unfortunately the poem is divided into 3.24 and 3.25 in the traditional numeration as well as in some of the manuscripts.

However, the verses are continuous in subject matter and in manner; and nothing is gained by treating them as a pair, whereas 38 (25.18) echoes 24.1, and the allusions* to 1.1, which are most prominent in '24' (11, 9–10 nn.), make most artistic sense if they come in the final poem of the Cynthia cycle.

1–2 Falsa: attention is immediately drawn to Cynthia's deception; ironically it is self-deception, brought on by the poet himself. **mulier:** for Propertius the word has none of the erotic connotations of *puella*, never mind *uita* (used as a vocative from 1.2.1 on) or *domina*, and this is the first time he has used it of Cynthia in his own mouth (a Cupid speaks at 2.29.9).   **olim:** the first of a number of markers of the passing of time: cf. *nunc demum* (17), *quinque annos* (23), *iam* (29), *facta anus* (36).   **elegis nimium facta superba meis:** 'made over-haughty by my elegies'. *elegis* (Schrader) leads into the sequence that follows (*laudes, uersibus, laudaui*), and introduces the notion that Cynthia is the poet's creation: she is *superba* because that is how he has described her. Not only her beauty but even her existence depends upon his writing: his curse will make her old (31–8). *oculis* is transmitted, and would make a link with Cynthia's eyes at 1.1.1; however, pride instilled by others comes not from their eyes, but their praise (2.1.8 *laudatis ire superba comis*) or subservience (1.18.25, 3.17.41).

3–4 tales . . . laudes seems to refer both back and forward: the praise was such that it made her haughty (2) and famous (4). We may think of the repeated comparison to the heroines of myth (1.3.1–6, 1.4.5–6, 1.19.13–16) and even goddesses (2.2.5–8), and passages such as 1.2.27–30, 1.4.11–14, and 2.3.9–44, e.g.:

> nec me tam facies, quamuis sit candida, cepit
> (lilia non domina sunt magis alba mea),   10
> nec de more comae per leuia colla fluentes,   13
> non oculi, geminae, sidera nostra, faces, . . .
> quantum quod posito formose saltat Iaccho . . .   17
> et quantum Aeolio cum temptat carmina plectro . . .   19

And it is not so much her beauty that has captured me, though she is fair (lilies are not whiter than my mistress), nor her hair flowing over her smooth neck in customary fashion, not her eyes, twin torches, our lodestars, . . . as much as the fact that she dances beautifully when Iacchus [i.e. wine] is served, . . . and as much as when she tries songs with the Aeolian [i.e. Sappho's] plectrum. . . .

uersibus insignem te pudet esse meis: this overturns the pride of claims such as 2.34.93 *Cynthia … uiuet uersu laudata Properti*, and 3.2.17 *fortunata meo si qua es celebrata libello*, and gives a new twist to the horrors of notoriety discussed at 2.5.1–3, and 2.24.4–7:

> aut pudor ingenuo est aut reticendus amor.
> quod si iam facilis spiraret Cynthia nobis,   5
>   non ego nequitiae dicerer esse caput,
> nec sic per totam infamis traducerer urbem.

A well-born man either has embarrassment or must keep quiet about his love. But if Cynthia were now blowing obligingly for us, I would not be called the fountainhead of iniquity, nor would I be paraded as infamous throughout the city like this.

Cf. also 21–2 n.

5–6 mixtam te uaria laudaui saepe figura: 'the you I often praised was concocted from various figures'. As we read the line, we lose any sense we have of Cynthia as a fixed identity: her appearance is put together from a variety of women. But we have heard far less about the details of her beauty than about her behaviour: typically vague is the list at 2.12.23–4 *qui caput et digitos et lumina nigra puellae | et canat ut soleant molliter ire pedes?* [who would sing the girl's head and fingers and dark eyes and how seductively her feet move]. So we may be inclined to read the collective singular* *figura* loosely as 'characteristics'.   **cum quod non esses esse putaret amor:** 'since love thought you were what you were not'. Love is the reason for P.'s inaccurate praise of Cynthia. *cum* (Dousa) has been replaced by *ut* at the start of the line (cf. p. 45). Neuter pronouns such as *quod* are used as easily in Latin as in English in such expressions: cf. 2.9.1, 2.25.36 *essem ego quod nunc tu* [I would be what you are now]; neuter plural is found when Theocritus puts a similar sentiment in the mouth of the lovesick Cyclops ἔρωτι … τὰ μὴ καλὰ καλὰ πέφανται (6.18–19: 'to love have things not fair appeared fair').

7–8 color est totiens … collatus: the opening verse of Book 2 (*Quaeritis unde mihi totiens scribantur amores*: 'you ask why I so often write of love') uses *totiens* to stress the repetitiveness of love elegy, and the adverb appears elsewhere of recurring features of the affair. Cynthia's complexion is praised (at least implicitly) in 1.2, 1.4.13, 2.3.9–10 (see 3 n.), 2.16.24 (*candida*), 2.18.23–30, 2.29.30 (*candida*); she is frequently compared to others (3 n., and e.g. 1.4.9, 2.28.9), and her behaviour contrasted with that of Aurora (Dawn) at 2.18.5–20. But this particular comparison is not found: as the addition of the pentameter shows, the poet invents specific examples to make his point: he praised her blush <and the whiteness of her skin>, though <the blush and> whiteness in her face were bought. *quaesitus* literally means 'sought': her beauty was not natural but acquired from some external source.　　　**roseo...Eoo:** as the Morning Star is not red, 'the rosy Dawn-star' must stand here for the blush of the dawn sky (*Il.* 1.477, *Od.* 2.1; *Aen.* 7.26).

11–12 haec...uerba loquebar: *haec uerba* refers to verses 5–8; as 9–10 interrupt the sequence, they have been transposed (see below). *loquebar* is a conjecture for the transmitted *fatebor*: an imperfect is needed to set the poetry in the past, and *fateri* is inappropriate, given that, elsewhere in P. at least, it always has some sense of confessing what is true, while 1–8 have stressed that his words have been false. **nunc ferro, nunc igne coactus:** 'now compelled by iron, now by fire'. He is forced to speak, like a slave giving evidence, under torture with heated irons. For *nunc..., nunc* = 'both...and' without temporal significance, cf. Ov. *Fast.* 4.138, 5.521, Lucan 3.684, Stat. *Silu.* 2.3.11. The phrase echoes 1.1.27–8 *ferrum saeuos patiemur et ignes* (cited 3.6 intro.). The main force there is 'endure treatment for madness': for the medical imagery see Ov. *Rem.* 229 *ut corpus redimas, ferrum patieris et ignes* [to recover physical health, you will endure surgery and cautery], Sen. *Ag.* 152; F. Cairns, *CQ* 24 (1974), 106; but torture is brought to mind too, and so are two frequent metaphors for suffering in love. In our passage too we might understand the falsehoods of 5–8 as uttered when P. was suffering the effects of Cynthia's 'ironheartedness' or his own 'burning passion'. *non ferro, non igne coactus* in the manuscripts is at odds with the stress on coercion in 12–14; there is a corruption of a pair in anaphora* also at 3.9.45.　　　**ipsa naufragus Aegaea...aqua:** the poet was not only tortured when he said such things, but also shipwrecked: for the image of love as a voyage, see 3.17.3 n., and 2.14.29–30:

> nunc a te est, mea lux, ueniatne ad litora nauis
> seruata an mediis sidat onusta uadis.

Now, light of my life, it depends on you whether the ship comes safe to the
shore or runs aground heavy-laden in the midst of the shallows.

The Aegean was regarded as a rough sea (it is where Paetus drowns,
3.7.57; cf. Hor. *Odes* 2.16.2, 3.29.63); it recalls 1.6.2 (where P. refuses
to sail: N) and perhaps evokes Venus (Stat. *Theb.* 8.477).

13–14 saeuo Veneris torrebar aëno: 'I was being roasted in Venus's
savage cauldron'. The image of legalized torture (or medical treatment) in 11 is replaced by cooking (cf. Theoc. 7.55, *Anth. Pal.*
12.92.7, Hor. *Odes* 1.13.1–8 [and see West], 1.33.6) or even roasting
in the bronze 'bull', invented for Phalaris, tyrant of Acragas in Sicily,
by Perillus, the first victim: 2.25.11–12 *nonne fuit satius duro seruire
tyranno | et gemere in tauro, saeue Perille, tuo?* [was it not better to
serve a harsh tyrant and to groan in your bull, savage Perillus?]. For
Venus's involvement in the punishment of lovers, cf. Tib. 1.8.5–6 *ipsa
Venus magico religatum bracchia nodo | perdocuit multis non sine uer-
beribus* [Venus herself bound my arms in a magic knot and educated
me with many a blow]. **uinctus eram uersas in mea terga
manus**: 'I had been bound with my hands twisted to behind my back':
like a slave awaiting a degrading punishment. *manus* is accusative of the
part of the body affected (G&L §338; Woodcock 1985 §19): it was the
hands that were bound, so they can remain in the accusative even when
the verb is in the passive.

9–10 quod will work best where it can pick up a general description
of love, and it is hard to see that a singular concept can be derived
from 5–8. Tremenheere's placing of the couplet after 14 addresses the
problems, and the homoeoteleuton* *terga man(us)/saga mari* explains the original omission.   **quod mihi non patrii poterant
auertere amici**: 'Family friends could not turn this away from me'.
The friends are those asked for help at 1.1.25–6 *amici, | quaerite non
sani pectoris auxilia* [friends, look for something to aid my love-sick
heart], just as the **Thessala saga** recalls the witches approached for
assistance in 1.1.19–24, though the request there is to make Cynthia
fall in love (*dominae mentem conuertite nostrae*, 21); cf. also 2.4.7–16
for apotropaic* magic and medicine. Thessaly is a traditional home

of witches: Aristophanes, *Clouds* 749, Plato, *Gorg.* 513a; Plin. *Nat.* 30.6–7, Apuleius, *Met.* 2.1; and especially Hor. *Odes* 1.27.21–2 *quae* **saga,** *quae te soluere* **Thessalis** | *magus uenenis, quis poterit deus?* [what witch, what magician will be able to free you (from love) with Thessalian potions, what god will]. **eluere aut uasto . . . mari:** 'or wash <it> away in the vast ocean': cf. Cic. *Leg.* 2.24.19 *animi labes nec diuturnitate euanescere, nec amnibus ullis elui potest* [a moral stain can neither disappear over time nor be washed away by any rivers]; *Aen.* 6.742; *Macbeth* II.iii.58–9 'Will all great Neptune's ocean wash this blood | Clean from my hand?' (though Macbeth has physical blood as well as guilt).

15–16 P. reveals that he is not shipwrecked in the sea of love any longer, but has reached port, having sailed across dangerous sand-banks: we may contrast 2.14.29–30, 2.26A and B. **ecce** gives a dramatic immediacy to the event. **coronatae portum tetigere carinae** echoes Vergil's analogy for the pleasures of winter after the labours of summer, *Geo.* 1.303–4: *ceu pressae cum iam* **portum tetigere carinae,** | *puppibus et laeti nautae imposuere coronas* [as when laden vessels have reached port and the joyful sailors have put garlands on the stern (i.e. to celebrate their arrival)]; cf. also Ov. *Am.* 3.11.29, *Rem.* 811. *carinae* (poetic plural) strictly means 'keels', but (as often) stands by synecdoche* for the boat as a whole (even though it is not the part that would be garlanded). **Syrtes:** 3.19.7 n.

17–18 uasto fessi resipiscimus aestu: the voyage image is combined with the notion of recovery from madness that has been touched on in 11, and in 9 through the allusion* to 1.1.25–6: *aestus* effects the move elegantly, as it means 'passion', 'feverishness', as well as 'stormy sea'. For tiredness induced by sailing, cf. 3.21.19, *Aen.* 3.78; Ov. *Ars* 3.748 (also metaphorical). **uulneraque ad sanum nunc coiere mea:** 'and my wounds have now come together to heal': cf. 2.12.12 *nec quisquam ex illo uulnere sanus abit* [nor does anyone come away unscathed from that wound (i.e. of Cupid's arrow)], 3.21.32.

19–20 Mens Bona: temples were established to Mens after the disastrous battle of Trasimene (Livy 22.9–10); she is one of the figures paraded as a captive with Ovid in Cupid's triumph (*Am.* 1.2.31–2). **si qua dea es:** 3.15.21 n. **tua me**

in sacraria dono: P. dedicates himself to serve in the shrine (*sacraria* is poetic plural), as if he were himself an offering from a sailor who has survived shipwreck (cf. 2.28.43–6, addressed to Jupiter; Hor. *Odes* 1.5.13–16). **exciděrunt:** 'have been uttered', or 'have perished' (*Ioui* then being dative of disadvantage). For the scansion, see p. 38. **surdo…Ioui:** at *Satires* 1.1.15–22 Horace imagines Jupiter refusing to listen to prayers, on the grounds that people keep asking for changes of role that they do not fundamentally desire. As a famously adulterous husband, Jupiter has in any case little interest in securing stable relationships (2.16.47–8), but apparently successful prayers have been made to him in 2.28.

21–2 [= 25.1–2] **risus eram:** 'I was a laughing-stock': cf. 2.21.7 *tu sermo es* [you are an object of gossip], 2.24.1 *cum sis…fabula* [though you are a byword]; 2.24.16 *fallaci dominae iam pudet esse iocum* [it shames me now to be a joke for a cheating mistress]. **positis inter conuiuia mensis:** 'when tables were set out in the middle of symposia', i.e. at parties.

23–4 [= 25.3–4] **quinque…annos** contributes to the historical realism of the affair: cf. *toto anno*, 1.1.7; 3.15.7 n. **ungue… morso:** collective singular*: lit. 'a nail having been bitten'. **meam…saepe querere fidem:** later Cynthia will be cast in the role of the elegiac lover as *exclusa* (35); here her future is aligned with behaviour described at 2.4.1 *multa prius dominae delicta* **queraris** *oportet*, and 3 *saepe immeritos corrumpas dentibus* **ungues** [it is inevitable that you should first complain about many sins of your mistress,… often spoil your innocent nails by biting them]. Ironically her complaint will be not about current *delicta*, but P.'s past fidelity, now lost to her: cf. her imagined lamentation over his bones at 2.24.36; *eheu tu mihi certus eras*. For *queri* implying elegiac complaint, see 3.6.18 n.

25–6 [= 25.5–6] **nil:** adverbial, 'not at all'. **lacrimis:** Cynthia's tears have made a rhetorically effective appearance at 1.3.46, 1.15.40. **ista sum captus ab arte:** P. has described himself as made captive already in 1.1.1—by Cynthia, but the use of *ab* makes *ars* an agent and lessens the distinction between the woman and her arts; cf. also 2.3.9, 3.10.15 n. *captus* here could also mean 'deceived' (*OLD capio* 20). Weeping is just one seductive art of which Cynthia is a mistress: see 3–4 n., and 2.1.9–10 *miramur, facilis ut premat arte manus* [we are amazed how she artfully applies her skilful hands]. *ars* has been a prime concern since 1.1.17, 1.2, where it already evokes love elegy (which in turn is identified with tears: 1.6.24).   **ad insidias**: 'for [i.e. to set] snares': 3.9.27 n.

27–8 [= 25.7–8] **flebo** is in contrast with *flere* (26): P.'s tears are for real.   **fletum iniuria uincit**: an inversion of 2.24.39 *numquam me iniuria mutat* [your wrong-doing never changes me]: here the wrongdoing overwhelms the sense of regret expressed by the weeping.   **tu bene conueniens non sinis ire iugum**: at 1.5.2 (in fact the last verse of poem 1.4) Bassus has been told to allow P. and Cynthia to continue to advance as a matched pair: *sine nos cursu quo sumus ire pares*; but at 2.5.14 the yoke is used as a symbol of unjust bondage round his neck and he must remove it (*iniusto subtrahe colla iugo*). If Cynthia will not allow the 'well-suited' pair to advance together, P. must lay aside the pairing also of the elegiac couplet as a symbol of love (Ov. *Am.* 1.1).

29–30 [= 25.9–10] **limina … ualeant**: he bids farewell not directly to Cynthia, but to her threshold and door, two of the most powerful symbols of their affair (1.8.22, 1.9.28, 2.7.9, 2.9.42, 2.20.23, 3.3.47).   **nostris … lacrimantia uerbis**: P.'s words are so powerful they make the threshold weep, just as the passing hours feel pain at the lover's plight (1.16.23–4—in a poem spoken by a door). **nec tamen irata ianua fracta manu**: 'and door not shattered by my hand, angry though it was': cf. 2.5.22 *nec mea praeclusas fregerit ira fores* [nor shall my anger have broken your closed doors]. *nec* = *et … non*; and *tamen* marks *irata* as concessive (3.15.35 n.).

31–6 [= 25.11–16] The imminence of old age, which will take away the desirability of the beloved, is a frequent motif of love poetry, especially the paraclausithyron* (which is brought into play by *exclusa* in 35): cf. Hor. *Odes* 1.25.9–20 (n.b. *inuicem*, 9), *Anth. Pal.* 5.23, 92, and 21 (= Rufinus 7 Page): 'Did I not say, Prodice, "We are growing old"? Did I not predict "The hairs that undo love will come soon"? Now wrinkles and grey hair and loose skin and a mouth that does not have its former charm. Does anyone approach you, haughty one, or beg you with flattery? Now we pass you by like a tomb.'

31 [= 25.11] **celatis...annis:** Tibullus 1.8.43–4 (33–4 n.) talks of 'hiding the years' with hair-dye. Though some hear the silent pacing of the years behind P.'s *celatis* (3.2.24 n.), we prefer the sense 'that you have hidden (with cosmetics)'.

35–6 [= 25.15–16] **fastus...superbos:** 'haughty rejection' will now be experienced by the woman who was not only *superba* in 2, but also cast down the *fastus* of P.'s eyes at 1.1.3.   **quae fecisti...queraris:** she shall complain about her own past behaviour: 24 n.   **facta...anus** echoes 2.9.8, where Penelope awaited the returning Ulysses, 'having become an old woman'; but *facta* also takes us back to 2, where it is P.'s writing that has made Cynthia *superba*: he threatens to write her in a different way—there was a tradition of abusive poetry about old women, illustrated in Latin by Hor. *Epod.* 8 and 12. More generally, compare 2.18.20 *ipsa anus haud longa curua futura die* [you are yourself to be a bent old woman at no distant day]; Ov. *Ars* 3.69–70 *tempus erit quo tu quae nunc excludis amantes | frigida deserta nocte iacebis anus* [the time will come at which you who now shut lovers out shall lie a cold old woman in the lonely night].

37–8 [= 25.17–18] **has...fatales...diras:** *dirae* are perpetrators of vengeance, curses as well as Furies: there is a curse poem in the *Appendix Vergiliana* called *Dirae*; cf. also Hor. *Epod.* 5.89 *diris agam uos*, Tib. 2.6.53 *tunc tibi, lena, precor diras* [then I call curses on you, bawd]. *fatales* can mean 'fated', and implies certainty in the outcome, but also 'deadly', which implies Cynthia's death.   **cecinit mea pagina** combines the two modes of publication, oral and written. As a perfect *cecinit* marks the completion of the curses, and of the book too: cf. Verg. *Ecl.* 10.70 (in the epilogue) *haec sat erit, diuae, uestrum cecinisse poetam* [it will be enough, Muses, that your poet has sung this].   **euentum formae disce timere tuae:** *disce timere* is repeated from 3.11.8, but in other respects this looks ahead. Book 4, with its aetiologies*, will prove to be more didactic, and *disce* is the first word of poem 8; Horos in 4.1B offers vague but threatening prophecies of the poet's future, and his final word is *timē* (fear). For *euentum* ('outcome') we may compare Canidia's words that close

Horace's *Epodes*: *plorem artis in te nil agentis exitus?* (17.81: 'am I to bemoan the end of an art that is achieving nothing against you'). She means witchcraft, but this is the end of Horace's iambics; P.'s *formae* likewise could mean 'genre' as well as 'beauty', and Book 4, at least to start with, moves away from the love elegy associated with Cynthia. And when eventually she does return it is as a ghost, and her beauty has been worn away by death (4.7.7–12).

[33–4 (= 25.13–14) That this couplet is interpolated is shown by (i) the unmotivated re-appearance of *ruga* in 34 as well 32; (ii) the utterly untypical use of exclamatory *a*; (iii) the fact that 33 is a slightly corrupted version of Tib. 1.8.45 (where the *tum*, pointless in P., is the third instance in a sequence):

> heu sero reuocatur amor seroque iuuentas,
>   cum uetus infecit cana senecta caput.
> tum studium formae est: coma tum mutatur, ut annos
>   dissimulet uiridi cortice tincta nucis;
> tollere tum cura est albos a stirpe capillos   45
>   et faciem dempta pelle referre nouam.

Alas too late is love recalled, too late youth, once white-haired old age has stained the ancient head. Then there is attention to appearance; then hair is transformed, dyed in order to hide the years with the green rind of a nut; then there is anxiety to remove white hairs by the root and to acquire a new face by removing skin.

The similarity of context explains why this verse was added in the margin or used as a model by someone wanting to rectify the absence of white hair in a passage on old age.]

Additional bibliography: G. W. Williams, *CR* 8 (1958), 8–9, A. W. Bennett, *CPh* 64 (1969), 30–5; G. L. Koniaris, *CPh* 66 (1971), 253–8.

AFTER BOOK 3

The closing sequence of Book 3, capped by 3.24, has announced separation from Cynthia, and implied a move to a different kind of poetry. The next book begins (4.1A.1–2):

Hoc quodcumque uides, hospes, qua maxima Roma est,
  ante Phrygem Aenean collis et herba fuit.

Everything you can see here, my friend, where the great city of Rome is,
before Phrygian Aeneas was hill and grass.

The address to a visitor makes a link with epigrammatic address of
the passer-by; but *maxima Roma*[8] and the mention of Aeneas give an
epic scope to the beginning. The metrical form continues to be
elegiac couplets; but the rest of poem says nothing about love, and
promises something more like a Latin *Aetia*: *sacra deosque canam* (69:
'I shall sing of rites and gods'). Though the astrologer in 4.1B adjusts
the programme, by reminding the poet of the advice to write erotic
elegy given to the young Propertius by Apollo (4.1B.135–46), the
book continues without Cynthia. Instead we find aetiological* poems
and character studies alternating as follows:

  4.1B: Horos, an astrologer, tries to sell a horoscope to P.
  4.2: a long epigrammatic poem on the changeable Etruscan god
    Vertumnus
  4.3: a letter from a *matrona* Arethusa, to her husband, who has
    deserted her for military service
  4.4: the story of the unchaste and treacherous Vestal Virgin Tarpeia
  4.5: a curse on the old drunken *lena* Acanthis, who is training the
    poet's *puella*
  4.6: a Callimachean* hymn to Palatine Phoebus on the battle of
    Actium.

Poem 4.5 is the closest to a Cynthia poem: we might wonder whether to
identify the *puella* with the former mistress, but nothing has suggested a
return, and the advice being offered would hardly have been needed by
Cynthia. Moreover, the poem fulfils something of the programme in
3.24.31–8, for Acanthis (whose name shares most of its letters with
Cynthia) is remembered as a dying old woman, and her tomb and ghost
are cursed (1–4, 67–78). Finally, in 4.7, the possibility hinted at in 4.1B
comes true, and in another character study Cynthia does return, but as
a ghost, visiting P. as he lies in bed at night after her funeral (like
Patroclus appearing to Achilles): he thus reprises his central character

---

[8] The opening does accurately indicate a return to Rome after the exploration of
the broader empire in Book 3.

without upsetting the narrative of confirmed separation established by
3.24 and the run of poems at the start of 4; and he overturns his
repeated fantasy of her presence at his own funeral. She is as vivid
dead as she has been alive, condemning him for his neglect, claiming to
have been murdered, criticizing his new woman, describing her place of
honour in the underworld, giving instructions for her tomb and the
disposal of the poems written in her name, and looking forward to the
time when she will once more possess him among the dead (*mixtis
ossibus ossa teram*, 94). As he tries to embrace her, her shade disappears
(as so often when alive).

The next elegy (4.8) upsets both the narrative and the alternation,
however. What starts as a poem on ritual at Lanuvium does not develop
into an aetiology*; Cynthia takes over once more, this time very much
alive and visiting the shrine on an outing with her latest lover. P. tries to
console himself by inviting round a couple of prostitutes, but the party
goes wrong, he can think only of Cynthia, and eventually she returns,
again like a figure from epic, but now an Odysseus clearing his house of
every sign of the suitors. The poem ends with peace restored, and the
lovers in bed together (*toto soluimus arma toro*, 88). The reader might
think this is simply to be placed in the past, at the height of their affair,
but *hac nocte* ('last night') in verse 1 obstructs that otherwise attractive
interpretation. Rather we should see this as further confirmation of
what has been said in 3.24: Cynthia is the poet's construction. He can
kill her off and he can bring her back to life again. He can turn her into
Acanthis, and (after two more aetiological* poems[9]) perhaps even into
Cornelia, the daughter of Augustus's ex-wife Scribonia; her ghost
speaks 4.11, and marks the end of the corpus* with her opening word
Desine ('cease').

---

[9] 4.9 on Hercules' founding of the Ara Maxima and the paraclausithyron* he
utters in an attempt to gain access to the shrine of the Bona Dea; 4.10 (improbably,
and very bloodily) on the *spolia opima*, trophies dedicated to Jupiter Feretrius by
Roman generals who kill the opposing general.

Appendix of Significant Intertexts*

A: Hesiod, *Theogony* 1–8, 22–34:

Μουσάων Ἑλικωνιάδων ἀρχώμεθ᾽ ἀείδειν,
αἵ θ᾽ Ἑλικῶνος ἔχουσιν ὄρος μέγα τε ζάθεόν τε,
καί τε περὶ κρήνην ἰοειδέα πόσσ᾽ ἁπαλοῖσιν
ὀρχεῦνται καὶ βωμὸν ἐρισθενέος Κρονίωνος.
καί τε λοεσσάμεναι τέρενα χρόα Περμησσοῖο   5
ἤ᾽ Ἵππου κρήνης ἤ᾽ Ὀλμειοῦ ζαθέοιο
ἀκροτάτωι Ἑλικῶνι χοροὺς ἐνεποιήσαντο,
καλοὺς ἱμερόεντας, ἐπερρώσαντο δὲ ποσσίν.

αἵ νύ ποθ᾽ Ἡσίοδον καλὴν ἐδίδαξαν ἀοιδήν,
ἄρνας ποιμαίνονθ᾽ Ἑλικῶνος ὕπο ζαθέοιο
τόνδε δέ με πρώτιστα θεαί πρὸς μῦθον ἔειπον,
Μοῦσαι Ὀλυμπιάδες, κοῦραι Διὸς αἰγιόχοιο,   25
"ποιμένες ἄγραυλοι, κάκ᾽ ἐλέγχεα, γαστέρες οἶον,
ἴδμεν ψεύδεα πολλὰ λέγειν ἐτύμοισιν ὁμοῖα,
ἴδμεν δ᾽ εὖτ᾽ ἐθέλωμεν ἀληθέα γηρύσασθαι."
ὣς ἔφασαν κοῦραι μεγάλου Διὸς ἀρτιέπειαι,
καί μοι σκῆπτρον ἔδον δάφνης ἐριθηλέος ὄζον   30
δρέψασαι, θηητόν. ἐνέπνευσαν δέ μοι αὐδὴν
θέσπιν, ἵνα κλείοιμι τά τ᾽ ἐσσόμενα πρό τ᾽ ἐόντα,
καί μ᾽ ἐκέλονθ᾽ ὑμνεῖν μακάρων γένος αἰὲν ἐόντων,
σφᾶς δ᾽ αὐτὰς πρῶτόν τε καὶ ὕστατον αἰὲν ἀείδειν.

Let us begin to sing from the Heliconian Muses, who inhabit the great and holy mountain of Helicon, and dance with delicate feet about the violet-coloured spring and the altar of the mighty son of Cronus. And when they have washed their youthful flesh in Permessus or Hippocrene or holy Olmius, on the top of Helicon they perform dances, beautiful, lovely ones, and move nimbly on their feet. . . .

They once taught Hesiod a beautiful song as he was pasturing his lambs beneath holy Helicon, and this speech first did the goddesses address to me, the Olympian Muses, daughters of aegis-bearing Zeus: 'Rustic shepherds, base reproaches, mere bellies, we know how to tell many lies that appear like the truth, and we know when we wish how to announce things that are true.' So spoke the ready-voiced daughters of mighty Zeus, and they plucked and gave me a staff, a branch of verdant laurel, a wonderful thing. And they breathed into me a divine voice, so that I might proclaim what is to be and what has been, and they told me to hymn the blessed race of the immortals, and ever to sing of themselves first and last.

B: Callimachus, *Aetia* fr. 1.1–36:

Πολλάκι μοι Τελχῖνες ἐπιτρύζουσιν ἀοιδῆι,
  νήιδες οἳ Μούσης οὐκ ἐγένοντο φίλοι,
εἵνεκεν οὐχ ἓν ἄεισμα διηνεκὲς ἢ βασιλ[η..
  ......]ας ἐν πολλαῖς ἤνυσα χιλιάσιν
ἢ ......].ους ἥρωας, ἔπος δ' ἐπὶ τυτθὸν ἑλ[ίσσω   5
  παῖς ἅτε, τῶν δ' ἐτέων ἡ δεκὰς οὐκ ὀλίγη
......].[.]και Τελχῖσιν ἐγὼ τόδε· "φῦλον ἀ[ηνές,
  ......] τήκ[ειν] ἧπαρ ἐπιστάμενον,
......]..ρεην [ὀλ]ιγόστιχος· ἀλλὰ καθέλκει
  .... πολὺ τὴν μακρὴν ὄμπνια Θεσμοφόρο[ς·   10
τοῖν δὲ] δυοῖν Μίμνερμος ὅτι γλυκύς, αἱ κατὰ λεπτόν
  ῥήσιες,] ἡ μεγάλη δ' οὐκ ἐδίδαξε γυνή.
......]ον ἐπὶ Θρήικας ἀπ' Αἰγύπτοιο [πέτοιτο
  αἵματι] Πυγμαίων ἡδομένη γέρα[νος,
Μασσαγέται καὶ μακρὸν ὀιστεύοιεν ἐπ' ἄνδρα   15
  Μῆδον]· ἀη[δονίδες] δ' ὧδε μελιχρότεραι.
ἔλλετε Βασκανίης ὀλοὸν γένος· αὖθι δὲ τέχνηι
  κρίνετε,] μὴ σχοίνωι Περσίδι τὴν σοφίην·
μηδ' ἀπ' ἐμεῦ διφᾶτε μέγα ψοφέουσαν ἀοιδήν
  τίκτεσθαι· βροντᾶν οὐκ ἐμόν, ἀλλὰ Διός."   20
καὶ γὰρ ὅτε πρώτιστον ἐμοῖς ἐπὶ δέλτον ἔθηκα
  γούνασιν, Ἀπόλλων εἶπεν ὅ μοι Λύκιος·
"......]... ἀοιδέ, τὸ μὲν θύος ὅττι πάχιστον
  θρέψαι, τὴ]ν Μοῦσαν δ', ὠγαθέ, λεπταλέην.
πρὸς δέ σε] καὶ τόδ' ἄνωγα, τὰ μὴ πατέουσιν ἅμαξαι   25
  τὰ στείβειν, ἑτέρων ἴχνια μὴ καθ' ὁμά
δίφρον ἐλ]ᾶν μηδ' οἷμον ἀνὰ πλατύν, ἀλλὰ κελεύθους
  ἀτρίπτο]υς, εἰ καὶ στεινοτέρην ἐλάσεις."
τῶι πιθόμη]ν· ἐνὶ τοῖς γὰρ ἀείδομεν οἳ λιγὺν ἦχον
  τέττιγος, θόρυβον δ' οὐκ ἐφίλησαν ὄνων.   30
θηρὶ μὲν οὐατόεντι πανείκελον ὀγκήσαιτο
  ἄλλο]ς, ἐ[γ]ὼ δ' εἴην οὐλαχύς, ὁ πτερόεις,
ἆ πάντως, ἵνα γῆρας ἵνα δρόσον ἦν μὲν ἀείδω
  πρώκιον ἐκ δίης ἠέρος εἶδαρ ἔδων,
αὖθι τὸ δ' ἐκδύοιμι, τό μοι βάρος ὅσσον ἔπεστι   35
  τριγλώχιν ὀλοῶι νῆσος ἐπ' Ἐγκελάδωι.

Often the Telchines grumble at me and my poetry, ignorant men who are no friends of the Muse, on the grounds that I did not produce one continuous poem in many thousands of lines on < ......> kings or < ......> heroes, but roll out a little poem, like a child, though the decades of my years are not few. < ......> and this I to the Telchines: 'Wearisome race, knowing how to make your liver waste away <......>, <......> of few lines; but the bountiful Demeter [a poem by Philitas] far outweighs the long [*or* tall] <......>. Of the two, it is the small-scale utterances that teach that Mimnermus is sweet, not the large woman [his poem the *Nanno*]. Let the crane, which rejoices in the blood of pigmies, fly from Egypt to Thrace, and let the Massagetae shoot a great distance at the Mede; but poems are sweeter like this. Be gone, baneful race of Envy; in future judge poetry by art, not by the Persian chain; and do not expect a loud-sounding poem to be born from me: it is not my duty to thunder, but Zeus's. For when I first placed a tablet on my knees, Lycian Apollo said to me: '<......> poet, feed the victim to be as fat as possible but, my friend, keep the Muse slender. I bid you this too, to tread where wagons do not trample, and not to drive your chariot in the common tracks of others, nor along a broad way, but on unworn paths, even if you drive a narrower course.' This I obey: for we sing among those who like the fine sound of the cicada, and not the hubbub of asses. Let another bray just like the long-eared creature, and let me be the light, the winged one, yes, absolutely, so that I may sing eating the dew, free sustenance from the divine air, so I may immediately slough off old age, which lies as heavy on me as the three-cornered island [Sicily] on baneful Enceladus.

C: Callimachus, *Hymn to Apollo* 105–12

ὁ Φθόνος Ἀπόλλωνος ἐπ' οὔατα λάθριος εἶπεν·   105
"οὐκ ἄγαμαι τὸν ἀοιδὸν ὃς οὐδ' ὅσα πόντος ἀείδει."
τὸν Φθόνον ὡπόλλων ποδί τ' ἤλασεν ὧδέ τ' ἔειπεν·
"Ἀσσυρίου ποταμοῖο μέγας ῥόος, ἀλλὰ τὰ πολλά
λύματα γῆς καὶ πολλὸν ἐφ' ὕδατι συρφετὸν ἕλκει.
Δηοῖ δ' οὐκ ἀπὸ παντὸς ὕδωρ φορέουσι μέλισσαι,   110
ἀλλ' ἥτις καθαρή τε καὶ ἀχράαντος ἀνέρπει
πίδακος ἐξ ἱερῆς ὀλίγη λιβὰς ἄκρον ἄωτον."

Envy said secretly in the ear of Apollo: 'I do not admire the poet who does not sing even as much as the sea <never mind as well>.' Apollo spurned Envy with his foot and said: 'The stream of the Assyrian river [the Euphrates] is great, but it carries down much filth of the earth and much rubbish in its water. But to Demeter the bees do not bring water from every source, but the little stream that springs up pure and undefiled from a holy fountain, the most perfect of waters.'

D: Lucretius 1.117–26:

Ennius ut noster cecinit, qui primus amoeno
detulit ex Helicone perenni fronde coronam
per gentes Italas hominum quae clara clueret;
etsi praeterea tamen esse Acherusia templa   120
Ennius aeternis exponit uersibus edens,
quo neque permanent animae neque corpora nostra,
sed quaedam simulacra modis pallentia miris;

unde sibi exortam semper florentis Homeri
commemorat speciem lacrimas effundere salsas   125
coepisse et rerum naturam expandere dictis.

... as our Ennius sang, who first brought down from pleasant Helicon a garland of
perennial foliage that might become famous among the races of Italian people;
although in addition, however, setting it out in everlasting verses, he explains that
there are regions of Acheron where neither our souls percolate nor our bodies, but
certain strangely pale phantoms; and he records that from here the image of ever
flourishing Homer appeared to him and began to pour out salt tears and to lay out
the nature of things in words.

E: Lucretius 4.1–5 [= 1.926–30]

Auia Pieridum peragro loca, nullius ante
trita solo. iuuat integros accedere fontes
atque haurire iuuatque nouos decerpere flores
insignemque meo capiti petere inde coronam
unde prius nulli uelarint tempora Musae;   5

I traverse the trackless places of the Muses, previously trodden by no foot. It
pleases to approach untouched springs and drink, and it pleases to pick fresh
flowers and to seek a distinctive garland for my head from the place from where
the Muses have veiled no one's temples in the past.

F: Gallus fragment

P.Qasr Ibrîm inv.78.3.11/1 (*ed.princ.*: *JRS* 69 (1979), 125–55) = 145 Hollis: a
papyrus fragment found in southern Egypt and attributed to the lost elegist
Gallus.

Gallus fr.2

            tristia nequit[ia ....]a, Lycori, tua.

<*e.g.* poems made> sad at your naughtiness, Lycoris

Gallus fr.3

            Fata mihi, Caesar, tum erunt mea dulcia, cum tu
                maxima Romanae pars eris historiae,
            postque tuum reditum multorum templa deorum
                fixa legam spoliis diuitiora tuis.

My fate will be pleasant to me, Caesar [*apparently* Julius], only when you will be
the greatest part of Roman history, and after your return I shall read [?] that the
temples of many gods are richer for being fixed with your spoils.

Gallus fr.4

> ....] ... tandem fecerunt carmina Musae
> quae possem domina dicere digna mea.
> .....] .atur idem tibi, non ego, Visce,
> . .] ..... Cato, iudice te uereor.

< ...... > the Muses have at last made poems such that I could utter them as something worthy of my mistress. < ...... > the same to you, I do not, Viscus, < ...... > fear with you as judge, Cato.

Gallus fr.5

>] Tyria.

Tyrian [probably a reference to purple cloth]

G: Horace, *Satires* 1.10.31–7:

> atque ego cum Graecos facerem, natus mare citra,
> uersiculos, uetuit me tali uoce Quirinus
> post mediam noctem uisus, cum somnia uera:
> 'in siluam non ligna feras insanius ac si
> magnas Graecorum malis inplere cateruas.'   35
> turgidus Alpinus iugulat dum Memnona dumque
> diffindit Rheni luteum caput, haec ego ludo.

And when I was writing light verse in Greek, though born this side of the sea [i.e. the Adriatic], after midnight, when dreams are true, Quirinus appeared and forbade me with a speech like this: 'It would not be more insane for you to carry timber into the wood than if you choose to expand the great ranks of the Greeks.' While turgid Alpinus is butchering Memnon, and while he splits the muddy mouth of the Rhine into different channels, I am writing these playful verses.

H: Vergil, *Eclogues* 1.1–5

> Tityre, tu patulae recubans sub tegmine fagi
> siluestrem tenui Musam meditaris auena;
> nos patriae fines et dulcia linquimus arua.
> nos patriam fugimus; tu, Tityre, lentus in umbra
> formosam resonare doces Amaryllida siluas.

Meliboeus: Tityrus, you lie back under the cover of the spreading beech tree and rehearse your woodland muse on a slender pipe. We are leaving the boundaries of our home and the sweet fields; we are fleeing the homeland; but you, Tityrus, at ease in the shade teach the woods to echo the beauties of Amaryllis.

I: Vergil, *Eclogues* 6.1–5:

Prima Syracosio dignata est ludere uersu
nostra neque erubuit siluas habitare Thalea.
cum canerem reges et proelia, Cynthius aurem
uellit et admonuit: 'pastorem, Tityre, pingues
pascere oportet oues, deductum dicere carmen.'   5

First our Thalea deigned to play in Syracusan [i.e. Theocritean] verse and was
not embarrassed to inhabit the woods. When I began to sing of kings and battles,
Cynthian Apollo tweaked me by the ear and advised: 'A shepherd, Tityrus, ought
to pasture the flocks to become fat, but to utter a refined song.'

J: Vergil, *Georgics* 2.39–46:

tuque ades inceptumque una decurre laborem,
o decus, o famae merito pars maxima nostrae,   40
Maecenas, pelagoque uolans da uela patenti.
non ego cuncta meis amplecti uersibus opto,
non, mihi si linguae centum sint oraque centum,
ferrea uox. ades et primi lege litoris oram;
in manibus terrae. non hic te carmine ficto   45
atque per ambages et longa exorsa tenebo.

And you, come and along with me run to shore the laborious voyage which I
have begun, o my glory, o deservedly the greatest part of my fame, Maecenas,
and, flying along, set sail for the open sea. I do not wish to cover everything in
my verses, not if I had a hundred tongues and a hundred mouths and a voice of
iron. Come and hug the shoreline; lands are close at hand. I shall not keep you
here with a fictitious poem and amid digressions and long preludes.

K: Vergil, *Georgics* 2.136–76

Sed neque Medorum siluae, ditissima terra,
nec pulcher Ganges atque auro turbidus Hermus
laudibus Italiae certent, non Bactra neque Indi
totaque turiferis Panchaia pinguis harenis.
haec loca non tauri spirantes naribus ignem   140
inuertere satis immanis dentibus hydri,
nec galeis densisque uirum seges horruit hastis;
sed grauidae fruges et Bacchi Massicus umor
impleuere; tenent oleae armentaque laeta.
hinc bellator equus campo sese arduus infert,   145
hinc albi, Clitumne, greges et maxima taurus

uictima, saepe tuo perfusi flumine sacro,
Romanos ad templa deum duxere triumphos.
hic uer adsiduum atque alienis mensibus aestas:
bis grauidae pecudes, bis pomis utilis arbos.   150
at rabidae tigres absunt et saeua leonum
semina, nec miseros fallunt aconita legentes,
nec rapit immensos orbes per humum neque tanto
squameus in spiram tractu se colligit anguis.
adde tot egregias urbes operumque laborem,   155
tot congesta manu praeruptis oppida saxis
fluminaque antiquos subter labentia muros.
an mare quod supra memorem, quodque adluit infra?
anne lacus tantos? te, Lari maxime, teque,
fluctibus et fremitu adsurgens Benace marino?   160
an memorem portus Lucrinoque addita claustra
atque indignatum magnis stridoribus aequor,
Iulia qua ponto longe sonat unda refuso
Tyrrhenusque fretis immittitur aestus Auernis?
haec eadem argenti riuos aerisque metalla   165
ostendit uenis atque auro plurima fluxit.
haec genus acre uirum, Marsos pubemque Sabellam
adsuetumque malo Ligurem Volscosque uerutos
extulit, haec Decios Marios magnosque Camillos,
Scipiadas duros bello et te, maxime Caesar,   170
qui nunc extremis Asiae iam uictor in oris
imbellem auertis Romanis arcibus Indum.
salue, magna parens frugum, Saturnia tellus,
magna uirum: tibi res antiquae laudis et artem
ingredior sanctos ausus recludere fontes,   175
Ascraeumque cano Romana per oppida carmen.

But neither Media's groves, richest of lands, nor the beautiful Ganges nor the Hermus, muddied with gold-dust, can vie with the glories of Italy—not Bactra nor India, nor all of Panchaia, enriched by incense-bearing sands. This land has not been ploughed by bulls breathing fire from their nostrils for the sowing of the teeth of the monstrous dragon, nor has it bristled with a harvest of warriors, their helmets and spears densely packed, but it has been filled with teeming crops and the Massic liquid of Bacchus [i.e. wine]. It is occupied by olive trees and thriving herds. From here comes the warhorse carrying itself proudly over the plain, from here come the white herds and the bull, noblest of victims, which, often bathed in your sacred waters, Clitumnus, have escorted Roman triumphs to the temples of the gods. Here spring never ceases and summer extends to months not her own. Cows calve twice a year, twice a year the trees fulfil their function with fruit. But here there are no raging tigers, no savage brood of the lion, no deadly nightshade to deceive the wretches who pick it. Nor does the scaly snake snatch his huge coils over the ground or gather himself into a spiral with so mighty a movement. Add so many outstanding cities, and the labour of effort, so many towns piled on top of sheer rocks by human hand and rivers gliding beneath ancient walls. Or should I speak of the sea which washes Italy's upper shore [i.e. the Adriatic] and the sea which washes the lower [i.e. the Tyrrhenian]? Or of her vast lakes? Of you, Larius, and you, Benacus, swelling with waves and a roar worthy of the ocean? Or should I speak of her harbours and the barrier added to the Lucrine lake and the sea howling in indignation where the Julian wave echoes from afar as the sea falls back, and the tide of the Tyrrhenian sea is let in to the Avernian waters? This land has also revealed streams of silver and mines of copper in her veins and flowed with an abundance of gold. She has produced a fine breed of men, the Marsi and Samnite warriors and the Ligurian, inured to misfortune, and the Volsci with their short darts; she has produced the Decii, the Marii and the great Camilli and the Scipios tough in war, and you, greatest Caesar, who, now victorious on the furthest shores of Asia, turn away the unwarlike Indian from the hills of Rome. Hail, great mother of crops, land of Saturn, great mother of men: for you I begin the themes and art of ancient praise, having dared to open up sacred fountains, and through Roman towns I sing a song of Hesiod [an early Greek poet, from Ascra in Boeotia, and a major model for the early part of the Georgics: see A].

L: Vergil, *Georgics* 3.8–48:

temptanda uia est qua me quoque possim
tollere humo uictorque uirum uolitare per ora.
primus ego in patriam mecum, modo uita supersit,   10
Aonio rediens deducam uertice Musas;
primus Idumaeas referam tibi, Mantua, palmas,
et uiridi in campo templum de marmore ponam
propter aquam, tardis ingens ubi flexibus errat
Mincius et tenera praetexit harundine ripas.   15
in medio mihi Caesar erit templumque tenebit:
illi uictor ego et Tyrio conspectus in ostro
centum quadriiugos agitabo ad flumina currus.
cuncta mihi Alpheum linquens lucosque Molorci
cursibus et crudo decernet Graecia caestu.   20
ipse caput tonsae foliis ornatus oliuae
dona feram. iam nunc sollemnes ducere pompas
ad delubra iuuat caesosque uidere iuuencos,
uel scaena ut uersis discedat frontibus utque
purpurea intexti tollant aulaea Britanni.   25
in foribus pugnam ex auro solidoque elephanto
Gangaridum faciam uictorisque arma Quirini,
atque hic undantem bello magnumque fluentem

Nilum ac nauali surgentes aere columnas.
addam urbes Asiae domitas pulsumque Niphaten   30
fidentemque fuga Parthum uersisque sagittis;
et duo rapta manu diuerso ex hoste tropaea
bisque triumphatas utroque ab litore gentes.
stabunt et Parii lapides, spirantia signa,
Assaraci proles demissaeque ab Ioue gentis   35
nomina, Trosque parens et Troiae Cynthius auctor.
Inuidia infelix Furias amnemque seuerum
Cocyti metuet tortosque Ixionis angues
immanemque rotam et non exsuperabile saxum.
interea Dryadum siluas saltusque sequamur   40
intactos, tua, Maecenas, haud mollia iussa:
te sine nil altum mens incohat. en age segnes
rumpe moras; uocat ingenti clamore Cithaeron
Taygetique canes domitrixque Epidaurus equorum,
et uox adsensu nemorum ingeminata remugit.   45
mox tamen ardentes accingar dicere pugnas
Caesaris et nomen fama tot ferre per annos,
Tithoni prima quot abest ab origine Caesar.

I must attempt a road by which I can raise myself too above the ground and fly as victor through the mouths of men. I shall be the first, provided there be life enough, to return from the Boeotian summit and lead down the Muses with me to my country; I shall be the first to bring back Idumaean palms [i.e. symbols of victory] to you, Mantua, and to place a temple of marble in the green meadow beside the water, where the large Mincius wanders, meandering slowly, and has covered its banks with youthful rush. I shall have Caesar in the middle, and he will inhabit the temple; for him I as victor and conspicuous in Tyrian purple [i.e. dressed as a *triumphator*] will drive a hundred chariots to the streams. For me all of Greece will leave Alpheus and the groves of Molorcus [i.e. Olympia and Nemea, famous locations for athletic festivals] and compete in running and with bloody boxing gloves. I myself, my head adorned with leaves of trimmed olive, shall bring offerings. Already now I delight in leading the solemn procession to the shrine and in seeing the bullocks slaughtered, or how the scene withdraws when the sets have been rotated and how the Britons raise the brightly coloured curtain into which they are woven. On the doors I shall portray in solid gold and ivory the battle with the orientals [i.e. the battle of Actium] and the arms of the victorious Quirinus [i.e. the Romans], and here the Nile in flood, billowing with war, and lofty columns adorned with the bronze beaks of captured ships. I shall add the conquered cities of Asia and routed Niphates [a mountain in Armenia, hence the Armenians] and the Parthian trusting in flight and arrows shot backwards; and two trophies seized by force from nations far apart, and races from both [i.e. eastern and western] shores, conquered in two triumphs. In addition statues of Parian marble will stand there breathing life, the lineage of Assaracus [Aeneas' great-grandfather] and the names of the race descended from Jupiter, and Tros, our parent, and Apollo, the creator of Troy. Wretched Envy will tremble before the Furies and the grim river of Cocytus and the twisted snakes and huge wheel of Ixion and the crag that cannot be overcome [by Sisyphus]. Meanwhile let us make for the Dryads' woods and untrodden glades, the difficult task, Maecenas, which you have imposed on me. Without you my mind can attempt nothing lofty; come then, break off sluggish delay. Cithaeron calls with a great clamour, as do the dogs of Taygetus and Epidaurus, tamer of horses, and the sound rings back redoubled by the applause of the groves. But one day I shall gird myself to speak of the fiery battles of Caesar and by my story to carry his name through as many years as Caesar is distant from the birth of Tithonus [the brother of Priam].

M: Horace, *Odes* 3.30

Exegi monumentum aere perennius
regalique situ pyramidum altius,
quod non imber edax, non Aquilo impotens
possit diruere aut innumerabilis
annorum series et fuga temporum.   5
non omnis moriar multaque pars mei
uitabit Libitinam: usque ego postera
crescam laude recens, dum Capitolium
scandet cum tacita uirgine pontifex:
dicar, qua uiolens obstrepit Aufidus   10
et qua pauper aquae Daunus agrestium
regnauit populorum, ex humili potens
princeps Aeolium carmen ad Italos
deduxisse modos. sume superbiam
quaesitam meritis et mihi Delphica   15
lauro cinge uolens, Melpomene, comam.

I have built a monument more lasting than bronze and loftier than the royal construction [but playing on *situs* = 'decay'] of the pyramids, which not gnawing rain could destroy, not the uncontrollable North Wind or the sequence of years beyond count and the fleeing of time. I shall not die entirely, and a great part of me will escape Libitina [goddess of funerals]. I shall grow ever fresh in future fame as long as the priest climbs the Capitol with the silent virgin [i.e. Vestal]. Where rough Aufidus resounds [the river near Horace's birthplace in Apulia] and Daunus [the legendary king of Apulia], poor in water, ruled over the country peoples, I shall be spoken of as the man who rose from humble beginnings, yet had the power to be the first to bring Aeolian song to Italian poetry. Take the proud tribute which I have sought by my services and with good will, Melpomene, circle my hair with laurel of Delphi.

Propertius 1.1.1–8: Introduction, p. 1
Propertius 1.3.1–8: Introduction, p. 2

N: Propertius 1.6

Non ego nunc Hadriae uereor mare noscere tecum,
    Tulle, neque Aegaeo ducere uela salo,
cum quo Rhipaeos possim conscendere montes
    ulteriusque domos uadere Memnonias;
sed me complexae remorantur uerba puellae   5
    mutatoque graues saepe colore preces.
illa mihi totis argutat noctibus ignes,
    et queritur nullos esse relicta deos;
illa meam mihi iam se denegat, illa minatur
    quae solet ingrato tristis amica uiro.   10
his ego non horam possum durare querelis:
    a pereat, si quis lentus amare potest.
an mihi sit tanti doctas cognoscere Athenas
    atque Asiae ueteres cernere diuitias,
ut mihi deducta faciat conuicia puppi   15
    Cynthia et insanis ora notet manibus,
osculaque opposito dicat sibi debita uento;
    et nihil infido durius esse uiro?
tu patrui meritas conare anteire secures,
    et uetera oblitis iura refer sociis.   20
nam tua non aetas umquam cessauit amori,
    semper at armatae cura fuit patriae.
et tibi non umquam nostros puer iste labores
    afferat et lacrimis omnia nota meis.
me sine, quem semper uoluit fortuna iacere,   25
    hanc animam aeternae reddere nequitiae.
multi longaeuo periere in amore libenter,
    in quorum numero me quoque terra tegat.
non ego sum laudi, non natus idoneus armis:
    hanc me militiam fata subire uolunt.   30
at tu seu mollis qua tendit Ionia, seu qua
    Lydia Pactoli tingit arata liquor,
seu pedibus terras seu pontum remige carpes,
    ibis et accepti pars eris imperii.
tum tibi si qua mei ueniet non immemor hora,   35
    uiuere me duro sidere certus eris.

I do not now fear to experience the Adriatic sea with you, Tullus, nor to spread sail on the swell of the Aegean, as with you I could climb the Rhipaean mountains [i.e. those of the extreme north] and to go <south> beyond the house of Memnon; but the words and embrace of my girl hold me back, together with her earnest prayers and frequently changing colour. She makes a shrill statement to me of her fire whole nights long and complains that, if she is abandoned, there are no gods. She tells me she is no longer mine; she makes the threats which an upset mistress often makes to an ungrateful man. [10] I cannot stand even an hour of these complaints: ah, may anyone perish who can love without passion. Would it be worth enough for me to get to know learned Athens and to set eyes on the ancient wealth of Asia, if Cynthia utter abuse at me as the boat is launched and mark her face with mad hands, and say that she owes the kisses to the adverse wind; and that nothing is more hard-hearted than a faithless man? You should try to go in advance of the axes your uncle has earned, and bring back old laws to forgetful allies. [20] For your life has never had the leisure for love, but always there has been a concern for your country and its arms. And may that boy never impose on you our labours and everything that is familiar to my tears. Fortune has always wanted me to lie prostrate; allow me to give up this soul to life-long misbehaviour: many have willingly perished in a long-lasting love: may I too be among their number when the earth covers me. I was not born suited to glory, nor to arms: this is the soldiering that the fates wish me to undergo. [30] But you, whether where luxurious Ionia stretches, or where the water of Pactolus colours the Lydian ploughland, whether you will cross land on foot or sea by oars, you will go and be part of an accepted rule. Then if any hour not entirely forgetful of me comes to you, you can be certain that I live under a dark star.

O: Propertius 2.1.1–16

Quaeritis unde mihi totiens scribantur amores,
    unde meus ueniat mollis in ora liber.
non haec Calliope, non haec mihi cantat Apollo:
    ingenium nobis ipsa puella facit.
siue illam Cois fulgentem incedere cerno,   5
    totum de Coa ueste uolumen erit;
seu uidi ad frontem sparsos errare capillos,
    gaudet laudatis ire superba comis;
siue lyrae carmen digitis percussit eburnis,
    miramur faciles ut premat arte manus;   10
seu cum poscentes somnum declinat ocellos,
    inuenio causas mille poeta nouas;
seu nuda erepto mecum luctatur amictu,
    tum uero longas condimus Iliadas;
seu quicquid fecit, siue est quodcumque locuta,   15
    maxima de nihilo nascitur historia.

You ask how it happens that so often I write of love affairs, how my book comes in elegiac form on to people's lips [*or* before the public gaze]. It is not Calliope who sings this for me, nor Apollo: it is my girl herself who creates my poetic talent. If I observe her out for a walk gleaming in Coan silks, the whole roll will be about [*and* of] Coan cloth; or if I have seen her hair undone and wandering on her brow, she rejoices to advance made proud by the praise of her locks; or if she strikes a song on the lyre with her ivory fingers, we are amazed how artfully she applies her skilful hands; [10] or if she ever lets drop her eyes that are demanding sleep, I the poet find a thousand new reasons [*and* themes]; or if her clothing is torn off and she wrestles naked with me, then to be sure I compose [*and* sheathe] long Iliads; whatever she has done, or whatsoever she has said, a grand history is born from nothing.

Propertius 2.1.17–19, 25–45, 71–8: Introduction, pp. 19–21

P: Propertius 2.10

sed tempus lustrare aliis Helicona choreis
  et campum Haemonio iam dare tempus equo.
iam libet et fortes memorare ad proelia turmas
  et Romana mei dicere castra ducis.
quod si deficiant uires, audacia certe   5
  laus erit: in magnis et uoluisse sat est.
aetas prima canat Veneres, extrema tumultus:
  bella canam, quando scripta puella mea est.
nunc uolo subducto grauior procedere uultu;
  nunc aliam citharam me mea Musa docet.   10
surge, anime, ex humili iam carmine; sumite uires,
  Pierides; magni nunc erit oris opus.
iam negat Euphrates equitem post terga tueri
  Parthorum, et Crassos se tenuisse dolet.
India quin, Auguste, tuo dat colla triumpho   15
  et domus intactae te tremit Arabiae;
et si qua extremis tellus se subtrahit oris
  sentiat illa tuas postmodo capta manus.
haec ego castra sequar; uates tua castra canendo
  magnus ero: seruent hunc mihi fata diem.   20
ut caput in magnis ubi non est tangere signis,
  ponitur his imos ante corona pedes;
sic nos nunc, inopes laudis conscendere culmen,
  pauperibus sacris uilia tura damus.
nondum etiam Ascraeos norunt mea carmina montes;   25
  sed modo Permessi flumine lauit Amor.

… But it is time to traverse Helicon with other dances and now time to give the plain to the Thessalian [i.e. Achillean] horse. Now it pleases both to record the squadrons valiant for battle and to tell of the Roman camp of my leader. But if my strength were to fail, the daring will certainly bring praise: even to have wanted is enough in big matters. Let the first age sing Venuses, the last disorder: I shall sing wars, since my girl is written. Now I want to advance more serious with a frown on my face; now my Muse teaches me a different lyre. [10] Rise, my spirit, from a song now humble; take strength, Pierides; now there will be need of a big voice. Already the Euphrates is refusing to protect the horseman of the Parthians behind its back, and grieves that it has held the Crassi. Nay, India bows its neck for your triumph, Augustus, and the home of untouched Arabia trembles before you; and if some land withdraws itself to most distant shores, let it in time to come be captured and feel your reach [*or* forces]. I shall follow these campaigns; in singing your campaigns I shall become an inspired poet and a great one: may the fates preserve this day for me. [20] As, where it is not possible to reach the head in the case of big statues, a garland is placed in front of their feet below, so we now, incapable of ascending the hill of praise, offer cheap incense in a poor man's rite. Not yet do my poems know the Ascraean [i.e. Hesiodic] mountains, but love has just washed them in the stream of Permessus.

Q: Propertius 2.13.1–16

> Non tot Achaemeniis armatur Itura sagittis
>   spicula quot nostro pectore fixit Amor.
> hic me tam graciles uetuit contemnere Musas,
>   iussit et Ascraeum sic habitare nemus;
> non ut Pieriae quercus mea uerba sequantur,   5
>   aut possim Ismaria ducere ualle feras,
> sed magis ut nostro stupefiat Cynthia uersu:
>   tunc ego sim Inachio notior arte Lino.
> non ego sum formae tantum mirator honestae,
>   nec si qua illustres femina iactat auos;   10
> me iuuat in gremio doctae legisse puellae,
>   auribus et puris scripta probasse mea.
> haec ubi contigerint, populi confusa ualeto
>   fabula: nam domina iudice tutus ero.
> quae si forte bonas ad pacem uerterit aures,   15
>   possum inimicitias tunc ego ferre Iouis.

Ituraea [or some other region of the East: the text is uncertain] is not armed with so many Persian shafts as Love has fixed arrows in my breast. He has forbidden me to disdain Muses as slender as mine are, and ordered me to dwell in the Ascraean [i.e. Hesiodic] grove in the way that I do; not in order that Pierian [i.e. Apollonian] oaks may follow my words, or so I can lead wild beasts through the Ismarian valley, but rather to stun Cynthia with my verse: then I would be better known for my art than Argive [i.e. Callimachean] Linus. I am not merely an admirer of a fine figure, nor of any woman who flaunts her illustrious ancestry; [10] I like to read lying in the lap of a girl of learning and to have my writings approved by pure ears. When this happens, I shall dismiss the confused gossip of the people: for with my mistress as judge I shall be safe. If she happens to turn her ears favourably towards peace, then I can bear the ill-will of Jove.

R: Propertius 2.34.51–66

harum nulla solet rationem quaerere mundi,
  nec cur frenatis luna laboret equis,
nec si post Stygias aliquid restabimus undas,
  nec si consulto fulmina missa tonent.
aspice me, cui parua domi fortuna relicta est   55
  nullus et antiquo Marte triumphus aui,
ut regnem mixtas inter conuiua puellas
  hoc ego quo tibi nunc eleuor ingenio.
me iuuat hesternis positum languere corollis,
  quem tetigit iactu certus ad ossa deus;   60
Actia Vergilio est custodis litora Phoebi
  Caesaris et fortes dicere posse rates,
qui nunc Aeneae Troiani suscitat arma
  iactaque Lauinis moenia litoribus.
cedite, Romani scriptores; cedite, Grai: 65
  nescioquid maius nascitur Iliade.

None of these girls is in the habit of seeking an explanation of the universe, nor why the moon labours with her horses curbed, nor if we continue to exist as something beyond the waters of the Styx, nor if crashing thunderbolts are sent deliberately. Look at me, a man with little wealth left at home and no triumph of forefather in ancient war, how I am king at the symposium amid a group of girls thanks to that ability for which you now belittle me. It pleases me to languish settled on yesterday's garlands: the god, certain in his aim, has touched me to the marrow. [60] It is for Vergil to have the power to tell of the Actian shores of Phoebus the protector and the bold boats of Caesar, Vergil, who now rouses the arms of Trojan Aeneas and the walls cast on Lavinia's shores. Give way, Roman writers; give way, Greeks: something greater than the Iliad is coming to birth.

Bibliography

Items relevant for single poems are cited *ad loc.*

Abbreviations

CAH = *Cambridge Ancient History*
Cynthia = Heyworth, *Cynthia: a Companion to the Text of Propertius* [see below]
G&L = Gildersleeve & Lodge [see below]
LIMC = *Lexicon Iconographicum Mythologiae Classicae* [see below]
GLK = *Grammatici Latini* (ed. H. Keil; 8 vols; Leipzig, 1857–80)
OLD = *Oxford Latin Dictionary*
OCD^3 = *Oxford Classical Dictionary* (3rd edition, ed. S. Hornblower & A. Spawforth; 1996)
PLLS = *Papers of the Liverpool* [or *Leeds*] *Latin Seminar*
Abbreviations for journals follow standard forms; where these are not easily guessed (e.g. *CPh* = *Classical Philology*), they can be found through internet searches, e.g. www.acronymfinder. com.

Commentaries on Propertius

(a) *complete*

Beroaldus, P. (Bologna, 1487)
Passerat, J. (Paris, 1608)
Broukhusius, J. (Amsterdam, 1702, 1727)
Burman, P. completed by L. Santenius, (Utrecht, 1780)
Kuinoel, C. T. (Leipzig, 1805)
Lachmann, K. (Leipzig, 1816)
Hertzberg, W. A. B. (2 vols, Halle, 1843–5)
Paley, F. A. (2nd edn, London, 1872)
Rothstein, M. (Berlin, 1898, 2nd edn 1920–4)
Butler, H. E., & Barber, E. A. (Oxford, 1933)
Richardson, L. (Norman, OK, 1976)

(b) *selected poems*

Postgate, J. P. *Select Elegies* (London, 1881)

(c) *Book III*

Camps, W. A. (Cambridge, 1966)
Fedeli, P. (Bari, 1985)

Other works cited

Adams, J. N., *The Latin Sexual Vocabulary* (London, 2nd edn 1987)
Allen, W. S., *Vox Latina* (2nd edn, revised reprint, Cambridge, 1989)
Ancona, R., & Greene, E. (eds), *Gendered Dynamics in Latin Love Poetry* (Baltimore, 2005)
Austin, C. & Bastianini, G., *Posidippi Pellaei quae supersunt omnia* (Milano, 2002) [= A.–B.]
Austin, R. G., commentaries on Vergil, *Aeneid*, Book I (Oxford, 1971); Book VI (Oxford, 1977)
Boucher, J.-P., *Études sur Properce: problèmes d'inspiration et d'art* (Paris, 1965)
Butrica, J. L., 'Propertius 3.6', *EMC* 2 (1983), 17–37
—— *The Manuscript Tradition of Propertius* (*Phoenix* suppl. 17; Toronto, 1984)
—— 'The *Amores* of Propertius: unity and structure in Books 2–4', *ICS* 21 (1996), 87–158
—— 'Editing Propertius', *CQ* 47 (1997), 176–208
Cairns, F., *Generic Composition in Greek and Roman Poetry* (Edinburgh, 1972)
—— 'Propertius 1.4 and 1.5 and the "Gallus" of the Monobiblos', *PLLS* 4 (1983), 61–103
—— *Sextus Propertius, the Augustan Elegist* (Cambridge, 2006)
Clausen, W., *A Commentary on Virgil, Eclogues* (Oxford, 1994)
Commager, S., *A Prolegomenon to Propertius* (Cincinnati, 1974)
Courtney, E., 'The structure of Propertius Book 3', *Phoenix* 24 (1970), 48–53
—— *The Fragmentary Latin Poets* (Oxford, 1993)
Enk, P. J., *Ad Properti carmina commentarius criticus* (Zutphen, 1911)
Fordyce, C. J., *Catullus: a Commentary* (Oxford, 1961)
Galinsky, G. P., *Augustan Culture* (Princeton, 1996)
Gibson, R. K., *Ovid: Ars Amatoria, Book 3* (Cambridge, 2003)
Gildersleeve, B. L., & Lodge, G., *Latin Grammar* (1st edn London, 1867; 3rd edn reprinted London, 2005) [= G&L]
Gold, B. K., 'Propertius 3.9: Maecenas as *eques, dux, fautor*', in B. K. Gold (ed.), *Literary and Artistic Patronage in Ancient Rome* (Austin, TX, 1982), 103–17
—— *Literary Patronage in Greece and Rome* (Chapel Hill, 1987)
Goold, G. P., '*Noctes Propertianae*' *HSCPh* 71 (1966), 59–106

—— 'Paralipomena Propertiana', *HSCPh* 94 (1992), 287–320

Gow, A. S. F., & Page, D. L., *The Greek Anthology: Hellenistic Epigrams* (2 vols, Cambridge, 1965)

Griffin, J., *Latin Poets and Roman Life* (London, 1985)

Günther, H.-C., *Quaestiones Propertianae (Mnemosyne* suppl. 169; Leiden, 1997)

—— (ed.), *Brill's Companion to Propertius* (Leiden, 2006)

Gurval, R. A., *Actium and Augustus: the Politics and Emotions of Civil War* (Ann Arbor, 1995)

Harmon, D. P., 'The poet's initiation and the sacerdotal imagery of Propertius 3.1–5', in C. Deroux (ed.), *Studies in Latin Literature and Roman History 1* (Bruxelles, 1979), 317–34

Heyworth, S. J., 'Notes on Propertius Books 3 and 4', *CQ* 36 (1986), 199–211

—— 'Propertius 2.13', *Mnemosyne* 45 (1992), 45–59

—— 'Some allusions to Callimachus in Latin poetry', *MD* 33 (1994), 51–79

—— 'Propertius: division, transmission, and the editor's task', *PLLS* 8 (1995), 165–85

—— 'Propertius, patronage and polities', *BICS* 50 (2007), 93–128

—— *Cynthia: a Companion to the Text of Propertius* (Oxford, 2007; corrected reprint, 2009) [= *Cynthia*]

Hinds, S., *Allusion and Intertext* (Cambridge, 1998)

Hollis, A. S., *Ovid*, Ars Amatoria *Book 1* (Oxford, 1977)

—— *Fragments of Roman Poetry: c.60 BC–AD 20* (Oxford, 2007)

Housman, A. E., *The Classical Papers of A. E. Housman* (3 vols., ed. J. Diggle & F. R. D. Goodyear, Cambridge 1972) [= *CP*]

Hubbard, M, 'Propertiana', *CQ* 18 (1968), 315–19

—— *Propertius* (London, 1974)

Hunter, R. L., *Theocritus: a Selection* (Cambridge, 1999)

—— *The Shadow of Callimachus: Studies in the Reception of Hellenistic Poetry at Rome* (Cambridge, 2006)

—— (ed.), *The Hesiodic Catalogue of Women* (Cambridge, 2005)

Innes, D. C., 'Gigantomachy and natural philosophy', *CQ* 29 (1979), 165–71

Jacobson, H., 'Structure and meaning in Propertius Book 3', *ICS* 1 (1976), 160–73

James, S. L., *Learned Girls and Male Persuasion* (Berkeley, 2003)

Kambylis, A., *Die Dichterweihe und ihre Symbolik* (Heidelberg, 1965)

Keith, A., *Propertius: Poet of Love and Leisure* (London, 2008)

Kennedy, B. H., *The Revised Latin Primer* (rev. J. Mountford; London, 1962)

Kenney, E. J., *Lucretius*, De rerum natura, *Book 3* (Cambridge, 1971)

—— *Ovid*, Heroides *16–21* (Cambridge, 1996)

Kershaw, A., 'Emendation and usage: two readings of Propertius', *CPh* 75 (1980), 71–2

Kidd, D., *Aratus*, Phaenomena *edited with Introduction, Translation and Commentary* (Cambridge, 1997)

Lexicon Iconographicum Mythologiae Classicae (Zürich/Dusseldorf, 1981–99)

Lightfoot, J., *Parthenius of Nicaea, Extant Works edited with Introduction and Notes* (Oxford, 1999)

Lyne, R. O. A. M., *The Latin Love Poets* (Oxford, 1980)

—— *Collected Papers on Latin Poetry* (Oxford, 2007)

Macleod, C., *Collected Essays* (Oxford, 1983)

Maltby, R., *A Lexicon of Ancient Latin Etymologies* (Leeds, 1991)

—— *Tibullus: Elegies. Text, Introduction and Commentary* (Cambridge, 2002)

McKeown, J. C., *Ovid:* Amores; *Text, Prolegomena and Commentary* (4 vols; Liverpool/Leeds, 1987–?)

Miller, J. F., *Apollo, Augustus, and the Poets* (Cambridge, 2009)

Morgan, J. D., 'Cruces Propertianae', *CQ* 36 (1986), 182–98

Murgatroyd, P., *A Commentary on the First Book of the Elegies of Tibullus* (Pietermaritzburg, 1980)

Mynors, R. A. B., *Virgil,* Georgics: *Edited with a Commentary* (Oxford, 1990)

Nethercut, W. R., 'The Ironic Priest. Propertius' *Roman Elegies,* 3.1–5: imitations of Horace and Vergil', *AJPh* 91 (1970), 385–407

—— 'Propertius 3.12–14', *CPh* 65 (1970), 99–102

Newman, J. K., *Augustan Propertius: the Recapitulation of a Genre* (Hildesheim, 1997)

—— 'The third book: defining a poetic self' in Günther (ed.) 2006, 319–52

Nisbet, R. G. M., & Hubbard, M., *A Commentary on Horace,* Odes, *Book 1* (Oxford, 1970); *Book 2* (Oxford, 1978)

Nisbet, R. G. M., & Rudd, N., *A Commentary on Horace,* Odes, *Book 3* (Oxford, 2004)

Osgood, J., *Caesar's Legacy* (Cambridge, 2006)

Page, D. L., *The Epigrams of Rufinus* (Cambridge, 1978)

Papanghelis, T. D., *Propertius: a Hellenistic Poet on Love and Death* (Cambridge, 1987)

Pelling, C., 'The Triumviral period' in *Cambridge Ancient History,* Vol. 10, *The Augustan Empire 43* BC–AD *69* (2nd edn, 1996), 1–69

Platnauer, M., *Latin Elegiac Verse* (Cambridge, 1951)

Putnam, M. C. J., 'Propertius' Third Book: patterns of cohesion', *Arethusa* 13 (1980), 97–113

Richardson N. J., *The* Iliad: *a Commentary. Vol. VI: books 21–4* (Cambridge, 1993)

Riesenweber, T., *Uneigentliches Sprechen und Bildermischung in den Elegien des Properz* (Berlin, 2007)

Ross, D. O., *Backgrounds to Augustan Poetry: Gallus, Elegy and Rome* (Cambridge, 1975)

Schmeisser, B., *A Concordance to the Elegies of Propertius* (Hildesheim, 1972)

Shackleton Bailey, D. R., *Propertiana* (Cambridge, 1956)

—— *Homoeoteleuton in Latin Dactylic Verse* (Stuttgart, 1994)

Skutsch, O., 'Readings in Propertius', *CQ* 23 (1973), 316–23

—— *The Annals of Quintus Ennius* (Oxford, 1985)

Smyth, W. R., *Thesaurus criticus ad Sexti Propertii textum (Mnemosyne* suppl. 12; Leiden, 1970)

Spanoudakis, K., *Philitas of Cos (Mnemosyne* supplement 229; Leiden, 2002)

Stahl, H.-P., *Propertius: 'Love' and 'War' - Individual and State under Augustus* (Berkeley, 1985)

Syme, R., *The Roman Revolution* (Oxford, 1939)

Thomas, R. F., *Virgil*, Georgics (2 vols; Cambridge, 1988)

Tränkle, H., *Die Sprachkunst des Properz und die Tradition der lateinischen Dichtersprache (Hermes Einzelschriften* 15; Wiesbaden, 1960)

Welch, T. S., *The Elegiac Cityscape: Propertius and the Meaning of Roman Monuments* (Columbus, OH, 2005)

Warmington, E. H., *Remains of Old Latin* (4 vols; Cambridge, MA; Loeb Classical Library, rev. reprints 1956–9)

Watson, L. C., *A Commentary on Horace's Epodes* (Oxford, 2003)

West, D. A., *Horace*, Odes 1: *Carpe Diem* (Oxford, 1995)

West, M. L., *Hesiod*, Theogony (Oxford, 1966)

—— *Greek Epic Fragments* (Cambridge, MA; Loeb Classical Library, 2003)

Williams, G., *Tradition and Originality in Roman Poetry* (Oxford, 1968)

Wills, J., *Repetition in Latin Poetry: Figures of Allusion* (Oxford, 1996)

Wimmel, W., *Kallimachos in Rom (Hermes Einzelschriften* 16; Wiesbaden, 1960)

Wistrand, E., *Miscellanea Propertiana* (Göteborg, 1977)

Woodcock, E. C., *A New Latin Syntax* (London, 1985)

Woodman, A. J., 'Propertius and Livy', *CQ* 48 (1998), 568–9

Wyke, M., *The Roman Mistress* (Oxford, 2002)

Zanker, P., *The Power of Images in the Age of Augustus*, trans. A. Shapiro (Michigan, 1988)

Index

Numbers in italics are page numbers (mainly of the introduction); other numbers refer to the commentary, single numbers in bold to whole poems, '1.1' etc. to notes on specific lines, 'int.' to the introduction to each poem, capitals in bold to passages in the appendix.

Readers are also directed to the glossary, which provides references for the explication or illustration of technical terms.

---

[1] There is no grammatical distinction between these datives but they are distinguished for convenience.

grammar, syntax, accidence (*cont.*)
  dative of person interested
    ('ethic') 7.19
  dative of purpose 13.36
  dative, possessive 2.11; 3.23; 5.3; 7.42;
    11.15, 55; 17.27; 18.15; 20.7;
    22.31; 23.8
  dative, predicative 11.34; 13.36
  dative with *causa* 13.3
  deliberative subjunctive 2.9; 15.22;
    16.5–6
  ellipse 21.33; 23.2
  epithet, compound 9.35; 13.17;
    21.18
  epithet, transferred 7.59, 9; 15.27;
    17.33; 22.14
  future in invitations 23.15–16
  future of -*ire* verbs 21.32
  generic subjunctive 8.19; 9.5; 16.11
  genitive after adjectives 11.25
    (*medius*); 13.62 (*uerax*); 17.7
    (*rudis*)
  genitive, defining 12.3
  genitive of destination 7.2; 13.4
  genitive of quality 14.26
  genitive of charges 11.3
  genitive of the sphere of
    operation 5.1
  genitive of value 12.3; 20.4
  genitive, partitive 17.19
  genitive plural of 3rd-declension
    adjectives, participles 13.25
  gnomic future 16.13–14
  Greek diction 14.1–2
  in + acc. without a verb of
    motion 9.59–60
  imperative, future or 'second' 13.45
  indicative in indirect questions
    5.27–8
  ne = *ut non* 12.4
  paratactic* clauses 6.1–2; 18.19–20
    (concessive)
  perfect of *esse* with past
    participle 10.29
  perfect subjunctive in laws 20.25–7
  pluperfect of *esse* 7.31; 8.1; 13.38
  poetic plural *41*; 9.30, 39, 49; 11.61;
    12.35; 16.21–2; 19.22; 24.15, 19
  present inf. after verbs of
    threatening 8.7

  relative + subjunctive expressing
    purpose 1.17–18; 3.20
  second person, use of *26–7*
  si introducing indirect question 5.31
  subjunctive after impersonal
    verb 7.72
  ut omitted in indirect wishes 4.12
greed 5.1–14; 7.34–8; 12.3–6; **13**
groves 1.2; 3 int., 41–2

hair 5.24; 6.9; 7.59–60; 8.5–8; 10.14; 14.28;
  15.13; 16.28; 19.21–2; 24.31–6
Hannibal 3.9–11; 11.67
Hardy, Thomas 10.15–16
Hector 1.28; 8.31
Helen 8.29–32; 14.15–20
Helicon 1.17–20; 3 int., 1–2; 5.19–20; A, D
Hellespont 22.5
Hercules *14*; 1.32; 6.32; 7.3; 11.16–20;
  18.3–6; 22.7–10
Hesiod 3 int.; 11 int.
Hesperides 22.10
Hesperia 18.5
Hippocrene 1.6, 19; 3.1–2, 32, 52
Homer see *Iliad* and *Odyssey*
hoop 14.5–6
Horace *11–12, 16–19*; 5.18; **9**; 13 int.
Horatius Cocles 11.63
Horatii 3.7
horses 2.7–8; 3 int.; 3.4.8, 17; 9.54,
  57–8; 11.61–4; 12.12; 19.3–10
humour 1 int.; 3.2–4; 8.39–40; 11.27–8,
  45–6; 13 int.; 14 int.; 18.12;
  21.27; 22 int.
hymns 17 int.

Iliad 1.25–34; 8.29–34; 9.37–42;
  10.5–10, 13–14; 18.29–30;
imagery 3 int.; 7.3–4; 24 int.; *see also*
  (*e.g.*) birds, fire, *militia amoris*,
  sailing, *seruitium amoris*, travel,
  triumph, water
impotence 6.34
India(ns) 4.1–2; 13.5–8, 15–22;
  18.19–20
inspiration 1.1–8; 3 int., 13–14, 31–2,
  51–2; 10.1–4; 13 int.; 17 int.
Io 22.35–6
Iphigenia 7.23–4; 22.34
Irus 5.17

Italy 7.43–4; **22**; K
Itys 10.10
ivy 17.29

Jason 11.9–12; 19.17–18; 20.17–26;
    21.11–14
Jugurtha 5.16
Julius Caesar *9–13*; 11.33–8; 18.31–4
Juno 10 int.; 17.5–6; 22.35–6
Jupiter 2.20; 4.6; 5.26; 9.15; 11.28, 66;
    13.7, 9; **15**; 17.21–2; 24.20
Juvenal 13; 19 int.

Lampetie 12.29–30
Lares 3.11
law, legal diction 6.19–20; 13.45; 14 int.;
    19.1; **20**; 23.3–4
Leucas 11.69–70
Liburnian ships 11.43–4
love *1–8, 19–33*; 5.1–2, 19–26; 6.37–40;
    7.71–2, 21–2; **8**; 10.27–32;
    11.1–32, 65–6; 13.1–2, 33–7;
    15.46; 16.11–16; **19**; **20**; **24**; *see
    also (e.g.)* Amor, *comus,* Cynthia,
    elegy, fire, *militia amoris,
    remedia amoris, seruitium
    amoris,* Venus
Lucretius **5**; 21.26
lust **19**
luxury 2.11–14; 5.2–6; 7.49–50; 10.22;
    12.18; 13 int., 1–12, 60; 18 int.,
    19–20
Lycinna 15.5–6
Lycurgus (of Sparta) 14 int., 3–4;
    (of Thrace) 17.23
Lycus 15 int., 11–12
Lydia 11.17–20; 18.28
Lygdamus **6**
Lysippus 9.9–10

Macaulay, Lord 11.63
madness of lover *1*; 12.7; 17.3; 24.11, 17
Maeander 22.16
Maecenas *13, 17, 19–20, 32*; **9**
maenads 8.14; 13.62; 17.22–4
magic *see* witchcraft
Malea 19.7–8
manuscripts *44–50*
Marcellus *15*; **18**
Marcian aqueduct *15–16*; 2.14; 22.23–4

Marius 3.43; 5.16; 11.46
marriage legislation **21**
Mausoleum 2.21–2
Medea 11.9–12; 17.11–12; 19.17–18;
    22.12
medicine 17 int., 4; 24 int.
Medusa 3.32; 22.8
Meleager (epigrammatist) **1–2**, *7*;
    17.3
Meleager (hero) 22.31–2
memorials 11.61–9; 3.16.23–30
Menander 21.28
Mens Bona 24.19
metapoetic* *30–1*; 1 int.; 9.35; 11.71–2;
    21.1; 22.1
metre *33–43*
  caesurae *36–8*
  correption 11.17
  dactylic line 21.11–12
  elegiac couplet *36, 42–3*
  elision (prodelision) *35, 38*;
    23.12
  enjambment* *43*
  et preceded by elision and followed by
    caesura 7.57–8
  hexameter, start/end *38–9*; 7.13
  hiatus *38*; 7.49
  ictus and accent *43*; 16.7–10
  internal rhyme *40*
  intractable forms 1.29; 3.7; 5.19–20;
    11.67; 13.25, 35; 16.2; 20.19–20;
    21.32
  –ne postponed 6.11–12; 16.5
  oddities in Prop. 3 *38*; 9.35
  pentameter, start/end *38–40*
  perfect infinitive metrically
    convenient 5.19–20; 14.30
  postponement of words to second half
    of pentameter 16.12
  quantity *33–5*; 1.27; 11.53
  spondaic line 10.1–2
  synizesis 6.35–6
militia amoris *1–2*; 5.2–6; **8**; 24.25–6; N
  (Prop. 1.6.30)
mimetic diction 3.30, 40, 41; 7.6; 10.1,
    4, 26; 21.11; *see also*
    onomatopoeia*
Minerva *see* Pallas Athena
Minos **19**
Misenus 18.3–4

Index of passages cited and scanned

Select index of passages cited [or, in square brackets, scanned]

Index of Latin Words